How the World's NEWS MEDIA Reacted to 9/11

Other Books of Interest from MARQUETTE BOOKS

Stephen D. Cooper, *Watching the Watchdog: Bloggers as the Fifth Estate* (2006). ISBN: 0-922993-46-7 (cloth); 0-922993-47-5 (paperback)

Ralph D. Berenger (ed.), *Cybermedia Go to War: Role of Convergent Media Before and During the 2003 Iraq War* (2006). ISBN: 0-922993-48-1 (cloth); 0-922993-49-1 (paperback)

Jami Fullerton and Alice Kendrick, *Advertising's War on Terrorism: The Story of the Shared Values Initiative* (2006). ISBN: 0-922993-43-2 (cloth); 0-922993-44-0 (paperback)

Mitchell Land and Bill W. Hornaday, *Contemporary Media Ethics: A Practical Guide for Students, Scholars and Professionals* (2006). ISBN: 0-922993-41-6 (cloth); 0-922993-42-4 (paperback)

Joey Reagan, *Applied Research Methods for Mass Communicators* (2006). ISBN: 0-922993-45-9

David Demers, *Dictionary of Mass Communication: A Guide for Students, Scholars and Professionals* (2005). ISBN: 0-922993-35-1 (cloth); 0-922993-25-4 (paperback)

John C. Merrill, Ralph D. Berenger and Charles J. Merrill, *Media Musings: Interviews with Great Thinkers* (2004). ISBN: 0-922993-15-7

Ralph D. Berenger (ed.), *Global Media Go to War: Role of Entertainment and News During the 2003 Iraq War* (2004). ISBN: 0-922993-10-6

Melvin L. DeFleur and Margaret H. DeFleur, *Learning to Hate Americans: How U.S. Media Shape Negative Attitudes Among Teenagers in Twelve Countries* (2003). ISBN: 0-922993-05-X

How the World's NEWS MEDIA Reacted to 9/11

Essays from
Around the Globe

Edited by
TOMASZ
PLUDOWSKI

MARQUETTE BOOKS LLC
SPOKANE, WASHINGTON

Printed in the United States of America

Library of Congress Cataloging-in-Publication Data

How the world's news media reacted to 9/11 : essays from around the globe
/ edited by Tomasz Pludowski.
    p. cm.
    Includes bibliographical references and index.
    ISBN-13: 978-0-922993-66-6 (pbk. : alk. paper)
    ISBN-10: 0-922993-66-1 (pbk. : alk. paper)
    ISBN-13: 978-0-922993-73-4 (hardcover : alk. paper)
    ISBN-10: 0-922993-73-4 (hardcover : alk. paper)
    1. September 11 Terrorist Attacks, 2001--Press coverage. 2. Terrorism--Press
coverage. 3. Terrorism in mass media. I. Pludowski, Tomasz.
HV6432.7.H69 2007
070.4'49973931--dc22

                                                    2007000100

Marquette Books LLC
3107 East 62nd Avenue
Spokane, Washington 99223
509-443-7057 (voice) / 509-448-2191 (fax)
books@marquettebooks.com / www.MarquetteBooks.com

DEDICATION

I dedicate this book to my father, who always stressed the importance of education and instilled in me an interest in other cultures and languages.

CONTENTS

PART I — EUROPEAN MEDIA

PART II — ASIAN MEDIA

PART III — ARAB/MIDDLE EASTERN MEDIA

ABOUT THE AUTHORS

Birol Akgün is an associate professor of political science at Selcuk University, Turkey. He earned a Ph.D. from Case Western Reserve University. Currently he is teaching courses on comparative politics, political sociology, political violance and terrorosism, American foreign policy, and human rights. His publications have focused on democratization, political behavior and terrorism.

Jesus Arroyave is a doctoral candidate in the School of Communication at the University of Miami. He earned a master's degree in communication and information studies at Rutgers, where he also was a Fulbright Scholar from Colombia. He also holds a master's degree in education from Universidad Javeriana-Norte in Colombia. He currently is an assistant professor at the Universidad del Norte (Barranquilla, Colombia). His research interests include Latin American media and journalism, communication and development, and communication and health.

Ralph D. Berenger is an assistant professor of journalism and mass communication at the American University in Cairo. He also is review editor and contributing editor to the *Transnational Broadcasting Journal* and guest editor of *Journal of Computer Mediated Communication*. He has published dozens of scholarly articles and edited *Global Media Go to War* (Marquette Books, 2004). He has lived and worked in the United states, Bolivia, St. Lucia, Kenya, and Egypt.

Nicolene Botha is a Ph.D. candidate in the Department of Journalism, Stellenbosch University, South Africa. She has co-published internationally on media coverage of war, and her present research deals with the American invasion of Iraq.

Gwen Bouvier earned her Ph.D. in broadcast journalism from the University of Wales, Aberystwyth. Her doctoral research involved "A Comparative Analysis of the Representation of 9/11 in BCC and VRT Television News." She is currently a member of the editorial board of *Media, War & Conflict* and is editorial administrator of the online journal

Particip@tions. She has taught courses at Metropolitan University, London, and has presented guest lectures at the University of Wales and at RITS, College of Audiovisual Media, Brussels. She also published a paper in *Journal for Crime, Conflict and Media Culture*.

Arnold S. De Beer is a professor extraordinary in the Department of Journalism, Stellenbosch University, South Africa. He is publisher and founding editor of *Ecquid Novi*, and an editorial board memer of inter alia *Journalism Studies*. His publications include *Global Journalism* (edited with John C. Merrilll, Pearson, 2004). De Beer is the research director of the Institute for Media Analysis in South Africa (iMasa).

Tine Ustad Figenschou is a research fellow at the Department of Media and Communication, University of Oslo. She is currently working on her thesis on Al-Jazeera International. She is a co-editor of *Babylon Magazine* and has worked as a journalist for various Norwegian publications. She lived in New York during the fall of 2001 and covered the terror attacks as a freelancer for Norwegian daily newspaper *Dagbladet*.

Mobo Gao works at the School of Asian Languages & Studies of the University of Tasmania. Gao has published widely on rural China and interpretation and reinterpretation of China's Cultural Revolution. *Gao Village: Modern Life in Rural China* is one of his numerous publications. In recent years, Mobo Gao has concentrated his research on media studies, particularly Western media reporting of China since 1989.

Brigitte Georgi-Findlay is professor of North American Studies at the University of Technology, Dresden. Her major areas of research include cultural history of the American West (Native Americans, women, urban West), travel writing, American photography, more recently also trans-Atlantic relations. She is the author of *The Frontiers of Women's Writing: Women's Narratives and the Rhetoric of Westward Expansion* (Tucson: University of Arizona Press, 1996).

Orhan Gökçe is professor of political communication at Selcuk University, Turkey. He is teaching courses on political communication, media and public opinion, and research methods in social sciences. He earned his Ph.D. in communication at Germany's Giessen University. He has just published a book, titled *The Images of the Terror* (in Turkish) in August 2004. His Web page can be found at *http://www.iibf.selcuk.edu.tr/yayinlar.asp?bolumu=kamu&kim=15*

Janet Fine is a journalist and author of five books. She has written extensively for Indian, Egyptian and international publications, specializing in writing on TV and film. After receiving her master's degree from the Columbia School of Journalism, she worked as a journalist and editor and has set up her own publishing company in Indiam, Classex Books. Some publications she corresponds for include *Video Age Int.*, *Variety Newspaper*, *TBS*, *Elan Magazine* and *The Economic Times*.

Cees J. Hamelink studied philosophy and psychology in Amsterdam and received his Ph.D. degree from the University of Amsterdam. He is professor emeritus of international communication (University of Amsterdam) and is currently professor of human rights and public health at the Vrije Universteit in Amsterdam. He is editor-in-chief of *The International Communication Gazette* and honorary president of the International Association for Media and Communication Research. He has published 17 books, including *The Politics of World Communication*, *The Ethics of Cyberspace*, and *Human Rights for Communicators*.

Sallie Hughes is an assistant professor in the School of Communication at the University of Miami. Dr. Hughes is the author of *Newsrooms in Conflict. Journalism and the Democratization of Mexico* (University of Pittsburgh Press, 2006), which examines that country's transition in politics and journalism in a comparative perspective. Her work on Latin American media has appeared in *Political Communication*, the *Latin American Research Review*, *Critical Studies in Media Communication* and the *Harvard International Journal of Press/Politics*.

Yahya Kamalipour is professor of mass communication and head of the Department of Communication and Creative Arts at Purdue University. He has 10 published books, including *Global Communication*, 2nd ed. (2006); *Bring 'Em On: Media and Politics in the Iraq War* (2005); *War, Media, and Propaganda: A Global Perspective* (2004); and *Globalization and Corporate Media Hegemony* (2003). Kamalipour is the founder and managing editor of *Global Media Journal* (www.globalmediajournal.com). He earned his Ph.D. in communication (radio-TV-film) from University of Missouri-Columbia, an M.A. in mass media from University of Wisconsin-Superior, and B.A. in mass communication (public relations) from Minnesota State University. For additional information, visit his personal Web site at www.kamalipour.com.

Anne Koenen was president of the German Association for American Studies from 1999-2002 and is professor of American Studies at Leipzig University. Her research has focused on African American literature, popular culture, and the fantastic. Her publications include monographs on Black women's literature, the fantastic in women's literature, as well as an interview with Toni Morrison and numerous articles. Her current research project is on mail-order catalogs as the primary media of modernization in the rural United States, 1880-1930.

Maria Teresa La Porte is professor of International Communication in the School of Communication of the University of Navarre (Spain). She also serves as the dean and is the director of a research project financed by the Spanish government on "Globalizatión and Pluralism in the European Public TV." She is also collaborating as an expert on global media and public diplomacy in another project funded by the BBVA Foundation on "The Social Experience of Time." She has been a research scholar at the London School of Economics and at the Center for International Affairs at Harvard University. She has also been a scholar at NATO. She is the author of the book: *The Foreign Policy of Franco's Regime: 1957-1963.*

Sam Lehman-Wilzig is vice chairman of the Department of Political Studies, in charge of the Public Communications Program, at Bar-Ilan University, Israel, and is a former chair of the Israel Political Science Association. He is editor-in-chief of *Patuakh,* Israel's Hebrew-language academic journal of mass media. His research interests include new media, political communication, and communications theory.

Ming Liang is a research assistant at the Center for Transforming Cultures, UTS, and is working in public relations in China and Australia.

Denis Mancevič was born in Belarus and is now living and studying in Slovenia. He has a university degree in Russian language and literature and in sociology of culture. He is finishing also an undergraduate program in International relations in the Faculty of Social Sciences, University of Ljubljana, Slovenia. His research interests are international relations, media studies, sociology of totalitarism. He works as a journalist and is author and co-author of many articles in Slovene newspapers and magazines, such as *Medijska pre a*, *Mladina*, *Delo* and *Večer*.

Maria B. Marron is professor and chair of the Department of Journalism at Central Michigan University. She holds a doctorate in journalism/mass communication from Ohio University, a master's in journalism from The Ohio State University, and a bachelor's in English, Latin and French from University College Dublin, Ireland. She has worked in journalism, public relations and academe in Ireland and in journalism and academe in the United States. Her research interests include investigative journalism with an emphasis on the British Isles, ethics, law and international communication.

Brian McNair is professor of journalism and communication at the University of Strathclyde in Glasgow, Scotland. He is the author of many books and articles on journalism, including: *Images of the Enemy* (1988), *Glasnost, Perestroika and the Soviet Media* (1991), *Journalism and Democracy* (2000) and *News & Journalism In the UK* (4th edition, 2003). His latest book is *Cultural Chaos: Journalism News and Power in a Globalised World* (Routledge, 2006).

Kirsten Mogensen is an associate professor at Roskilde University, Denmark. She was a visiting professor at the Manship School of Mass Communication, Louisiana State University during the 2001-2002 academic year. On September 11, she was in the United States, where she initiated a research project about the coverage of the first 24 hours after the events on the five major TV-stations from the perspective of learning how to handle crisis coverage. She has been a journalist for more than 30 years, where she has worked in print as well as broadcast and in many different functions such as reporter, editor, copy editor and anchor. The last 15 year she has taught journalism at the Danish School of Journalism and at Roskilde University. Her main research interest is the norms, philosophies and ethics of journalists who work within a liberal or a social liberal press system. Mogensen holds degrees at university level in journalism, Danish, psychology and management. She has studied at universities in Denmark, United States and Sweden.

Greg Noble is a senior lecturer in cultural studies in the School of Humanities and a member of the Centre for Cultural Research at the University of Western Sydney. His research interests include youth, ethnicity and identity; material culture, technology and subjectivity; and the sociology of intellectuals. He has published widely on various topics and is co-author of *Kebabs, Kids, Cops and Crime: Youth, Ethnicity and Crime* (Pluto, 2000) and *Bin Laden in the Suburbs: Criminalising the Arab Other* (Institute of Criminology, 2004).

Rune Ottosen graduated with a degree in journalism in 1973 (Norwegian College of Journalism) and one in political science in 1984 (University of Oslo). He worked for many years as a journalist in various Norwegian media. From 1984-89 he was engaged as a lecturer and research fellow at the Norwegian College of Journalism. From 1989-1993 he worked as a

Information Director and research fellow at the International Peace Research Institute, Oslo (PRIO) where he was in charge of the research project "Enemy Images in Norwegian Media Since the Thaw in East-West Relation." From 1994-1996 he worked as a research fellow at the Norwegian Journalist Federation, writing the professional history of Norwegian journalists. Since 1996 he has worked as an associate professor at the Journalisteducation, Oslo University College, and became a full professor at the same institution in 1999. From 2001 to 2005, he has served as the president of The Norwegian Non-fiction Writers and Translators Association. Professor Ottosen has published several books, is a member of the research project "Journalism in the New World Order," and has, together with professor Stig Arne Nohrstedt of Sweden, edited three books on international conflicts.

Ross Perigoe is associate professor of journalism at Concordia University in Montreal, Canada. A former radio and television reporter and producer, Perigoe was the director of television for the Canadian Broadcasting Corporation in the nation's capital, Ottawa, before joining the faculty of Concordia University in 1985. In 2005, he completed his doctoral thesis on racist representations of Muslims at RMIT University in Melbourne, Australia.

Tomasz Pludowski, Ph.D., is currently a Fulbright Senior Research Scholar in the Department of Communication at Stanford University. He also is editor-in-chief of *Global Media Journal* (Polish edition), published online by the Collegium Civitas, Warsaw. His publications include *American Politics, Media, and Elections* (Collegium Civitas Press, 2005), *Terrorism, Media, Society* (Collegium Civitas Press, 2006), and *The Media and International Communication* (Peter Lang, 2007). Dr Pludowski is a former Kościuszko Foundation Visiting Scholar at New York University and has taught at universities in the Netherlands and the United Kingdom.

Jacques Portes is professor of North American History at the University de Paris 8 Vincennes Saint Denis and is also a member of a CNRS-EHESS research unit. Professor Portes' work focuses primarily on mass culture and American political life. He is interested in contemporary American life and its concept of democracy, as well as in the cultural relations between the United States, France and Québec. He has published several books, most notably, *Les États-Unis: une histoire à deux visages* (Bruxelles, Complexe, 2003), *Buffalo Bill* (Paris, Fayard, 2002) and *Une fascination réticente: les États-Unis dans l'opinion française, 1870-1914* (Nancy, PUN, 1990), which was awarded many distinguished prizes. His most recent book is *Une génération américaine* (Paris, Colin, 2004).

Scott Poynting is an associate professor in the School of Humanities at the University of Western Sydney. He is co-author of *Bin Laden in the Suburbs: Criminalising the Arab Other* (Institute of Criminology, Sydney, 2004) and *Kebabs, Kids, Cops and Crime: Youth, Ethnicity and Crime*, Pluto Australia, Sydney, 2000).

Dmitry Alexadrovich Ruschin is associate professor and director of the International Journalism Summer School and Winter School on Public Relations at St.Petersburg State University, St. Petersburg, Russia. He is author of many articles in newspapers and scholarly publications and has been speaker at numerous congresses, conferences and seminars. He also is a member of the St. Petersburg Union of Journalists and St. Petersburg Philosophical Society.

Teresa Sádaba is an associate professor in the School of Communications at the University of Navarra, Spain. She is also the vice director of the master's program on political and corporate communication, which is run in collaboration with George Washington University. Her research and teaching focus on political communication, and she is a former visiting professor at the University of Texas at Austin and a former Fulbright Fellow in Salzburg. She also teaches courses at the University Paris XII, and University Complutense in Madrid and is the editor of "Periodistas ante conflictos" (Eunsa, 1999) and several works about communication and terrorism.

M. Zenaida Sarabia-Panol is a professor at the School of Journalism, College of Mass Communication, Middle Tennessee State University. She teaches public relations and advertising at both the graduate and undergraduate levels. Dr. Sarabia-Panol is the immediate past head of the International Communication Division, Association for Education in Journalism and Mass Communication (AEJMC). A published author, her research interests are international communication, public relations, disability advertising, new technologies, academic quality rankings, and media content and effects. She obtained a bachelor of journalism degree, *magna cum laude*, from Silliman University; a master of arts in communication from the University of the Philippines at Diliman and a doctorate in mass communication from Oklahoma State University.

Yoichi Shimatsu is former editor of *The Japan Times Weekly* in Tokyo and has taught journalism and media studies at The University of Hong Kong and Tsinghua University in Beijing. As an independent video producer and freelance journalist, he covered the Kashmir conflict and Afghan War.

Qustandi Shomali is an associate professor at Bethlehem University, where he teaches journalism and literature. With degrees from universities in Algeria, Canada and the Sorbonne in France, he possesses a wide range of personal and academic interests that include history, literature and arts. He published many books including a series of academic studies about the Palestinian Press.

Ksenija Vidmar Horvat is an assistant professor at Department of Sociology, Faculty of Arts, University of Ljubljana. She completed her master's and Ph.D. at University of California, Davis. Her research includes analysis of cultural representations of gender and identity, global mass media, multiculturalism and global culture. Her most recent work addresses questions of globalization, post-socialism and post-feminism, including "Globalization of Gender: *Ally McBeal* in Post-Socialist Slovenia," *European Journal of Cultural Studies* 8:2; 2005.

FOREWORD

Yahya R. Kamalipour

*The only way in which a human being can make some
approach to knowing the whole of subject is by hearing what
can be said about it by persons of every variety of opinion and
studying all modes in which it can be looked at by every
character of mind. No wise man ever acquired his wisdom in
any mode but this.*

—John Stuart Mill

In 2006, America is not, nor is the world, the same
as it was prior to the September 11, 2001, terrorist attacks. Suspicion and
distrust of "others," fear of the unknown, and unease about the role and
status of the United States permeates the air. The so-called "War on
Terrorism," against a vague and undefined enemy, rages on in Iraq,
Afghanistan, and elsewhere. The media hint at the possibility of another pre-
emptive attack against Iran and its nuclear power plants which are reportedly
intended for making atomic weapons.

The contemporary "Electronic Age," as Marshall McLuhan envisioned
in the 1960s, has interconnected the entire world, but this interconnectedness
has not ostensibly contributed to improved intercultural communication and
international relations or a cooperative "global village." Rather, it has
presented an array of previously inconceivable challenges and obstacles vis-à-
vis media, culture, economy, and politics. "Increasingly removed from
personal experience," writes Mark Slouka (1995), "and over-dependent on
the representations of reality that come to us through television and the print
media, we seem more and more willing to put our trust in intermediaries who
"re-present" the world to us" (1995, pp. 1-2). This situation is indeed
intensified during conflicts and wars in which highly sophisticated
propaganda campaigns and emotionally charged terms such as
"fundamentalism," "terrorism," "jihad," and "evil" are coined and used by

the mass media to influence public opinion in favor of a particular government agenda (Kamalipour, 2004). Regarding global media coverage, Douglas Kellner (2004) writes:

> The 2003 Iraq War was a major global media event constructed very differently by varying broadcasting networks in different parts of the world. While the U.S. networks framed the event as "Operation Iraqi Freedom" (the Pentagon concept) or "War in Iraq," the Canadian CBC used the logo "War on Iraq," and various Arab networks presented it as an "invasion" and "occupation." (p. 69)

In the aftermath of the first and second Persian Gulf Wars and 9/11, scores of books have been published in the United States and elsewhere about the role of mass media during wars and global conflicts, including: (1) media coverage of the 9/11 attack, (2) media coverage of the war on Afghanistan and Iraq, (3) media complicity with the U.S. administration, (4) media framing and debates, (5) media censorship and embedded reporting, (6) media construction of reality, (7) media manipulation of public opinion, (8) media and public diplomacy, (9) media and social-political responsibly, 10) media, patriotism and democracy, (11) media and objectivity, and (12) media and dehumanization of war.

The well-orchestrated 9/11 attacks shattered the perceived invincibility and invulnerability of America vis-à-vis foreign invasion and permanently altered the international and intercultural relations of this contemporary superpower with the rest of the world.

The information age has transformed everything in people's lives, whether they live in a remote village in Africa, America, Asia, Australia, or Europe. Provided that they have some of the necessities of the modern life, such as electricity and a telephone and access to the electronic media, they unknowingly have become a member of the global village. In a global village where distant voices and images, transmitted via the electronic and print media, can be used as powerful means of psychological warfare and propaganda weapons, its inhabitants inevitably form their perceptions of "other" people and places — their thoughts, behavior, expectations, preferences, likes or dislikes — based on what they receive through the mass media. Furthermore, by acquiring skills in reading and writing and having access to a computer and a global network, such as the Internet, they can quickly become full-fledged participants, not just observers, of the world community in which they can interact with millions of people around the globe.

Global capitalism and global media have now penetrated the tribal way of life in the Amazon jungles via satellite-receiving dishes that adorn the elite's huts. Quite possibly, the members of the tribe may now dream of having a Pizza Hut, driving a Toyota, drinking a Budweiser beer, and owning other goods trumpeted on their TV sets.

We live in a world that is intensely information-driven, in which "knowledge is power," and in which mass media play a key role in our social, economic, and cultural affairs. With the concentration of global media in the hands of a few transnational corporations (i.e., Time Warner, Disney, Murdoch's News Corporation, Bertelsmann of Germany, and Viacom), it is possible to use the media to provoke both positive or negative human emotions or create a divisive and polarized political and cultural environment within and without nations. In other words, we live in a media-induced global environment in which carefully manufactured and packaged images play a decisive role in our daily lives — images that can sell, as well as enhance, and images that can conjure hate and despair. Clearly, the communication-information-technology revolution continues to alter, redefine, and restructure human societies and lives throughout the world.

Apropos the above, this multifaceted book, *How the World's News Media Reacted to 9/11*, examines the global media's reaction to the 9/11 attack. The editor, Tomasz Pludowski, has done a commendable job of bringing together an impressive cast of media experts, scholars, and professionals from throughout the world to assess global media reaction and coverage of 9/11. This book adds a fresh and welcome dimension to the existing literature on international communication, media and war.

The reader of this timely volume will note that the contributing authors have carefully studied and analyzed the global media's reactions to the 9/11 from a non-American perspective. In so doing, they have skillfully woven their personal insights and expertise into their research analysis of the media coverage of a given country and produced a series of critical essays that are easy to read, informative and thought-provoking.

Any meaningful step toward devising a better world requires shared goals and coordinated actions in reversing the current destructive, divisive, and anarchistic global trends. The first step in that direction must be based on education, awareness, and reliable information. Hence, this multi-faceted and multi-cultural volume makes a significant contribution by providing the reader with diverse perspectives that hopefully will provoke thoughtful analysis and discussions vis-à-vis human reactions to 9/11, media coverage, cultural interpretations, and global implications of war and violence.

How the World's News Media Reacted to 9/11 should prove to be a valuable book for disciplines, such as international communication, international affairs, cultural studies, political science, journalism, and mass communication in general. This timely volume should also be beneficial to media professionals and policy makers.

REFERENCES

Kamalipour, Y. R. (2004). Language, media and war: Manipulaing public perception. In R. D. Berenger, (ed.), *Global media go to war: Role of news and entertainment media during the 2003 Iraq War.* Spokane, WA: Marquette Books.

Kellner, D. (2004). Spectacle and media propaganda in the War on Iraq: A critique of U.S. broadcasting network. In Y. R. Kamalipour & N. Snow (Eds.), *War, media, and propaganda: A global Perspective.* Boulder, CO: Rowman & Littlefield.

Slouka, M. (1995). *War of the worlds: Cyberspace and the high-tech assault on reality.* New York: Basic Books.

INTRODUCTION & ACKNOWLEDGMENTS

Tomasz Pludowski

Hundreds of books on 9/11 have been published, covering global terrorism (e.g. Hoge and Rose 2001), U.S. media coverage of September 11 (e.g., Berenger 2004), media framing (Norris, Kern, & Just 2003), communicating terror (Tuman 2003), U.S. journalism after 9/11 (Zelizer & Allan 2002), understanding 9/11 (Calhoun, Price, & Timmer 2002; Hershberg & Moore, 2002), U.S. hegemony (Chomsky, 2002; Chomsky 2003), etc. However, nearly all of those provide the U.S. perspective. This study aims to bridge that gap by being more inclusive and representative of the world's scholarship.

The idea for this book grew out of a panel discussion at the 2002 convention of the Association for Education in Journalism and Mass Communication (AEJMC) in Miami Beach, to which I was invited by Debra Mason, director of the Religion Newswriters' Association. The discussion, titled "The World Watched Us", was thought-provoking but it covered only a handful of geographic areas. Moreover, virtually all perspectives presented were those of American scholars.

Afterward, I decided to continue the project and bring together a more diverse group of scholars to offer a wider range of views on the world's reactions to 9/11. Maria Marron and Zeny Sarabia-Panol were part of the original line-up. Brian McNair and I met during a 1997 conference on "The Images of Politics" organized by the University of Amsterdam, where we both spoke. He seemed a natural choice to offer an analysis of the British media reaction to the attack. The other authors included in this publication were either selected by me or suggested to me as possible contributors.

This volume is unique in its approach and scope. It bears some resemblance to *Communication and Terrorism* (Greenberg 2002), but it clearly distinguishes itself by expanding on the non-American responses to the attacks. To that end, virtually all chapters that presented American scholars' analyses of American reactions to 9/11 were taken out of this publication and will appear elsewhere (Pludowski, 2006). While the other volume is intended to bring American perspectives on 9/11 and terrorism to European audiences, this collection serves the opposite purpose — namely, it brings non-American persepectives to the attention of mainly American audiences. In short, *How the World's News Media Reacted to 9/11* fills a void in academic scholarship.

CHARACTERISCTICS OF THIS STUDY

The working intention behind this project was to make this anthology:

- *International.* As noted before, the purpose is to fill a gap in global English-language scholarly literature by providing a volume on reactions to 9/11 in the mass media of communications around the world.
- *Interdisciplinary.* The perspectives presented include a variety of disciplines: journalism, political science, media and communication, and international relations. A multitude of research methods have been used ranging from personal interviews with journalists covering 9/11, discourse analysis of media coverage, content analysis, semiotic analysis, statistical analysis, and general informed commentary. While many authors provide succinct national overviews, a number of contributors offer detailed and more narrowly-focused analyses of select aspects of media coverage in a country or region of their choice.
- *Comparative.* A number of studies go beyond analysis of individual countries by making cross-national comparisons. That is most notably true of the chapters dealing with Latin America, the Far East, and Britain and Ireland.
- *A combination of scholarly theory and journalistic practice.* The authors represent some of the most accomplished media analysts in their home countries. While most of them are academic scholars, several are also or primarily journalists.
- *Cross-generational.* The authors range from established experts to junior faculty, in most cases working together to marry experience with a fresh view.
- *Native-like.* Every effort was made to ring true by including perspectives written by scholars native to the area under study, or at least ones with long-term, first-hand, near-native experience with that area and culture.
- *Accessible.* Given the all-encompassing nature of 9/11, this study is intended for the general reader as well as the academic community. One of the aims was to interest scholars, researchers, politicians, media executives, as well the general reader. To this end, and for reasons of space and economy, discussions of theory and reviews of literature have been limited to the minimum and presented at any length only in several

chapters (e.g. Bouvier, Vidmar Horvat, Sarabia-Panol, Hughes) and in some caes entirely omitted.

The Structure of this Volume

The book begins with a Foreword by Yahya Kamalipour, an internationally noted scholar of international communication and executive editor of all national editions of *Global Media Journal*, including the Polish edition for which I am editor-in-chief.

The chapters are structured by continent, with the European analysis constituting the most numerous group and, thus, coming first. Individual chapters are devoted to British and Irish, French, German, Spanish, Norwegian, Polish, Slovene, and Russian media. Then analysis focuses respectively on Asia (a comparative study of the seven nations of China, India, Indonesia, Japan, Malaysia, Pakistan, and the Philippines, followed by individual studies of China, a comparison of Japan and China, and a look at India). The remaining sections focus on Arab and Middle Eastern countries (Egypt, Palestine, and Turkey), Australia, South Africa, and the Americas (U.S., Canada, and an extensive comparison of Latin American data).

In the Afterword, Cees J. Hamelink, former president of the International Association for Mass Communication Research, faces the difficult, if not impossible, task of making sense of the extensive amount of information this volume provides. One cannot help but agree that this study bears out the flaws of the vision of journalism as a mirror of multi-faceted reality by showing how journalism falls victim to political and economic pressures, local cultural values, recent history, and the current state of international relations.

The text will appeal to the general reader and anyone interested in journalism, international media, global studies and current affairs. Also, by offering new information and filling a niche in American scholarly literature the volume will be interesting to researchers in those areas. The anthology can be used in classes in international journalism, international relations, media and terrorism, political communication, American Studies and sociology.

Acknowledgments

In all likelihood, the idea for this book would not have occurred had it not been for Debra Mason of AEJMC, who invited me to a panel on world reactions to 9/11 back in 2002. I would like to thank her for that invitation and for her support.

Several individuals put me in touch with other scholars doing work in the area. Those helpful souls were: David Goodman and Stephanie Donald of the University of Technology Sydney, Janet Trewin of BBC, Robin Larsen and Ahlam al-Muhtassib of California State University San Bernardino, Richard Nelson of the Manship School of Mass Communication, Toby Miller of New York University, Marie Lienard of University de Paris 8, Ralph D. Berenger of the American University in Cairo, Bogusława Dobek-Ostrowska of Wrocław University, and, last but not least, Lidija Herek of Slovenian Government. I would like to thank them all greatly.

Tal Azran of Melbourne University, a fellow NYU visiting scholar, should be thanked for drawing my attention to Marquette Books, an energetic and open-minded publisher interested in international communication, which resulted in a contract. From the day I approached him with this project, Marquette Books' *spiritus movens*, David Demers has been a very supporting and encouraging editor to work with. When I was adopting his book, *Global Media: Menace or Messiah?*, for my seminar in late nineties, I never suspected he would be my editor and publisher several years later.

This is the longest-running project I have ever worked on—it took several years to complete. Consequently, over that period many individuals have helped in a number of ways and their help and contribution are gratefully acknowledged.

Tomasz Pludowski
Kolumna, Winter 2007

REFERENCES

Berenger, Ralph D. (Ed.). (2004). *Global media got to war: Role of news and entertainment media during and after the 2003 Iraq war*. Spokane, WA: Marquette Books.

Calhoun, Craig, Paul Price, and Ashley Timmer. (Eds.). (2002). *Understanding September 11*. New York: Social Science Research Council.

Chomsky, Noam. (2002). *9-11*. New York: Seven Stories Press.

Chomsky, Noam. (2003). *Power and terror. Post-9/11 talks and interviews*. New York: Seven Stories Press and Tokyo: Little More.

Greenberg, B. S. (Ed.). (2002). *Communication and terrorism*. Creskill, NJ: Hampton Press, Inc.

Hershberg, Eric and Kevin W. Moore (Eds.). (2002). *Critical views of September 11: Analyses from around the world*. New York: Social Science Research Council.

Hess, Stephen and Marvin Kalb. (Eds.). (2003). *The media and the war on terrorism.* Washington, D.C.: Brookings Institution Press.

Hoge, James F. and Gideon Rose. (Eds.). (2001). *How did this happen?* Washington, D.C.: Public Affairs.

Nacos, Brigitte L. (2002). *Mass-mediated terrorism.* New York: Rowman & Littlefield Publishers.

Nacos, Brigitte L. (1994). *Terrorism and the media.* New York: Columbia University Press.

Norris, Pippa, Montague Kern, and Marion Just. (Eds.). (2003). *Framing terrorism. The news media, the government and the public.* New York and London: Routledge.

Palmer, Nancy (Ed.) (2003). *Terrorism, war, and the press.* The Joan Shorenstein Center on the Press, Politics and Public Policy, John F. Kennedy School of Government.

Pludowski, T. (Ed.). (2006). *Terrorism, media, society.* Toruń and Warsaw: Adam Marszałek and Collegium Civitas Press.

Tuman, Joseph S. (2003). *Communicating terror.* Thousand Oaks: Sage.

Zelizer, Barbie and Stuart Allan (Eds.). (2002). *Journalism after September 11.* London and New York: Routledge.

Part I

EUROPEAN MEDIA

Chapter 1

UK MEDIA COVERAGE OF SEPTEMBER 11

Brian McNair

More than twenty years ago, French philosopher Jean Baudrillard referred to terrorism as the "theatre of cruelty" (1983, p. 143). He meant that in so far as its perpetrators set out to fill news media with horrifying, attention-grabbing images of bodies and buildings blown apart, (post)modern terrorism can be understood as staged spectacle, intended to command the political agenda and fill the enemy's hearts with disgust and fear. The British public saw the tactic in action over some 30 years in Northern Ireland, where it contributed to the decision of the UK government to enter into negotiations with the various armed factions and, eventually, the Good Friday agreement of 1998. The Spanish have seen it in their cities and coastal resorts, where, at the height of the holiday season in 2002, an ETA bomb killed a child and the resulting publicity seriously damaged the local tourism industry. But the spectacular, theatrical quality of terrorism has never been more skillfully deployed than on September 11, 2001, when Osama bin Laden used the immediacy and global reach of 24-hour real-time news to send his defiant message to the United States and its allies, and to rally his own supporters across the world. On that day in New York, in the most obscene snuff movie of all time, the transnational television audience watched nearly 3,000 people die.

The event triggered military attacks — first on Afghanistan, then on Iraq — and led to controversial policy developments, such as the Patriot Act in the United States and a proposal to introduce identity cards in the United Kingdom. It was a devastating first strike in what quickly became known as the "war on terror," sharpening and making visible to all what Samuel Huntington had already called "the clash of civilisations" in his 1996 book of that name. Islamic fundamentalism and Osama bin Laden, in particular, in interviews with CNN and other media, had declared holy war — *jihad* — on non-Islamic civilizations and values in the 1990s. In that context,

September 11 was Pearl Harbor and Guernica rolled into one — an audacious, ruthless, hitherto unimaginably violent act designed to decapitate and demoralize. As John Gray's 2003 essay on globalization and terrorism put it: "The attack on the Twin Towers demonstrates that Al Qaida understands that twenty-first century wars are spectacular encounters in which the dissemination of media images is a core strategy" (2003, p. 76).

Dissemination of those particular images was immediate and all-encompassing. Real-time news media such as CNN and Fox News, network news organizations such as NBC and the BBC, Internet news sites and bloggers, and radio and print outlets all were given over to blanket coverage of events in New York and Washington for several days and weeks. The story commanded the global news agenda, bringing into being a transnational public united in consumption of information about its significance and impacts.

I was on sabbatical study leave in the far north east of Australia, twelve thousand miles from my home in Scotland, when the first plane hit the World Trade Center.[1] It was approximately 10:45 p.m. in that geographically isolated part of the world, and my wife and I were eating pizza with a friend at a local restaurant. When we got home just after 11 p.m., I switched on CNN, as I often did at that time of night while down under, to enable me to keep up with events on the other side of the world. Like all those who were not in the immediate vicinity of the twin towers, I missed the first strike, tuning in to the live TV coverage at a point when the north tower was already burning, but nobody as yet knew why. CNN's correspondents were speculating about the possible causes of the fire clearly visible on camera, but without firm information. Along with the hundreds of millions of people by now following CNN and other broadcasters, I witnessed the second strike as it happened a few moments later. I stayed with CNN throughout a night of journalistic confusion, panic and disbelief.

From that remote outpost in tropical Queensland, I joined a global audience of spectators to an act of mass murder that would shape the course of world events for the foreseeable future. The sense of connection between my location in Australia, my home in Scotland, and events occurring 15,000 miles and fourteen time zones away on the east coast of the United States was both exhilarating and unsettling. My feelings of anger, incapacity and impotence in the face of such an act were similar, I imagine, to those experienced by CNN correspondents narrating the drama from their Manhattan offices, although we were half a world apart.

For all that it was global in impact, however, the news media of different countries reported the events of September 11 in different ways, reflecting the relationships to and perceptions of their media and political elites about the United States, the Republican administration of George W. Bush, and the Middle East conflict. This essay assesses coverage in the United Kingdom, the United States' closest ally on September 11, 2001, as it has remained in the ensuing period. It notes that British news media shared many of the premises and assumptions of U.S. journalists as they sought to make sense of the attacks. While dissenting views as to the meaning of 9/11 were reported in the UK media, British journalists tended to respond, as did their colleagues in the USA, to the event as the inauguration of a new era — an era of war on global Islamic terror.

September 11 in the British Media

There is general consensus among observers of Western media that on September 11, 2001, the conventional rules of newsgathering and reportage ceased to apply. As Zelizer and Allan put it in their introduction to *Journalism After September 11*, "shaken to their foundation have been familiar notions of what it means to be a journalist, how best to practice journalism, and what different publics can reasonably expect of journalists in the name of democracy" (2002, p. 1). September 11 meant "the death of detachment" (Ibid., p. 16). While long-standing critics of liberal journalism bemoaned the fact that "the media system" on this occasion proved to be, as it had been in the past, "a superior propaganda organ for militarism and war" (McChesney, 2002, p. 93), the majority of journalists and their audiences recognized that September 11 was different, both in scale and intent, from the terrorist atrocities of, say the IRA.

IRA terrorism always had a political objective, holding out the possibility of negotiation and resolution. Thus, it was that even American right-wingers and Republicans could support it with money and resources. Al Qaida's declaration of war, on the other hand, was non-negotiable, an act of pure violence designed to destabilize and, if possible, begin the process of bringing down global capitalism itself. Just as objectivity was not expected of the Western news media toward the Nazis in 1939-45, it would not be forthcoming in coverage of September 11. This was manifest in the tears shed by usually detached anchors as they sought to make sense in their own minds and for their audiences the scale of the atrocity. It also generated the kind of uncritical journalistic solidarity with government normally associated with wars of national survival, which is precisely how the attacks quickly came to be perceived — as a declaration of war. It was understood from an early stage in the drama that this was a new kind of war, fought by nonstate actors with weapons made available by and symbolic of globalization — real-time news and cheap air travel in particular — against the world's leading economic power. But it was war nonetheless. Early in its coverage, CNN adopted the rubric "Attack On America."

Academic analysts have documented and criticized the manner in which American coverage of September 11 so quickly and unquestioningly became a narrative about war. Sandra Silberstein notes that "through emblems of patriotism, the media endorsed, and indeed helped produce, 'America's new war'" (2002, p. xiii). Martin Montgomery notes that "even though other expressions were available, which could have provided competing currencies of description, war quickly came to dominate public discourse and ultimately thereby to dominate events" (2005, p. 239). Through "a process of discursive amplification," the American media, as Montgomery sees it, marginalized alternative narratives for making sense of the event, such as that which stressed the sense of helplessness and desperation experienced by the peoples of developing countries, and the Palestinians in particular, as they sought to battle poverty and injustice.

Such criticisms have empirical substance, as all viewers of the coverage will recall. They neglect the emotional dimension of September 11, however, as if journalists in a newsroom five kilometres (or 3000 miles) away from where thousands of people were dying in real time could be expected to have reported the story dispassionately or without bias towards the victims. On September 11, journalists left their objectivity at the newsroom door because this, in a manner never seen before, was an attack on them and theirs: their city, their country, their values, and their media.

There was, of course, dissent from this view in some quarters. Only two days after the attacks, the late Susan Sontag wrote a piece for the *New Yorker* magazine which defended the "courage" of the September 11 terrorists.[2]

> Where is the acknowledgment that this was not a "cowardly" attack on "civilization" or "liberty" or "humanity" or "the free world" but an attack on the world's self-proclaimed superpower, undertaken as a consequence of specific American alliances and actions ... [I]f the word "cowardly" is to be used, it might be more aptly applied to those who kill from beyond the range of retaliation, high in the sky, than to those willing to die themselves in order to kill others. In the matter of courage (a morally neutral virtue): whatever may be said of the perpetrators of Tuesday's slaughter, they were not cowards.

One scholar pointed out that "dominant coverage" of 9/11 in the United States did not include "historical assessment of the structural violence that went into building [New York and Washington]" (Karim, 2002, p. 104). Indeed, it did not, although it seems naïve in the extreme to think that journalists reporting such an event would pause to consider the "structural violence" involved in the construction of a modern city as a causal factor in a terrorist attack upon that city and its working people. Noam Chomsky, while accepting that the September 11 attacks were "major atrocities," qualified this statement by asserting that "in terms of number of victims, they do not reach the level of many others, for example, Clinton's bombing of the Sudan with no credible pretext."[3] Seen from the purely human perspective, however, it is difficult to imagine in what ways the response of U.S. media to this unprecedented event could have been other than what unfolded — shock, confusion, anger and grief.

Beyond America's borders, on the other hand, so close a journalistic identification with the events in New York and Washington was not so predictable. It was present, however, especially in the media of the country traditionally closest to the United States politically. In Britain, too, after the initial confusion about what exactly was happening at the World Trade Center buildings had been clarified, September 11 was reported as an act of war, rather than a mere act of terrorism. BBC News embraced the "Attack On America" rubric. September 12 headlines in the British press included:

War on America (*Daily Telegraph*)
War on the World (*Daily Mirror*)
Declaration of war (*Daily Express*)
Assault on America (*Financial Times*)
Apocalypse (*Daily Mail*)

As in the United States, there were a few exceptions to this pattern. In an article written for the *Guardian* two days after 9/11, UK-based journalist Seamus Milne blamed the American people themselves, including those killed in the World Trade Center buildings that morning, for the atrocity. By their "unabashed national egotism and arrogance," argued Milne, and their failure to address "the injustices and inequalities" that, in his view, motivated the bombers, they had gotten more or less what they deserved, "once again reaping a dragon's teeth harvest they themselves sowed."[4] A contributor to the *London Review of Books* declared in an essay a few days later that "however tactfully you dress it up, the United States had it coming. World bullies, even if their heart is in the right place, will in the end pay the price."[5] The September 13 edition of the BBC's public participation current affairs program, *Question Time*, included anti-American comments directed toward the U.S. ambassador (who had appeared as a panel member on the show) from some members of its studio audience (the BBC later apologized for the incident). Such dissent from the overwhelming consensus that September 11 was an attack without justification or excuse was rare, however.

To a greater extent than was true of the American media, British coverage of September 11 focused not just on the events in the United States but on the global response. International solidarity with the American people and their government was reported as almost universal, while rare expressions of support for the attacks, as displayed by West Bank Palestinians filmed celebrating and cheering, were highlighted by Independent Television News, Channel 5 News and other outlets. BBC World reported that "in the Palestinian refugee camps all over the Middle East there has been jubilation — chanting, cheering, celebratory gunfire, people have been handing out sweets; they're ecstatically happy. They are saying, now, at last, America is having a taste of the same sort of suffering that we, the Palestinians, have had."[6]

Such coverage has arguably had lasting effects on global perceptions of the legitimacy of the Palestinian cause. Just as Yasser Arafat's support for Saddam Hussein's occupation of Kuwait in 1991 was at the time and continues to be seen as a major strategic error, so coverage of apparent Palestinian pleasure at the deaths of so many innocent civilians — including those several hundred Muslims who had been in the World Trade Center at the moment of the attacks — had a complex but pronounced impact on global public opinion, especially as the tactic of suicide bombing became more popular among Palestinian militants during the second Intifada.

There was, then, a rare degree of journalistic consensus around the meaning of the September 11 events. With a few exceptions, such as those cited above, they were read by the British media, as they had been in the United States, as a declaration of war — an unprovoked and mystifying assault upon ordinary people going about their daily business in downtown New York, and an event that fully warranted a military response by the American government. This consensus would not survive the build-up to and execution of war on Iraq 18 months later, coverage of which was often critical of the Blair government's WMD-focused rationale for war (Tumber and Palmer, 2004), but on September 11 and in the days and weeks that followed, including the invasion of Afghanistan and the ousting of the Taliban from power, few beyond the ranks of the anti-American left challenged this reading.[7]

CONCLUSION

In Britain, as in the United States, media coverage of the September 11 attacks was dominated by journalists' genuine feelings of horror and outrage. Expressions of dissent, such as the *Guardian* article quoted above by Seamus Milne, were the exception to the rule and tended to reflect the long-standing anti-Americanism of many on the British left, including the view that "they had it coming." Such dissent was not typical, however. Certainly, the British media were somewhat freer to speculate on the underlying roots and causes of the attacks, simply because they had not occurred on British territory, but Tony Blair's early declarations of solidarity and sympathy with the American people, as well as the fact that several hundred British citizens died in the Twin Towers, defined the event as an assault on "us" as much as "them."

Then, and later in Afghanistan and Iraq, British media coverage reflected the degree of political consensus around the meaning of the events being reported. September 11 was reported as an act of homicidal terror not just against America but against civilized humanity in general, to which no response but journalistic outrage was justified. The attack on Afghanistan some weeks later was reported as a legitimate response to 9/11, validated by the United Nations and carried out by a broad coalition of countries. The attack on Iraq was less consensual and was fiercely opposed both inside and out of the leading Coalition countries, and the British media reflected this in coverage that was much less accepting of the government's rationale for and declared aims in war against Iraq (Tumber and Palmer, 2004). Content analyses show that the UK media were often critical of the Blair government in the run-up to and then the actual invasion of Iraq. They were even more so in the occupation phase, as the Andrew Gilligan affair and other stories exposed the evidential flaws (some called them lies) in the case for war against Saddam.

Since those interventions, and especially since the London bombings of July 2005, the British media have been heavily focused on the issue of Islamic fundamentalism within the country (its capacity to inspire terrorist attacks such as the July 7 bombings) and the policy challenges associated with integrating Muslims into British society. As this essay went to press, the British media were covering the trial of Abu Hamza, the radical cleric accused of inciting racial hatred and murder in speeches delivered at public meetings and religious services in London. Because of September 11 and its aftermath, the present and future status of such individuals, and of the Muslim community in general, had become a much more newsworthy and contentious issue for Britain's journalists than ever before. News media were also engaged in running coverage of governmental efforts to make such activities as "glorifying terrorism," and on the merits of identity cards, phone-tapping and other security measures deemed necessary by the Labour government post-September 11. In all these ways, the impact of that day on the British media has continued to be felt by journalists and their audiences.

CHAPTER ENDNOTES

[1] This paragraph is an extract from McNair, B. (2006). *Cultural Chaos: Journalism, News and Power in a Globalised World.* London: Routledge.

[2] Sontag, S., 'A Mature Democracy', *New Yorker*, September 24, 2001.

[3] Chomsky, N., 'A quick reaction', *Counterpunch*, September 12, 2001.

[4] For the full text of the article see www.guardian.co.uk/comment/story/ 0,3604,551036,00. html.

[5] Beard, M., 'Reflections on the present crisis', *London Review of Books*, September 20, 2001.

[6] Reported in Michalski and Preston, 2002, p. 11.

[7] British-based media did not monopolize coverage of the 9/11 events in the UK. The rise of real-time satellite news stations and a growing online journalism sector had, by late 2001, already created a substantially different media environment from that which accompanied the IRA's bombing campaign of the 1970s and 1980s. A study conducted under the joint auspices of the Broadcasting Standards and Independent Television Commissions (Michalski and Preston, 2002) notes that public knowledge of events such as the September 11 attacks is formed not merely by UK print and TV news media. "For an increasingly large number of viewers satellite news channels have offered a broader range of views and sometimes, when originated outside the UK, a different sensibility and analysis of these events." Their research found that Muslim and Arab residents of the UK perceived UK media coverage to be biased in favor of the Israelis and against the Palestinians as compared with that of Al-Jazeera and other Arab-language channels, although the researchers found no evidence of actual bias (as opposed to the perception of it) in their analyses.

REFERENCES

Allan, S., ed. (2005). *Journalism: Critical Issues*, London, Open University Press.
Baudrillard, J. (1983). *In the Shadow of the Silent Majorities*, New York, Semiotext.
Gray, J. (2003). *Al Qaeda and What It Means to Be Modern*, London, Faber and Faber.
Hess, S., Kalb, M., eds.(2003). *The Media and the War on Terrorism*, Washington, Brookings Institution Press.
Hiro, D. (2002). *War Without End: The Rise of Islamist Terrorism and Global Response*, London, Routledge.

Huntington, S. (1996). *The Clash of Civilisations and the Remaking of World Order*, New York, Simon & Schuster.

Karim, K.H. (2002). "Making Sense of the 'Islamic Peril': Journalism as Cultural Practice," in Zelizer and Allan, eds., 2002, pp. 101-116.

McChesney, R. (2002). "September 11 and the Structural Limitations of U.S. Journalism," in Zelizer and Allan, eds., 2002, pp. 91-100.

McNair, B. (1988). *Images of the Enemy*, London, Routledge

McNair, B. (2005). "The Emerging Chaos of Global News Culture," in Allan, ed., 2005, pp. 151-166.

McNair, B. (2006). *Cultural Chaos: Journalism, News and Power in a Globalised World*, London, Routledge.

Michalski, M., Preston, A. (2002). *After September 11: TV News and Transnational Audiences*, London, Broadcasting Standards Commission/Independent Television Commission/British Film Institute.

 Montgomery, M. (2005). "Talking War: How Journalism Responded to the Events of 9/11," in Allan, ed., 2005, pp. 239-260.

Silberstein, S. (2002). *War of Words: Language, Politics and 9/11*, London, Routledge.

Tumber, H., Palmer, J. (2004). *The Media At War*, London, Palgrave.

Zelizer, B., Allan, S., eds. (2005). *Journalism After September 11*, London, Routledge.

Chapter 2

Elite British and Irish Newspapers Reflect Ideology in Framing the 9/11 Catastrophe

Maria B. Marron

Much has been written about media coverage of 9/11. The winter 2003 edition of *Newspaper Research Journal*, for example, devoted the entire issue to studies of 9/11 media coverage under the title, "Reflections on an American Tragedy: Media Studies of September 11, 2001." Writing in that edition, Guido H. Stempel and Thomas Hargrove noted: "Much has been written and said about television's coverage of the terrorist attack Sept. 11, 2001, but a national survey by Ohio University and the Scripps Howard News Service shows that newspapers also played an important role" (Stempel and Hargrove, 2003, p. 55). In the same edition, Dominic Larosa concludes that on September 11, 2001, and on subsequent days, "The news media appear to have fulfilled the surveillance function reasonably well" (Larosa, 2003, p. 18). A study by Xigen Li and Ralph Izard found that "broadcast and print media focused coverage of the Sept. 11 terrorist attacks on facts" (Li and Izard, 2003, p. 204), but differences were manifest in frames and use of sources.

What is missing from this volume and, indeed, from much of the scholarship on 9/11 media coverage is a focus on international media coverage. This study will attempt to narrow that gap, specifically by exploring content from three key newspapers in England and Ireland, namely, the *Times* and *Sunday Times* (London, referred to hereafter collectively as the *Times*), the *Guardian* (Manchester/London), and the *Irish Times* (Dublin). These newspapers were selected for their "elite" status and because they are newspapers of record.

LITERATURE REVIEW

The Newspapers

England and Ireland have a long history of print media (Oram, 1983). There is a proliferation of media — print, broadcast and electronic — in both England and Ireland, and the media continue to play a powerful role in national life. In England, for example, the BBC last year broke a story about alleged malfeasance by Prime Minister Tony Blair's government in relation to the weapons of mass destruction in Iraq. The story, which led to the apparent suicide of one of its sources, prompted "the worst crisis in the corporation's 80-year history" in 2004 (Plunkett, 2004). The story was responsible for the launch of the Hutton Inquiry and ultimately led to the resignation of BBC chairman Greg Dyke and reporter Andrew Gilligan. Also in 2004, Piers Morgan, editor of the *Daily Mirror*, resigned his job when photos of alleged Iraqi prisoners were deemed false. But aside from the BBC and the *Mirror*, other important media include Channel 4, ITV, the *Daily Telegraph*, the *Independent*, the *Sun*, and Rupert Murdoch's Sky News satellite channel.

In Ireland, the *Irish Times*, traditionally considered the newspaper of the management and professional classes (Oliver, 2004, p. 17, and Ashdown, 1991, pp. 56, 46) continues to be so with some 79 percent of senior business executives reading the paper every day (Oliver, 2004, p. 17). The average readership of the *Irish Times* was 319,000 in 2003, an increase of 14,000 readers or 4.6 percent over the previous year (Oliver, 2004, p. 3). The *Irish Independent* had 532,000 readers in 2003; the *Sunday Independent*, 1,064,000 readers; the *Sunday World*, 827,000 readers; the *Sunday Tribune*, 219,000; the *Sunday Business Post*, 158,000; the *Examiner*, 206,000; and the *Star*, 437,000. In circulation terms, the *Irish Independent* has a circulation of about 168,000; the *Irish Times*, about 119,000, and the *Evening Herald*, about 104,000, with these figures representing an overall increase in daily newspaper readership attributable to Ireland's economic boom, according to Lianne Fridriksson in *Global Journalism* (Fridriksson, 2004, p. 198). Furthermore, "About one out of every four dailies sold in Ireland is British, as British newspapers are widely available throughout the country," Fridriksson notes (p. 198).

In England, the London press has become the national news source over the years. The BBC and the *Times* are preeminent, with the *Guardian*, Manchester and London, having a prominent role. The book, *The Function of Newspapers in Society*, notes that "in England, the London press became increasingly the national news source (augmented, of course, by the British Broadcasting Corporation) along with some provincial additions, most notably the Manchester *Guardian*" (Martin and Copeland, 2003, p. 98). Fridriksson (2004, p. 198) notes that

> The print media of Great Britain comprise about 130 daily and Sunday newspapers, more than 2,000 weekly newspapers, and about 7,000 periodicals, constituting more national and daily newspapers for every British citizen than in most other developed nations. Traditionally divided into qualities and populars, or broadsheets and tabloids, 13 national morning newspapers appear daily in Britain and nine appear Sundays. The *Times*, the *Daily Telegraph*, the *Guardian*, and the *Independent* are among the world's most respected newspapers.

In the 1960s, John C. Merrill, in *The Elite Press: Great Newspapers of the World*, described the elite press:

> It is aimed at the educated citizen who is aware of, and concerned about, the central issues of his time, and undoubtedly it is read by more opinion leaders than are other types of newspapers (Merrill, 1968, p. 11).

Merrill added that the elite press appealed to the intelligentsia, was well-informed about government matters, had a reputation for reliability and "even for presenting the most accurate image of governmental thinking" (Merrill, 1968, p. 12) He included both the *Times* and the *Guardian* in his primary elite tier of newspapers. Neither the *Irish Times* nor any other Irish newspaper was included, perhaps because at the time of the book's publication, the *Irish Times* did not enjoy the elite status it has enjoyed for the intervening years.

Tracing the evolution of both the *Times* and the *Guardian*, Merrill portrayed them to be exact opposites of each other: "Where the *Guardian* is brash and liberal, the *Times* is staid and conservative; where the former is a gadfly, the latter is a defender" (Merrill, 1968, p. 161).

Agenda Setting and Framing

The power of the media to set the agenda, to tell people what to think about, has been well documented since the seminal 1972 study by Maxwell McCombs and Donald Shaw (McCombs and Shaw, 1972, pp. 176-187). People not only acquire information from the media about issues, they also learn what importance they should attach to various issues based on the emphasis placed on topics in the news. The salience of topics usually is indicated by prominence in the newspaper (e.g., front-page placement vs. inside- or back-page placement, large headline vs. small, number of inches devoted to the topic, etc.). Each topic, or object, has attributes, characteristics and traits that tell us more about it. The media emphasize some, give less attention to others and none at all to more.

Chyi and McCombs note that while the first level of agenda-setting research focuses "on the transfer of object salience from the media agenda to the public agenda, the second level deals with attribute salience in the media and its impact on both object salience and attribute salience among the public" (Chyi and McCombs, 2004, p. 23). The selection of key attributes is regarded as framing. As different attributes of an event are recorded over time, "frame-changing" occurs (Chyi and McCombs, 2004, p. 22). Given that space and time are two of the most important dimensions of news coverage, frames may be grounded in those dimensions; i.e., coverage moves across levels from the micro to the macro, from the individual, community, regional, and societal to the international.

Stephen Reese has suggested that framing is the way in which media, media professionals and their audiences organize and make sense of events and issues (Reese, 2001, pp. 7-31). Unlike Entman, Goffman and Bateson, all credited with introducing framing, Gamson focused on the construction of issues, the structuring of discourse and the development of meaning (Reese, 2001). Shah et al. have suggested that the norms of newsworthiness, along with "the routines of media production, encourage journalists to organize — to frame — their reports in predictable ways" (Shah, Domke and Wackman, 2001, p. 227). What Shah et al. term the "episodic and strategic framing" (p. 227) of news influences information processing and political judgments.

Focusing on the measurement of frames, James Tankard suggested that framing is a multidimensional concept (Tankard, 2001, pp. 95-107). Pan and Kosicki explore the "discursive community" and show that framing involves "defining and redefining the actors-speakers" (Pan and Kosicki, 2001, p. 43). Kosicki does not regard framing as an extension of agenda-setting "because framing begins from an explicit cognitive perspective" (Maher, 2001, p. 83). Michael Maher has noted that despite their differences, both agenda-setting and framing have converged in recent years (Maher, 2001, p. 83).

RESEARCH QUESTIONS

This framing analysis of coverage of 9/11 in its immediate aftermath in three international newspapers will attempt to answer five questions: (1) What type of coverage existed in these newspapers from Sept. 12-19, 2001? (2) Were any particular frames or themes manifest during that week, and, if so, what were they? (3) How did these newspapers narrate the tragic event of 9/11 (i.e., in what sort of tone and language)? (4) Were the newspapers similar or different in their coverage? (5) Did the newspapers reflect their traditional identity or affiliation?

NEWS MEDIA DATA

News stories were drawn from the *Times*, the *Sunday Times*, the *Guardian*, and the *Irish Times* in the Lexis Nexis database and the newspapers' own archives from Sept. 12-19, 2001, inclusive. Stories were identified as relevant if they contained any of these words in relation to the World Trade Towers: "crash," "WTC," "World Trade Center," "tragedy," "terrorist," "terror," "September 11," "New York," "Osama bin Laden," and "attack."

The search produced a total of 93 stories. Of these, 28 came from the *Times/Sunday Times*; 52 came from the *Guardian*; and 13 came from the *Irish Times*. The most intense day for coverage in the *Guardian* was Sept. 12, with 44 of the 52 stories; the *Times* carried five stories on Sept. 12. The *Times/Sunday Times* coverage was most intense on Saturday, Sept. 15, with 11 stories. The *Irish Times* carried five 9/11-related stories on Sept. 12 and four on Saturday, Sept. 15, which were its days of most intense coverage.

Clearly, each of these newspapers devoted significant coverage to the 9/11 attacks. This study focuses only on narrative coverage (stories and opinion pieces) from a framing analysis perspective.

ANALYSIS OF COVERAGE

Narrative of the 9/11 catastrophe can be explored from a framing perspective with the major theme or frame being that of the terrorist attack and the minor theme that of the global implications of the disaster (i.e., the superpower "brought low," the effect on international trade, on security and the aviation industry, on the perpetrator and his reasons for causing the tragedy, and ultimately, on the superiority of the Western powers over others).

The actor-speakers in the 9/11 drama form a discursive community in so far that the key political leaders — President Bush and Prime Minister Blair — are involved directly from the first frames as the statesmen who will bring the terrorist perpetrator to justice and who will form an international alliance to fight evil. Juxtaposed with the framing of these two political actor-speakers is Osama bin Laden, suspected from initial frames as the mastermind of the attack. bin Laden and his Al-al-Qaeda counterparts immediately acquire the image of terrorists, of evildoers, of non-Western, Islamic radicals bent on jihad.

The key political player, however, was that of the United States itself, the superpower "brought low," the behemoth framed as a now-vulnerable entity.

As the first week's coverage unfolded, other political players entered the drama as did ordinary people and the media themselves. Again, the narrative of good versus evil, of West versus East, of pro-United States versus anti-US played out. Ordinary people, those who witnessed the tragedy as innocent bystanders and those who became victims of it, are framed as individuals and as social groups whose lives have been altered by the attack. The media themselves became embroiled in the drama, framed as being pro-U.S. or anti-U.S., radical and left or moderate and right.

Times

The *Times* immediately focused on the hijacked airplanes and their doomed flights, on "the inferno" of the World Trade Center and on the "many surreal sights" on the streets of Lower Manhattan (Ayres, 2001). The newspaper's diplomatic editor, Richard Beeston, attributed the attack to Osama bin Laden, reporting that "several extremist Middle Eastern groups and governments have the motivation to launch devastating attacks against the United States, but only one man has the experience and audacity to cause so much bloodshed" (Beeston, 2001, p. 5). The newspaper provided a profile of bin Laden, discussing his public appearances at his son's wedding, his poetry reading, his al-Qaeda training camps and his videotape in which he is shown with a Yemeni dagger. Bin Laden was bestialized with the emphasis on seizing him from his lair. The suspected terrorist was depicted as the enemy of the free world, and there was a call for a coalition to prevail against this evil.

The Taleban (the *Times'* spelling) was mentioned in the context of the United States seeking retaliation against the regime for housing bin Laden. Stories focused on the immensity of the disaster, comparing it with Pearl Harbor and paralleling the hijackings with the Northern Ireland strife of the 1970s. The leading article (editorial) on Sept. 12, titled "Terror for All," noted: "The United States, its allies and the civilised world are at war today against an enemy which, while undeclared is as well organised and as ruthless as any that a modern state has confronted" (Leading Article, 2001, p. 13). In a prescient sentence, the editorial commented that the world would feel the implications of New York's "urban avalanche" (Leading Article, 2001, p. 13).

Personal first-hand accounts of what it was like to be in the World Trade Center at the time of the strikes appeared on Sept. 13. The Trade Center's magnitude was portrayed and the leaping of people from this tower of steel and glass to their deaths was unwound as if through the movie, "Inferno." The image of the disaster was that of a bad movie, so surreal that its dimensions were hardly understood.

The following day, the *Times* ran more on bin Laden, Mullah Omar and Ayman Al-Zawari, immediately identifying those responsible for the attacks. On Sept. 15, the newspaper's coverage of the three minutes of silence observed around the world the previous day reflected on the attacks as "the worst terrorist outrage in history" (MacIntyre, 2001). That same day, the *Times'* Michael Gove lambasted his journalistic colleagues in the *Guardian* for their left-wing comment and analysis of the week's events. Dubbing them the Guardianistas, Gove argued, "The radical Left retains an antipathy to our common Western values which still finds its expression in anti-Americanism, anti-Zionism and the romanticism of revolutionary violence" (Gove, 2001).

Roland Watson and Damian Whitworth in Washington covered President Bush's walkabout among rescue workers in New York and his address at the memorial service in the National Cathedral. James Bone in New York reported on the president's "first visit to the first battlefield of what he has called 'the first war of the 21st century'" (Bone, 2001, p. 1). The president at Ground Zero was paralleled to Dwight Eisenhower after World War II and Winston Churchill after the Blitz.

In "A Time to Mourn," Hugh McIlvanney on Sept. 16 suggested the prospective world-class golf tournament, the Ryder Cup, which was to be held at the end of September, would resemble the 1972 Olympic Games when eleven Israelis were killed by Arab death squads. Holding the golf competition in the United States at a time of global catastrophe would be like having "a circus in a graveyard" (McIlvanney, 2001). Every newspaper page devoted to the tragedy chronicled the worst days in history, a time of unabashed grief when the world was in mourning.

Guardian

The *Guardian* focused immediately on bin Laden, on the air strikes and on those killed in the tragedy, among them "Frasier" creator David Angell and CNN commentator Barbara Olson, wife of the U.S. solicitor general Theodore Olson. It described the Pentagon, the world's largest building, and talked about the shift of banking operations from New York to London. It looked at the National Missile Defense system into which the United States was pouring money as no defense against terrorist hijackers and cited an expert's calling on the United States to abide by international law in this game of Star Wars. It explored aviation security, the employment of baggage screeners, and the differences between the government-run screening in Europe and the private company-contracted screening in the United States and concluded that the former is superior to that of the United States. It talked about the world's greatest superpower being "laid low" and called on President Bush to resist the clamor for retaliation and to think long-term.

"The hijacking heralded the start of a series of appalling attacks which reduced America's two most important cities to war zone-like scenes of carnage and threw the entire nation into a panic-fueled state of siege," reported the *Guardian* on Sept. 12 (Borger, Campbell, Porter and Millar, 2001). Bystanders were quoted on the kamikaze nature of the hijacking, including Joe Trachtenberg, who watched the disaster from his building; Omar Campo, a Salvadorean; Afework Hagos, a computer programmer; Tim Timmerman, a pilot; Mike Smith, a fire marshal; Navy Commander Tom O'Loughlin; Tom O'Riordan, an elderly man; Paul Begala, Democratic consultant; AP reporter, Dave Winslow; and Tom Seibert, a network engineer.

Writer Simon Tisdall predicted in the immediate aftermath that the implications of the tragedy would be dramatic (Tisdall, 2001), and Polly Toynbee hit out at the United States, commenting:

> The nation that is the world's great fount of technological, financial, artistic and intellectual brilliance is fatally burdened by a primitive and unsophisticated political culture. Its warped political institutions, its leaders' debilitated and febrile dependence on hour-by-hour polling, its constitutionally split powers, reliance on big business and its perpetual cycle of elections all add up to a politics unfit to bear such responsibility (Toynbee, 2001).

Derek Brown noted that Anti-Americanism was becoming a new world power, that the agenda of the hijackers was "driven chiefly by an insensate hatred of America and all things American" (Brown, 2001). He noted that innumerable people shared such antipathy.

The *Guardian*'s saturation coverage on Sept. 12 included a look at how the tabloid media reported the event, how Palestinians displayed their joy at the attack; how Prime Minister Blair responded; how America would hunt down the perpetrators; how the United States was on a war footing; how the financial markets coped with the disaster; how Hollywood closed down; how Arab journalists reported that bin Laden had warned only weeks before that he would launch a large-scale attack on the United States and how the tragedy epitomized "the sum of all our fears" (Leader, 2001).

Irish Times

Like its British counterparts, the *Irish Times* immediately covered the airplane-directed devastation of the World Trade Center, the victims, the survivors, the impact on financial markets, and the likelihood that Osama bin Laden masterminded the tragedy. Writer Fintan O'Toole predicted that the consequences of the attack would be "huge, ubiquitous and long-lasting" (O'Toole, 2001). In tone and sentiment similar to that of Polly Toynbee in the *Guardian*, O'Toole wrote:

> The scale of the loss will evoke a Blitz spirit, a determination to rebuild, not just Lower Manhattan, but the fragile sense of community and solidarity that may emerge ... But there will almost certainly be a dark side. For there is in American culture a fundamentalism no less strong than that of those who may have plotted yesterday's carnage. The tendency to divide the world between the forces of God and the forces of Satan, the elect and the damned, is, ironically one of the things that America shares with its most ferocious enemies (O'Toole, 2001).

Jonathan Eyal, director of studies at the Royal United Services Institute in London, discussed how the missile defense program would not provide refuge against acts of terrorism. He reported that "Washington knew for a few days that something was afoot; its embassies in Asia and Europe were warned of an impending attack" (Eyal, 2001), but it had failed to penetrate the terrorist organization thought responsible. Frank Millar, London editor, focused on Prime Minister Tony Blair's commitment to stand "shoulder to shoulder" (Millar, 2001) with the United States and looked at the cessation of trading at the Stock Exchange and the evacuation of the City of London.

Subsequent coverage in the *Irish Times* included the story of Martin Price, an Irishman who escaped "from the fortieth floor of hell" (Price, 2001); e-mails to the newspaper about the experiences of the Irish writers on the day of the attack in New York (Cremin, 2001); a focus on the Irish and Irish-Americans killed in the catastrophe, particularly on Ruth Clifford McCourt and her four-year-old daughter Juliana and Fr. Mychal Judge of the New York Fire Department; the candle-lit prayer ceremonies throughout Ireland for victims of the disaster and for global peace; and New York correspondent Conor O'Clery's insight into the effect of the tragedy on the global economy (O'Clery, 2001).

All three newspapers under scrutiny in this study shared frames or themes in the aftermath of 9/11. They immediately identified the perpetrator of the attack on New York on 9/11, focused on the enormity of the tragedy, the victims – including the personified United States, and the response of key political figures. Horror-laden terms such as "carnage," "terror," "tragedy," "apocalypse," "sum of all fears," and "catastrophe" were used to describe the devastation. Parallels were drawn to Pearl Harbor and to bad and surreal movies. In secondary frames or minor themes, the global implications of the disaster were explored; the implications for stock markets, currency exchange, trade, security, and the aviation industry were examined; and the partnership of bin Laden and al-Qaeda was chronicled.

Throughout its narratives, the *Times* displayed greater objectivity, perhaps a more tempered treatment of the tragedy than did the *Guardian* and the *Irish Times*. The *Times* did not display any anti-American sentiment, a matter that is not surprising given its Murdoch/News Corp. ownership. Both the *Guardian* and the *Irish Times* did, pointing to the tragedy almost as the result of the great hubris of America. Both newspapers, in broad sweeps, painted the United States as an isolationist country that thought it could use money and technology to protect itself, a bastion of capitalism too mean to pay baggage screeners a decent wage to do the job properly, a populist continent where people hop on an airplane as though it were a bus. In chronicling such differences, both the *Guardian* and the *Irish Times* pointed to the weakness of the American system, of the American mindset, and in so doing, juxtaposed elitist Europe with populist America. Through tone and context, both the *Guardian* and the *Irish Times* framed Europe as superior to the United States. What all three newspapers shared, however, was the framing of the World Trade Center strike as a tragedy, a disaster, a catastrophe, thus aligning themselves with Western values versus Middle Eastern jihad.

In what can be regarded as a struggle between discursive communities — political figures versus terrorists, ordinary people, West versus East, and even the media themselves — the tragedy of 9/11 played out from a disarticulation of normalcy and everyday reality to a rearticulation of the bizarre and the surreal or unreal. After 9/11, the world awakened to a new reality, a new dawning — the realization that rogue states (such as Iraq) are not all that is to be feared but that terrorists who pass as regular citizens in our midst may present the greatest threat.

Ideologically, the dominant capitalist, powerful Western nations were seen as threatened by the authoritarian, nonpowerful, underdeveloped and unknown Middle Eastern terrorists, individual and collective. The *Guardian* and the *Irish Times* framed British culture as superior to American, and with the *Times*, posited that a new ideology involving an international alliance of world powers, including the Saudis, might be one of the consequences of the tragedy.

Conclusion

This study of 9/11, through framing analysis, shows how the media frame an event, focusing initially on the key elements of the event — who, what, where, and when — and later digressing to the how, the why and future implications. It delineates how the media change frames or focus over time and how major and minor themes emerge from the narrative.

Coverage of 9/11 in the British media as exemplified by the *Guardian* and the *Times* and the Irish media through the *Irish Times* demonstrates that these newspapers, long-established as they are, continue to reflect certain political ideologies: the *Times*, right wing; the *Guardian*, left; and the *Irish Times*, usually moderate, more left of center in this particular case.

This examination of 9/11 is a snapshot of one week's coverage in the aftermath of the disaster, as opposed to an in-depth longitudinal analysis of the tragedy and its evolution through the drama of the invasion of or preemptive strike on Iraq, dubbed the "Fight for Freedom" by the Bush administration. Further study could be undertaken on how the evolution has been framed in terms of Chyi and McComb's space-time continuum. It also would be worthwhile from a scholarly perspective to explore how coverage in the British and Irish media of the post-9/11 reality compares with that of the Arab media, perhaps that of the Gulf's former "Trucial States," once an outreach of the British Empire.

References

Ashdown, P. (1991, January 26). Ireland's troubled press, *Editor & Publisher*, pp. 56, 46.

Ayres, C. (2001, September 12). I watched as people leapt from flames to death. *Times*. Overseas News.

Beeston, R. (2001, September 12). Bin Laden heads list of suspects; Terror in America. *Times*.

Bone, J. (2001, September 15). Bush tours the New York battlefield; Terror in America. *Times*.

Borger, J., Campbell, D., Porter, C. and Millar, S. (2001, September 12). Everyone was screaming, crying, running. It's like a war zone. *Guardian.*

Brown, D. (2001, September 12). Anti-Americanism: a new world power. *Guardian.*

Chyi, H. I. and McCombs, M. (2004). Media Salience and the Process of Framing: Coverage of the Columbine School Shootings. *Journalism & Mass Communication Quarterly. 81*(1): 22-35.

Cremin, N. et al. (2001, September 15). Email voices. *Irish Times.*

Eyal, J. (2001, September 12). Epic horror puts US intelligence and defence [sic] to shame. *Irish Times.*

Fridriksson, L. (2004) Western Europe. In A. S. De Beer and J. C. Merrill (Eds.). *Global Journalism: Topical Issues and Media Systems.* Boston: Pearson Education, Inc.

Gove, M. (2001, September 15). Willing guardian of the designer terrorist. *Times.*

Larosa, D. (2003). News Media Perpetuate Few Rumors About 9/11 Crisis. *Newspaper Research Journal. 24*(1), 10-21.

Leader. (2001, September 12). The sum of all our fears. *Guardian.*

Leading article. (2001, September 12). Terror for all. *Times.*

Li, X. and Izard, R. (2003) 9/11 Attack Coverage Reveals Similarities, Differences. *Newspaper Research Journal, 24*(1), 204-219.

MacIntyre, B. (2001, September 15). When the world stood still in mourning; On a memorable day; Terror in America. *Times.*

Maher, T. M. Framing: An Emerging Paradigm or a Phase of Agenda Setting? in Reese et al. *Framing Public Life: Perspectives on Media and Our Understanding of the Social World.*

Martin, S. E. and Copeland, D. A. eds. (2003). *The Function of Newspapers in Society.* Westport, CT: Praeger.

McCombs, M. and Shaw, D. (1972). The agenda-setting function of mass media. *Public Opinion Quarterly, 36*, 176-187.

McIlvanney, H. (2001, September 16). A time to mourn. *Sunday Times.*

Merrill, J.C. (1968). *The Elite Press: Great Newspapers of the World.* New York: Pitman Publishing Corporation.

Millar, F. (2001, September 12). Blair pledges to stand shoulder to shoulder with US. *Irish Times.*

O'Clery, C. (2001, September 19). Masters of financial universe manage to avert crash. *Irish Times.*

Oliver, E. (2004, September 25). Irish Times still paper of choice for business executives. *Irish Times.*

Oliver, E. (2004, March 10). Significant rise in numbers reading Irish newspapers. *Irish Times.*

Oram, H. (1983). *The Newspaper Book: A History of Newspapers in Ireland, 1649-1983.* Dublin, Ireland: MO Books.

O'Toole, F. (2001, September 12). Terrorists slash their way into the heart of the American Dream. *Irish Times.*

Pan, Z. and Kosicki, G. M. Framing as a Strategic Action in Public Deliberation. In Reese et al., *Framing Public Life: Perspectives on Media and Our Understanding of the*

Social World.

Plunkett, J. (2004). All Change. *Guardian Unlimited: MediaGuardian.co.uk,* Special Reports, July 12, 2004 [http://media.guardian.co.uk/top100_2004/story] 22 October 2004.

Price, M. (2001, September 13). An Irishman's escape from the fortieth floor of hell. *Irish Times.*

Reese, S. D. (2001). Prologue — Framing Public Life: A Bridging Model for Media Research. In Reese, S.D., Gandy, O.H., Jr., and Grant, A.E. (Eds.). *Framing Public Life: Perspectives on Media and Our Understanding of the Social World.* Mahwah, NJ: Lawrence Erlbaum Associates.

Shah, D. V., Domke, D. and Wackman, D. B. The Effects of Value-Framing on Political Judgment and Reasoning. In Reese et al., *Framing Public Life: Perspectives on Media and Our Understanding of the Social World.*

Stempel, G. H., III and Hargrove, T. (2003) Newspapers Played Major Role in Terrorism Coverage. *Newspaper Research Journal, 24*(1), 55-57.

Tankard, J. W., Jr., The Empirical Approach to the Study of Media Framing. In Reese et al., *Framing Public Life: Perspectives on Media and Our Understanding of the Social World.*

Tisdall, S. (2001, September 12). How will America respond? *Guardian.*

Toynbee, P. (2001, September 12). The rule of reason over madness died along with the victims. *Guardian.*

Chapter 3

"Breaking News": The First Hours of BBC Coverage of 9/11 as a Media Event

Gwen Bouvier

"Whoever decided to go down this route was aiming for maximum publicity on the world stage and […] in drawing a major attention to what they are doing" —*Brian Hanrahan, diplomatic editor BBC, 9 Sep 2001*

W hen, on Tuesday September 11, 2001, television programs across the world were interrupted by 'breaking news' about the attack on the World Trade Center in New York, many journalists were unprepared.[1] There were no scenarios for how to conduct television journalism and balance facts under such circumstances, not even in newsrooms that had been reporting on terrorism regularly (Zelizer & Allan, 2002; Alexander & Picard, 1991). Everyone had to improvise.

As a consequence, most reports on 9/11, and especially live broadcasts, show an acute tension between a sense of directness and unmediatedness of experience of what is being reported (seeing it as if you were there), and a constructedness and deliberation typical of any report that claims to convey meaning (telling you what it means). In the case of 9/11, the negotiation of this tension became paramount for the ways through which 9/11 acquired meaning.

Such a tension is typical for "media events," and to understand 9/11 it is useful to analyse it *as* a media event (Fiske, 1996). Focusing on the discourses in the first few hours of broadcasting by the BBC, the British public broadcaster, I explore how the tension between directness and construction governs the 9/11 broadcast. September 11 also provides a unique opportunity for studying television journalism in action. The directness and improvisation would now reveal assumptions and beliefs that would otherwise have remained hidden beneath rhetoric and procedures.

In a first section, I give an overview of the existing reading on media events and frame 9/11 theoretically as a media event. There are differences, of course, especially with respect to the coherence and rhetorical structure of the broadcast, but the backgrounds of these differences are tellingly similar to those that govern media events. I will particularly draw on John Fiske's views of a media event as a network of different statements, crossing and contradicting each other, captured into a final broadcast version. In practical terms, the first hours and days of the dissemination of 9/11 present us with a site in which we can clearly distinguish the social discursive debates that took place as the world was trying to come to terms with the event. Rather than presenting a consistent image of the event, the broadcast of 9/11 comprises a number of struggles. First, we can trace what was said (and consequently what was left out). Second, we can ask what the role of the (technological) media are through which these different statements were negotiated. On top of all this comes the observation that the very characteristics of the BBC coverage present several challenges to this coherence — especially in terms of immediacy ("it is happening now") and fluidity ("it is forever changing").

It is all very well to theorize 9/11 as a media event, but does the actual empirical material substantiate such claims? The empirical part of the paper first describes the "narrative flow" of the BBC coverage and highlight the most salient elements of its discourse. Next, I isolate three key moments in the coverage in which the discourses shift, using Althusser's and Balibar's observations of looking for a history's "breaking points," its lapses and silences, its "structuring absences" and constitutive lacks (Althusser & Balibar, 1979, pp. 30, 205). In analyzing the moments, I put particular emphasis on the (changing) use of key terms, and on how their use is accompanied and interrupted by what I would like to call, following Roland Barthes, "reality effects" (apparently inessential details as guarantors of authenticity and trauma, Barthes, 1977, pp. 30-31). While acknowledging that the first hours of coverage are perhaps too soon to single out what Douglas Kellner has called "Manichean discourses of good and evil ... in dominant media codes of popular culture" (Kellner, 2003), I still try to uncover how the BBC coverage has treated such blunt distinctions.

In conclusion, I elaborate on how seeing the 9/11 broadcast as a media event, especially in its traumatic nature and struggling form, allows for its framing as the live televising of history, and as a defining moment for the world we now live in.

9/11 AS MEDIA EVENT:
STATUS, IMPACT AND NATURE

The belief that media events are artificial, not really reporting on, but constructing reality is often traced to Daniel Boorstin. He was the first author to corner the idea of a "media event." In his 1961 monograph on pseudo-events in American public life, he argues that most events that occurred in America's society were false and artificially crafted. These pseudo-events were mere illusions, divorced from any possible underlying reality (Boorstin, 1961). With Boorstin, media only played a minority role in facilitating knowledge on events. The work which appears to have been most influential on later fine-tuning of the definition of a media event was written by Daniel Dayan and Elihu Katz (Dayan & Katz, 1992). Authors such as Maurice Roche and Nick Couldry draw on the volume (Roche, 2000; Couldry, 2003). Couldry notes that Dayan and Katz represent "one of the most important cruxes for assessing the media's social consequences" (Couldry, 2003, p. 17) and "pose[s] more clearly than anywhere else the advantages and the difficulties" of a study of media events and media rituals (Couldry, 2003, p. 55).

Dayan and Katz present very clear markers for what can or cannot be considered a media event. By comparing these markers with the event of September 11, I have found it to fit the authors' definition up to a certain point. The "matching" key characteristics as defined by Dayan and Katz can be grouped in three main categories. The first and second are closely related; they specify the media event's exceptional and extraordinary status, and the impact of the media event and its broadcast. The third category looks at the nature of the broadcast itself.

(1)   A media event has to be perceived as exceptional and extraordinary.

  (1a) A media event has to mark a historic moment and be recognized as such by both broadcasters and audience (Dayan & Katz, 1992, pp. 1-9). The many socio-political changes that have occurred in world politics since 9/11 have established the event as a historical marker. It is often said that "America changed on September 11" (White, 2002, p. 284). The name "9/11" has become popular shorthand, indicating not only the date of the event but also serving as a container term for more complex meanings of the event[2] (Branston, 2003).

  We can deduce that broadcasters saw the event as exceptional because of the time and effort committed to the subject. The 9/11 news program was an exception to regular broadcasting both in format and in content. An example of format is that BBC1 switched over to 24-hour news broadcasting, cancelling its planned programming (announcement on BBC1, 2.08pm, 11/09/01). An example of exceptional content is the live broadcasting of the collapse of the south tower of the World Trade Center (BBC1, 3.05pm, 11/09/01).

Viewing figures gathered by broadcasters indicate the audience watched the 9/11 broadcasts in great numbers: "On 11 September, 33m[illion] people — 52% of the UK population, turned to BBC TV News" (Thomson, 2001). In addition to generating massive interest, an investigation undertaken in 2003 by PEW, the independent research center,[3] points out the paradigmatic change 9/11 brought about. Its study of American audiences for two years after 9/11 indicates a heightened public concern about international threats. Following 9/11, American audiences felt more worried and threatened. I believe this indicates both quantitatively and qualitatively the historical importance of 9/11.

(1b) The event has to transform daily life into something special, and be watched in one or several nations, or even on a global scale, to such an extent that the experience integrates societies and evokes a renewal of loyalty (Dayan & Katz, 1992, pp. 1-9). Previous research conducted on the online discussion list CultStud_L has pointed out how the normal flow was interrupted as discussion focused on one single subject for three days straight. List members from all over the world unilaterally perceived 9/11 as an exceptional event, and advised each other to "watch the news" (Gajjala, 2001; Bouvier, 2003). International outreaches of solidarity were sent; for example, "We are dazed here on the other side of the world too" (Di, Australia), and "A word of sympathy to all Americans" (Pina, Portugal). These reactions indicate the international forum in which 9/11 took place (quoted in Bouvier, 2003).[4]

In addition, BBC foreign correspondents reported on reactions in many places, such as in the United States, Israel, Palestine, and other countries. Whether communities reacted in terror or joy,[5] the experience was communally shared. One example of this is in the United States, which experienced a surge of nationalism and patriotism after the event, resulting in a unification of loyalty to the then newly elected President Bush (Apple, 2002; Rizvi, 2003). September 11 integrated a society which was up to that point often politically divided on many issues.[6]

(2)   The second category of matching characteristics deals with the impact of a media event and its broadcast.

(2a) The broadcast interrupts everyday social routines and represents a monopolistic interruption (Dayan & Katz, 1992, pp. 1-9). It is hard to say specifically how far people's daily lives were interrupted on 11/09/01. This requires thorough qualitative research and interviews. It is likely, however, that daily routines were interrupted as people paused to watch the news on television or listened to the radio, at home or in a public place, and learned what had happened. People might have simply paused their activities to take in the news, or they might have changed their schedule altogether to pay full attention to watching the news and following up on the events. As Henry Bean reflects on how 9/11 interrupted his plans: "I wanted to do all that and more that I've forgotten, but this event on television seemed to swell, obscuring my plans" (Bean, 2001, p. 26).

As mentioned before, BBC switched its regular programming around, and offered live, continuous, and single-focused reporting of the event. Other programs were canceled, or moved to alternative channels. The interruption of the television flow was pervasive to the extent that certain broadcasters stayed on the story for more than 24 hours straight (e.g. VRT, the Belgian, Flemish public service broadcaster). The interruption monopolized not one channel, but many; few channels did not modify programming to report on 9/11.

(2b) The broadcast of the media event presents an almost obligatory, communal viewing (large audiences), in which the manner of viewing is one of focused concentration (Dayan & Katz, 1992: 1-9). Depending on time and location, some viewers were in a public place such as work or a pub. Many gathered communally around television screens and other media output to follow what was happening. People who were alone tended to call family or friends to share the news. In Italy, phone lines were busy with family trying to contact each other to communicate what had happened (Morcellini, 2002).

As mentioned before, BBC viewing figures of that day demonstrate the surge in viewers watching the 9/11 broadcast. These numbers, however, do not specify the way in which people watched. It can be said that because of the nature of the event, the broadcast demanded (and received) focused and prolonged attention.[7] Viewing figures of other channels, such as VRT TV1,[8] corroborate the massive attention the event attracted: 51.3% of the

Belgian population watched the event on the public service broadcaster.

(3) The third category focuses on the nature of the broadcast of a media event.

(3a) The broadcast has to be live (Dayan & Katz, 1992, pp. 1-9). The BBC 9/11 broadcast made regular use of live feeds and included several live updates. The frequency of live images was what contributed to the broadcast's aura of seeing history in the making. In the empirical part of this paper I further elaborate on the broadcast's use of "reality effects," another device which enhances its "liveness."

(3b) The narrative is to be highly dramatic and rich in symbolic values (Dayan & Katz, 1992, pp. 1-9). The event in itself was highly dramatic and so was its mediation. The timing of the attacks made for a constant development and updating of the story, heightening the drama: *The first tower of the World Trade Center is on fire! The second tower has been hit by a plane! The Pentagon is under attack! There are still flights in the air! A plane has come down in Pennsylvania!* And so on. The dramatic qualities of the event were heightened by the symbolic richness of its targets. First, targets such as the World Trade Center and the Pentagon are symbols that represent the financial, economical, and military position of the United States. Second, the composition of certain shots, such as rescue workers raising the flag in a manner reminiscent of the raising of the flag in Iwo Jima, made for rich symbolic representations.

(3c) The broadcast should feature heroic actions and individuals (Dayan & Katz, 1992, pp. 1-9). It could be argued that the efforts and emotional involvement of the rescue workers lent them to archetypical portrayal as the heroes of the hour. The brave firemen laid down their lives in the pursuit of rescuing the helpless, trapped victims. President Bush appeared as the strong, revengeful, if not somewhat absent, leader. The presence of these representations, bordering on stereotypes, lent the broadcast its heroic actions and performers.

In addition to these key characteristics of a media event, Dayan and Katz discuss two theoretical concepts. The first is the "aesthetics of compensation," and the second is that of the sense of "centre." The "aesthetics of compensation" deals with the idea that in trying to make up for the fact that the viewer is limited in her or his witnessing of the event as compared to an eyewitness, broadcasters provide extensive verbal and visual information. This information is compared to what an eyewitness could experience (Dayan & Katz, 1992, pp. 92-100). In light of the extent of reporting (the story dominated channel output for many hours) and the excess of visual information and commentary (e.g. the frequent repetition of the plane's impact on the World Trade Center), I would argue that the BBC's 9/11 broadcast fits such an "aesthetics of compensation." It especially refers to the visual repeats of the moments of impact (the most dramatic and, in a sense, "aesthetic" moments). As Zelizer and Allan put it: "If the coverage, especially the repetition of images showing the towers being hit, was too much to handle for some viewers, for others it somehow authenticated their experience" (Zelizer & Allan, 2002, p. 4). It is also worth quoting Bean here again, who also remarks on the visual excess of the 9/11 reports:

> [A] pair of televisions showed the endlessly recurring shot of the second plane slamming into the south tower … When did the towers fall? Did I see them go down? I saw footage of it, but not 'live'. Or maybe I saw the second one live, that is, on television … Many people claim to have seen these things, and no doubt many did, but by now the images have become so iconic we all possess them and it seems less important how we came by them in the first place (Bean, 2001, pp. 27-28).

The recurrent shots and repeats compensate for not being there in the flesh, and the images become iconic because they replace, in a sense, direct experience. For German composer Karheinz Stockhausen, this visual excess even made 9/11 a cruel piece of art (a remark for which he was heavily criticized).

The second concept deals with how media aspire to create the sense of a certain event being society's "centre"; the event is perceived as the core of cultural experience of that moment. During the broadcasting of an event such as 9/11, eyewitnesses recount their experiences from "where it is happening" (the centre) to the (remote) viewers. The role of newsmakers, thus, seems to merely consist of bridging the gap between society's centre and viewers at home. This role, however, is more invasive than it seems. The media frame and, therefore, translate the event (e.g. through selection of what is said, which voices are heard, which images are shown, what is absent in the reporting, etc.) (Dayan & Katz, 1992, p. 58). The media present their subjective view of the event, rather than relaying "reality as it is." Television seizes the opportunity to name reality (e.g. by circulating discourses that name the event) while operating under the cloak of servicing as relay between the social centre and the viewers (Couldry, 2003: 43).

Differences? Preplanning and Consensus

Up to this point, 9/11 appears to seamlessly fit Dayan and Katz' definition of a media event. Both its content, manner of broadcasting, and impact on society adhere to the criteria set out by the authors. As we explore their definition further, differences occur. The two most important ones are those of (1) pre-planning and (2) the consensual role of the "centre." However, these differences between a media event and 9/11 contain much more similarities than we would say at first sight.

(1) A core difference between a media event and 9/11 lays in the pre-planning and organization of the event.

The term preplanning here involves much more than just the logistics of preparing for the (broadcast of an) event; it also includes the rhetorical structure and the inherent coherence of both event and broadcast. This distinction sparks off a number of other differences. I first discuss the preplanning and organizational nature of a media event, and will then examine the further range and nature of the differences between 9/11 and a media event.

According to Dayan and Katz, any media event is preplanned. Its planning lies in the negotiation between three partners who have closed a contract (Dayan & Katz, 1992, pp. 7, 54-77). There are a number of different themes in this description: three partners, who are in negotiation together, and whose relationship is described as a contract. Dayan and Katz name these three partners as the event organizers (who bring together the elements for the event), the broadcasters (who reproduce the event), and the audience at home (who invest time and interest by watching the broadcast) (Dayan & Katz, 1992, p. 54). Their relationship is one of negotiation. Each party has to be willing to offer an input to make the event work. The organizers provide the set up of the event, which is disseminated by the broadcasters. The audience then has to accept the proposition from organizer and broadcaster that this event is worth their time and interest (Dayan & Katz, 1992, pp. 17, 65-6).

At first sight, this was not the case on 9/11. The organizers (the terrorists, who provided the agency for the event to happen) did not announce or agree on any aspect of the event with the other two parties: the broadcasters (who gave the event its worldwide platform), and the public (who watched the broadcast). It might be said that, instead of making clear agreements, each party counted on their knowledge of the other's interest and routines. As such, the terrorists might have counted on the broadcaster's values of newsworthiness to give airtime to their event.[9] Then the broadcasters noted the event's newsworthiness and estimated the interest of their audience to be high enough to grant the event the platform that they did (interruption and cancellation of other programs, change of format to 24-hour news, and staying with this single subject for a number of hours). The audience, alerted by the media, agreed on the remarkableness of the event and watched the news program in great numbers.

Whereas this negotiation is, in accordance with Dayan and Katz, a cooperation between three partners, the contract was only semi-voluntary, inasmuch as mutual services were forced rather than agreed-upon. The event was an attack against proper ethics, and its terrorist/organizers were anti–establishment (whereas Dayan and Katz note that event organizers should be "well within the establishment" (Dayan & Katz, 1992, p. 6). It was, therefore, not possible to turn the broadcast of the event into a celebration or reconciliation (Dayan & Katz, 1992, p. 8), although unification was reached through solidarity among global/Western victims. As a consequence, the nature of the event and its organizers prohibited an open discussion on any consensus about the meaning of the event.

This lack of negotiation and consensus means the terrorist/organizers had no control over the execution of the broadcast, and the broadcasters had no idea of how the event was going to develop. The terrorists could but offer a "cue" to prompt interpretation by the media. The media, in turn, created a broadcast, presenting their interpretation of the event to their audience. Rather than a consensual agreement, 9/11 involved an implicit complicity. The limit of this complicity lies in the inability to control the outcome of the interpretation of the event by the organizers.

This left the broadcasters with an organizational problem and an opportunity. Their organizational problem consisted of being unable to plan ahead and prepare for the broadcast. They could not foresee the development of the story and were not fully informed on what was going on. This resulted in the broadcasters having to improvise a great deal, and, dealing with unforeseen changes in the development of the story, they had to "learn" 9/11 on screen. At the same time, the event presented an opportunity to interpret and "make meaning of reality" without being too restricted on the political and ideological tone of the broadcast: The subsequent cultural struggle for meaning of the event was dominated by media, government and audience, but only influenced in a very limited capacity by the perpetrators of the attack. To a certain extent, each channel was able to define the boundaries of the event. They were able to highlight particular meanings and opinions by adding certain features to their coverage, some of which were channel-specific (for instance, the Belgian broadcaster VRT was quick to offer a story on the connection between 9/11 and the Palestine/Israeli conflict).

Dayan and Katz note that television coverage of media events provides interpretation and definition (Dayan & Katz, 1992, pp. 80-9). Rather than asking the event's organizers (the terrorists) to come and explain their actions (an impossibility in every sense), coverage focused on a variety of descriptive and analytic questions that omitted any direct input by the terrorists. Because the event was anti-establishment, it might not have been seen appropriate to offer a platform to perpetrators of such an act. Another important absence in the television coverage of the event is the lack of investigation into the conflicts that lay at the source of the attack. This avenue of investigation was suggested in retrospect by Noam Chomsky (Chomsky, 2001, p. 24).

In all, the issue of preplanning, although real in technical terms, is hardly as big as Dayan and Katz seem to put forward. As James Carey observes, they appear to concentrate too much on a description of media events as "celebratory," and ignore "traumatic" events which qualify as easily as media events (Carey, 1998). Tamar Liebes seems to join Carey when she compares media events to what she calls "disaster marathons," televised events that contain a "shared collective space" with a "chaotic exploitation of pain of participants on screen." She points to the lacking of a "script" as a significant difference, yet one which does not invalidate the "marathon" as a media event (Liebes, 1998, pp. 71-72). Tellingly, and probably linked to this lack of preplanning, Liebes refuses to agree with Dayan and Katz that journalists are in charge of the meaning-making process of the event. Rather, she calls this an "illusion" — one illustrated by the observation made above that several networks and channels chose to offer different interpretations.

(2)   This issue of the 'illusion' of journalists taking charge of the event brings us to the second major difference between Dayan and Katz' view on media events and 9/11: the supposedly consensual role of the "centre."

Dayan and Katz speak of a consensual centre, implying that meaning on the core of the event is undisputed. This is certainly the case for celebratory media events, and even in the traumatic ones that Carey discusses such a core consensus may be present (the shared shock for instance). But the "illusion" to which Liebes refers, and the examples of deviant interpretations on different channels, also reflects a struggle at the centre of the meaning-making of media events. This struggle closely relates to John Fiske's view on the centre of meaning of media events. As he points out, it is theoretically wrong to speak of a consensus. A consensus implies a shared view, something to which all parties agree. This is not necessarily the case with media events.

In his 1996 *Media Matters*, Fiske looks at how struggles over cult
meaning are conducted in American popular culture. Through th
examination of the media treatment of the O. J. Simpson trial, the L.A
riots and other (ethnically linked) media events, Fiske examines the wa
in which minority voices make themselves heard against dominant
"mainstream" voices in society. As such, Fiske argues, it is through the
struggle of competing voices in media debates that the nation makes
sense of the events (Fiske, 1996). This makes media events "a composite
reality comprising everything from the process of videoing the original
event through to its uncountable viewings and reviewings ... around the
world" (Fiske, 1996, p. 126). As a result any consensus is (more likely)
a locus where diverse, potentially contradicting discourses, opinions,
etc., meet. I want to argue that the meaning over 9/11 needs to be
perceived, in first instance, as a media event in Fiske's sense; that is, as
a locus of conflicting opinions, and that it only gradually shifts to the
shared view Dayan and Katz have in mind.

If meaning of a media event is only gradually moving toward such
a consensus, then it follows that media events are not instantaneous.
According to Fiske, media events are indeed bound to strict limits of
time, but, when read carefully and especially with the immediacy and
development of 9/11 in mind, still allow for shifts over time. Fiske says:

> A media event, then, as a point of maximum discursive
> visibility, is also a point of maximum turbulence. ... It also
> invites intervention and motivates people to struggle to
> redirect at least some of the currents flowing through it to
> serve their interests; it is therefore a site of popular
> engagement and involvement ... Its period of maximum
> visibility is limited, often to a few days, though the discursive
> struggles it occasions will typically continue for much longer
> (Fiske, 1996, p. 8).

In the case of 9/11, the moving of meaning toward a core
consensus took only a few hours and with some networks even not that
long. But in those few hours, the struggle, as one within media (rather
than between the media and the organizers), was very much present. In
the analysis of key moments in the broadcast of the first hours of BBC
coverage, I make this clear.

For now, it suffices to reiterate the exceptional status, interrupting
impact, and live nature of media events, and to stress how the
complicity in organization (rather than preplanning), and the short
struggle before a core consensus is arrived at, make for the theoretical
classification of 9/11 as a media event.

As a scene for playing out the media event and the tensions between those involved, the first hours of the 9/11 broadcast are of essential importance. It is there and then that the discourse about what 9/11 means is being forged, and that viewers are offered the tools to make sense of it as a media event. In what follows, I analyze instances of the television broadcast that, in my view, demonstrate how the discourse of the event is being constructed. I first give an account of the flow of the narrative being composed; next I analyze three key moments in the coverage in which the discourse shifts.

Before moving to those key moments it is necessary to sketch the overall flow of the first hours of BBC coverage. The first hour of the broadcast runs from 2:07 p.m. until 3:08 p.m. It begins with the announcement of a change in schedule: "This is BBC1. Now a change to the schedule as we join BBC News 24." At 2:36 p.m., another announcement in the form of a banner points out that CBBC and other programs have been moved to BBC's second channel. The remaining three hours consist of uninterrupted rolling news without referral to the status of the program, with one exception: an announcement made by one of the anchors in the BBC24 studio at 4:58 p.m.: "This is a BBC special, broadcasting as well on BBC1."

The broadcast starts with images of the second impact (on the south tower of the WTC). These images, which comprise the entire first hour, are in voice-over format: The anchors are giving comments, but all the viewer sees is a feed, often live, consisting of shots over Manhattan. Bush delivers his first speech at 2:28 p.m. When at 2:41 p.m. the image changes unannounced to smoke billowing out of the Pentagon in Washington, anchors are struggling to catch up. At about 3:00 p.m., viewers see a live feed of the south tower collapsing. There seems to be some confusion among the anchors as to what the images are, but this eventually gets cleared up. Guests that are featured in support of the commentary by anchors consist of BBC correspondents (correspondents in New York and Washington, a transport correspondent, the diplomatic editor, an economic correspondent, and a foreign affairs correspondent). Viewers only hear their voices; they never see any of the people speaking, including the anchors.

At 3:07 p.m. the Pentagon has partly collapsed. At 3:08 p.m. more variation is introduced in the pattern of the format: a division of the screen into two image boxes of equal size. One shows the Prime Minister Tony Blair making a statement, while the other shows views of the WTC, a repeat of the second impact, and views of the Pentagon. This format will be used more regularly from now on, be it in slight variations of theme and volume of boxes. Another subtle change occurs: the Breaking News banner has, since the start of the broadcast, read: "Explosions in America." At 3:17 p.m. this is changed into "Terrorists attack America." The continuous wide shots over Manhattan are now varied with on-the-ground action of fleeing people and rescue workers. At 3:18 p.m. this is followed by the first eyewitness reports. Moments later, for the first time, anchors are shown in duo presentation in a BBC24 studio. From this point on the broadcast becomes more routine: It appears to run smoother and the anchors seem to be more in control. Much of the confusion and hesitation is gone, although technical errors persist. Examples of this gain in organization and control are the emergency number that is presented at 3:27 p.m. and the announcement of the imminent collapse of the north tower three minutes before images of the collapse are shown at 3:33 p.m.

In addition to the BBC guests (as mentioned above), a variety of non-BBC guests are now introduced: a former spokesperson for the U.S. state department, a terrorism specialist, an aviation expert, etc. Yasser Arafat condemns the attacks, but he is the only world leader to appear besides Bush and Blair. At 3:49 p.m. the Pennsylvania crash is announced. At around 4:00 p.m. the broadcast has become very routine. There are hardly any professional mistakes, and technological errors are few. It is worth taking note of the images that were absent in these three hours of coverage: No images of cheering Palestines were shown, nor were images broadcast of people jumping from the WTC towers. Both incidents were, however, reported: The first incident was brought up in a conversation with the Israeli foreign correspondent, and the second was mentioned several times by eyewitnesses in Manhattan. No images were shown in support of these reports.

BREAKING MOMENTS

More important than the overall flow of the broadcast, however, are the "breaking moments": key moments in which the underlying rhetoric of the broadcast (and the event) comes to the fore. The use of "breaks" is important here. It refers to Louis Althusser's and Etienne Balibar's use of the term and their discussion of the underlying rationale and continuity in the philosophy of Karl Marx (Althusser & Balibar, 1979). All stories of history and science are, in retrospect, told as continuous flows, with an inherent logic, rhetoric, and an embedded purpose; in short they are told teleologically, much in the same vein as I have done above with the BBC broadcast. But, they seldom were so at the moment of their inception and construction, when they were much more chaotic, spontaneous, uncontrolled. For Althusser, this observation leads him to plead for an attention to whatever is significantly absent from official discourse: "Certain silences in its discourse, certain conceptual omissions and lapses in its rigour, in brief, everything that 'sounds hollow' to an attentive ear, despite its fullness" (Althusser & Balibar, 1979, p. 30). In terms of 9/11 this means that the moments in which the BBC broadcast seems to doubt itself, when chaos and contradiction, silence and improvisation are present, should not be seen as clumsy interruptions of the flow, but as telling signs of the struggle between competing and still-forming discourses and meanings. As Balibar puts it: "The forms of vagueness of their articulation" itself becomes significant (Althusser & Balibar, 1979, p. 207).

In such a context, breaks become extremely important. On the one hand they are the result of deliberate attempts to structure the rationale of the broadcast; on the other hand they are signs of the lack of editorial control, or official rationale (much in the same way as Liebes or Carey had in mind). In what follows, I offer examples of three kinds of breaks appearing in the 9/11 broadcast. The first involves the opening (the breaking of the news), when journalists' first attempts occur to offer some interpretation; the second concentrates on the gradual taking shape of structuring the rationale, through usage of different, associated terms; and the third is an example of how the traumatic nature of the event allows a particular kind of image (a "reality effect") to become both an interruption and confirmation of discourses operating in the flow.

Moment 1: Opening

The start of a broadcast of a media event is always a key moment. It gives the opportunity to set the tone and agenda for the discourse to follow. As described above, preplanning usually allows for the careful preparation of such openings. This obviously was not the case for 9/11. Not only was the event not planned or foreseen, there were also no scenarios to deal with the eventuality of it. As Zelizer and Allan observe: "News organizations — together with their sources — lacked a ready-made 'script' to tell their stories, a frame to help them and their audience comprehend the seemingly incomprehensible" (Zelizer & Allan, 2002: 1).

As a result, the opening moments of the 9/11 broadcast appear less rhetorically smooth and much clumsier than regular media events. In what follows I lay out how the first elements of the discourse are introduced chronologically in the broadcast and how tentative meanings are explored and linked to each other. I focus on four aspects: (1) the attempt to offer factual information and descriptions of the event (including on its style); (2) the first attempts to define the event as an attack, and the first mention of the term "terrorist"; (3) the erroneous identification of the first plane; and (4) the first effort to link the attack to other discourses (the 1993 bombing of the WTC and Osama bin Laden). In each case I use quotes from the broadcast to illustrate the creation of the discourse.

(1)   After the interruption of the normal television flow on the BBC, the first moments of the broadcast of 9/11 are devoted entirely to offering viewers information and descriptions of what happened. Within the first seconds, the time and place of the event are defined, and the reporters offer very basic comments on what is shown:

Anchor X (X): We are interrupting normal programs to bring you extraordinary pictures from the United States where the both towers of the World Trade Center are now on fire. [caption: Live/ Breaking news/ World Trade Center on fire/ Two planes have crashed into the World Trade Center in New York setting it on fire]. Shortly before 2 o'clock United Kingdom time, the north tower of the World Trade Center was hit by a twin-engine passenger plane. The north tower immediately went on fire. A few moments ago the south tower was also hit by a plane and went on fire as well, so the pictures that you are now seeing are both towers of the World Trade Center hit by passenger planes. The first plane shortly before 2, which is 9 a.m. in the United States. We are about to show you a repeat of the picture when the second plane crashed. Now this is the second plane crashing in the south tower of the World Trade Center. This is in the financial district of the U.S., on Wall Street. U.S. of course on the east coast, 5 hours before us. So it's 2:10 in the United Kingdom, 9:10 in the U.S. Wall Street busy, many, many people at work. We, as yet, have no details of fatalities.

(2)   After the basic where and how, comes the who; the broadcast moves on to inform about casualties and possible victims and perpetrators. After briefly mentioning office workers and tourists, foreign correspondent David Lyon immediately makes the connection with the perpetrators and introduces the view that what happened must have been a terrorist attack. What is significant here is not so much that he does this so early in the broadcast. After all, the argument he uses that two planes hitting the two WTC towers within a short span of time can be no coincidence is logical. What is significant, then, is the fact that he arrives at the connection by inference to the 'symbolic' status of the WTC towers:

> David Loyn (DL): … It's one of the prime tourist sights of New
> York. You get this incredible view, right over Manhattan from the
> tops of those towers. Because they are so tall. They stand right at
> the end of the island. Rather prominently as some sort of symbol
> in a way of American power. And that is what makes them such a
> potential target for terrorists. And certainly looking at that second
> plane, I think we are now talking about a terrorist attack unless that
> was some bizarre coincidence. The timing, people still coming into
> work, those offices would have been filling up, the escalators
> would have been full of people coming into work … .

Interestingly, the reporter first arrives at the acknowledgment of the
symbolic status of the WTC via an attempt to explain why they are so
attractive for tourists (a possible groups of victims or targets), and then
uses that same status as a possible first explanation for making a guess
about who could have been the perpetrators, namely terrorists. The
symbolic status of the WTC hence becomes a binding tool between
arguments (at this point nothing more than educated guesses) about
effects (victims) and causes (terrorists).

Apart from offering basic information and introducing some basic
cause-and-effect guesses, the opening also functions to familiarize
viewers with the style of the broadcast. As the first quote shows,
viewers are gradually introduced to what will become the standard
visual style of the broadcast: the endless repeats of the second plane
crashing into the tower. Sentences like "so the pictures that you are
now seeing" and "we are about to show you a repeat" offer a way of
linking factual information (where, when, who) with ways of seeing it
happen. This is important as it will determine how images can be used
for making meaning of them — how they become evidence rather than
just illustration. This becomes clear when a second repeat of the second
plane is used to investigate the guess that it was no accident but a
terrorist attack:

> Valerie Sanderson (VS): Well I think we can look again at that
> second crash [1min on from first broadcast]. And there we see the
> plane advancing, towards the building. Here it is in slow motion.
> And there is that explosion. Now that looked pretty deliberate to
> me David.

In itself, the image is, of course, no more indicative of intent than any
other, but with the information on the symbolic status of the WTC,

and its consequent attractiveness for terrorists still fresh in the mind, it is easy, indeed logical, to infer a sense of deliberation from the second plane impact. In fact, it confirms the claim I made above about the implicit complicity (the "contract") between media and organizers that is so typical for a media event in Dayan & Katz' view. What the quote and line of reasoning above demonstrates, then, is the eagerness of reporters to see the status of the WTC and the images of the second impact as deliberate elements: as an incentive or a "cue," offered by the terrorists to prompt the interpretation of an attack.

(3)   At first instance, the development of this interpretation is hindered by the information that the first plane (of which up until then no images have been shown) was a small plane — a "small twin engine passenger plane," "no large passenger plane," or a "small executive jet." As such, this lack of information does not necessarily invalidate the terrorist-argument, but because information is still missing, the reporters return to the basic task of looking for facts — in this case the type of planes involved — before even attempting to go further in their speculation about causes and reasons.

> DL: … It's difficult to say what that plane was. It wasn't a large passenger plane — it was — it looked like some small executive jet which you can charter pretty easily from American airports and therefore the kind of thing that's flying in the air over New York all the time. It's impossible to imagine terrorists having unauthorised flights over a city like New York City. But they might well have got permission to fly over. There's all sorts of planes that fly over all sorts of times and have got permission to fly these two planes. And then flown them straight into the towers. That is pure speculation but it does, from that second plane, look as if that might have been one of the possibilities.

Seconds later, the identity and type of the second plane is also cast into doubt:

> DL: Well the second, I don't know about passengers, but the second one is the sort of jet which takes about 8 or 10 people. With, again, twin engine plane, you know, a Lear jet, something of that sort. I'm not an aviation expert but a plane of that size. The sort of thing that's very common flying over the skies in New York.

The identification of the first plane becomes crucial to the argument that this was a terrorist attack, not only because it leaves open other interpretations, but also because it leaves open the issue of the degree of intent and deliberation, and the scale of the attack that the reporters had started speculating on.

(4)   A few moments later, however, the interruption of the initial argument is resolved when two new pieces of information are introduced. The first is a link with the past, bringing into mind the bombing of the WTC in 1993; the second is the new information that one of the planes had been hijacked.

> VS: And after all, the towers have been struck by bombists before, in February 1993.

> DL: Well they were struck in an attack by a group of men who, most of them are Pakistani origin, but in a bomb attack which was certainly planned by Osama bin Laden, the Saudi-Arabian terrorist leader, who is currently living in Afghanistan.

> VS: Let me just tell you, some news' just come in: We understand that one of the planes anyway, David, was hijacked before the crash. That would fit in with the scenario that you were suggesting. Well, absolutely. That must have been the first one. It's thought that that was a passenger plane and hijacked and flown into the towers.

The link with the past abruptly ends the speculation about the types of planes involved, and brings the issue of the perpetrators back to the foreground. Importantly, it also offers a framing of the event in a bigger scheme: suddenly the interpretation extends over almost a decade, encompassing a well-known legitimized discourse about the antagonism between Middle East terrorism and U.S. involvement in the region. Without making it explicit, it creates a frame of reference within which the entire event can be explained and seen as part of a larger chain of events, as part of an ongoing conflict (something the U.S. administration was at pains to stress in its subsequent mentioning of "war").

The second piece of information, although seemingly a mere factual piece of knowledge, functions in the same way. The very mention of the term "hijack" brings into effect a framework of terrorism which stretches back to the early seventies, connects again with Middle East terrorism, and infers a course of operation usually associated with violent actions of movements against nation states (the PLO hijackings for instance). Finally, even the mention of the term "bombing" (twice) evokes such connotations (it is worth noting in this context the particular British connotation "bombing" has, specially in BBC reports on IRA activities in previous years — e.g., the Omagh bombing). All in all, within seconds a framework for interpretation is offered through which the entire 9/11 event can be seen. Loose ends remain in this interpretation: There is still no definite certainty on the identity of the planes (their size begins to matter), and the information about the Pakistani origin of the hijackers is incorrect, but the foundation for what will become the main interpretation of 9/11 is cemented.

Moment 2: Warning, Risk, Threat

The subsequent key moments still involve a lot of factual fine-tuning, and new information is continuously introduced throughout the broadcast. But after the initial moments, there is a gradual increase in the proportion of interpretation in the broadcast. Now the basic "where," "what," "when," and "who" are solved, the "why" and "how" must be addressed. As interpretations go, these involve much more inference, analysis and speculation from reporters. This is when, I argue, the broadcast enters its interpretive stage. To illustrate the development of discourses in this stage, I analyze the gradual process through which reporters frame the event (i.e., through mentioning and discussing "warning," "risk," and "threat").

The key elements of this framing are already present in the opening of the 9/11 broadcast: There is talk of a disaster involving airplanes, and the question is raised as to how such flights over New York could be authorized. A little later the likelihood of a terrorist attack is put forward, and, again, questions are raised concerning the security failures that must have led to the hijacking of the airplanes. The term security itself, however, is not used. Instead, there is a curious development of terms and inferences related to it, including words like "warning," "risk," and "threat." These three terms are discursively connected throughout the broadcast, and they form stages in the gradual process of the broadcast discourse. They parallel a move from the description of 9/11 towards steps to interpret it. In short, I show how the use of the word "warning" is descriptive and very factual (a warning is something you hear, see). The use of the word "risk" involves a more abstract conceptualization (although still very tangible but less connected with technology or the senses). The use of "threat" not only introduces the element of "bad intent," which is not necessarily present with "risk," but also broadens the scope of interpretation in the discourse to a much wider extent, allowing 9/11 to be seen as a symptom of a wider, historical evolution and, hence, as a media event, covering a historical "break."

Let us begin with the use of the word "warning." It is first used a few minutes into the broadcast, when the scope of the attack is not yet clear and there is still a sense that not all the facts are known (this is, for instance, before the reporters hear about the attack on the Pentagon):

> John (J): Steven we understand the United States State Department had warned Americans traveling abroad to be on their guard. Do you know anything further about this?

> Steven Cviic (SC): Yes I mean that's, er, that's something I hadn't heard about, yeah. But I think these warnings are issued from time to time. And I don't necessarily think we should read into that that they knew something like this was going to happen. Of course the U.S. is the world's only super power. U.S. interests are under threat. A lot of the time there are a lot of people around the world — various groups who would like to hit at US targets. And I, as we saw in the embassy bombings in Africa, just 3 years ago, the attack on the World Trade Center in 1993, to a certain extent I think U.S. interests are always a little bit under threat, and that for warnings that are issued from time to time don't necessarily always mean that some big attack is coming. So I think people — it's quite possible that the authorities here will have been completely taken by surprise. If indeed this was some sort of attack.

It is clear from this quote that much of what has happened has not yet been validated. Reporters "learn" about facts in real broadcast time and struggle to provide a bigger picture within which this all fits, even though there are, like in the opening moment, already some attempts to bring in points of comparison (the WTC bombing of 1993 and the embassy bombings being obvious examples). As a measure of being sure about what interpretation they offer viewers, the reports then resort to discussing the most immediate, direct, and physical aspect of the attacks. With the basic facts about what happened more or less established (who, where, what) this leads to questions about who is in immediate danger of becoming a victim (or being affected otherwise) or what immediate measures against other attacks can be taken. At its most basic, this means the broadcast operates almost uniquely on a descriptive level of interpretation, looking only at the closest (literally) environment. The second time "warning" is used is in a similar context, 23 minutes into the broadcast, which is the first time diplomatic editor Brian Hanrahan is introduced.

> VA: … No doubt then, at the highest echelons, Brian, that this is a terrorist attack?

> BH: No, I think everybody jumped to that conclusion very quickly. You noticed he [President Bush] did say apparent. He's left himself the possibility, but it seems hard as anything else and, in fact, I was just checking back four days ago, the United States issued a worldwide alert saying that they had information, I mean, they were very vague about it, that their citizens and interests were at risk all around the world and putting everybody onto a heightened state of alert. That was accompanied with a kind of specific warning about the far east: Korea and Japan and military interest there. … there have been attacks against American people which have been stepped down the last years, but nevertheless there's been repeated warnings they might come, and if you remember there have been repeated American attacks on people.

Although there is less talk here about the immediate physical dangers, and the question to the diplomatic editor clearly addresses the bigger meaning of the attack, there is still a tendency to draw the whole event back to the very specific element of warnings. In his discussion, Hanrahan covers much more than the WTC environment, actually drawing attention to warnings across the world, but he still adamantly connects it to physical and tangible events (the actual "worldwide warning"), and is, at this point, careful not to infer anything else. Instead of speculating, he admits the "warning" was "vague" and leaves it at that.

Next to "warning," the word "risk" also appears in the broadcast, but in a slightly different context and with somewhat different implications. Overall, the use of the word "risk" is still closely related to that of "warning." Both refer to direct dangers, for victims, for potential new attacks, etc. The very first time the word is used, in the second quote of this section, its use is almost equal to that of warning (or alert). But there is also a sense that "risk" allows for a little more generalist framing. This becomes clear the second time "risk" is used, 19 minutes into the broadcast:

> VA: And Steve, looking at the towers now and how damaged they are, there must be a very real risk that they'll fall and, onto buildings surrounding (them). I mean, not only must there be a huge rescue operation on now, they must want to evacuate the area, too.

> SE: Well, they've evacuated to within I would have thought 200 meters

of the towers. I presume some kind of assessment of the risk of those buildings falling down has been done. But having said all that, all the engineering work was being done when they were built for all kinds of eventualities. These explosions gave those buildings, or the building I was in, one almighty [twat], and it did move, but it didn't feel like it was going to fall down. As I said, initially I thought there had been a bit of an accident on a construction site very, very near. I can't tell you what the risks are. I can tell you that the area immediately around the buildings has been evacuated, but not the area beyond about half a mile, which is where I'm standing.

Instead of referring to particular instances (like warnings at airports), potentially wider impacts are addressed. It is important, of course, that this new term is introduced before the collapse of the first tower, but at a point where there is a sudden realization the towers *can* collapse. This draws away attention from airports and potential other targets to the dangers of what can still happen to the targets already hit. In a way, what the term "risk" does, then, is to offer the possibility for widening the interpretation of the dangers assessed. They no longer only concern people and targets but also the building itself and the immediate urban area (hence the reference to a "construction site"). In itself, such a widening is logical. It is both an almost literal widening (notice the reporter talks about where he is standing "about half a mile" farther) and an abstract widening. After the immediate dangers are covered, reporters will start to look for deeper and more hidden aspects of the story. The damage to the first tower has reminded them of the fact that there are very real risks for people still in the other tower, as well as in the neighborhood. But the embedded potential of "risk" to abstract from "warning" to something less circumstantial and instantaneous (encapsulated in the admission by one reporter that he "can't tell what the risks are") will also allow for other, even more general interpretations to appear. This happens when the word "threat" is introduced.

Next to "warning" and "risk" the word "threat" is gradually introduced. It first appears when physical dangers (of being a victim, of being on one's "guard" at airports) are discussed (see the first quote of this section). The reporter at this point immediately realizes the symbolic meaning the word "threat" can carry, and he qualifies his use of it by stating that what he intends to convey is not the symbolic meaning. In fact, his use of qualifying terms as "of course," "to a certain extent," "always" prevents from jumping to this symbolic meaning. Rather, the two times he uses the word "threat" he immediately links it to present dangers: "a lot of the time there are a lot of people around the world" (referring to the fact that American citizens need to be warned everywhere, not just at New York airports) and "warnings are issued from time to time" (referring to a system of looking out for possible dangers). It is telling that in the last instance the reporter immediately follows his remark by stating that this "doesn't necessarily mean that some big attack is coming" and asking "if, indeed, this was some sort of attack," effectively preventing any further elaboration of the symbolic meaning of the word "threat."

Now compare this use of the word threat in a quote about 30 minutes further on in the broadcast. It is worth noting that, at this point, the consensus has been reached that it was a terrorist attack (acknowledged by President Bush's reference to it) and that the target has a particular function, as a symbol.

> SC: This seems to be a very, very coordinated operation and one does wonder, you know, is there anything more coming? You know, this is, this is absolutely quite remarkable and I think it's going to give, give Americans a sense of really, of being under threat. If not in physical terms for the whole population, the symbolical power is remarkable.

Note how this use of the term "threat" is very different from how the word was first used about 10 minutes earlier. In the first mentioning, the emphasis was still very much on the physical danger of becoming a victim of a terrorist attack — a physical threat. In the mention quoted above, the emphasis has shifted toward a symbolic use of the word. Because it is employed in a discussion on how the United States and the WTC were a likely target because of how they symbolize financial, military, and political power, it becomes less of a physical denominator and more of a symptomatic one.

When Cviic mentions that Americans must now be experiencing a feeling of being under threat, he means not necessarily that there is physical danger of Americans becoming victims of attacks, but, rather, he identifies a less tangible, more general "feeling" (and the use of this word here is key to its symptomatic use). As he goes on to explain, this feeling relates "not in physical terms to the whole population," but its "symbolic power" is "remarkable." In this instance, the term "threat" is recruited, as it were, into an emerging discourse on the more general and abstract (yet politically very important) symbolic meaning of "being under threat." It means that, for one of the first times in history Americans are experiencing a sort of general fear — a "feeling" that does not disappear once the physical threat is removed.

David Bordwell's schema of levels of interpreting film (Bordwell, 1989, pp. 8-9) provides a speculative framework for the developments sketched above. According to Bordwell, any first comprehension of film will try to establish referential meaning — i.e. the kind of "who," "where," "what" and so on that were typical for the opening. Next, Bordwell argues, an explicit meaning will be established, a discourse in which an explanation will be suggested about what this all is about, in first instance. This is, I argue, what happens when the "warnings" and "risks" are introduced. They are logical deductions from the information available to the reporters, but they remain, in themselves, fairly descriptive, linked to specific information. When the "threat" is introduced, especially in the latter meaning, as described above, the discourse moves to what Bordwell calls implicit meaning, in which the symbolic elements of the text are discussed, and in which speculation on the abstract meaning becomes more important.

The final step in Bordwell's schema is that of "symptomatic interpretation," a term also used by Althusser & Balibar. As Althusser and Balibar explain, any symptomatic interpretation is much more likely to cover territory initially not meant to be part of the discussion (or even part of the text — the broadcast or the event) (Althusser & Balibar, 1979, p. 28). The gradual introduction of comparisons between the 9/11 attack and other terrorist attacks, facilitated amongst others by elaborating on the word "bombings," or on bin Laden's involvement (not just in the 1993 attacks but his attacks on American embassies as well), or on the Middle East, makes this broadening beyond the broadcast possible. Importantly, it also allows for the framing of the broadcast in a larger, historical context; hence, making it a media event by virtue of its place as a historical marker — a historical "break."

This discursive development, from warning over risk to threat, is a significant one. It demonstrates how the narrative discourse around the event gradually took shape and how shifts and moves from one emphasis to another were linked to each other. In itself, such moves are not unusual; indeed, they belong to the routines of organization of the flow of news broadcasts. But in this case, when the meaning of what is happening is being discovered (and is being speculated on) while the broadcast is being aired, it shows the close link between the development of discourse and its inherent meaning; in other words, the move from warning over risk to threat has implications for the approaches taken and the opinions formed.

The important thing here is that the outcome of the move (the established meaning) is not known in advance by the broadcasters (something which is usually the case). What the move from warning over risk to threat shows, then, is the "invention" of the discourse — the crystallization of awareness into meaning (the getting their head around it). This also means these moves expose the implicitly held opinions of the broadcast.

Moment 3: Hesitation — Reality Effect

It is important to note that developments as the one described above, in Moment 2, are not part of an uninterrupted flow usually associated with news broadcasts. Because the reporters and presenters were "learning" the news as the broadcast went on, there are sudden breaks and lapses. With the 9/11 breaking news broadcast in mind, this means that whatever moves and developments I sketched above are accompanied by (and indeed interrupted and corrected by) hesitations and moments of acknowledged uncertainty. Ideologically speaking, such moments can be seen as attempts at self-correction, as instances of intervention in the organization of the direction of the flow. Needless to say, such instances are more prone to happen in a live broadcast than in pre-recorded flows. And given the immediacy of the 9/11 breaking news broadcast, and its consequent lack of newsroom preplanning, they occur quite frequently. It would be unfair and wrongly opportunistic to see in their very frequency signs of the "breaking down" of emergent discourses and meaning of the event.

Nevertheless, they are special. Their presence and impact is closely related to how Roland Barthes describes the additional code of "truly traumatic photographs" (Barthes, 1977, p. 30). For Barthes such photographs succeed in capturing a kind of directness which invokes (next to the always present connotations and denotations of perception and cognition) the "lived" experience. Barthes sees these photographs as images "about which there is nothing to say" (Barthes, 1977, p. 31). This both means they are devoid of meaning (they do not offer any additional information) and they require no further comment (they are too powerful to be reduced to mere information). This simultaneity in being less and more is typical for many moments in live reports of traumatic events. Liebes refers to it when she discusses disaster marathons as media events (Liebes, 1998). But in the case of 9/11, it takes on a particularly interesting status.

I want to argue that many of the moments in which the flow of the broadcast seems to stall and reporters seem to struggle for words — and indeed sometimes lack basic information because the pictures do not offer them any further knowledge — qualify as the kinds of images Barthes describes as truly traumatic. Images like the second plane hitting the south tower or the collapse of the first tower, indeed, leave nothing to say. However, in the bigger context of the broadcast they not only interrupt the flow, they also enhance the broadcast's status as "real" ("lived" as Barthes has it). Because they are so powerful, and because their information value is as yet undecided (devoid of meaning), they are, at the same time, traumatic and fatic/redundant. I would like to call such moments "reality effects," because their presence has the effect of making the broadcast appear more real.

"Reality effects," by other names, are not entirely new to media analysis. It has been argued, by Roman Jacobson and Barthes amongst others, that such fatic moments are ideologically inherent to all images; in fact, a certain degree of redundancy helps ascertain the legitimacy of the image (Barthes, 1977). In relation to the developments and interpretations sketched above, it would mean that "reality effects" play a rhetorical role in assisting the interpretation achieve validity and momentum. However, when these moments are of a direct traumatic nature, the extremity and impact of "reality effects" break up the flow (to bring Althusser's and Balibar's term back in mind). This is the case with several moments in the 9/11 broadcast.

It is interesting to see how reality effects operate in quite distinct ways, and relate to particular breaks, during the 9/11 broadcast. Let us focus on two telling examples: the first images of the Pentagon being hit and the live collapse of the south tower. Let us tackle them chronologically. Thirty-four minutes into the 9/11 broadcast a sudden break in the coordination of image and sound occurs. Up until then, and even given the overall confusion, the anchors and their guests have been coping well in linking images (mostly of the burning WTC towers) and sound (their comments on what is happening — a combination of incoming news reports and describing the images to viewers). The use of guests in the broadcast, foreign correspondents of all sorts (as mentioned above in the narrative flow), has been a valuable aid in this. When the images suddenly change from New York to a clearly different area (government buildings and trees, with smoke rising in the background), it takes the audio flow a few moments to realize there has been a change and to adjust their comments to the new images. It is worth quoting the broadcast at length here:

> Brian Hanrahan (BH): I'm hesitating cause I, I, I see, another building on fire, and we are not quite sure what it is at the moment, coming from …
>
> VS: Washington [whispered]
>
> BH: Washington apparently.
>
> VS: Washington.
>
> X: It looks very much like Washington doesn't it?
>
> BH: And in fact it almost looks as though it's the area around the White House. But I'm not sure of the, at this stage, just glancing at it.
>
> VS: This apparently is the Pentagon we are seeing.

BH: [long pause] It sh.. doesn't look like the normal shot of the Pentagon it looks more like some of the executive buildings in downtown Washington …

X: It looks more like…

BH: … er, not very far away from the White House itself.

X: It looks much more like the area round about the Vice President's…

BH: Exactly.

X: … residence doesn't it, erm, from those sort of pictures.

BH: At the moment we have, we really don't know what this is about.

It is very difficult to see a "break" in the flow of the broadcast like the one above as a rhetorical tool reinforcing the already-present discourse. In fact, what happens above is that there is so much absence of context that even the reporters have to admit they "don't know what this is about." All the technical elements of the reality effect are still in place: There is a live and powerful image of smoke rising in the Washington administrative area, and the speechlessness of the reporters can well be seen as the Barthesian image "about which there is nothing to say." But what we see here is also the capacity of the reality effect to overtake the broadcast altogether. It no longer plays a supporting role, but instead prevents any discourse from taking place (or continuing) at all. It is the break down of the reality effect, even when the image itself is of a less traumatic nature (compared at least to the plane hitting the tower or the towers collapsing).

Throughout this moment, the reporters and editors struggle to regain control. In their rush to appear in control and attribute meaning while trying to remain fluent, the commentators struggle to keep up a professional appearance. In order to explain what is being shown, whilst not being fully informed themselves, they make additions and interrupt each other until they have established amongst each other what is going on. Much of their interruptions are about the identification of the image. Some confusion arises about what site in Washington is being shown. In defending his point, Hanrahan makes reference to "the normal shot" of the Pentagon; in other words, images that have been established in the past to refer to the Pentagon. Supporting BH's link to previous meanings, X agrees "those sort of pictures" recall images of the vice president's residence rather than the Pentagon. Even while they are improvising, the professionalism of the reporters demands they give the impression that there is a fluent coordinated coherence between sound and image. This is essential for the reality effect to function in support of the discourses being developed. It is the lack of this which makes for a good example of the breaks and lapses in the flow. This is exemplified by the sudden appearance of other voices, stuttering, whispering, suddenly broken off sentences, and on-screen acknowledgment of hesitations. The ensuing discussion demonstrates how the commentators are working together to reach consensus. Interestingly, in order to find agreement on the meaning of the images, they backtrack to previously established references to create discursive unity. Finally, they agree upon the subject of the image. But the only way to reach consensus on the exact area in Washington, without getting further information themselves, is to admit they "are not sure." This effectively halts all further interpretation and interrupts the discourse, much in the same way as the traumatic effect does.

Eventually, following the above scene, the reality effect gets restored. At first, this happens through acknowledgment of the impact of the image: "Startling," "extraordinary," and "remarkable" are frequently used terms. The fact that it takes some time before the flow is restored demonstrates the importance of the "reality effect." Seemingly devoid of meaning it becomes an important carrier of the rhetorical unity of the flow — in effect, a core tool in the transport of meaning across it. And when it breaks down it still opens possibilities. Even through the confusion, it allows reporters, commentators and editors to re-use, re-address and re-emphasize already mentioned points of attention, hence turning them, by repetition, into more established facts. This creates the discursive unity and the legitimization, as discussed above, but in a different way.

The second moment, the collapse of the south tower, occurs 52 minutes into the broadcast. It features the same characteristics as the Pentagon-images, but the eventual recuperation of the reality effect as supporting the flow happens in a more direct way.

X: Steven, what was it like to be in the World Trade Center when it was hit?

Steven Evans (SE): [Oh my God! — heard in background] There's something, there's another explosion happening as we speak!

X: We are seeing another explosion as we speak [hesitant]. We, we, the pictures that you are seeing now are of the World Trade Center in New York. [microphone makes high pitched sound] These are live pictures, however, that we are now seeing — we are now seeing live pictures of another building exploding in New York. Steven, I know you are at the World Trade Center. There have been two explosions there, but a third explosion has now taken place in New York. Steve, what can you see?

SE: [long silence]

X: Steven are you with us? What can you see in New York? [pause] Well we seem to have lost erm, Steven Evans in New York, we will try to get him back as soon as we possibly can. But just to update you, we now have two explosions in the World Trade Center in New York. We have an explosion in the Pentagon in Washington. The Pentagon has now been evacuated, and we are now getting pictures, these are live pictures that you are seeing of a third building in Manhattan now collapsing it appears, after being hit as well. That's a — a third explosion in Manhattan. These are quite extraordinary scenes.

[Caption: live/moments ago World Trade Center/ New York]

VS: Let's bring in our diplomatic editor Brian Hanrahan. In your long career, have you ever seen anything like this?

BH: No, this is clearly a terrorist spectacular which is intended to hurt and humiliate the United States. This is the center of, if you like, of, of the symbol of America. The, the, these twin towers of the World Trade Center which dominate now Manhattan islands, and there they are, shrouded in smoke, er, the American defenses against this. There's the idea that they're a continent, isolated in the troubles of the world, broken down with a few simple hijackings. And this enormous picture of devastation and destruction, which has been mirrored in Washington by an attack on the Pentagon, the center of military power. Er, it, it is quite astonishing and clearly quite deliberate the intended, to, er, to put this on television around the world, so everybody can see what the people who did this think of America.

As with the Pentagon image, there is a sudden break down of the flow, as a result of the powerful live image of the south tower collapsing. Although the risk of such a collapse had been addressed in the broadcast previously, it still comes so sudden the reporters need some time before they establish what is going on. There are mistakes, hesitations, silences, and even technical difficulties (also in the banners at the bottom of the screen, where, at one time, there are three overlapping each other). But, unlike the Pentagon images, where it was left to the reporters to find an agreement (even if it was on what they were unsure about), and restore the flow, we here have an explicit intervention from an editor, through which the diplomatic editor Brian Hanrahan gets introduced again. His comments do not really seem to address the images, nor do they really restore the flow to or reduce the power of the image to a regular reality effect (for instance by giving a logic to them). Rather the opposite, his exposition, using highly symbolic and charged language, seems to acknowledge the traumatic nature of the images, enhancing as it were their powerful impact. Under usual circumstances, Hanrahan's monologue would have been interrupted much sooner by an editor, to allow the flow to regain momentum. But because everyone is busy finding out what is happening exactly, his comments go on, their symbolic weight reinforcing the break down of the reality effect — calling into attention even the possibility that these kinds of images were exactly what the terrorists aimed for. Bearing in mind the issue of preplanning and complicity essential for seeing the broadcast as a media event, Hanrahan comes close to acknowledging this. At the same time this intervention also buys time, during which additional information is sought, and after which the flow is, finally, restored. Once it is clear the images are of the south tower collapsing, there is a brief, factual acknowledgment; the banners are also corrected (actually the BBC banner replaces the ABC banner).

Both moments show to what extent reality effects play an important role in the 9/11 broadcast. In moderate form they help legitimize the ongoing flow; the small breaks make the flow appear more real and, hence, more truthful. In extreme form, however, they break up the flow and make visible some of the underlying, usually invisible, elements of its construction (hesitations, contradictions, off the cuff acknowledgements about the role of television). But even here, the reality effect ultimately confirms the status of the flow as real. When the reality effect breaks up the flow, and especially when it is sudden and to an extent that cannot be ignored (or immediately recuperated), the consequence is that it looks even less mediated. Ironically, the complete breaking up of the flow then also functions as an enhancement of its rhetoric: It becomes more real. Because the way in which the traumatic reality effect makes the broadcast look more real in a *non-routine* and *non-procedural* way (it looks extraordinary real), it also reinforces the status of 9/11 and its television broadcast as a media event: The event is so exceptional, television has trouble fully mastering it.

Returning to Fiske's view that the meaning of media events is the result of competing voices only gradually reaching a consensus, this means the reality effect, and its analysis, allows for the specific identification of such voices. It not only points to how the 9/11 broadcast already is a media event, the attention it puts on "breaks" (the breaking up of the flow) makes it one.

CONCLUSION

In conclusion I want to return to the importance of framing 9/11 and its broadcast as a media event. Because of the live nature of the broadcast, the historical significance, and its interruption of social routines, such a framing seems logical in itself. But, by insisting that even in the differences with Dayan & Katz' original description of media events, this framing still remains accurate, it becomes possible to uncover an underlying belief in their view on the construction of history.

The two main differences between Dayan and Katz's and my own view on 9/11 and its broadcast as a media event are its planning and the consensual nature of its meaning. I have demonstrated how 9/11, if only implicitly, seems to show a kind of complicity between the organizers and the broadcasters. In fact, as some of the reporters themselves remarked, the event almost seemed to be "aiming for maximum publicity on the world stage." I tackled the second difference by referring to Fiske's view on the broadcasting of history, demonstrating that media events are more likely to be the result of struggles over their meaning than Dayan and Katz are prepared to admit.

Such struggles are at the core of the 9/11 broadcast. The discourse of meaning of 9/11 was formed in the first couple of hours of its broadcast, when journalists had to improvise on-screen. When investigating just *how* this discourse developed, I found those first few hours to consist of a curious mix of flow and breaks. The *flow* seemed logical, in fact, not any different from how Raymond Williams first theorized it (Williams, 1974). The concept of *breaks*, however, is new in this context. In terms of the broadcast it refers to moments in which the broadcast's continuity seems to break up; moments when the reporters themselves seem confused, hesitant, struggling for words. Interestingly, some of these breaking moments contain the most traumatic and powerful images of the broadcast (the hitting of the towers, the first images of the Pentagon, the collapse of the towers). They also have the effect of making the broadcast appear more "real," because they seem to offer a more direct, immediate "feel" of the traumatic nature of the event. Building on Barthes' discussion of traumatic images, I have called breaking moments of this kind "reality effects." Because reality effects both abruptly break up the flow, and open up the possibilities of other meanings (more direct ones, traumatic shock), and because the broadcast clearly shows reporters struggling to overcome these moments, they, too, are examples of the struggle for meaning that I believe is at the center of media events.

Finally, seeing 9/11 and other media events as sites of struggle harbors an important view on the construction of history. In their view of media events as celebrations of which the center of meaning is consensual or undisputed, Dayan and Katz display a belief that the broadcasting of history represents what everyone agrees upon. As the struggle over meaning in the first hours of 9/11 demonstrates, however, the broadcasting of history contains many breaks and disruptions. The concept of breaks reminds of

Althusser's and Balibar's critique of the constructions of history: Breaks unveil telling signs of struggle between competing and still forming discourses and meanings. This not only confirms to Fiske's view on media events, ultimately it also carries the belief that history is not borne out of consensus, but out of struggle, trauma.

CHAPTER ENDNOTES

[1] I would like to thank Ernest Mathijs, Martin Barker, and the ccprg reading group of the University of Wales, Aberystwyth for their valuable comments and criticism on this paper and the underlying research. I also thank the several BBC staff who were willing to share their views with me. Some of them remain deliberately anonymous.

[2] Branston notes that the term '9/11' is a postmodern sign, detached from the complexity of the event. The term functions as shorthand for many aspects that deserve closer attention and critical study (Branston, 2004).

[3] The PEW research center is an independent opinion research group. It studies attitudes toward the press, politics and public policy issues. Their most frequent output includes national (U.S.) surveys on public attentiveness to major news stories, and polls that indicate trends in values and fundamental political and social attitudes.

[4] Two chapters in Zelizer & Allan (2002) address the relationship between online forums and 9/11: Stuart Allan's 'Reweaving the Internet: Online News of September 11', and Bruce Williams' 'The New Media Environment, Internet Chatrooms, and Public Discourse after 9/11'. I refer to these for a more specific literature on discussion lists and 9/11.

[5] I am referring to the controversial images of people celebrating in Palestinian refugee camps.

[6] This pull for integration was felt by the U.S. media to the extent that whoever failed to blindly support the United States' cause was regarded no less than a traitor. This resulted in mainstream media converging in one voice (Allan, 2002, p. 119).

[7] See also Liebes and Katz (1993), "The Export of Meaning."

[8] Flemish Radio and Television, a Belgian public service broadcaster

[9] I believe the event's 'newsworthiness' lies in its remarkableness: choice of geographical and socio-political place (an attack on American soil), symbolical value of the targets (WTC as a financial and economic symbol, and the Pentagon as a symbol of military might), spectacle (high visibility guaranteed by presence of cameras and time interval between the impacts), and possible high number of victims (American victims).

REFERENCES

Alexander, Y. & Picard, R. (Eds.). (1991). *In the Camera's Eye: News Coverage of Terrorist Events*, London: Brassey.

Allan, S. (2002). Reweaving the Internet - Online News of September 11 *Journalism After September 11*, Zelizer B. & Allan S. (Eds.). London: Routledge, 119-140.

Althusser, L. & Balibar, E. (1979) *Reading Capital*, London: Verso.

Apple, M. (2002). Pedagogy, Patriotism, and Democracy: on the educational meanings of 11 September 2001 *Discourse, 23:3*, 299-308.

Barthes, R. (1977). *Image, Music, Text*, London: Fontana Press.

Bean, H. (2001) Everything has Changed *Sight & Sound, 12*, 26-29.

Boorstin, D. (1961). *The Image — A Guide to Pseudo-Events*, New York: Harper Colophon.

Bordwell, D. (1989). *Making Meaning*, Cambridge MA, Harvard University Press.

Branston, G. (2003). *Out of a Clear Blue Sky: '9/11', Media Study and Memory*, University of Coventry.

Carey, J. (1998). Political Ritual on Television: Episodes in the History of Shame, Degradation and Excommunication *Media, Ritual and Identity*, Liebes T. & Curran J. (Eds.). London: Routledge, 42-70.

Couldry, N. (2003). *Media Rituals: A Critical Approach*, London: Routledge.

Chomsky, N. (2001) *9-11*, New York, NY: Seven Stories Press.

Dayan, D. & Katz, E. (1992). *Media Events: The Live Broadcasting of History*, Cambridge, MA: Harvard University Press.

Fiske, J. (1996). *Media Matters — Race and Gender in US Politics*, London: University of Minnesota Press.

Gajjala, R. (2001). *Cultstud-L New York and D.C.*, [e-mail].

Kellner, D. (2003). *9/11, Spectacles of Terror, and Media Manipulation: A Critique of Jihadist and Bush Media Politics.* http://www.gseis.ucla.edu/faculty/kellner/ essays/ 911terrorspectaclemedia.pdf accessed 04/01/05

Liebes, T. (1998). Television's Disaster Marathons: a Danger for Democratic Processes? *Media, Ritual and Identity*, Liebes T. & Curran J. (Eds.). London: Routledge, 71-86.

Liebes, T. & Katz, E. (1993). *The Export of Meaning: Cross-Cultural Readings of Dallas*, Cambridge: Polity.

Morcellini, M. (2002). *Torri crollanti: communicazione, media e nuovi terrorismi dopo i'11 settembre*, Milan, Italy: Franco Angeli.

Pew Research Center, Two Years Later, the Fear Lingers, 2003. http://people-press.org/reports/display.php3?ReportID=192, accessed 04/01/05

Rizvi, F. (2003). Democracy and Education after September 11 *Globalisation, Societies and Education, 1:1*, 25-40.

Roche, M. (2000). *Mega-Events and Modernity*, London: Routledge.

Thomson, C. (2002) *The Future of Public Service Broadcasting - An International Perspective*, [speech given at the Broadcast Magazine/Commonwealth Broadcasting Association Conference].

Williams, R. (1974). *Technology and Cultural Form*, London: Fontana.

White, J. (2003). *Terrorism*, London: Thomson Wadsworth.

Zelizer, B. & Allan, S. (2002). Introduction, *Journalism After September 11*, Zelizer B. & Stuart A. (Eds.). London: Routledge, 1-24.

Chapter 4

"We Cannot All Be Americans": French Media Reception of 9/11

Jacques Portes

Afirst and well-known French answer to the tragic attack on the United States has been Jean-Marie Colombani's editorial on Sept. 12, 2001: "We are all American" (2001, p. 1). At the time, about 90 percent of the French agreed more or less with this astounding phrase, which came from a daily paper often considered leftist and anti-American in the tradition of its founder Hubert Beuve-Méry, who despised the United States as early as 1944 (Greilsamer, 1990, p. 283) and said: "Americans present a clear danger for France. It is economic and moral."[1]

But this approbation was short-lived. About a day later other pundits questioned it, making a distinction between American people and the Bush administration, finding a link between a revolting attack and some frightening American initiatives in the recent past as before. Finally, a solid hostility toward the United States replaced quickly the immediate sympathy.

We Are All American

As in many other countries in the world, the French reacted emotionally to 9/11. The TV images were frightening. Philippe Roger (2002, p. 579) was in New York on September 11:

> From this morning, I keep first an audio memory: the incredible rumor which arose two times over the town, when each of the towers collapsed ... coming from a City engulfed by horror. The images of the tumbling down towers resumed ad nauseam can lose their meaning, if they never had any. That unheard scream, so different from a stadium clamor or

from a roaring riot, covered forever for me the sound of all "intelligent" comments.

In France, as in the United States, most people live in cities and quite a few worked in towers and huge office-building so the Twin Towers collapse, accompanied by people running in the dust and others jumping from windows, triggered strong sympathy, which might not have been the case in other parts of the world where most people still live in villages or in shantytowns near cities devoid of skyscrapers. That sympathy also drew upon the December 1994 incident in which an Air France Airbus flying between Algiers and Paris was taken by GIA pirates but stopped in Marseilles. Special Forces assaulted the plane, killed the men and found some documents about their intent to crash the plane into the Eiffel Tower. The parallel with New York was striking and strengthened French sympathy (Colombani, 2001):

> At this tragic time, when words seem so inadequate to describe the shock we are feeling, the first thing that comes to mind is: We are all American! We are all New Yorkers, as sure as John Kennedy said 'Berliners' in 1963 in Berlin. Indeed, how not to feel, as in the gravest moments in our history, deep solidarism with this people and this country, the United States, to which we are all so close and to which we owe our freedom, and therefore our solidarity.

On Sept. 12, a similar reaction was expressed by President Chirac, by the General Secretary of the Communist Party, as well as by François Hollande for the Socialist Party or Dominique Voynet for the Greens and François Bayrou for the Center. The attack on the American soil arose "indignation," "compassion," "fear," was seen as a "nightmare" justified by no fact nor event: The solidarity with the U.S. was more or less unanimous. Only the Trotskyites (Ollivier, 2001) said immediately that they could have empathy towards victims but in no way could they support the American government: "We cannot express any sort of solidarity to a government which again could attack civil people with the purpose to strengthen its position of first global power."

On the following days, such a consensus began to crumble. Some said they could not be American, except at an emotional level. Divergence with the Bush administration was widening. George W. Bush invoked God on his side, but explanation of the terrorist attack were being attributed to "the act and words of Bush" and his "new order" (Joxe, 2002, p. 103).[2] Such opinion came from the left and center, but other explanations also emerged.

From the 1960s, France has tried to keep contacts with Arab countries and had her links with French-speaking African people: So some observers were immediately aware of the limits of the sympathy towards America. On Sept. 15, the daily *Libération* noticed the large discrepancy between different countries: "If you draw new meridian lines on the world, one could be resumed by two numbers: 78% of Danes would support the U.S. in their military initiative, but 65% of Brazilians think that Americans deserved what happened to them. And the divide between the occidental world and the Arab-Muslim is steeper."

And even in the developed world, emotions were divided (Badie, 2001, *Libération*, September 15-16):

> I have not seen this week many reactions towards the death of some Palestinians ... And when we'll be able to look at the genocide of 500,000 Rwandans in the same way we have reacted to the tragedy of the New York victims, we'll advance on the road of an international regulation. But we are still in a world where one human being is not worth another, that's why the South has reacted to the New York catastrophe.

Such postmortem indicated that the unanimity was fragile; no event, as impressive as 9/11 was, could erase negative opinions of the United States.

A CRITICAL VIEW OF THE AMERICAN WAY

Nevertheless, since the 1990s French people have became less anti-American but more critical of American society, American motive and values, and that is why they could appreciate Hollywood movies as entertainment but find them violent and childish. Generally speaking, very few differences existed between elites and common people, but officials and politicians could still use anti-Americanism as an easy traditional explanation to be understood by a plurality of the citizens.

In 1999, Hubert Védrine, then Minister of Foreign Affairs and without being categorized as an anti-American, forged the concept of "Hyperpuissance" to explain how the United States was dominant, as Kuisel quoted (2004, p. 24):

> The United States has assets not yet at the disposal of any power: political influence, the supremacy of the dollar, control of the communications network, "dream factories," new technology. Add these up — the Pentagon, Boeing, Coca-Cola, Microsoft, CNN, the Internet, the English language — the situation is virtually unprecedented.

The 9/11 attacks could not change such a context, as they could be related to some effects of "Hyperpuissance":

America had been hit by heart, as victim of her "Hyperpuissance." The United States wanted to be seen as the good cop of a new world order. His (Bush's) incoherent policies have facilitated a chaos, provoking frustrations which were the nourishing bed of terrorism. (Tolotti, 2001)

People well-informed of the situation of the Middle East argued that the United States often acts like a bully. In a letter written a few days after the attack, Jean d'Ormesson gave his advice to President Bush (2001, September 15, *Le Figaro*):

Your demoniac enemies have not only hit the symbols of all what they hate in this world. Their calculus goes much farther. Your own reaction is part of their plan. We live in a time when victims replace heroes and they count on your repression for bringing to their side the still vacillating masses. If I dared, Mr. President, I'll pray you to not be for the Islamic masses from Morocco to Indonesia what Ariel Sharon has been for the Palestinians.

Some specialists went farther. Gerard Chaliand (2001, September 18, *Le Monde*) explained that such a terrorist attack was not new by itself but only as a final phase of what he called "classical terrorism" and that it could not be met by a war but by a multi-level reaction: "Terrorism will be weakened by the destruction of its sanctuaries. It'll not be eradicated. Even if terrorism is not able to put on its knees a strong State, we'll have to live with as a recurrent cause of harm."

Claude Roy and a few others who understood the necessity of an American rapid-response denied any clash of civilization. Such moderates were rapidly troubled and choked by the language used by George W. Bush and his neo-conservatism oriented team: The "crusade against terrorism" employed on Sept. 16 by the president could not be more accepted than the unilateralist approach highly assumed. As in the Islamic World, many French pundits were scornful about Bush's lack of historical sense and anxious of what he could mean by this word. This lapse has been rapidly corrected, but soon came other expressions, which arose indignation and anxiety. The famous speech on the State of the Union 2002, denouncing an "axis of evil" was met by similar outcry, and the best analysts made all the distinction between Iraq, Iran and North Korea and discussed this idea of "rogue states" as too simple.

For these intellectuals, George W. Bush was a typical uneducated

American, and he could be dangerous as he affirmed his will to act alone and counting only on American mighty military forces. Nevertheless, the "victory" in Afghanistan had been accepted, as this war was seen as legitimate and because in France as in other countries there has been a general outcry against the Taliban in the previous years. But the result of the war could have been more heartily acknowledged if the President had stopped his revenge there and tried to find a political solution to confront terrorism. Bernard-Henri Lévy (2001, December 21, *Le Monde*) even predicted that the old French anti-Americanism had suffered a severe blow, after a victory which did not provoke any uprising in Muslim countries, but he was too optimistic.

It was not long before this perspective was scattered and destroyed by the overt choice of force by the Bush administration, which held to his "war against terrorism" as a way of uniting his people behind him, without giving them anytime nor anything to think about. This evolution of the pundits and experts was always mixed with discussions and caveats especially critical of the neo-con around the president, of the influence of the religious right. So, even when they stayed moderate in their expression, their comments could be seen as anti-American.

In the general public, whose opinion has been apparent in different surveys and who got their information mostly from TV, such intellectual reserve and nuances were unintelligible. During 2002, the proportion of French people hostile to the United States climbed from 30 percent in the beginning of this year to 60 percent when the Iraq war was being discussed at the United Nations. France did not differ from other countries, and suspicion of a hidden American ambition in the region was frequently assumed: Oil was the principal culprit.

A general suspicion of the U.S. motive gave way to some extreme opinion: a cartoon presented Phan Thi Kim Phuc, the little naked girl running after be burnt by napalm in Vietnam in 1972, with the World Trade Center Towers crumbling in the background. It made a troubling relation between two very different events: "They deserve it." More startling has been the success of Thierry Meyssan's book (2002), which sold more than 200,000 copies in a few weeks and has been translated in many languages: Spanish, German, Arabic and English. In this book, Meyssan pretended that the Mossad was at the origin of the attack on the Twin Towers and that no plane never crashed on the Pentagon. All the fuss being created and manipulated by a faction of the American government on its way for a fascist "coup d'état'."

Such cases were examples of a profound hostility even of a sort of hate towards America. It was directly caused by 9/11 — interpreted as a revelator of the "normal" harmfulness of the United States. This dark vision did not arise suddenly in September 2001; it has its roots in the recent past.

A GREATER DIVIDE
BETWEEN FRANCE AND AMERICA

French opinion of the United States has been fluctuated during the 20th century. In the early 1900s, the Left definitely became hostile to a country which was seen as the golden land of capitalism, and the far right was always critical of American vulgar manners and lack of sophistication (Portes, 2000).

After the Vietnam and from 1968 to the 1980s, the two countries have been converging in some ways, with a sort of Social Democracy gaining ground to challenge the consumer culture. The decline and disappearance of the USSR weakened the Communist Party and the Marxist Left. The anti-American current was also marginalized by increasing tourism. At the beginning of Nineties, the United States was the first country visited by one million of French people every year. Trade agreements and the development of American movies and television series gave the French a superficial knowledge of American life   one that emphasized violence in the streets and racial tensions — but did not bring a better understanding between France and America.

But this helped explain why there was no more an active political anti-Americanism — just a critical view of American society. The end of communism as a common threat and the conservative backlash in America provoked a form of realignment in their relations. On the political side, French officials could be critical of American initiatives in Kosovo or of Washington for refusing to pay its dues to the UN, and they could distance themselves from an international policy which has lost its moorings with the end of the Cold War. On the social side, French people were upset by the frequent use of the death penalty in American States, by the lack of a real social policy — especially after 1994, with the failure of President Clinton health plan. In May 2000, a French polling agency posed the question (Kuisel, 2004): "Are you, with respect to the United States, rather sympathetic, or neither sympathetic nor antipathetic?" More than 4 of 10 (41%) said "sympathetic," 10% "antipathetic" and the rest (48%) said "neither the one nor the other."[3]

During the Clinton years, many controversies arose between France and the United States. The president was not so much Europe-oriented as his predecessor and it took him a long time to get his footing in international affairs. The war in the Balkans illustrated this evolution; until 1995, the American administration kept aloof and did not want to intervene, but after the Serb shelling of Sarajevo, Bill Clinton changed his position and followed President Chirac lead seeking an end to the war. When this decision was taken, the belligerents accepted the cease-fire agreement imposed by the Americans in Dayton (Ohio), because they were Americans: They acknowledged American power, as negotiators of the Oslo agreement between Israel and Palestinians have done in 1993. In such cases, American power have been benevolent, but it could also been seen as oppressive: a vacillating determination in Kosovo had been criticized by French pundits, who wanted at the same time an American determination and feared its probable effect.

The war in Kosovo gave an example of the new American military forces, much more powerful than their European counterparts. That is why, in 1999, Hubert Védrine spoke for the first time of a "hyperpuissance" and such a power can be feared, as a "machine that would go by itself" (2002, January 1st, *Le Monde*).

> The United States have spent much more in the military domain than any other country: much more even than Russia, China, France, Germany and Great-Britain put together. Such an exceptional power feeds a permanent anxiety for partners of the United States. He could be inclined to use this force in despise of the law or by crossing the limits of a self-defense?

The contested 2000 election came in this context. An obscure democratic process puzzled French observers, as many others in the States as in other parts of the world, and nobody knew George W. Bush well. It was not very long before the new President antagonized many Europeans and especially the French with his decision to build an anti-missile shield, to drill in the proximity of national parks, to refuse to ratify international agreements (international court or Kyoto treaty on pollution), to give tax cuts to the wealthy and to give an increased role to the churches in social problems and in education.

All these initiatives offended most Europeans, who believe in international peace and respect the environment and social programs. In France, the divide between sympathy for the America people and hostility toward their President was widening every day.

The unanimity caused by 9/11 was fragile. Nevertheless, President Bush had the opportunity to build on that large emotion in favor of his country. It would have been difficult but the magnitude of this moment could have made this orientation possible (July, 2001, September 16, *Libération*).

> Bush has to practice a strategic u-turn. He will have to radically break the United States twenty years alliance with Islamic countries as Pakistan, Saudi Arabia, Emirates, and Afghanistan ... The president can also, in the present state of shock, give a new impetus to the peace process in Middle East and impose peace to Israelis and Palestinians ... Anyhow the United States will have to reorient all its strategic plan: to abandon isolationism and get rid of an all-economy agenda, but to use all his weight on the political side ... America has no choice.

Such a bold program, which summarizes what many pundits thought, has not been implemented. The choice of force by President Bush and, in the spring of 2002, his decision to make war in Iraq destroyed the unanimity of September 2001, as Kuisel (2004) as demonstrated:

> A year after the attacks French respondents attributed mainly negative consequences, except for the war against terrorism, to the actions of the U.S. and its allies after 9/11 (…) with respect to mitigating sources of international tension or creating a more just international system.

In 2003, France was leading other countries against war in Iraq and the United States responded with French-bashing. In a sense there has been a long tradition of French misgivings of the United States, which explains the recent evolution. But 9/11 provoked a strong disappointment after a short moment of hope. There was a real opening at the time, which could have permitted a better understanding between both countries, but President Bush chose his own way and preferred to act alone to promote his vision of national security. The unanimity of September 2001, as ephemeral as it was, was spoiled.

CHAPTER ENDNOTES

[1] All translation from French to English is made by Jacques Portes.

[2] Alain Joxe, in Sylvie Kaufmann dir., *11 septembre, un an après*, Paris: Le Monde & éditions de l'Aube, 2002, p. 103.

REFERENCES

"Un monde de silence." (2001). *Libération*, September 15-16.

Badie, B. (200, September15-16). La puissance américaine condamnée à la modestie, *Libération*.

Chaliand, G. (2001). It's not a war….. *Le Monde*, September 18.

Colombani, J.-M. (2001, September 13). *Le Monde.*,(p. 1)

D'Ormesson, J. (2001). "Lettre ouverte au président Bush."*Le Figaro*. September 15.

Greilsamer, L. (1990). *Hubert Beuve-Méry*. Paris: Fayard, (p. 283).

Joxe, A. (2002). in Kaufmann Sylvie (Ed.), *11 septembre, un an après*. Paris: Le Monde & éditions de l'Aube, (p. 103).

July, S. (2001). "Le bouleversement américain." *Libération*, September 16.

Kem, H. (2002). "Ce qui est bon pour les États-Unis l'est-il pour le monde?." *Le Monde*, January 1st.

Kuisel R. (2004). "French Opinion and the Deteriorating Image of the United States, 2000-2004." *French Politics, Culture and Society*, XXII (3). This paper is also available on the web under the author's name.

Lévy, B.-H. (2001). "Ce que nous avons appris depuis le 11 septembre." *Le Monde*, December 21.

Meyssan, T. (2002). *L'effroyable imposture*. Paris: Carnot.

Ollivier, F. (2001, September 20). "Tous internationalistes." *Rouge*.

Portes, J. (2000). *Fascination and Misgvings. The United States in French Opinion, 1870-1914*. New York : Cambridge University Press.

Roger, P. (2002). *L'ennemi américain. Généalogies de l'antiaméricanisme français*. Paris: Seuil (p. 579).

Tolotti, S. (2001)." L'Amérique frappée au cœur….." *Télérama*. 2697., September 19.

Chapter 5

REACTIONS TO 9/11 IN THE GERMAN MEDIA

Anne Koenen & Brigitte Georgi-Findlay

Before analyzing German reactions to September 11, 2001, one should probably sketch the context in which they took place. First, one needs to consider that German-American relations, for various, mostly security-related reasons, have changed, if not cooled down, since the end of the Cold War. Not too many seem to have noticed the new strains and conflicts accompanying trans-Atlantic political cooperation in the 1990s, considering the internationalist and multilateralist rhetoric of the Clinton administration and due to the focus on internal problems on both sides of the Atlantic. Germans in particular turned their energies to German reunification and the strengthening of the European Union, and interest in U.S. foreign policy seems to have been relegated to the margins (despite some hotly debated issues, such as the Gulf War) on both sides of the Atlantic. Trans-Atlantic issues seem to have been subsumed under the debates over economic globalization, transnational politics, and global cultures (within which, of course, one could argue over the role of the United States in terms of the "Americanization" of international communication, globalization, etc.).

In August 2001, an opinion survey (conducted by the *International Herald Tribune* and Pew poll) in Britain, Italy, Germany, and France found wide disapproval of President George W. Bush's conduct of foreign policy. Disapproval of Bush's international policy was strongest among Germans (65%, compared to 46% among Italians and 59% among the French). Disapproval focused on his "positions on global warming and missile defense," his pursuit of "American interests in a narrow sense," and his "support for the death penalty in the United States." Other controversial issues were "Mr. Bush's decision to abandon the Kyoto Protocol," his repudiation of "a Clinton administration decision to sign an accord to establish an International Criminal Court," the administration's withholding of support "for efforts to complete or enforce a biological weapons treaty, an international ban on land mines, a small-arms control pact, an anti-money laundering effort and United Nations population control programs" (Knowlton 1,7). Although it is doubtful whether the latter issues were central every-day concerns for the German public, a majority of Germans agreed with the poll's suggestions that Europe and the United States were growing apart because they "need each other less for security reasons since the end of the Cold War" (77%), because of the "growing power of the European Union" (71%), because "American multinational corporations are creating resentment in Europe" (68%), and because "Europeans and Americans have increasingly different social and cultural values these days" (68%) (Knowlton 7).

Mark Siemons reacted to this poll in the English edition of the conservative *Frankfurter Allgemeine Zeitung* by suggesting that the "new anti-Americanism is beginning to gain a clearer profile. ... there is a more fundamental uncertainty about what America really stands for." At the same time, the United States "has returned to its former role of villain." While the United States under Clinton's leadership "seemed to be Europe's twin, but with power," under Bush "it looks once again like a twilight zone of the strange and frightening." Siemons adds that the new anti-Americanism, unlike the old version,

> does not deny the United States its leadership role; on the contrary, it demands more leadership. It is Bush's lack of interest in giving the West guidance that raises most suspicion. Fueling this is the idea of the new world order that arose after the fall of communism — the belief in the possibility of a world government capable of enforcing peace, human rights, ecology and economic equity in equal measure (Siemons).

While during the Clinton presidency "the illusion that the United States was the ideal candidate for such a job could survive," the Bush administration "has made clear that the United States is much less universalistic than Europe has willed it to be. It could well be that the new anti-Americanism is primarily an expression of disillusionment over Europe's own self-deception" (Siemons).

Then came the shock of September 11, with the spontaneous outpouring of sympathy for the United States. Television images of the attacks, first mistaken by many Germans as commercials for disaster movies, could be seen in seemingly endless repetition on all channels, on public as well as on commercial TV. Regular programming was suspended, commercials were banned. Music channel Viva stopped all its music programs, only showing a still "out of respect." German news channels like n-tv and phoenix attracted more viewers than ever (n-tv reached an unprecedented 9.3 % of viewers during 4 and 5 p.m. on September 11 — LVZ, 13.11.01, p. 12; *Frankfurter Rundschau*, 13.11.01, p. 23). Radio stations banned comedy as well as game shows, aired more sedate programs, and invited listeners to phone in their condolences. While these immediate reactions were characterized by outpourings of sympathy, disbelief, and helplessness, reflections about the events and the media's reporting of the attacks followed with a time-lag of only a few days. Analyses of the attacks were circulated in experts' rounds and ranged from criticism of U.S. politics (on September 17, a leader of the German Muslim community, shown on phoenix, identified the United States as being responsible for the terrorists' acts and host Martin Schulze did not object) to warnings of rash political actions and references to Germany's fear of war.

The same pattern — sympathy followed by analysis — emerges in the print media. The tabloid *Bild*, describing the attacks as the worst terrorist acts in the history of mankind, asked in its headline on September 12: "Thousands Dead in America! The World in Fear! Will There be War?" and added: "May God Help Us!" The paper claimed that "we are all afraid!" The world was seen as united in shock, mourning, and anger *(Bild* September 12, 2001, 1-2). Editor Kai Diekmann interpreted the attacks as a declaration of war against all humanity and declared that the world will never be the same again (1). Another commentator, Franz Josef Wagner, was certain that World War III had begun, and that everybody was now an American willing to defend America (1). The German chancellor, Gerhard Schröder, declared the attacks a declaration of war against the whole civilized world, while the German President, Johannes Rau, predicted that this day would change the world (6).

Germans mourned, prayed, laid flowers at the doors of U.S. embassies (12). German politicians interrupted their election campaigns (*Bild* Hamburg, September 12, 2001, 8). Many saw the attacks not directed at America but at "us" (Wolf Heckmann, "Angriff auf uns," *Hamburger Morgenpost* September 12, 2001, 2). There was no doubt that America would have to hit back and America's allies would have to signal their solidarity and support (Olaf Jahn, "Ein schwarzer Tag für die Welt," *Berliner Morgenpost* September 12, 2001, 3). Others, such as the chairwoman of the PDS (Party of Democratic Socialism, successor party of the state party of the GDR) called for a balanced U.S. reaction, reminding America of its responsibility for peace ("Normaler Betrieb ist nicht mehr angesagt," *Berliner Morgenpost* September 12, 2001, 9). One hotly discussed subject was whether sports events should continue or be canceled.

Major dailies took the attacks as an opportunity to review earlier terrorist attacks targeting the United States or U.S. forces abroad in the past twenty years (Kurt Kister, "Der Terror sucht Amerika heim," *Süddeutsche Zeitung* September 12, 2001, 2). Stefan Kornelius drew attention to the scorn Europeans had earlier poured over Washington's anti-terror planners who were preparing for the worst scenarios imaginable ("Amerika im Krieg," *Süddeutsche Zeitung* September 12, 2001, 4). Again there was no doubt that the world would never be the same again. The "clash of civilizations" described by Samuel Huntington was already a bloody reality. NATO countries, particularly Germany, would have to face this reality by reforming their armed forces and revising their distrust of a strong state. American security fears, scorned by German officials as exaggeration at best, as hysteria at worst, had proven to be legitimate. Europeans had only escaped — for now — the catastrophe because they were not taken seriously by the terrorists.

But the declaration of war should be taken seriously as a warning to Europeans, too (Michael Stürmer, "Das ist der Ernstfall," *Die Welt* September 12, 2001, 8). Konrad Adam suggested that the attacks brought America closer again since they helped everybody to distinguish between friend and foe (Konrad Adam, "Sicherheit und Freiheit," *Die Welt* September 12, 2001, 8). Günther Nonnenmacher claimed: "Not only has the United States been hit, the entire Western world has been shaken in its self-assurance, shaken to its psychological foundations" ("The Future We Have," *Frankfurter Allgemeine Zeitung* English Edition September 13, 2001, 1). Berthold Kohler reiterated this: "At this moment, Europe knew that as part of the community of Western values it had been attacked itself" ("A Show of Hands Is Not Enough," *Frankfurter Allgemeine Zeitung* September 13, 2001, 1). Others suggested in their headlines — "War against the Superpower" — that only the United States was meant ("Terror gegen die Supermacht," *Frankfurter Rundschau* September 12, 2001, 2).

For days and weeks after the attacks, the pictures and personal stories of loss and suffering dominated the media coverage. Germans everywhere were in a state of heartfelt mourning, lit candles, wrote letters of sympathy and condolences to America, and demonstrated against terror and for peace. Magazines like *stern* and weeklies like *Die Zeit* dedicated special editions to the attacks. Even the most popular teenie-magazine, *Bravo*, replaced the usual pop star-portrait with an American flag on its cover (*Bravo*, No. 39, Sept. 19). German states like Hessia and companies like Porsche, Bertelsmann, and Siemens as well as banks ran full-page memorial notices in national newspapers like *Bild* and weeklies. Dresdner Bank, for example, wrote (in German and in English) that they wanted "to pay their respects to the victims of the terrorist attacks in the United States of America. Our deepest sympathy goes to the relatives of those who died. In these hours of mourning we stand together with our friends in the United States" (*Die Zeit*, special edition Sept. 17). German victims of the attacks were mourned.

On September 14, *Bild* had the picture of Mohamed Atta on its cover, screaming: "Terror Fiend Lived in Germany For Eight Years." German politicians and media increasingly awoke to the realization that Germany may have harbored radical Muslims involved in terrorist acts — some of the alleged terrorists had been students at the Technical University of Hamburg. *Bild* also asked: "Will Germany Have to Go to War?" — a question that was answered in the negative by German Minister of Defense Rudolf Scharping. Already, NATO's announcement that it was willing to invoke the treaty's mutual defense principle was met with criticism by the Greens, the coalition party in the German government (6; the tabloid did not refer to the text of the resolution passed by the Greens council which warned that an "unreasonable response by the United States could lead to the escalation of violence, which is what the terrorists are counting on" *Frankfurter Allgemeine Zeitung* English Edition September 14, 2001, 2).

At the same time, a survey disclosed that more than 57 percent of Germans supported the use of military force against those responsible for the terrorist attacks (*Bild* September 15, 2001, 5). Yet the calls for a prudent response became louder (Claus Strunz, "Mr. President, bleiben Sie besonnen!" *Bild am Sonntag* September 16, 2001, 2). On September 18, *Bild* asked: "Can War Still Be Avoided?" The next day, the tabloid opened with the headline: "War-Fears! Chancellor, How Bad Will It Be For Us?" A report on U.S. Special Forces bore the title: "Will They Conquer Evil?" — which demonstrated that the U.S. President's use of manichaean distinctions was not particularly American (*Bild* September 19, 2004, 5). The next day, the German chancellor calmed fears of war: "We are not in a state of war" (*Bild* September 20, 2001, 1). Commentators emphasized that the U.S. government was reacting prudently, and not at all (as many had feared?) in the manner of cowboys shooting without thinking (Rafael Seligmann, "Vier Zeichen der Hoffnung," *Bild* September 20, 2001, 2). There were also interesting curiosities. On September 18, the local tabloid *Dresdner Morgenpost* had a local politician on its cover, stating that she had just now heard of the attacks.

In conservative dailies, critiques of the German government's reaction rose. The terror attacks led to the realization "that Germany has obviously been shutting its eyes to the danger in recent years." The chancellor's words of sympathy for the United States were interpreted as masking the attempt "to evade the pressures of concrete action by talking big ... Solidarity with the United States was convenient as long as neither partner was put to the test. Now that partnership is called for, Mr. Schröder finds himself doubly punished for his ignorant treatment of the German armed forces: The troops are weak, and it is too late to reinforce them" (Georg Paul Hefty, "Rude Awakening," *Frankfurter Allgemeine Zeitung* English Edition September 14, 2001, 1).

Commentators doubted whether Germany was prepared for the action required in the days ahead: "Having long ago grown unaccustomed to acting seriously and accepting responsibility, German politicians face ... decisive tasks" (Volker Zastrow, "The Steps Ahead," *Frankfurter Allgemeine Zeitung* English Edition September 22, 2001, 1). Thomas Schmid pointed to the first members of the German government "to ascribe — ever so discreetly — a measure of culpability to the victims," implying that the United States, "with its support for globalization and its self-interested foreign and security policy, is not free from blame for the attack carried out against it. ... All this shows that it was only the murderous impact of the attacks that silenced the old anti-Americanism for a few moments. A certain gloating will begin and become fashionable. Since many who feel this way belong to or are close to the governing elite, such schadenfreude carries great political weight" (Thomas Schmid, "Blaming Victims," *Frankfurter Allgemeine Zeitung* English Edition September 14, 2001, 2).

Conservative commentators emphasized that the U.S. President's reaction to 9/11 "contradicts the cliché of the trigger-happy cowboy from Texas. The president has not acted precipitately, nor has he yielded to the pressure for swift, immediate retaliation. His administration is systematically preparing for a sustained campaign, holding out against public outrage and calls for revenge" (Klaus-Dieter Frankenberger, "State Action?" *Frankfurter Allgemeine Zeitung* English Edition September 15, 2001, 1). This assertion was important in the context of a survey released on the same day, revealing that 66 percent of Germans were "confident that the German government is responding/will continue to respond appropriately to the situation," but only 36 percent were "confident that President Bush is responding/will continue to respond appropriately to the situation" (*Frankfurter Allgemeine Zeitung* English Edition September 15, 2001, 2). In contrast, Berthold Kohler suggested that the constant warning to Washington "not to overreact was mainly based on the cliché-ridden world view of which they are fond of accusing America. However, there is more rationality in the U.S. political system than some erstwhile peace activists and theoreticians of imperialism might like to believe" (Berthold Kohler, "Europe's Turn," *Frankfurter Allgemeine Zeitung* English Edition September 22, 2001, 1).

Considering the above survey's results (and the slightly overwhelming use of the word "peace" in political arguments in Germany), one might suggest, however, that the latter still wielded quite some influence within the

German public. At the same time, the security threat posed by the attacks in New York began to shake, as some saw it, the pacifist pillar of the Greens' philosophy, threatening to weaken their political credibility: "That the Sept. 11 attacks have rendered their party's positions on security policy irrelevant is now dawning on the Greens' leaders, as they scramble to reinterpret, adapt and reformulate — while at the same time putting a cautionary foot on the brakes, to a very unconvincing effect. ... It is strange indeed that a political movement could play for so long on fears of the Apocalypse while at the same time taking a deeply irreverent attitude toward one of the basic human experiences: that of being under threat" (Thomas Schmid, "Looking for a Way Out," *Frankfurter Allgemeine Zeitung* English Edition September 26, 2001, 1). It was indeed ironic that a party that had never found a commitment to NATO a necessity and had in effect wanted to disband NATO, now would find it necessary, as a member in a government coalition, to defend the Atlantic alliance.

In many media, images predominated over text. Personal stories were at the center of most reports. Interspersed were allusions to war on an international scale. Images, reconstructions of the events, personal stories of victims and witnesses, and talk of war also shaped the extra coverage of German weeklies such as *stern*, which ran its stories under the caption "terror-war" (*stern* 39, September 17, 2001). A few days later, its headline ran: "Will the World Explode? Why War Would Be Insanity" (*stern* 39 September 20, 2001). The editorial suggested that German solidarity with the United States could not be unlimited (although the German chancellor had emphasized that German support would be just that: unlimited). The defense of the values of the Western world could not include any bombing attacks on children, women, men and old people (5). Interestingly, the editorial was illustrated by the picture of an American pick-up bearing hastily scribbled calls for "Revenge" (a call which, as the picture's caption suggested, was shared by a "majority" of Americans). Letters to the Editor emphasized fears of war and called for U.S. caution (11).

The first story, on U.S. war preparations for its campaign against Afghanistan, was titled "Countdown to Insanity" (14-15). Mario R. Dederichs criticized the United States, saying that it was already talking of war before all the facts were clear. Facts were ignored, he suggested. "This is no war, and this was no declaration of war" (*our translation*, 25; note: all *stern* reports on 9/11 in this issue bore the headline "terror-krieg"= "terror-war"). Rather, he declared, the attacks were a criminal act. The world was just as afraid of the American reaction as of acts of terror (26). The author explained his skepticism about U.S. policy by pointing to a history of foreign policy failures: Korea, Vietnam, Iran hostage crisis, Latin America, Lebanon,

Somalia, Iraq (27). The article used an interview with a specialist in international law to suggest that an attack against Afghanistan violated international law (28). It concluded that this war wasn't "our war" but a war that would only breed hatred and more violence (29). The issue included a portrait of Osama bin Laden, a report on the "Hamburg connection" of terrorists and an article critical of the German Interior Minister's harsh regime and attempts to strengthen anti-terror laws in Germany (42ff.). Criticism was also levied against Chancellor Schröder's willingness to grant unconditional support to the United States, if necessary, with military help in America's war of retaliation. Tensions within the "red-green" government coalition of Social Democrats and Greens were repeatedly alluded to (48).

On September 29, the *stern* cover warned of terror dangers in Germany from radical Muslim groups (reflecting a debate that increasingly focused on Germany's immigration policies). The editorial was now a bit less skeptical of the chances of a U.S. campaign against terrorism, under one condition: Military operations must be limited and precise. Terrorism should be conquerable by way of intelligence and information. However, skepticism against large-scale military operations was seen as legitimate and by no way anti-American. The editorial even suggested that President Bush and his team had so far acted prudently (3). One article warned of the collapse of the red-green coalition if Chancellor Schröder held on to his support of U.S. military operations (65). It also referred to an ominous passage in the chancellor's parliamentary address (Regierungserklärung) in which Schröder categorically rejected any participation in "adventures" (70).

It took only two weeks after the attacks until American commentators registered a divided European response: "A debate has begun over whether the inconsistencies of U.S. foreign policy and the sheer weight of American dominance in the world mean that resentment of the United States and even, in extreme cases, hatred are inevitable." A report from Berlin suggested that not only did Europeans hold the U.S. partially responsible for the attacks, but that they even gloated secretly over America's pain:

> it has also become clear that some Europeans feel that ordinary Americans have largely floated on a tide of prosperity, triumphalism and indifference to the world since the collapse of the Soviet Union. ... For those critics, Americans are viewed as now facing unsurprising retaliation ... Some Europeans also contend that many Americans have a blinding confidence in their own goodness and so do not see that U.S. reactions are regarded in many quarters as driven by the domineering pursuit of national self-interest (Erlanger).

By mid-October, 2001, after the beginning of the campaign against Afghanistan, anti-war demonstrations became the daily fare of reporting. One headline in the *Frankfurter Allgemeine Zeitung* stated: "The Big, Bad American Imperialist Is Back: More than Western Germans, Easterners Are Skeptical About U.S. War on Terrorism." Letters to the editor in eastern Germany were united by one point: "While all sympathize with the victims of the terror attacks in New York and Washington, most reject unqualified solidarity with the world's sole superpower." People see the "evil American, heartless world sovereign" rising again. Despite the fact that "eastern Germans are in many respects even more 'Americanized' than western Germans," signs of "gratitude toward the Americans are rare." People do not feel indebted to the United States: "Even German reunification is attributed primarily to Mikhail Gorbachev's policies of détente."

According to a survey conducted in mid-September, "two-thirds of western Germans, but only one-third of eastern Germans, regard as justified German participation in military actions aimed at agents of terror." Another poll "showed a third of eastern Germans sharing the view that the United States to some degree provoked the attacks 'with their superpower politics.' Half the respondents … was convinced that they had not 'earned our full solidarity.'" Although one should not be surprised at one interviewee's description of Americans as "friendly, but superficial" (one of the mantras repeated incessantly by some of our East German students), the rest of the article could raise some concern, since what was suggested here by most interviewees is that 9/11 was not, as many Americans saw it, an attack on the concept and common values of the West, but strictly an American superpower affair (Janert).

There were, it is true, countercurrents to this trend. Most surprisingly, they came from some Alliance 90/The Greens members of Germany's parliament, including not only German Foreign Minister Fischer but a delegation of three parliamentarians who visited the U.S. in October 2001. "On Capitol Hill in Washington the three almost sounded like a miniature general staff. 'We see it as our duty,' Mr. Berninger said at a dinner with the Congressional Group on Germany, 'to make it clear to the German people that they need to be afraid of a second terror attack and not of the U.S. counterstrike.' 'There is nothing to criticize about President Bush,' Mr. Ozdemir [sic] added. 'He's no cowboy'" (Buchsteiner 2).

In its mid-October issue, the weekly *DER SPIEGEL* described a German republic evenly divided into supporters and critics of the United States. One of the news anchors of German public TV, Ulrich Wickert, had compared George W. Bush with Osama bin Laden, the fashion designer Wolfgang Joop had stated that he did not regret the fall of the Twin Towers

— after all, they only symbolized capitalist arrogance (88). At the same time, the German chancellor promoted "unconditional solidarity" with the United States, the writer Ralph Giordano suggested that the Germans had reasons to feel bad since Germany had become the privileged place of residence for "Islamic" terrorists (90). Dirk Kurbjuweit suggested that those suspected of anti-Americanism were much more on the defensive: Their camp, he argued, was traditionally a small, yet well organized one, since it was tied to other movements of the Left (90). Interestingly, although the author was able to portray quite a number of "anti-Americans," he could only come up with one "pro-American" example — a sociologist who admired the "American actionism" without, however, thinking too much of American culture (92). At the end of the day, Kurbjuweit claimed, no Germans were whole-heartedly for or against America. Rather, the fact that Germans categorized each other as such was evidence of Germany's obsession with America (92). While the example of a high school class in Berlin showed how calmly young Germans could look at a country whose culture they shared, the same could not be said of the world of politics and parts of the media — in these areas an open debate about the United States and its war on terror was no longer possible (93) (Dirk Kurbjuweit, "Böser Onkel, lieber Onkel," *DER SPIEGEL* October 22, 2001, 88-93).

Germany also provided a fertile soil for conspiracy theories. In July 2003, the *International Herald Tribune* reported that "almost one in three Germans below the age of 30 believes the U.S. may have sponsored the Sept. 11, 2001, attack, a poll conducted for the weekly Die Zeit found" (*International Herald Tribune* July 24, 2003, 5). The most prolific generator of conspiracy theories after 9/11 was Andreas von Bülow, a former official in the German Ministry of Defense (1976-1980) and German Minister of Research and Technology (1980-1982) who argued that the four planes weren't hijacked by 19 young Muslims. Their job was only to act suspiciously and divert attention. Rather, the planes were flown into the Twin Towers by remote control — a feat that can only be undertaken by American specialists. In the end it wasn't the planes that brought the WTC down but bombs in the towers' interior. The attacks on the Pentagon were carried out by a cruise missile. Ergo: The attacks were carried out by some intelligence commando structure in the service of U.S. elites intent on coopting the masses in their hegemonic striving for world conquest (Wilfried von Bredow, "Entlarvung als Lachnummer: Andreas von Bülow konstruiert sich seinen 11. September," *Frankfurter Allgemeine Zeitung* August 4, 2003, 6).

REFERENCES

Buchsteiner, Jochen. "Three Green Parliamentarians in George Bush's Court: U.S.-Sympathetic Bundestag Members Visited America as Their Party Balked on Issue of Retaliation." *Frankfurter Allgemeine Zeitung*, English Edition, October 9, 2001, 1, 2.

Erlanger, Steven. "In Europe, Some Scold 'World's Policeman': Critics Decry Inconsistencies of U.S. Conduct." *International Herald Tribune* September 26, 2001, 7.

Janert, Josefine. "The Big, Bad American Imperialist Is Back." *Frankfurter Allgemeine Zeitung*, English Edition, October 15, 2001, 3.

Knowlton, Brian. "Bush Gets Low Marks in Europe: Poll Finds Wide Disapproval of President's Conduct of Foreign Policy." *International Herald Tribune* August 16, 2001, 1, 7.

Siemons, Mark. "Of Thee We Kvetch: Europeans Distrust Uncle Sam the Bogeyman." *Frankfurter Allgemeine Zeitung*, English Edition, August 18, 2001, 7.

Chapter 6

September 11 in the Spanish Press: War or Terrorism Frame?

Maria Teresa La Porte & Teresa Sádaba

On September, 11, 2001, mass media, through live broadcasts of the attacks on the Twin Towers, succeeded in creating the "global village" that was forecast decades earlier by Canadian scholar Marshall McLuhan. A global audience, watching in disbelief, tried to come to grips with what was actually happening in downtown Manhattan.

In an attempt to define the events unfolding before them on the television screen, journalists soon labeled them as "attacks," even though after several hours few were able to form a clear picture of what was happening. Indeed, the precise nature of the attacks was an issue that sparked off an initial debate in international public opinion. Some saw the events as a declaration of war and some viewed them as acts of terrorism.

The first words spoken by President George W. Bush on September 11 were about terrorist attacks. That is, his first speech contextualized the attacks as acts of terrorism. However, on the next day, after a meeting with the National Security Team, he said: "The deliberate and deadly attacks which were carried out yesterday against our country were more than acts of terror. They were acts of war." On Sept. 20, in his address to a Joint Session of Congress and the American People, he made an official declaration that these were acts of war: "Enemies of freedom committed an act of war against our country."[1]

As Robert Entman has shown, Bush strategically used the frame of war, which then "overwhelmingly dominated the news" (2003, p. 416). Frames help to define situations, identifying causes and endorsing remedies. In the case of the frame selected by the Bush administration, Entman said: "For September 11, the problematic effect was of course the death of thousands of civilians in an act of war against America; the cause was terrorists; the moral judgment condemned the agents of this assault as evil; and the remedy quickly became war against perpetrators" (2003, p. 417).

Nonetheless, the debate raged on as people around the world waited to see what interpretation the United Nations would place on the attacks. On Sept. 28, the United Nations Security Council unanimously declared "that such acts on the previous 11 September, like any act of *international terrorism* constitute a threat to international peace and security" (Resolution 1373 of September 28, 2001). With this resolution, the United States' legitimate defense against the attacks of Sept. 11 was recognized and the also the "terrorist attacks" were described as "a threat to peace." Specific action measures to be adopted would "require the active involvement of the states within the internal limits of their jurisdictions." It also left the way open to combat by any means "the obligation of all states ... to watch over and defend the security and liberty of their citizens" (Resolution 1373 of September 28, 2001).

Thus, the United Nations, acting under Chapter VII of the Charter, introduced a new legal concept when it interpreted the attacks as terrorism and allowed for them to be combated as in war. "War against terrorism" was, then, an eclectic and conciliatory stance which showed a new reality yet to be defined.

Therefore, during those days in September, the media echoed this debate and, insofar as they themselves are political actors, opted for and supported that position. Generally, for the American media, this was quite clearly an "act of war"("Acts of War," the front page of *USA Today*, September 12, 2001; the same in *San Jose Mercury News, New York Post*. "War at home," *The Dallas Morning News*, September 12, 2001). Another of the words repeated most on the front-pages was "attack" (*Philadelphia Inquirier, Idaho Statesman, Dayton Daily News*, at September 12, 2001*)*. What is more, some authors point out that the media, especially television, "promoted the war fever and military solutions for the problem of global terrorism" in their wish to close ranks with their government's stance (Kellner, 2002, p. 143).

In this sense, the media were shaping reality before it was defined in a legal concept. This is what Ulrich Beck calls the role of media in a "risk society," when there is a discrepancy between realities and concepts because reality surpasses language (Beck, 2003).

The media, insofar as they shape the public space, have an important function in the defining of social phenomena, especially while they are still emerging, as in the case we are dealing with here. In this process of formation, the experience that each nation has of political violence has an explicit influence. For this reason, it is interesting to examine coverage given by other countries and political cultures and to know exactly what definition they adopted. In this way, we will be able to see whether there are aspects of the political culture which help to define events.

This paper explores the definition that was advanced by the Spanish media for the 9/11 attacks. This analysis will specifically focus on the coverage given by the Spanish press. In this country, the pairing of terrorism-media has been in existence for more than 40 years, and it still remains one of the most intense and enduring partnerships.[2] Also, it is interesting to note that although the type of terrorism in Spain differs from 9/11, the Spanish Prime Minister of the time, José Mª Aznar, noted that "we know what all terrorists want, and we know it is impossible to distinguish between different types of terrorists" (Statement to the *Congreso de los Diputados* by José Mª Aznar, September 26, 2001).

MEDIA CONSTRUCTION OF REALITY

The conceptual framework of this paper rests on the assumption that media help to construct social reality (Altheide, 1987; Wasburn, 2002). This is not because they invent new realities, but rather because they re-invent or re-present social phenomena when these are judged to be more or less news-worthy, when they are explained in a certain way, or when they are contextualized with specific images. It has been shown that through news selection (gatekeeping theory), the selection of the key issues (agenda-setting) or the adoption of certain approaches (framing theory), the media help to create the meaning of reality (Sádaba, 2001).

William Gamson defines frame as the "central organizing idea for making sense of relevant events and suggesting what is at issue" (1989, p. 157). The theory of framing explains how it is not enough for frames to organize meanings: Meanings also have to be understood socially. An interaction occurs between the journalist and his/her audience. On the one hand, thanks to media discourse, individuals build meanings, and on the other, public opinion is part of the process through which journalists develop these meanings. According to this, media frames are successful in that they combine three factors: cultural echoes; promotional or public relations activities around the subject; and adjustments to news norms and practices (Gamson & Modigliani, 1989).

At present, perception of reality passes through the media perception, so that individuals use what they have just seen on the news about a natural catastrophe to interpret what they consider a disaster of this kind should mean (First, 1997). In this way, the frames are associated with individuals' experience about similar realities. When there is no such experience, the frame covers for its absence, not only by providing information about a new issue, but also bringing together all the symbols which this issue contains. When audiences or consumers are looking at known situations, the frame helps them to describe events synthetically, and when the events are new, it provides the necessary elements to understand the issue for the first time.

MEDIA IN CONFLICTS: TERRORISM AND WAR

The relationship between the media and conflict is another area that has interested researchers (Rodríguez and Sádaba, 1999). Specifically, terrorism is essentially a media phenomenon. Of all the expressions of violence, it is only the genesis and dynamics of terrorism that become meaningless if we do not take into account the role of the media. In this respect, academic research has shown, as an initial premise, that terrorism and the media appear to constantly feed off each other (Nacos, 2003; Reinares, 1998; Livingston, 1994; Schaffert, 1992). Whether it has a political, social or economic cause, terrorism is a form of violence that needs the media to gain legitimacy, win supporters for its cause and obtain publicity[3] (Paletz, 1995); and it is defined as "the new form of violence carried out with the aim that the act will automatically become news" (Clutterbuck, 1985, p. 13).[4] At the same time, the media find spectacle and drama in terrorist attacks.

The word terrorism, which derives from the Latin *terrere* (to frighten, to leave frozen), has been defined as "the exercise of physical force, with or without arms, to cause injuries or damage to people and their property" (Paletz, 1995, p. 332). However, a debate rages about the ends of this type of violence and its legitimacy. For this reason, it is necessary to address this issue not so much in terms of the aims, which are often quite diverse, but in terms of the means used to achieve the end, which include use of sophisticated arms directed at places, people or symbols, their psychological effects, and the attempt to propagate particular ideas.

With regard to terrorism, the use of violence appears to be more unilateral. Its aim is to provoke terror in the civilian population. It involves sporadic acts with a public aim and has not only real but more symbolic impact. One also is generally less sure about the forces terrorists have to carry out attacks. Terrorists also have a manifest intention to use the media to achieve their goals.

The media's effects on the origin, expansion and mediation processes during war also have been investigated (LaPorte, 1999). The media's role in the Gulf War also is now well documented (Iyengar & Simon, 1997; Bennet & Paletz, 1994; Mowlana, Gerbner, Schiller, 1992) and has been described by some as "a news war with no in-depth news" (Quiñonero, 1999) and by others as a war of misinformation (Muñoz-Alonso and Rospir, 1999). There have been numerous studies of the media as propaganda platforms for states at war (Taylor, 1993; Pizarroso, 1991).

From a theoretical point of view, war has a different nature from terrorism: it is a concept that has long been studied and that has been defined well by political science. From a practical perspective, however, this is undergoing a certain revision process, because more and more acts of violence do not fit the conditions of the classic term. For the purposes of the present study, we shall use a definition which comes precisely from research into coverage of armed conflicts. Boyd-Barrett understands war as follows: "These occasions of massive, violent conflict, nearly all involve organized, "regular" armed forces of distinguishable enemies, often nation-states, or of warring regions, ethnicities or social classes within nation-states whose legitimacy is contested" (2004, p. 3). The differences between war and terrorism can be illustrated in the following table:

War	Terrorism
Recourse to armed forces	Unilateral, no armed forces
Visibility and definition	Lack of definition
Development of stages	Sporadic acts
Media relations	Targets the media

The table shows how the concepts of war and terrorism can be distinguished at the theoretical level. However, the lines between them melt away in some ambiguous events; then it becomes a problem of interpretation to explain them as war or terrorism. As different authors point out, in that situation, the simple choice of a term already implies a definition of the event[5] (Doornaert, 1993; Livingston, 1994; Miller, 1982). Moreover, the terms, expressions and concepts acquire different meanings in each cultural or social context. For this reason, in view of the aims of the present analysis, it is necessary to examine how political violence has been defined in Spain. In this way, we shall be able to identify the use of the "cultural resonances" which framing theorists point to in the frames which the press uses for war and terrorism.

THE SOCIAL CONCEPT OF 'POLITICAL VIOLENCE' IN SPAIN

The concept of "political violence" present in each nation's media is no more than a reflection of the way in which it is understood by its society. And societies shape their ideas according to their historical experience and their day-to-day reality. For this reason, it is important to bear in mind that every country's idiosyncrasies must be added to the general concept of "political violence" which is commonly accepted in political science (La Porte, 2004).

In Spain, as in the rest of the countries in Western Europe, violence in any form is an illegitimate expression of aggression and its capacity to act as an instrument of social communication is not accepted. Therefore, it is also rejected as a means of pursuing political goals (Delgado, 1998). The only accepted violence is the use of force by the state or by institutions (e.g., police) delegated this function by the State.[6]

As well as social consensus, historical experience also is important in order to understand a society's stance on political violence. In present-day Spain's case it is important to remember that it is a country marked by two violent conflicts: the Spanish Civil War (1936-1939) and the terrorist acts perpetrated by the Basque independent group, ETA. Both conflicts took place and take place in Spanish territory and were caused by internal tensions: the first of which has a political and military nature and the second of which has nationalistic and secessionist causes.

With respect to the Spanish Civil War, it can be stated that today it lives on in the memory of the old, while for younger people it is a historical event relived in its anniversaries. However, during Franco's regime it divided Spanish society for 40 years. Although the peaceful transition to democracy showed that the Spanish had managed to overcome antagonisms, these feelings are still significant enough for political parties to make political capital out of them during electoral campaigns.

On the other hand, a distinct terrorist conflict has troubled Spanish society since the late 1960s. ETA was formed in 1959 and two years later it made its first appearance in public. It demanded an amnesty and self-determination for the Basque people, based on a nationalist and Marxist ideology. After the establishment of a democracy, ETA's goals were rejected by Spanish society (Sádaba, 1999). Opinion polls show constantly that terrorism is seen as one of the main problems for Spanish people: this is confirmed by surveys carried out by the Centre for Sociological Studies over the last 20 years.

METHODOLOGY

This study employed quantitative and qualitative approaches to content analyzes three Spanish newspapers ten days after 9/11, from Sept. 12-21, 2001. This coincides with the time when the debate on the nature of what had occurred was raging and the technical or legal response from the United Nations had still not been issued.

During this period, the three newspapers analyzed produced a total of 1,297 unevenly distributed analytical specimens, which means a news item with its own headline and content. Thirteen variables was measured. To confirm the legitimacy and the actors involved, we analyzed the sources; to check the scope of the conflict, we used the variables of the section and place from which the news was covered; and lastly, to complete the idea of the frame used, we examined the language and symbols. The aim of this quantitative analysis was to identify the general lines of coverage.

For the qualitative analysis, the newspaper's editorials were analyzed. The assumption was that the editorial "is the key piece not only of the opinions section but of the whole newspaper and it is here we find an evaluative interpretation of newsworthy events and their meaning and transcendence are transmitted. The editorial is where we can find the publisher's ideological standpoint on the news reported and it also brings together the standards ruling the rest of the sections" (Gárate, 2002, p. 7. And also Santamaría, 1997; Diaz Andino, 1994).

The three newspapers examined are the most important national newspapers in Spain, in terms of circulation as well as in terms of their social and political influence: *El País, El Mundo* and *ABC.*

El País is the general newspaper with the largest circulation in Spain; it follows a progressive-liberal line and is clearly in tune with the Spanish Socialist Party (Partido Socialista Obrero Español, PSOE). As a defender of democracy and pro-European newspaper, it is a basic point of reference in the definition of public opinion and its international section is considered to be the highest quality in Spain. *El Mundo* defines itself as anti-imperialistic and anti-military, a radical defender of human rights and civil liberties. It tends to be more favourable to the Partido Popular, conservative, center-right party, although the newspaper itself has claimed that its ideological space was center-left. Finally, *ABC* is a conservative newspaper founded by the Luca de Tena family; it defines itself as a defender of the Spanish tradition, it is monarchist, liberal and independent, advocates the unity of Spain, is Catholic, and favors a free-market economy. It has a marked editorial style and usually accompanies information with evaluation and assessment by the journalist who wrote the article. This is also true of its international section, which is mainly written by veteran correspondents.

Our first task was to identify the distinguishing traits that typify their standpoints on terrorism as well as on the United States and its government. With regard to the terrorism perpetrated by ETA, they are all firm in their outright condemnation and are actively opposed to radical nationalism — in this area they closely adhere to the government's line of argument (Idoyaga and Ramírez de la Piscina[7], 2001). As far as the policies of the United States are concerned, *El País* is the newspaper which is most vocal in its criticism of the United States and the Bush administration.

FORMAL ASPECTS AND ACTORS IN THE NEWS: TRENDS IN COVERAGE

To distinction between frames of war and terrorism, a first reading[8] was made of the 1,297 specimens and subjected to analysis. These were spread as follows: 435 from *El País* (33.5%), 343 from *El Mundo* (26.4%) and 519 from *ABC* (40%). The fact that in ten days such a volume of news was published gives us an idea of the importance that the media placed on such an event which was also present on every page because stories related to 9/11 appeared in any section (Opinion, Economy, Culture and Television, International and even Domestic News). The choice of sections varied from one newspaper to another: *El País* showed a clear preference for international news (with 62.2% of its stories printed in this section) while *El Mundo* and *ABC* preferred to prepare special sections for the occasion. Also of significance were 22 stories related to 9/11 that appeared in the Domestic section of *El Mundo* (6.5% of the total of the newspaper).

The next phase of the analysis involved examining the language used in the stories, with the goal of distinguishing the type of conflict covered in the media. More specifically, the explicit appearance of words related to "war" and "terrorism" was quantified. Some examples of warlike language would be words such as: enemy, army, combat, battle, invasion. Words that appeared relating to terrorism were: terror, terrorist attack, terrorist organization, terrorist band, terrorise. *ABC*'s use of terrorist terms is striking since they appeared in over half the pieces analyzed, with the significant fact that on 17 occasions express reference was made to Basque terrorism. In the case of *El País*, more "war" related terms were used (36.3% of the stories as opposed to 31.7% related to terrorism) and in *El Mundo* the appearance of both terms was less frequent and more evenly distributed (around 15% in both cases). However, the front page on the first day the newspaper was unequivocal in its use of the term "terrorist attack."

In terms of the actors in the news, the American president was given priority over anyone else. His appearances almost doubled those of the next most mentioned actor who was Osama bin Laden. In *ABC*, the percentage of references to the latter was almost the same as those referring to Bush (40% and 41.5% respectively). In *El Mundo* and *El País* the American president dominated the pages over half the times. Another important actor was Aznar who appeared on 18% of the occasions in *ABC* and 11% of the time in *El País*.

APPROACHES AND CONTEXTS

By means of a qualitative analysis our aim was to discover what lines of thought were adopted in the reporting of 9-11, using the model followed by Akiba Cohen and Gadi Wolfsfeld in their study of the *Intifada*. The authors point out that the approaches found in the media are projected onto a situation of conflict and are the result of their interaction with the public and even the antagonists (Cohen and Wolfsfeld, 1993). This means that these lines of thought are not entirely the newspaper's own, nor are they generated independently, but are, rather, the result of a combination of factors involving the newspaper, the journalist, the readers targeted, and the cultural context in which reporting was carried out. These approaches have been analyzed in the 34 editorials for those days with a specific examination of the contextualization of arguments expressed. The main conclusions of this qualitative analysis are the following:

ABC: The Terrorism We Endure

In *ABC*'s editorials, the newspaper appeared to move from its initial stance where it described the attacks as terrorism, following the Spanish president's thesis, to defining it in terms of war, consistent with its support for the United States' actions. In any case, the newspaper followed the general trend by combining the two concepts in an editorial published on Sept. 12 titled "Terrorist War," which was then used as the heading of a special general section on 9/11. In this editorial we could find a mixture of comparisons with other wars and a vocabulary relating to terrorism and its advocates that was familiar to the Spanish: "Islamic terrorism has brought the world to a crisis similar to that provoked by the Japanese attack on Pearl Harbour"; requiring an international response: "It is no longer just enough for people to say they reject and condemn violence if, at the same time, *they welcome, give shelter and permit the funding and training of terrorists*" ("Terrorist War," *ABC*, September 12, 2001, p. 5. The italics are ours).

When terrorism was discussed, frequent comparisons and identifications were made. Following Aznar's line of argument, it was repeatedly claimed that Spain already had experience in this area because it had suffered the dreadful effects of terrorism for years. It stated that the opportunity should be seized upon to put a stop to the problem, open people's eyes and nudge the consciences of those who were complaisant and soft on Basque terrorism. In the comparison of 9/11 with Basque terrorism, several opinion columns appeared at this time: "World Trade Center and the terrorism of ETA," "The guilty ones," "Faces and clouds," "The intellectual and violence," "Mourning and dynamite." The attack in New York was compared to the ETA attack on Hypercor (a popular supermarket). "The dynamite of Zarauz (a Basque village) and the suicide planes of Manhattan" or the call for dialogue to put an end to terrorism which, according to the newspaper's collaborators, was a futile endeavor.

On the thirteenth, the editorial "Democracies against terror" spoke about the fight against terrorism as "the great threat in this century to freedom and democracy" ("Democracies against terror," *ABC*, September 13, 2001, p. 13); thus, terrorism perpetrated by ETA was included, of which this type of rhetoric was frequent. This decision to define the events of 9-11 as acts of terrorism was reaffirmed when the editorials were given the blanket heading of "Lay siege to terrorism"(editorials that appeared on September 14, 2001), an expression that the newspaper would eventually make its own but to begin with was placed in inverted commas. In the second editorial, the word terrorism appeared described by different adjectives: Islamic, militarized (this closely resembles "an act of war"), genocidal ("Another NATO," *ABC*, September 14, 2001, p. 13). However, it is interesting to note that when, later on, reference was made to Russian collaboration, the words "Chechen guerrilla force" were placed in inverted commas. This was far removed from the thesis of Putin's administration regarding the essential terrorist nature of the Chechens ("Afghanistan castled," *ABC*, September 18, 2001, p. 11).

Another theme related to terrorism that appeared in editorials on 9/11 was how the media were covering the events. The decision of the American channels not to broadcast any further scenes of horror was welcomed and this was linked up to how the Spanish press respond to Basque terrorism. With the exception of a few publications, the editorial maintained that Spanish newspapers have always based their coverage on the principles of freedom, justice and individual rights. When faced with terror, neutrality was not an option, it contended ("The press does not give up," *ABC*, September 15, 2001, p. 13).

In keeping with its usual editorial line, *ABC* closed ranks with the Spanish government and it supported the EU joint arrest warrant for the pursuit of terrorist crimes, which would prove useful in the fight against ETA ("Without fissures," *ABC*, September 15, 2001, p. 13). It was from this moment that the definition of the acts took on a more warlike tone, even including references to a Third World War ("Religious terror," *ABC*,

September 16, 2001, p. 13). The concept of war was also reinforced by some opinion articles (such as "A basically long war," *ABC*, September 20, 2001, p. 24). The newspaper justified the response of the United States and also condemned those who had spoken about American imperialism as a justification for what had happened on 9/11.

On Saturday the nineteenth, *ABC*, in its defense of American policies, included an article on Henry Kissinger, former American Secretary of State, titled "A new policy is needed for victory over terrorism." In this respect, the newspaper viewed Spain's support for the Americans' response as logical, combining the concept of a justified war with the argument that Spain had suffered this same evil and that all terrorism was aggression, and a war initiated against terrorism was a just one ("Spain in its role," *ABC*, September 19, 2001, p. 13). At this point the blanket heading "Lay siege to terrorism" disappeared.

El País: The Alliances of the New International Order

From the first day of coverage, *El País* would adopt an approach that it would come back to again and again: What kind of international alliances and coalitions would be established after 9/11? In its first editorial it stated that the attacks were not against the United States but against civilization and that they could be repeated in Europe. The newspaper argued for international co-operation between democracies to combat it and Spain's active role as an ally ("A strike at our civilisation," *El País*, September 12, 2001, p. 26). Although *El País* initially defined the attacks as "terrorist," on the following day it did not venture a definition of them since it claimed that prior to this the "enemies" should be identified. It pointed out that "even if suspicions are confirmed that some fundamentalist Islamic group has been responsible it would be a historic mistake to give a punitive response on a general scale" ("Response to a scattered enemy," *El País*, September 13, 2001, p. 28).

However, the very fact that the word coalition was used appeared to place this newspaper's editorials closer to a warlike type of vocabulary. In any case, it maintained that, rather than a war, the coalition should promote political action on a global scale and international justice should be given priority. The fact that it had been an unconventional act of aggression meant that not only would there have to be international military cooperation but also media cooperation ("Worldwide insecurity," *El País*, September 13, 2001, p. 28; "A grand coalition against terrorism" and "Full powers," *El País*, September 15, 2001, p. 22).

This global action also implied economic measures: "Global threats require global responses, and if a grand international coalition is constructed against terrorism, another economic one must be promoted to combat recession (...) ." ("A grand economic coalition too," *El País*, September 18, 2001, p. 24). After stating the case for global actions, it then went on to criticize America´s Manichaeism with its "you're either for me or against me" attitude and its demand that Pakistan "unequivocally align itself" with the international coalition against terrorism. "The United States should be flexible and understand that it cannot insist on suicidal loyalties from a poor country with demands made on it by formidable political and social forces, situated at a geographical crossroads of high tension." ("Pakistan in the eye of the storm," *El País*, September 19, 2001, p. 24; "Everyone firm," *El País*, September 20, 2001, p. 26).

The newspaper also maintained a critical stance on the kind of war to be pursued and spoke of the danger of a "pre-emptive war": "It is an aim worthy of praise but although we know how pre-emptive wars begin we do not know how they will end." The lead writer contended that the war against terrorism should be one of information rather than conventional military attacks and he reminded readers that until then any power that had tried to go into Afghanistan had come out worse for wear ("Full powers," *El País*, September 15, 2001, p. 22).

In its criticism of the American government it also spoke in passing of the ever-widening gap with poorer nations. "It is vital that the coalition is not perceived as an attack of the North on the South. (...) This world cannot carry on allowing injustice to grow and the already huge differences between rich and poor to become even greater. That is the breeding-ground for global violence" ("A tenacious fight," *El País*, September 16, 2001, p. 26). But it was not only the United States that came under fire, the Spanish government's opportunism was also criticized for seizing "any opportunity for electioneering purposes" ("The strength of a society," *El País*, September 17, 2001, p. 28).

On the last day analyzed, Spain was the main subject of the editorials. According to the newspaper, it had a great deal to contribute: "Many years of having to endure ETA's violence and that of other terrorist groups means that Spain has developed more than just a special sensitivity for this terrible menace. For years it has sought greater international collaboration to combat it. And, in this case, the Spanish secret services (...) must have special knowledge of the networks that may have been set up by Islamic terrorists in Spain." In addition, "this will also be an opportunity to concentrate every effort on something that Spain has been seeking since 1995: the creation of a common security space with the removal of EU borders" ("Spanish bases," *El País*, September 21, 2001, p. 26). The international context in which it placed Spain was as a member of the European Union. That is to say, Spain was not presented as an actor functioning on an individual basis (as it was presented by ABC) but rather as working within the European Union framework ("Air aid," *El País*, September 21, 2001, p. 26).

Lastly, it should be mentioned that the first time ETA terrorism was explicitly named was on the Sept. 16 and in a very specific context. The main idea of that editorial was related to the grand coalition that had been formed around the United States. Europe had also shown its solidarity, and the newspaper stressed the hope that the tidal wave of indignation will also wash ETA away. "In Spain we know that the fight against terrorism requires tenacity" ("A tenacious fight," *El País*, September 16, 2001, p. 26. Later on, as had occurred in *ABC*, 9/11 issues would be used in defining Basque terrorism, see for example: "ETA, globalised," where the "Taliban Arzalluz" is spoken of, *El País*, October 25, 2001, p. 28).

El Mundo: Justified Response

El Mundo's first editorial shied away from taking up any kind of stance on the nature of the attacks. Rather, it sought to find keys to make sense of events, turning to the Middle East and the risk of conflict while underlining the important economic repercussions ("An infamy that will change our world and mark our lives," *El Mundo*, September 12, 2001, p. 21). This approach would be maintained by the newspaper throughout the ten days analyzed: It steered clear of either terminology except when someone was quoted.

In any case, "legitimate defense" ("In favour of a concerted response and under parliamentary control," *El Mundo*, September 14, 2001, p. 23) or "powder keg" ("Afghanistan, a powder keg to be handled with care by the US," *El Mundo*, September 15, 2001, p. 21), with the warlike connotations these bring to mind, were spoken of because the most recurring theme for this newspaper was the legitimacy of the United States to take action. Even though the approach adopted by *El Mundo* in its editorials was more international, it frequently sought the voice of Spain in this conflict, with the advantages and disadvantages that its acts could bring, including in economic terms ("In favour of a concerted response and under parliamentary control," *El Mundo*, September 14, 2001, p. 23; "Unconditional solidarity but not blind involvement," *El Mundo*, September 16, 2001, p. 23.).[9] If, in *ABC*, the justification for intervention was terrorism, also endured in Spain, in *El Mundo*, Spanish participation was referred to in terms of its membership of NATO and as a strategic point on the route to the Middle East ("Unconditional solidarity but not blind involvement," *El Mundo*, September 16, 2001, p. 23).

In a strategy designed to attract a certain type of reader, *El Mundo* gave a more in-depth treatment of economic issues than the other newspapers, backed up by the stories on 9/11 in the Economy section ("Cheaper money to prevent the collapse of Wall Street," *El Mundo*, September 17, 2001, p. 23. "Wall Street collapses," *El Mundo*, 18 September, 2001, p. 23). It should also be noted that this was the only newspaper whose editorials did not just refer to 9/11 during this period but also spoke about one of its favorite themes: corruption during Felipe González's mandate ("Secret funds: unadulterated corruption," *El Mundo*, September 19, 2001, p. 23).

CONCLUSIONS

The attacks of 9/11 produced a rupture in the classic concepts of war and terrorism and led to a new way of understanding conflicts, and the lines drawn between war and terrorism were becoming increasingly blurred. The media were participants in this new debate. In the first weeks after 9/11, they were unclear as to who the enemy was and what its intention was: Nobody had claimed responsibility for the attacks, speculation was rife and various possibilities were considered such as the involvement of states which had given their backing to the attacks. After this initial stage, the frame of "war on terrorism" came to dominate the agenda of both politicians and media (Wasburn, 2002).

What distinguished the Spanish media from the American, as shown by this study, was that, on the one hand, the Spanish media were not always clear about the concept of the attacks and, on the other hand, there was no uniform opinion on the definition of the conflict. This last point could be attributed to the influence of the editorial line and the newspapers' political affinities, which in Spain tended to focus on terrorism.

"Terrorism" was preferred when there was an attempt to "domesticize" the issue, whereas a war focus was used in talking about support and loyalties with regard to the United States. The subject of terrorism was introduced more frequently because of its familiarity to readers and also because it was the explanation of the events offered by Prime Minister Aznar. That is, the cultural resonance and political discourse (which also made use of this resonance in order to gain effectiveness) helped to generate media frames during the first moments of coverage.

"Terrorism" was preferred when there was an attempt to "domesticize" the issue, whereas a war focus was used in talking about support and loyalties with regard to the United States. On this point, *El País* was more "international" in its approach to the facts.

This analysis also illustrates the different editorial approaches of the three main newspapers in Spain. When we look at *El Mundo* and *ABC*, this can be seen not just in formal questions (such as language or sections) but also in arguments of context. The case of *ABC* is particularly interesting with its continued references to terrorism, the parallels that were made, the fact that neutrality was not to be considered, and use of a vocabulary similar to that used to discuss Basque terrorism. In this, it followed the arguments of Aznar's cabinet after 9/11, to which it gave unconditional support. In contrast, *El Mundo*, although referring to Spain with regard to the subject of terrorism, used a different framework to legitimize the government's action: NATO and the European Union. Lastly, *El País* spoke of world confrontation and alignments, demanding global action and often criticizing American policy. It frequently used the latter as a source but did not follow its strategies or arguments. Although *El Mundo* also adopted this approach, it was not so critical of the United States, considering that it had a legitimate right to respond. Also, as we have said, *El Mundo* gave Spain a greater leading role, but in a different way to *ABC* where clearly terrorism was the enemy to be beaten, both in America and in Spain. When the latter newspaper moved toward using the terminology of war, this was done in defense of the actions of the United States.

We can therefore affirm that, although there were few express definitions, the elements of coverage provide clues as to the newspapers' understanding of the attacks of 9/11. For *ABC,* it was more a terrorist phenomenon; for *El País*, it was a war; and *El Mundo* maintained a more ambivalent position. In any case, the three standpoints address issues of a political and cultural nature which differ substantially from those held by the American media.

In the public debate on 9/11, the Spanish press attempted to bring the phenomenon closer to their readers with arguments true to the world view they have always held. It would seem clear that it is precisely at such moments of lack of definition that media frames call on cultural resonance, seeking for clues as to how to understand the emerging reality. As we have shown, it is also easier at that stage for the politicians' frames to penetrate the media agenda, as also occurs in the case of the U.S. media (Hutcheson et al., 2004).

In this way, the media contribute decisively to the socialization and assimilation of phenomena at the embryonic stage, but run the risk of over-simplifying them. Since they do not offer new frames of reference which bring out the novelty of the events, the reality is often present only in a reduced form in public debate. Finding frames that combine cultural resonance with a sensitivity toward what is new and unique constitutes the current challenge that the media in this global-risk world are facing.

CHAPTER ENDNOTES

[1] For the President´s speeches, go to <http://www.whitehouse.gov>.

[2] After the attacks of March, 11, 2004, in Madrid, the terrorist threat in Spain was broadened to other groups and objectives.

[3] However, as Altheide points out, terrorists are good communicators but access to the media does not mean "a good press"; it has been shown that what the media really do is to provide television coverage but they do not confer legitimacy (Altheide, 1987).

[4] Clutterbuck takes this definition from Jacques Ellul work.

[5] For example, the British press would never call a terrorist a "commando" because such a term could give terrorists a legitimacy conferred upon British commandos who fought in World War II. Equally, when it is said that a police officer has been "executed" or simply "perished" at the hands of terrorists, the media have created the idea of something that is not a murder (Miller, 1982). Recently, Reuters has grappled with the same problem when trying to distinguish between "terrorist" and "freedom fighter." The international agency has decided not to use either of them, unless they are in direct quotes, because "emotive terms" should not be used in pursuit of objectivity. Instead, facts should be presented and the reader should be allowed to decide (see Demers, 2002, p. 11). In wars, there are also difficulties with the terminology used by sources, since sometimes governments talk about "collateral damage" when they could be talking about innocent battle victims.

[6] And, even in this case, as has been shown in the Spanish public opinion's reaction to the Government's position on the conflict in Iraq, this power has its limitations and an armed intervention or a police action is only accepted when it is the last available option, always and only to defend individual and collective security in proportion to the threat (Alvira, 1992). According to data from the Centre for Sociological Studies, Spanish public opinion is one of the most pacifist in Europe.

[7] In the study, carried out by Professors Idoyaga and Ramírez de la Piscina, only *ABC* and *El País* were analyzed, but there is no doubt that *El Mundo*'s line on terrorism is equally clear, to the point that some of its journalists are targeted by the terrorist band.

[8] A first reading takes in headlines, subheadings, photographs, photograph headings, leaders, summaries and subtitles and is what at least the majority of newspaper consumers manage to read.

[9] The front page of September 16 issue is highly significant — even though the headline (five columns) was "Bush targets bin Laden and the Taliban threaten whoever assists in an attack against them," the accompanying photograph showed Aznar signing the book of condolences in the American embassy in Madrid.

REFERENCES

Altheide, D. (1987). Format and symbols in TV coverage of terrorism in the United States and Great Britain. *International Studies Quarterly*, 31, 161-176.
Alvira, R. (1992). Opinión pública, servicio militar y Fuerzas Armadas en España. *Política Exterior*, VI (26), 163-170.

Beck, U. (2003). *Sobre el terrorismo y la guerra*. Barcelona: Paidos.

Bennet, W. L. and Paletz, D. (1994). *Taken by storm. The Media, public opinion and US foreign policy in the Gulf War*. The University of Chicago Press.

Boyd-Barrett, Oliver (2004). Understanding: the second casualty. Paper presented at the conference on *Communication & Globalization*. Center for Global Media Studies and the Korean Press Foundation, Seattle, July 16-17, 2004.

Clutterbuck, R. (1985). *Los medios de comunicación y la violencia política*. Pamplona: Eunsa.

Cohen, A. A., & Wolfsfeld, G. (1993). *Framing the Intifada. People and the Media*. New Jersey: Ablex Publishing Corporation, Norwood.

Demers, D. (2002). When Is a Terrorist a Terrorist? Reuters Policy Exposes Parochialism in U.S. Media. *Global Media News Reader,* 4(1), 1, 11.

Diezhandino, P. et alia (1994). *La elite de los periodistas*. Bilbao: Servicio Editorial de la Universidad del País Vasco.

Doornaert, M. (1993). The ethical considerations underpinning he media in situations of conflict and tension. *Proceedings of the Seminar on the Media in Situations of Conflict and Tension*. Strasbourg 29-Nov.-1-Dec.

Entman, R. M. (2003). Cascading Activation: Contesting the White House's Frame After 9/11. *Political Communication*, 20, (4) 415-432.

First, A. (1997). Television and the construction of social reality: an Israeli case study. In McCombs, M.; Shaw, D., Weaver, D. (Eds). *Communication and Democracy* (pp. 41-50). New Jersey: Lawrence Erlbaum Associates.

Gamson, W. A. (1989). News as Framing. *American Behavioral Scientist* 33 (2), 157-161.

Gamson, W..A. & Modigliani, A. (1989). Media Discourses and Public Opinion on Nuclear Power: A constructionist Approach. *American Journal of Sociology* 95 (1), 1-37.

Gárate, M. L. (2002). *La prensa como configuradora del nuevo orden internacional: análisis del tratamiento del concepto en los editoriales sobre la guerra en la antigua Yugoslavia*. Unpublished doctoral dissertation, Universidad de Navarra, Pamplona. *Global Media News*, Winter 2002.

Hutcheson, J.; Domke, D., Billeaudeaux, A. & Garland, P. (2004). US National Identity, Political Elites and a Patriotic Press following September 11. *Political Communication* 21, 27-50.

Idoyaga, P., & Ramírez de la Piscina, T. (2001). Política informativa de El País y ABC ante la nueva situación política del País Vasco (1998-2000). *Zer. Revista de Estudios de Comunicación*, 10, 257-279.

Iyengar, S., Simon, A. (1997). News coverage of the Gulf Crisis and Public Opinion. *Communication Research*, 20 (3), 365-383.

Kellner, D. (2002). September 11, the Media, and War Fever. *Television & New Media*, 3 (2),143-151.

La Porte, M. T. (1999). Efectos de los medios en las controversias internacionales. In Rodríguez, R., & Sádaba, T. (Eds.) *Periodistas ante conflictos* (pp. 79-94). Pamplona: Eunsa.

La Porte, M. T. (forthcoming, 2006) The Bosnian War in Spain: The Media's Representation of a Distant Violent Conflict, in Nossek, H., Swanlaker, Sreberny, A., (Eds.) *Media and Political Violence*, Hampton Press: New Jersey, USA.

Livingston, S. (1994). *El espectáculo del terrorismo*. Boulder: Westview Press.

Miller, A. H. (1982). *Terrorism. The media and the law*. Dobbs Ferry, USA: Transnational Publishers.

Mowlana, H., Gerbner, G., Schiller, H. (eds.) (1992). *Triumph of the image: the media's war in the Gulf. A global perspective*. Boulder, CO: Westview Press.

Muñoz-Alonso, A., & Rospir, J. I. (1999). *Democracia mediática y campañas electorales*. Barcelona: Ariel.

Nacos, B. (2003). The terrorist calculus behind 9-11: a model for future terrorism?. *Studies in conflict and terrorism* 26, 1-16.

Paletz, D. L. (1995). Los medios de comunicación y la violencia. In Muñoz-Alonso, A. & Rospir, J. I. (Eds.) *Comunicación Política* (pp. 331-367). Madrid: Editorial Universitas.

Pizarroso, A. (1991). *La guerra de las mentiras*. Madrid: Eudema.

Quiñonero, J. P. (1999). Goya y el periodismo del mañana. In *Periodistas ante conflictos* (pp. 95-98). Pamplona: Eunsa.

Reinares, F. (1998). *Terrorismo y Antiterrorismo*. Barcelona: Paidós.

Rodríguez, R., & Sádaba, T. (1999). *Periodistas ante conflictos*. Pamplona: Eunsa.

Sádaba, T. (1999). Comunicación y conflicto terrorista: la segunda Transición de los medios. In Rodríguez, R., & Sádaba, T. (Eds.) *Periodistas ante conflictos* (pp. 125-140). Pamplona: Eunsa.

Sádaba, T. (2001). Origen, aplicación y límites de la teoría del encuadre (framing) en comunicación. *Comunicación y Sociedad*, XIV,143-175.

Santamaría, L. (1997). *Géneros para la persuasión en periodismo*. Madrid: Fragua.

Schaffert, R. (1992). *Media coverage and political terrorism. A quantitative analysis*. New York: Praeger.

Taylor, P.m. (1993). *War and the media: propaganda and persuasion in the Gulf War*. Manchester: Manchester University Press.

Wasburn, P. C. (2002). *The social construction of international news. We're talking about them, they're talking about us*. New York: Praeger.

Chapter 7

September 11 in Norwegian Media: Images of the Local Threat

Rune Ottosen & Tine Ustad Figenshou

After September 11, media all over the world and, in particular, in the United States were severely tested. How were they to deal with a situation whereby the whole nation was in shock over the mass murder of close to 3,000 people in what is best characterized as a crime against humanity?

This test included ethical issues such as how simultaneously to be a channel for the strong feelings in American society — reporting on the anger and trauma of millions — and also to assist the authorities in distributing information to suppress panic while preparing for possible new attacks. At the same time, the media were obliged to defend the classic values of a democratic society, such as freedom of the press and of expression.

The attacks represented the first test case for U.S. media since the World War II, the last time an attack took place on U.S. soil (i.e., the Japanese attack on Pearl Harbor on December 7, 1941). And the test had global implications, since the development of satellite technology and the modern global media infrastructure now automatically make modern wars into global media events.

Images are distributed to a world audience minutes after dramatic events such as the attack on the World Trade Center (Nohrstedt & Ottosen, 2001). Of course, this also has ethical implications on a global scale, since major news organizations such as CNN and Fox News are controlled from U.S. territory.

One of the key objectives in the following analysis is to look more closely at how Norwegian mass media represented a global media event like 9/11.

In the days following the September 11 terrorist attacks, U.S. Defense officials prepared the media for an early display of secrecy in the all-encompassing American campaign against terror by characterizing the "war on terrorism" as something other than a global conflict (The Reporters Committee for Freedom of the Press, 2003). By calling for a war on terrorism, the United States was initiating an open-ended and global conflict — one that could be directed against any adversary anywhere in the world. U.S. Defense officials described the war as having multiple battles along multiple fronts and possibly against multiple and sometimes unknown enemies.

According to Höijer, Nohrstedt and Ottosen (2004, p. 1), the war on terrorism can be understood as a propagandistic and rhetorical device in order to establish power over discourses constructed and exchanged about the terrorist attacks. In this context, anything but media support for the U.S. leadership may be interpreted as anti-Americanism.

This position influenced international media coverage of the terrorist attacks and the following war on terror, particularly in the mainstream U.S. media. September 11 drove the U.S. media into a sphere of consensus in which professionalism, critical coverage and oppositional opinions were seen as inadequate (Schudson 2002, p. 40).

Traditionally there are three occasions that cause U.S. journalists to abandon reporting from a neutral stance in favor of patriotism: in moments of tragedy, in moments of public danger, and during threats to national security. The terrorist attacks suggested all of these (Schudson, p. 41). In addition, some journalists liked the new intimacy of the consensual "we," feeling connected and important to their audience.

In this sphere of consensus, U.S. National Security Advisor Condoleezza Rice convinced U.S. networks to be careful when broadcasting the speeches of Osama bin Laden and other controversial material aired on Al-Jazeera. All major mainstream U.S. networks and newspapers signed the agreement (El-Nawawy and Iskandar 2002, p. 178). This self-censorship within the U.S. media raised broad criticism from international media and human rights groups.

Most of the U.S. media focused on the September 11 incidents instead of on their broader causes, which constituted a dominant framing of the events as stereotypical acts of Muslim terrorism instead of leading to investigation of the root causes of anti-U.S. sentiments (Karim 2002, p. 106). There is evidence that various new laws introduced after September 11 in several countries have challenged the commitment to traditional civil liberties. Two such examples are the Patriotic Act in the United States and the Terrorism Act in the United Kingdom (Vetlesen, 2005).

These issues are background for this article but will not be dealt with in detail here since we will focus on the events and media coverage in the days immediately after September 11.[1]

CHALLENGES FOR THE NORWEGIAN MEDIA

The Norwegian media faced other challenges, primarily access to the action. In the first days after the terrorist attack, all U.S. airports were closed for security reasons and no journalists could enter the country by plane, so Norwegian media had to rely on their staff already based in New York and Washington. This included their correspondents and also freelancers and other journalists who were in the vicinity when the planes hit the World Trade Center and the Pentagon. Among them is an author of this article (Figenschou), who was writing as a freelance journalist for the Norwegian daily *Dagbladet* at the time (see her story in the Appendix).

WHEN THE GUARDIAN IS ATTACKED: NORWAY AND THE UNITED STATES

Norway has been a loyal member of NATO since the foundation of the organization in 1949. During the Cold War, close ties between Norway and the United States were confirmed on several occasions, including bilateral military agreements to place heavy U.S. military equipment on Norwegian soil. Polls have repeatedly confirmed that NATO membership has a solid basis in Norwegian public opinion. In short, the close ties between Norway and the United States, both at a bilateral level and through NATO, have been a cornerstone of Norwegian security policy.

It is well known that the security policy in a given country is reflected and defended in the mainstream press (van Dijk, 1988). In times of crisis and war, the mainstream media tend to be even more loyal toward their own country (Nohrstedt & Ottosen, 2001). Earlier content analyses of the media coverage of wars and conflicts that involve the United States, Norway and NATO support the claim that the Norwegian mainstream media are reluctant to criticize the United States, even for controversial interventions such as the invasion of Panama in 1989 (Ottosen, 1994). A comparative analysis of the coverage of the 1991 Gulf War in five countries documented a correlation between the coverage of international issues in a given country and its security and political orientation. Thus, the coverage of the Gulf War in the mainstream press in NATO countries like Norway and Germany were closer to official U.S. policy and to the coverage in the U.S. press than that of the media in non-NATO countries like Sweden and Finland.

In a situation like 9/11, where Norway's closest ally was under attack, it was expected that the Norwegian media, like the population in Norway and in most other countries, would be fully behind the United States and, indeed, broad initial support was expressed through empathy and solidarity in the media. The question to be analyzed in this article is how it was expressed in the coverage during the dramatic days following September 11.

SAMPLE AND METHODOLOGY

This study content analyses television and newspaper overage of 9/11 during the first week after that event. Two Oslo-based national newspapers *Aftenposten* and *Verdens Gang (VG)* were chosen. The former is Norway's largest and potentially most influential morning paper and the latter is Norway's largest tabloid and the largest newspaper overall. Both newspapers are owned by Schibsted, one of three companies in control of the majority of the Norwegian newspaper market.

Also included in the study is coverage of the first week after 9/11 by the previously state-owned public broadcast company NRK, mainly financed by a compulsory annual fee paid by all Norwegians in possession of a television set, and coverage of the first four days by the commercial TV2 channel, financed mainly through advertising. TV2 was established in 1992 following a new media law, lifting the broadcast monopoly of the then state-owned NRK. TV2 can operate on the basis of a license with a commitment to incorporate certain public service features in its program policy, including the broadcast of a certain amount of, for instance, Norwegian-produced dramas, culture programs, and educational programs (Syvertsen 1997).

In this study we combined quantitative and qualitative research. The presence of different genres and use of sources has been registered and coded to a database. We have also registered the framing of articles and news stories in television by coding the messages expressed by the different sources in a coding scheme, with pre-defined positions in five different categories:

U.S. *Hatred.* The United States was attacked because it is, itself, the largest evil-doer and terrorist. In the 9/11 attacks, the United States tasted its own medicine. The attacks on U.S. targets will not stop before the Americans have left Saudi Arabia, Israel has left Palestine, and the sanctions against Iraq are lifted.

U.S. Critical. The United States was attacked. The terrorists are criminals who should be prosecuted by an international court and the conflict should be solved through diplomacy. This is an issue for the United Nations and should not be dealt with by the United States or NATO on their own. The enemy is not a nation, but a loose network of individuals; thus, Article 5 in the NATO charter is irrelevant. (This position might be combined with a critical stand against the Taliban and al-Qaeda.)

U.S. Friendly. The United States was attacked by terrorists. The attack was a declaration of war and the United States has the right to strike back with military means. Article 5 in the NATO charter should be activated and the attack should be regarded as an attack on the whole NATO alliance. As a NATO-allied and friend, Norway has a duty to support a U.S. military action. The terrorists must be caught, punished and killed. Taliban must take responsibility for any military attack and Taliban-bases are legitimate targets. Any civilian casualties should be regarded as collateral damage.

Norwegian Angle. What is the consequence for Norway? Norwegians are at the center of the events because we are also threatened, as a Western nation and NATO member. As a nation we must take precautions to defend ourselves. The story justifies its place because it focuses on Norwegians. (Stories in which Norwegians are interviewed or comment are not included.)

Neutral. Straightforward situational description of events, comments on facts, rescue operations, etc.

Framing of news involves selection and salience. According to Entman (1993, p. 52), "to frame" is to "select some aspects of a perceived reality and make them more salient in a communicating text, in such a way as to promote a particular problem definition, causal definition, moral evaluation, and/or treatment recommendation for the problem described." Frames select and call attention to particular aspects of the reality described, which means that at the same time they direct attention away from other aspects (p. 54). Journalists may follow the rule of "objective reporting" and still convey a framing of the events that only emphasizes parts of the story. Politicians seeking support are compelled to compete with each other and in the media over news frames.

According to Tuchman (1978, p. 182), it is important to acknowledge that news coverage is a constructed reality developed through a series of choices made by journalists and editors every day. The social construction of news involves the construction of frames — the process of choosing which perspectives and news angles to give the news stories in order to make them newsworthy. It must be stated here that this coding is not according to what Teun van Dijk calls a "main story" (title and lead) but reflects the clearly expressed positions of the sources or the reporters. In principle, an article or news item can include several frames. Since these frames do not express the main story, they should be interpreted with care and analyzed with a more qualitative textual analysis.

It is fair to say that the dramatic events on 9/11 dominated the media in the following days, leaving other news stories in the shadows. If we look at the two newspapers included in the study, we find that news articles dominated the coverage in both, with an equal share of 83 percent. Both newspapers, however, also printed several commentaries, a few more in *Aftenposten (28)* than in the *VG* (6). *VG* printed more features (17 vs. 7).

Two of the most significant characteristics of the Norwegian coverage were the high number of stories in which the presence of Norwegians at the scene of action seem to be the central news value of the stories, and the high number of Norwegian sources used by the media covering the catastrophe taking place on U.S. soil. Nearly three-fourths of the sources in both newspapers were Norwegians. Americans represented only about 1 in 6 sources.

Most of the stories in both the newspapers and the television news programs fit the "neutral" frame, meaning that they focused on facts surrounding the attacks as opposed to issues (see Table 7.1). They represented about half of the stories. There were no major differences between the media on this measure. Fewer than 1 of 10 stories took a "U.S.-Hatred" or "U.S.-Critical" frame. About the same number were "U.S.-Friendly."

Next to the "neutral" frame, the "Norwegian" frame was most popular, characterizing about a third of the total stories. Television was somewhat more likely to use this frame than the newspapers (38% vs. 28%). These news stories focusing on national interests consisted mainly of two basic groups: a) Stories of Norwegians who were in danger abroad because of the dramatic events, and b) the consequences of the events for Norwegian interests at home. Norwegian sources also particularly dominated in the TV coverage, where as many as 73 percent of the sources was Norwegian compared to only 17 percent American (data not shown). In the newspaper coverage, by contrast, the use of sources was more balanced between American (42.4 per cent) and Norwegian (37.2 per cent).

Table 7.1
Framing of the September 11 in Norwegian Media
(Percent of Stories)

	Newspapers			Television		
	Aftenposten N=452	VG N=295	Total N=747	NRK N=403	TV2 N=270	Total N=673
U.S.-Hatred	3.3%	1.4%	2.5%	1.2%	1.9%	1.5%
U.S.-Critical	7.1%	2.4%	5.2%	4.2%	1.1%	3.0%
U.S.-Friendly	11.1%	5.1%	8.7%	6.9%	6.3%	6.7%
Norwegian Angle	23.7%	34.2%	27.8%	39.7%	34.8%	37.7%
Neutral	54.9%	56.9%	55.7%	47.9%	55.9%	51.1%
Total	100.0%	100.0%	100.0%	100.0%	100.0%	100.0%

Note: Totals may not add to 100% because of rounding.

A) Norwegians in Danger in the United States

The September 11 attacks caught the media around the world by surprise. In Norway, the commercial national channel TV2 started its first coverage of the attacks at 3.30 p.m., one-and-a-half hours ahead of the public broadcast company NRK. Many of the first stories were frantic situational updates as politicians, media, and experts gradually realized that what seemed a tragic accident was in fact a grotesque terrorist attack. Then the media started to focus on how the events were experienced by Norwegian citizens in the United States.

During the first news updates, there were a number of interviews, with Norwegian eyewitnesses in New York and Washington giving their versions of the events, as well as interviews with the authorities speculating about Norwegian casualties. Norwegian students and freelance journalists were among the most popular voices from New York. Their accounts were more emotional than professional reporting, but the commercial channel TV2 in particular gave these reports high priority in the first couple of days. As the days went by there were no reported Norwegian casualties and the number of missing Norwegians was gradually reduced.

On Sept. 18, the *Aftenposten* wrote that the last missing Norwegian was probably not in New York at the time of the attack. But even though there were no reported Norwegian casualties, the focus on Norwegian accounts of the events remained high throughout the first week, and in the days following the attacks there were several interviews with Norwegian celebrities in New York — artists, photographers, sports heroes, and TV personalities, all of them sharing their thoughts and feelings with their countrymen back home.

Furthermore, there were interviews with several Norwegians indirectly involved in the tragedy including Norwegian pilots and flight attendants working with American Airlines, Norwegian economists and financial experts with contacts in the World Trade Center, and Norwegian firefighters in New York. Similarly, as the identity of the hijackers came out, tabloid daily newspaper *VG* tracked down several Norwegians who had been in contact with the terrorists before the attacks. On Sept. 14, they printed an interview with Norwegian architect Martin Ebert titled "Studied with death pilot,"[2] in which he revealed that he studied for four years with hijacker and pilot Mohammed Atta. On Sept. 16, there was a similar story about Norwegian pilot Øivind Pedersen, who studied in the United States at the same flight school as the hijackers ("Went to the same flight school as the hijackers").[3] On Sept. 17, *VG* followed up with more stories, including "Threatened by the death pilot,"[4] which quoted Norwegian pilot Jonas Tingstad, who studied with hijacker Marwan el-Shehhi, saying that el-Shehhi hated Americans, was loaded with money and once threatened to kill him. And on Sept. 18, there was another article titled "Morten failed terrorist suspect,"[5] which focused on Norwegian flight instructor Morten Engstrøm, who failed suspected terror pilot Hani Hanjoor. In all of these stories, the Norwegians, who were indirectly or nearly or almost victims of the attacks, received much more media attention than those from other countries who were actually directly involved in the events.

B) Norway in Danger

From day one, the Norwegian media put a lot of effort into analyzing whether national security in Norway was sufficient and whether the authorities had done enough to adapt it to the new terrorist threat. In the first TV coverage, in particular, the national security issue was among the most important in the Norwegian media. There were interviews with the prime minister, the foreign minister, army generals, police officers, NATO officers, intelligence officers, and so on.

During the first day, some stories were repeated again and again on national TV: the constant updates on the security measures taken outside the American Embassy in Oslo, security measures taken at the Norwegian

Table 7.2
Types of Sources in Norwegian Media 9/11 Coverage
(Percent of Stories)

	Newspapers			Television		
	Aftenposten N=452	VG N=294	Total N=746	NRK N=403	TV2 N=270	Total N=673
Experts	39.6%	28.6%	35.3%	9.4%	7.8%	8.8%
Politicians	29.9%	30.3%	30.0%	27.3%	27.4%	27.3%
Man in street	19.9%	5.1%	14.1%	13.4%	11.1%	12.5%
Victims	4.0%	15.3%	8.4%	7.9%	10.0%	8.8%
Editorial	0.0%	0.3%	0.1%	31.5%	35.2%	33.0%
Other media	6.2%	12.2%	8.6%	0.5%	0.0%	0.3%
Other	0.4%	8.2%	3.5%	9.9%	8.5%	9.4%
Total	100.0%	100.0%	100.0%	100.0%	100.0%	100.0%

Note: Totals may not add to 100% because of rounding.

Parliament, security measures taken at the NATO Headquarters in Stavanger, Norway, and security measures taken at Oslo Airport Gardemoen. From the TV coverage on 9/11, with such a heavy focus on Norwegian national security, it almost seemed as if Norway was the next potential target for the terrorists.

In the newspapers the following day, these stories were somewhat reduced, but the feeling of being under threat was present in Norwegian coverage all week — an approach that produced a strong representation of sources from the upper echelons, both in television and newspapers (see Table 7.2). This was particularly the case in the newspapers, where 65 percent of the sources were experts and politicians. The contrast between how newspapers and television use expert sources is interesting. In the television newsroom, senior reporters were upgraded to experts themselves and interviewed by colleagues. This is one of the reasons why the category "editorial source" is the largest category of sources in both NRK and TV2, with shares of 31 and 35 percent respectively of the sources.

There were, for instance, several interviews with the head of Norwegian Intelligence, who asked the public for information about international terrorism. As a result of this call for information, Intelligence received much information about suspected terrorist connections and activities in Norway, and on Sept. 15 TV2 sent a report focusing on the information that terrorist leader Osama bin Laden had direct links to Norwegians. Although the terror experts and security advisers interviewed generally tried to counter the impression of Norway as a potential target for international terrorism, the stories about potential terror targets on Norwegian territory remained. One example is the lengthy article titled "This is how the terror can harm Norway,[6] which *VG* published Sept. 18. The article was based on reports from the Norwegian Defense Research Establishment (FFI) and stated that Norwegian society is vulnerable to terrorist attacks targeting electricity and telecommunications.

Media attention was also directed toward how Norwegians in Norway reacted to the gruesome, almost surreal, images of the attacks. Since none of the victims was Norwegian, one can say that Norwegian experts and politician got the job of analyzing the victims' situation when they had little personal knowledge of those experiences. As a consequence of the character of the attacks (crashing passenger airplanes into large buildings), there were several stories on air safety and the fear of flying, and polls showed that two out of three Norwegians were afraid of going to the United States. Another significant feature in the news was the large amount of attention given to how Norwegian children in Norway reacted to the news of the terrorist attack. There were several interviews with Norwegian children both in the papers and on TV, as well as crisis psychiatrists giving advice to teachers and parents on how to explain the attacks to children.

The attack on the United States in general, and the World Trade Center in particular, hit the financial markets globally. *Aftenposten* focused most on the economic consequences of the attacks for Norwegian businesses and economic interests. The hardest hit sectors were tourism (particularly Norwegian-owned cruise lines, travel agencies specializing in the United States, and the major airlines such as Scandinavian SAS), while there was a continuing discussion on how the attacks would influence oil prices and thus the national economy. Furthermore, *Aftenposten* produced several interviews with financial analysts on the general implications for the Norwegian national economy (such as the interest rate, insurance policies, national markets, etc.).

PROVINCIALISM OR A NATIONAL AGENDA?

In the introduction to this chapter, we tried to explain why the political and structural conditions around the event must inevitably be colored by the national agenda. We find no reason to be critical that, to a certain extent, the national agenda and national sources dominate such a dramatic occurrence, even though it took place on the other side of the Atlantic Ocean. Still, we find it interesting to raise the question whether the Norwegian framing went too far, ending in what might be called a narrow-minded provincial outlook.

For the sake of argument we mention here that a few years ago the German scholar Hans Magnus Enzensberger was invited by the Norwegian journal *Samtiden* to review the foreign coverage of several Norwegian newspapers for a certain period of time. Even though some aspects of his methodological approach are open to criticism,[7] his judgment was harsh. In his conclusion, he pointed out that foreign coverage in Norwegian newspapers was narrow-minded and nationalistic compared to that of the quality newspapers in Europe. He censured the newspaper for underestimating its readers by analyzing global events as seen from a Norwegian angle and was particular critical of the tabloid newspapers, including *VG*, which is represented in our sample. The other newspaper in our sample, *Aftenposten*, was also criticized, but was regarded by Enzensberger as the most internationally oriented of the Norwegian newspapers (Enzensberger, 2002).

THE RATIONALE BEHIND THE HOME-RELATED STORIES

September 11 was been labeled a global media event because of the enormous media exposure the attack received around the world. Why, then, was the national Norwegian perspective so dominant in Norwegian coverage?

As mentioned above, it is not unusual for foreign news stories to appeal to the special interests of the home audience (Hannerz, 2004, p. 136) — home-related stories which often have to do with specific connections between home and abroad. There are many explanations as to why the media turned to Norwegian voices, sources, and stories. Many of them seem so obvious to journalists that they are quite hard to explain; they are almost built-in mechanisms of the social construction of what is considered "good news." According to Norwegian editor Per Egil Hegge,

> a central journalistic principle is grounded in closeness and in what is told, should concern the reader. This is formulated in many ways; the first I heard as a newcomer in a Norwegian local newspaper went like this: "One person from Nord-Trøndelag [a Norwegian province] is equivalent to half a million Chinese." This was a way of measuring the

size of the headlines, supposedly not human value. But — there is a large "but" in the air after such comparisons (Hegge 1998 in Eide, 2002, p. 45).

We have tried to sum up some of the explanations for this built-in framing of events. First, the Norwegian angle has to do with identification. In her study of identification and otherness in media texts, Eide (2002) asks if the media's focus on Norwegians as individuals, and foreigners as members of a group or a mass, could be due to a perception among reporters of its being much easier for Norwegian readers to identify with Norwegian "heroes" or "victims" than try to cope with the greater challenge of identification across inherited divides (Eide, 2002, p. 200). The Norwegian framing of the terrorist attacks is, therefore, used to help the audience back home make sense of an almost unreal catastrophe. To help the audience understand the gruesome images and reports, Norwegian media chose to use Norwegian sources, faces, and framing to make the stories easier to connect with and absorb. This is because many Norwegians feel that what happens to other Norwegians is perceived to be more important than what happen to other people on the other side of the world. The Norwegian angle is, thus, recognized as important information that brings news value and newsworthiness to stories. Norway is a small country where everybody knows someone who knows someone who was indirectly involved in the terror attack. Another element is the fact that the journalists themselves identify with their countrymen.

Second, the working conditions of journalists in the days after the attacks influenced the coverage. During the first days the situation was very chaotic and Norwegian journalists in the United States had to find interviewees quickly. It was more convenient for them to get in touch with the sources and people, many of whom were Norwegians, that they knew already. Many Norwegians in the United States associate mainly with other Norwegians. Similarly, in the newsroom back home, journalists needed to interview as many sources and eyewitnesses as possible during the first days after the attack and the easiest way out was to call Norwegians over there and ask for their stories. One should not forget that most Norwegian journalists in the United States, working for small publications compared to the large U.S. networks and newspapers, have limited access to senior officials whereas back in Norway, on the other hand, most experts and politicians line up to comment on the latest events. These limitations on working conditions contribute to strengthen the dominance of the Norwegian angle.

Third, it is important to acknowledge that the terrorist attacks actually influenced the Norwegian economy and local economic interests. The strong focus on the economic influence of the terror attack on Norwegian business interests, therefore, may be interpreted as an effect of the increasingly connected global economy.

CONCLUSION: A GLOBAL EVENT, A NATIONAL NEWS SPHERE?

Obviously, the events of 9/11 must be characterized as a crisis. But as Raboy and Dagenais (1992) point out, the intensity of a crisis determines the means one chooses to meet it. The line between reaction and overreaction is in itself an ethical issue. Here, of course, the working conditions for the media during the crisis are a central issue. During previous research on the Gulf War and the Kosovo War, the issue of a "global discursive order" has been raised, involving the interests of the different parties in a conflict, the media as a channel for information, and the audience as a concerned receiver of the media discourses (Nohrstedt, Höijer, and Ottosen, 2002).

As we have shown in the Norwegian media coverage of 9/11, a great deal depends on the discourse that the individual media and journalists choose to present to the public. As illustrated in this article, the Norwegian angle dominated the first week of the Norwegian coverage of 9/11 even though not a single one of the more than 3,000 victims was Norwegian and the events took place on the other side of the globe. We, thus, have raised the issue of whether such national framing went too far in the direction of provincialism.

In the literature on globalization of media and communication, there has been talk of the evolution of a global public sphere in which issues of international significance are articulated through mass media. The validity of such a concept, however, has been contested (Thussu, 2000, p. 71). The notion that the rise of global media has managed to establish a global public sphere has been both proclaimed and denounced by media scholars. Recent research indicates that, owing to growth in transnational and global news media, public opinion formation occasionally transcends national borders and acquires a political life of its own on the global level. Still, compared to the globalization of politics, economy and culture, the public sphere and the formation of public opinion are still very much tied to the national level and oriented toward national political institutions (Hjarvard, 2000, p. 19). Today, both newsrooms and audiences have access to news services at different levels, from local to global news. This, however, has not resulted in major changes in the consumption patterns of audiences. The majority in most countries are still closely tied to local or national media (op. cit., p. 32). The production and reception of media are mostly shaped by local, national, and regional forces, as by the macro-economies of the media industry (Magder, 2003, p. 35).

However, the availability of transnational news has influenced editorial decisions, presentation formats, and the narrative techniques within the national media, and thus transnational news provides an incentive for increasing adaptation of transnational formats to national contexts. Furthermore, increased transparency also stimulates the synchronization of editorial decisions between news services in different countries (primarily during major international events or crises) (p. 33). These developments indicate a homogenization of the news media around the world. Hjarvard (2000, p. 34) argues that the globalization of the media does not entail the creation of one global public sphere media but, rather, the development of a multi-layered structure of publicity. New transnational forums develop, but local, national, and regional spheres continue to play important roles in the global public sphere. Thus, globalization also implies a gradual differentiation of the public sphere.

CHAPTER ENDNOTES

[1] See Ottosen, 2002, for more details on these issues.

[2] Studerte med utpekt dodspilot, *VG* September 14, 2001.

[3] Gikk på samme flyskole som kaprerne, *VG*, September 16, 2001.

[4] Drapstruet av dodspiloten, *VG*, September 17, 2001.

[5] Morten ga terrormistenkt stryk, *VG*, September 18, 2001.

[6] Slik kan terroren ramme Norge, *VG*, September 18, 2001.

[7] In a public meeting where Enzensberger's report was presented, the foreign editor of *Aftenposten*, Nils Morten Udgaard, rightly pointed out that since Enzenberger only analyzed the foreign pages he missed many of the relevant debates on foreign issues introduced in the cultural pages.

REFERENCES

Eide, E. (2002). 'Down there' and 'up here': Europe's 'others' in Norwegian feature stories. *HiO-report 2002 nr 31*. Faculty of Journalism, Library and Information Sciences, Oslo University College.

El-Nawawy, M., & Iskandar, A. (2002). Al-Jazeera. *How the free Arab news network scooped the world and changed the Middle East*. Boulder: Westview Press.

Entman, R. M. (1993). Framing: Toward clarification of a fractured paradigm. *Journal of Communication, 43*, 51-58.

Enzensberger, H. M. (2002). Verden skrumper på avispapiret. Innblikk i norsk presse, *Samtiden*, no. 1 2002.

Hannerz, U. (2004). *Foreign news: Exploring the world of foreign correspondents.* Chicago: University of Chicago Press.

Hjarvard, S. (2000). News media and the globalization of the public sphere. In Hjarvard (Ed.), *News in a globalized society.* Göteborg: Nordicom.

Höijer, B., Nohrstedt, S. A., & Ottosen, R. (2004). Introduction: Media and the 'War on Terror'. In Nohrstedt, S. A., & Ottosen, R. (Eds.). (2004). *U.S. and the others: Global media images on "The War on Terror."* Göteborg: Nordicom.

Karim, K. H. (2002). Making sense of the 'Islamic peril'. In Zelizer, B. and Allan, S. (Eds.). *Journalism after September 11.* London & New York: Routledge.

Magder, T. (2003). Watching what we say: global communication in a time of fear. In Thussu, D. K. & Freedman, D. (Eds.). *War and the media.* London: Thousand Oaks & New Delhi: Sage Publications.

Nohrstedt, S. A., & Ottosen, R. (2001). *Journalism and the new world order. Volume I: Gulf War, national news discourses and globalization.* Göteborg: Nordicom.

Ottosen, R. (1994). *Mediestrategier og fiendebilder i internasjonale konflikter. Norske medier i skyggen av Pentagon.* Oslo: Universitetsforlaget.

Ottosen, R. (2002). Pressefriheten under press etter 11. September. *Redaktørforeningens årbok 2002.*

Raboy, M., & Dagenais, B. (1992). Media and the politics of crisis. In Raboy, M., & Dagenais, B. (Eds.) *Media, crisis and democracy.* London: Sage Publications.

Schudson, M. (2002). "What's unusual about covering politics as usual," In Zelizer, B. and Allan, S. (Eds.). *Journalism after September 11.* London & New York: Routledge.

Syvertsen, T. (1997). *Den store TV-krigen. Norsk allmennfjernsyn 1988-96.* Bergen: Fagbokforlaget.

The Reporters Committee for Freedom of the Press (RCFP). (2003). *Homefront confidential: How the war on terrorism affects access to information and the public's right to know* (4th ed.). http://www.rcfp. org/homefrontconfidential/

Thussu, D. K. (2000). *International communication: Continuity and change.* New York: Arnold & Oxford: Oxford University Press.

Tuchman, G. (1978). *Making news: A study in the construction of reality.* New York: The Free Press.

Vetlesen, J. (2005). Umuliggjøring av en annen verden. *Aftenposten* January 11, 2005.

Van Dijk, T. A. (1988). *News analysis: Case studies of international and national news in the press.* New Jersey: Lawrence Erlbaum Associates.

APPENDIX

Notes by Tine Ustad Figenschou after witnessing the events on September 11 in New York:

I sat at my desk at the U.N. headquarters in New York on this beautiful sunny Tuesday morning. Still alone in the office I was in the process of turning on my computer when the phone started ringing. I was exited and happy at first when I realized it was the news desk at the national newspaper I used to work for back in Norway, then shocked when they told me a plane had crashed into the World Trade Center. I ran into the restroom and from the large windows on the 35th floor I could see the towers burning. Minutes later the entire U.N. staff was evacuated down in the basement. A few hours later I was out on the streets of Manhattan. It was a surreal chaos. An endless group of people were walking northwards, away from the towers downtown. People were crying silently, walking in their business suits with their shoes in their hands, some of them covered in dust. Others were screaming, "oh my God," "oh my God." Phones were down. Public transport didn't move. People gathered around TVs and radios trying to grasp what were going on. There were news stories of car bombs exploding around town, of a truck full of explosives and more hijacked airplanes headed towards us. We did not know then that these news stories were all false. We were scared and overwhelmed. I did not even know where to start my coverage. I felt incredibly focused and disoriented at the same time. I was almost relieved when I finally got through on a public phone and my boss at the news desk back home gave their orders: Go to the Norwegian Seaman's Church! Go find some Norwegians!

Chapter 8

September 11 in Poland: America's Most Enthusiastic Ally in Europe

Tomasz Pludowski

For all of the 20th century, Polish people have had a special affinity for Americans. During a recent radio show broadcast, a middle-aged man who had just won a ticket to see a popular Polish rock band at a concert in Chicago said: "I'm so excited — they're my favorite band." "And you get to see them in Chicago," added the radio host. The winner replied: "I don't know what to say. It is every Pole's dream come true — to visit America, isn't it?"

According to some data, Warsaw is the second biggest Polish city in the world after Chicago. In public opinion polls conducted among Poles, Americans invariably score highest on the list of best-liked peoples. The Poles' liking for America goes so far that the leader of one of the parties, which is currently not represented in the Parliament, called for Poland joining North American Free Trade Agreement rather than the European Union. Even though this policy is not usually taken seriously, Poland is often seen as the most pro-American country in Europe, possibly with the exception of the United Kingdom, which has a special relationship with the United States. In fact, Poland is sometimes referred to as America's Trojan horse in the EU. The special status of America is reflected, too, in coverage of 9/11 by the Polish media and in Polish reactions to the terrorist attack. In the words of Bronislaw Geremek (2006), former foreign minister of Poland and a renowned academic,

> Poland, like other Central European countries, has long perceived the
> United States as a patron of the international order and guarantor of the

fundamental values of the West. Superimposed on that political myth —
a myth strongly reinforced during the Cold War — was the image of
America as the country that offered the greatest opportunities for
personal advancement and economic success. The huge number of
Polish-Americans — estimated at more than ten million — consolidated
the "American myth" in the Polish awareness to the point that
communist propaganda, despite its best efforts, was never able to
engender widespread anti-American sentiment in Poland. Anti-
Americanism of other kinds, too, has had its ups and downs in Europe,
but none has had a significant effect on Polish public opinion. This was
the case during the Cold War and in more recent years, too: As
demonstrations against the war in Iraq swept through many European
cities, Poles by and large distrusted the mix of anti-Americanism and
pacifism that animated them. This cultural and political predisposition
continues to inform current Polish-American relations and Polish view
of American policies. (p. 53)

THE COVERAGE

Immediately after the attacks on the WTC and the Pentagon (i.e. after 3 p.m.
CET), regular television programming was interrupted with CNN footage
from New York and Washington, D.C. After the second tower was hit, the
regular TV schedule was abandoned altogether. What followed was day-long,
continuous coverage of the events unfolding in America, including
discussions with experts in the studio. The footage of the second plane
hitting the second tower and the subsequent collapsing of the towers was
repeated throughout the day.

One of the private TV stations, which is usually characterized by its
eagerness to copy American style of news presentation, put together a
dramatic jingle with the image of the plane hitting the second tower
superimposed onto the American flag. The footage was accompanied by a
big headline: "Attack on America." The station's coverage contained a
mixture of CNN footage (simultaneously translated), live presentations by
the station's own correspondents, interviews with experts, and anchors
delivering the latest information from wire services. The evening news shows
were extended from the usual half an hour to between one and two hours.

In a matter of two days, *Wprost*, a Polish newsmagazine, and *Newsweek
Polska* had special 9/11 issues out. Picture-oriented, they highlighted the
emotional and human drama at the expense of the political. On Sept. 12,
newspapers followed in the footsteps on the previous day's TV news shows
and dramatized the events to the point of overstating facts by using big, red-
ink headlines like: "War with the U.S." and "America at War."

Gazeta Wyborcza, the biggest and most influential Polish quality daily, devoted the first half (or all 12 nonbusiness sections) of the Sept. 12 issue to the attacks. The front page included three pictures from lower Manhattan. Unknown terrorists were mentioned. CIA officials were quoted as pointing to Osama bin Laden. Richard Holbrook was quoted as saying an international coalition was needed to combat terrorism — a coalition ranging from Canada to Russia. The op-ed was titled, "Tak się zaczyna XXI wiek," or "That's the 21st Century Starting." To give an idea of the tone and rhetoric, I'll quote from the newspaper's editor-in-chief, Adam Michnik:

> What happened in New York is a sign of terror that the greatest pessimists warned against. The attack was a work of madmen, who, whoever they are, do not need any justification, any legitimization. All it takes is money and dead conscience. They killed entirely innocent people in order to achieve a goal that obviously cannot be achieved this way. The devil that the world of progress, democracy and knowledge wanted to bury showed its ugly face.
>
> We in Poland have directly experienced the tragedies and triumphs of the 20th century. Today we join the American people in their pain and despair. We contribute our scream of protest.

One of the reports in the issue praised Americans for how well they took it — they were calm, well-organized, and willing to help each other out. People did not panic; the spirit of community was present.

The front page of the Sept. 13 issue included a big picture of the WTC debris and the headline: "Who's done it?" Interestingly enough, what was missing for a long time was an analysis of why they might have done it. The reason for this and the underlying assumption seems to be that this kind of action cannot be justified.

Thursday was a day of solidarity with America. Until Friday, all state and public institutions lowered the national flag to half the mast in sign of mourning. The op-ed said:

> We are all New Yorkers. It is a good thing that both the president and the prime minister (who represented a Polish example of *cohabitation*) announced the Polish day of solidarity with the American people. [...] It is a good thing that Poland, which gave the world "Solidarność," should offer solidarity to America, the country attacked by terrorists. America has offered solidarity to us on numerous occasions. It was thanks to America that we heard free speech from Polish language radio stations in communist Poland. America supported us during martial law and then in the building of the Third Republic. It is she that we owe joining NATO. Those who attacked New York and Washington attacked the

whole free world. They made people watch the skies not for stars, but for madmen-operated torpedo-airplanes. They started a new kind of war. Today the target is America, tomorrow Europe, each of us can be a victim. Today we are all New Yorkers.

Arguably, a sociologist or mass communication theorist might label this commentary propagandistic, but since Poland shares the ideology of the victim, not the aggressor, this interpretation was not offered.

The emotional aspect of the coverage was heightened by reports of the last phone calls passengers of the planes made to their beloved right before the planes crashed: "We have been kidnapped. I want to tell you I love you and the boys." The newspaper was careful to point out that although the terrorists were all Arab, we should not blame all Arabs for terrorism. It was not a matter of race or religion.

On Sept. 14, the day of the solidarity with the United States, *Gazeta Wyborcza* published photographs of 32 victims of the attacks on the front page with the title: "Polowanie," or "The Hunt." The following day the front page contained a large photograph of an American girl crying. The headline: "America in tears." The front-page article created the impression of unanimous sympathy for the United States by enumerating the places where the victims are mourned. From the United States to the Vatican, to London, to Paris, to Moscow and to Teheran, people give tribute to the victims.

Nine days after the attacks, on September 20, *Gazeta Wyborcza* eventually looked at the big picture, including the politics behind 9/11, by quoting Zbigniew Brzezinski who said:

- the war on terror should not turn into a war on Islam
- U.S. foreign policy will have to change
- Unconditional support of U.S. government for any Israeli action against Palestine is dubious. The solution to the Israeli-Palestinian conflict needs to come from the outside
- Moscow wants to use its contribution to the war on terror to gaining Western support for the war with Chechnya

Even popular media such as the glossy, picture-oriented celebrity magazine *Viva* joined in by putting out a special issue called "Apocalypse Now." The subtitle stated, "Photographs scream, witnesses speak."

THE IMPACT

The 9/11 coverage triggered a highly emotional response on the part of the Polish people, who lit candles and left flowers and even their own poems outside the American Embassy in Warsaw. The Americans I know who live in Poland were contacted by their Polish friends with words of consolation. In extreme cases, they were offered alternative accommodations should they feel uncomfortable or insecure living in University housing, under known addresses, or next to people of other nationalities.

Some elderly Polish citizens coming with flowers to the U.S. Embassy in Warsaw spoke in highly emotional terms about the associations they had with World War II and the Warsaw uprising, both of which left many of people homeless, suffering or missing at least one family member.

The events of 9/11 took place amid a parliamentary campaign — 12 days prior to election — and they had a strong impact on the campaign's focus and outcome. Many candidates abandoned their political agenda, refused to run the previously scheduled and prepared TV broadcasts or participate in scheduled programming on public TV. Instead, they offered statements of support for the American people and against terrorism, trying to tap into the public sentiment. Running a political campaign during such a tragedy was improper, they said. As a result, the election was practically brought to a halt.

Some political observers argue that the atmosphere of insecurity and threat helped *Samoobrona* [Self-defense] and *Liga Polskich Rodzin* [League of Polish Families] — the two populist, nationalist, isolationist, and anti-EU parties — pass the five-percent threshold needed to get into the Sejm, the lower house of the parliament, which marked the first time an isolationist party gained significant support in the Polish parliament since 1989, the year Poland regained its independence after 54 years of Soviet-imposed communism and six years of World War II.

Until the end of the war in Afghanistan, the "war on terror" continued to be a major front-page story in the Polish media. Mainstream Polish media had correspondents both in the United States and Afghanistan. The controversial "collateral damage" was covered, but the frame was clearly pro-American. The bombings of Afghanistan and the campaign of airlifts were given equal footing, and a propagandistic/public relations frame for the food airlifts was not offered, except in the post-communist daily, *Trybuna*.

The social democratic government and the social democratic president, both referred to in the Western media and in the Polish media by their opponents as post-communist, offered full and unconditional support for the war effort, again along the lines of that by the British government. A NATO member since March 1999, the Polish army sent "our boys" to Afghanistan, among other things, to help disarm mines. This decision was not questioned in mainstream media and the justification offered was two-fold: 1) Poland is a loyal NATO member, and 2) in the attack on the WTC, Polish lives were claimed as well. Poland also symphatized with the Iraqi people under Saddam and, more or less explicitly, saw parallels to its own fate in times of communism and most of the Nazi occupation when no outside military deliverence was offered despite the Polish people's hope to the contrary.

The Poles' emotional reaction to the attacks led the U.S. Ambassador to write a thank-you letter, which was published on the front page of the Sept. 22-23 issue of *Gazeta Wyborcza*. Poland's support for the United States also played a role in President Bush's invitation to President Aleksander Kwaśniewski to visit the United States in mid-July, which marked the second state visit during George W. Bush's presidency. Naturally, President Bush had his political and economic agenda, which included gaining the support of a million Polish Americans living in Michigan, where he lost marginally to Gore in 2000, and exerting pressure on Poland to buy F-16 fighter planes.

THE AFTERMATH

Poland did buy America's F-16 planes and it provided the fourth biggest contingent of soldiers in Iraq, after America, Britain, and Australia. The country also administered one of Iraq's occupation zones, although the official status of the Polish military was that of a stabilizing not an occupational force. The support for joining the United States in ridding Iraq of Saddam Hussein was almost unanimous, at least among the biggest political parties and the president. With every month and every Polish casualty, the support diminished, but Polish troops have not been withdrawn and are expected to stay in Iraq at least until the end of 2007 despite public sentiment to the contrary.

The special relationship between Poland and the United States became somewhat of a problem when the country was negotiating rules of accession with the EU and later the budget (Matera & Matera 2005). Accusations of Poland acting as America's "Trojan horse" emerged in Western European press, particularly in France. The Polish-EU relationship suffered a clear setback.

The Polish sentiment has always been that those accusations are unbased and untrue — Poland does not plan to act against the EU, but it also does not wish to make a choice between having a close relationship with the United States and with the EU (like choosing between your mother and your father, some commentators would say, half-jokingly). The fact is that the Polish-American relationship is extremely close, and Poland remains one of the least critical European allies of the United States and President Bush. The coverage of 9/11 by the Polish media attested to that.

At the same time, criticism of current U.S. policy in Iraq is clearly on the increase and ever more pronounced in elite Polish media discourse. While some commentators call the policies of the leading states of Western Europe "infantile and cynical" and detect "the clear feeling of Schadenfreude characteristic of their political elites" (Bolechóów, p. 81), a growing number of publications say the war in Iraq is a failure. Brigadier General Marek Ojrzanowski — commander of the 12th Mechanised Brigade, CO of 1 BCT/MND CS in 2003 in Iraq — claims in 2005 that "at the moment, it is difficult to resist the impression of total political chaos in the conflict in Iraq" (p. 61). He goes on to say: "Assessing whether the price we pay and costs that we bear for our involvement in Iraq is worth the results achieved constitutes a real challenge for the politicians who make the decisions" (p. 61). Geremek elegantly summarizes the transformation 9/11 and its aftermath has had on Poland and its relationship with the United States.

> The essentially moral view of the Iraq war has not changed; Poles are no fans of dictatorship and appreciate the American determination to support fundamental Western values. But at the same time, more and more Poles want their soldiers back home. The Iraq war has also undermined the image of America as a competent and effective global superpower. Public discourse in Poland has slowly begun to rethink fundamental geostrategic issues, including the legitimacy and effectiveness of American unilaterism, and the challenges posed by international terrorism (p. 55).

REFERENCES

Bolechów, B. (2005). 9/11 Today. *The Polish Foreign Affairs Digest*, Vol. 5, No. 4 (17), 77-93.

Geremek, B. (2006, Summer). Among Friends. *The American Interest*, Vol. I, No. 4, 53-56.

Matera, P., Matera, R. (2005). Links and Obstacles in Transatlantic Relations after 9/11. In T. Płudowski (Ed.), *American Politics, Media, and Elections* (pp. 161-179). Warsaw: Collegium Civitas Press & Toruń: Wydawnictwo Adam Marszałek.

Michnik, A. (2001, September 12). Tak się zaczyna XXI wiek. *Gazeta Wyborcza*.

Ojrzanowski, M. (2005). Iraq — an Unfullfilled Challenge? *The Polish Foreign Affairs Digest*, Vol. 5, No. 1 (14), 51-61.

Wszyscy jesteśmy Nowojorczykami. (2001, September 14). *Gazeta Wyborcza*.

Chapter 9

GLOBAL NEWS, LOCAL VIEWS: SLOVENE MEDIA REPORTING OF 9/11

Ksenija H. Vidmar & Denis Mancevič[1]

During the past two decades, many scholars argue that media around the world have become more monopolized (Bagdikian, 1990; Lee & Solomon, 1990; MacBride & Roach, 2000). The interrelatedness of financial interest and news-making which this new media monopoly exhibits produces a growing concern over the quality of the information we get. "The truth of the matter is that financial interests play a major role in determining what we see," Lee and Solomon write (p. 59). Furthermore, corporate-controlled information has made the prospect of being able to rely on a variety of sources dim in the global contexts as well. The concentration of news media within a narrowing field of global news corporations has limited access to world events, and the selection of "news-worthy" information or production of "news on demand" (Diamond, 1991) has channeled the interpretive lenses for local audiences.

As the center of media monopoly has been most often located in the West, and the United States in particular, it is rightfully assumed that the meanings that get produced in the U.S.-based news corporations are globally shared, whereas global audiences' views become "Americanized." This can certainly be argued on the case of reporting on 9/11, which, through a handful of news and press agencies providing the main images and narratives, structured the global ways of seeing the event. In our paper, we track this global flow of news on the 9/11 as it was accommodated by the Slovene news media.

We also want to turn lenses and ask how, through globally pre-selected ways of seeing, Slovene news media contributed to the formation of the local views on the 9/11. Postcolonial theories of globalization, cultural studies and audience research have questioned a strictly one-dimensional relationship between global media and local audiences and provided new ways of understanding the entwinement of global and local cultures. Instead of seeing globalization as "simply an ideological mask for Americanization or Westernization" (Waters, 2001, p. 223), which forges hegemonic forms of consciousness, scholars have argued for a more complex and dynamic understanding of the relationship between the global and the local.

A global product does not "simply slip[s] into some local context," where it is superficially consumed, Daniel Miller has argued. On the contrary, it can partake in the "refinement of the concept" of local culture (Miller, 1992, pp. 179, 180). Arjun Appadurai also writes that the global flow of media imagery operates in disjunction with different realities (or scapes, as he calls them), which "can and do get disaggregated into complex set of metaphors [...] as they help to constitute narratives of the 'other' and proto-narratives of possible lives, fantasies which could become prolegomena to the desire for acquisition and movement" (Appadurai, 1990: 299).

In this chapter, we want to point to just such a desire that was articulated by the Slovene news media and arrived from the restructuring of the local cultural and political field. The 9/11 attacks were a tragic story that was brought to Slovene audiences in a globally shared way. By providing visual and narrative framing of the attack, the global coverage pre-defined the meaning of the tragedy. A comparative look at three major news media in Slovenia — public television *TVS*, the national daily *Delo* and weekly magazine *Mladina* — also uncovers discrepancies in articulating local meanings of the 9/11. In the paper, we reconstruct the three respective stories that the selected media constructed for the Slovene public and provide an account for the different views at the events on the 9/11 and aftermath.

METHOD AND CONCEPTUAL ANALYSIS

Our analysis is based on collecting a sample of articles and visual materials from the 9/11 attacks to the U.S. coalition's attack of Afghanistan on Oct. 7. Our sample included reports from the TVS major news bulletin, broadcast daily at 7:30 p.m. and a special presented on the day of the attack; a special edition of *Delo;* and articles, comments and opinions as well as reprints from other media published between the same period in *World* and *Opinion* sections of the daily (a total of 137 written articles and 118 items of visual materials). Finally, we read four issues of weekly *Mladina*, which had 23 articles and 13 visual materials.

Our main conceptual tool has been the "thematic analysis" described by Philo and Berry (2004). The main assumption on which the thematic analysis is based is that in "any contentious area there will be competing ways of describing events and their history" (p. 95). In this ideological struggle for meaning, mass media play an important role, most notably by providing the "explanatory themes" that frame an area of coverage. We closely followed the explanatory themes as they were articulated in articles, main headlines and subtitles. We also looked at the visual framing of the 9/11, which added an analytic angle that often reinforced but also contested the main narrative "thematic" findings.

Taken together, the explanatory themes in the reporting on the 9/11 and the thematic differences among the three Slovene news media provide distinct local interpretive views. Embedded in local political and ideological struggles, the three views add to and contest the meaning of the 9/11 as constructed by the global news.

TVS: APOCALYPTIC DIMENSIONS

The first news medium to report 9/11 was *TVS*, a national public broadcasting service. TVS was given public service status by a law passed in parliament in 1994. Its rating share in prime time scores around 30 percent. In the main news bulletin at 7 p.m., *TVS* competes for the audiences with the commercial, American-owned Pop TV. On the second day of reporting of 9/11, *TVS* proudly displayed charts which showed it gaining an increase in viewers.

TVS first reported the attacks on the "Today" program. The reporter in studio began with the words: "The United States of America has been attacked. The consequences of the carefully planned terrorist attacks are horrible." After the "Today" program, *TVS* interrupted its regular programming and joined the international reporting. Two commentators in the studio announced that they were "joining various visual sources" as they tried to provide an account of what was happening. *CNN* and *Euronews* proved to be the main sources of information. On the very same day of the attacks, the theme of the terrorist attack and the most likely figure of Osama bin Laden responsible for it were introduced. *TVS* broadcast U.S. President George W. Bush's speech and U.K. Prime Minister Tony Blair's instant reiteration of the theme of "terrorism as the new evil of our world." Visually, the station included images from Manhattan and Pentagon on the one hand and from the streets of Lebanon on the other. In the former, witnesses' narratives testified of horror and trauma; in the latter, the global screens were filled with celebration and joy.

As mentioned earlier, global sources were used as a background stage through which the two commentators developed their own "reading" of the 9/11. Many themes appeared and changed as new information arrived. They included worldwide solidarity with the United States; well-coordinated and organized nature of the attacks; and hints that the American security and intelligence were unable to foresee the attacks. An instant retaliatory action by the United States was forecast ("quite possibly already tonight!") whereas visual sources continued to display testimonies of horror by the people near the collapsing towers.

Most importantly, both commentators repeatedly expressed the view that the epochal nature of the attacks would dramatically alter the course of world history. We define this view as the apocalyptic view. Writing of the apocalyptic war, John R. Hall has defined the notion of the apocalyptic as socially constructed. "In the most extreme cases, the established social order itself comes to define its struggle in apocalyptic terms, or acts in ways that lead others to believe that it has joined such a struggle" (Hall, 2004, p. 2) Various parties can lay claim to unleashing or defining an apocalyptic mission. By dramatizing the nature of the action, mass media, being part of the established social order, interactively reinforced the apocalyptic meanings. "This is a terrorist attack without a precedent in world history," the commentator said. By placing the attacks in a broader historical perspective, the commentator reiterated the theme that "the world would never look the same" — a theme frequently recycled in mass media since 9/11. The same commentator also pointed to the irony of the date, which he read as the "evidence that they [the attackers] don't respect any civilized norms."

The theme of the epochal, historically dramatic dimension of the attacks, and the irony of the date signifying the world peace in the *TVS* special report subtly introduced the theme of radical discontinuity and difference. The discord concerned the understanding of the moral order and the notions of peace and democracy. The interpretation of the symbolic exploitation of the 9/11 to send across the globe a terrorist message projected a vision of the worlds before and after the attack. In this view, the two worlds were radically different and changed. Although the perception of the abrupt cut into the flow of history was no doubt a product of the commentator's disbelief and emotional terror experienced by the scope of the tragedy, it nonetheless inscribed a vision of a harmonious past that was taken away by the terrorists. This vision, as we will see later, was radically questioned in *Mladina*. Although *TVS* included a report by a journalist who argued that the United States played a role in the making of the Osama bin Laden as a terrorist figure, the station never made an attempt to revisit its starting position. Instead, taken by the flow of the subsequent events, the notion of the radical break in world history was silently adopted and visually reinforced in an endless series of replay of the images of the Twin Towers hit by the planes (16 times during the first two days of reporting, and 23 times in the four-week period).

In its early days of reporting, TVS introduced the themes of "rapid retaliation acts" by the United States. In its main news, TVS also provided a comparative historical view by refreshing the memory with past and more recent foreign and domestic terrorist attacks against the United States. The global broadcasting of the speeches of President Bush and U.S. Secretary of State Colin L. Powell, as well as Tony Blair, framed the narrative of the war of "good versus evil," in which the "good" signified the United States and the West. While the theme was well pre-tuned by the leaders of the coalition against terrorism, local selection of the news reinforced the division, for instance, by broadcasting the speech of Slovene Foreign Minister Dimitrij Rupel, who said that "terrorism is the No. 1 enemy of this world and this civilization."

The selective inclusion/exclusion of reports from home and around the world also contested the simplified divisions. *TVS* broadcast Sheik Jasin said that "America is harvesting the injustice and corruption which it itself sowed." The Slovene foreign correspondent spoke of the "America that is wounded but not humiliated," embarking on Bush's ideological discourse of unity and strength. The news also presented local views of people on the streets of the capitol of Ljubljana, who made clear distinctions between "American people" and the "American politics." Whereas many found compassion for the former, the later was also blamed for the tragedy. "Those who did evil will have to feel it on themselves" was one's person commentary.

As already stated, the attacks on the 9/11 were given the connotations of apocalyptic change of history. The change signified a new map of divisions and alignments in which Slovene public and political discourses parcelled their own local ideological space. For instance, when NATO Secretary General George Robertson spoke of the attack as an act directed "against the whole civilized world," the Slovene foreign minister joined the chorus by adding his own voice of identification with the "civilized": "Terrorism, or, if you want, barbarism, is the worst threat to civilization. Slovenia belongs to the block of the civilized states." The announcement can be seen as part of diplomatic discourse rooted in a different context. Namely, on occasion of talking to the candidates for the membership in NATO, George Robertson some time later spoke of the Afghanistan as a "black hole" — a pocket in the geo-political map of the world which clearly lacked a stable state structure. "That is why," he continued, "NATO is interested in South — East Europe, because it doesn't want black holes to emerge at its front door." In this respect, identifying with the "civilized" by the Slovene foreign minister may have been a public appeal to be recognized in and by the imagined and real community of the states which decided on the fate of the Slovenia and other candidate states. The minister's pointing of the terrorist attack as "an attack against normalcy, against normal foreign politics" was a rhetoric tautology; it also subtly inscribed the desire that Slovenia was worthy of such recognition.

But this self-proclaimed image of the "civilized" produced its own fractures of meaning. Later, *TVS* reported on Italian media mogul and Prime Minister Silvio Berlusconi's problematic statement which produced resentment throughout Europe and Islamic world: "We have to be aware of the power of our civilization," he said and warned against paralleling "our" civilization with the Islamic ("ours" being committed to freedom and love for the other). Berslusconi's view contested the notion of the civilized world, making it a tradeable category prone to various ideological appropriations. *TVS* included the response by president Milan Kučan, who in a radio interview added his own understanding of the "civilized" as deployed in public discourse and world politics. "With a public person, politician, words leave mouth and become public property. Interpretations vary. My stand on this is that this cannot be about the war of civilizations, war of cultures."

The attacks on the 9/11 and the consequent course of events were an exploitable terrain that could be ascribed different meanings and invested with different political stakes. Given the alternative views presented by two leading Slovene politicians, it can be argued that *TVS* reflected a splitting of the Slovene political body in the field of the international politics. Embarking on the epochal discourse of discontinuity, it also helped to frame the local public view and structure the alternative outcomes of two politics of identification. Finally, by combining the local political struggles with the visual replay of the attack, it was undertaking its own little war — one for the audiences. In this war, as it will become clear from a comparative view presented below, Slovene news media added local tones to the construction of the global narrative of the 9/11.

THE DAILY *D*ELO: A EUROPEAN VIEW

Delo is one of the three major Slovene dailies (together with *Dnevnik* and *Večer*), but because of its specific "national" character, reflected in six different regional editions, maintains the top position. Its latest main shareholder since the daily was privatized in 1991 has been brewery company Pivovarna Laško (25%), although the state remains present indirectly (20%).

With the circulation figures of 80,000 to 90,000, *Delo* remains the nation's leading newspaper and has served as both a source of information as well as a forum for various political and intellectual debates. This role proved vital in the context of reporting on the events of 9/11 as well.[2]

Looking at *Delo*'s representation of 9/11, one can hardly identify a single line of editorial politics that would be determinant of the ways the newspaper framed its reporting. Instead, a cacophony of views can be found which competed for the primacy of interpretation and none prevailed. More importantly, the interpretative nuances were articulated in a number of layers. Most notably, though, a sharp contrast could be found between the front and the inside pages. Similarly, antagonistic was the relationship between the main headlines and the photographs on the one side, and the commentaries and opinions on the other. Finally, while the headlines, photographs and commentaries competed for the dominant meaning of the 9/11, the political caricatures (a permanent feature of *Delo*)[3] contested all three of them and added another layer of interpretation.

Throughout the period of our analysis, the front pages displayed an image of 9/11 that made the attack and the consequent actions taken by the United States and/or the international community intrinsically linked and "logical." On the first days after the attack, the reports focused on the tragedy itself and the shock experienced by the Americans. However, a special edition published on the Sept. 12 outlined a map of representation that would define the governing structure of reporting. After summing up the chronology of the attacks, the report noted the irony of the date proclaimed by the UN as a day of world truce and nonviolence. Although the report dealt primarily with the tragedy and the U.S. administration composing its course of action, the picture included Osama bin Laden on the front page, beside the Twin Towers image. The visual-narrative display of the front page suggested that the main interpretative frame to the 9/11 will unfold in identifying the person responsible for the attack, finding and punishing him accordingly and, most importantly, subordinating the terms and conditions of the international politics to that mission. Once the chain of causation was established as inherently consistent and self-evident, the subsequent reports — which focused on the preparations of the U.S. military forces to attack Afghanistan as well as to discipline the countries that did not comply — seemed "expected" and "common sense."

The mission involved many aspects that, as displayed on the front pages, created new definitions of security, the legal frames of action, human rights and democracy, war, crime and terrorism. Following international and U.S domestic politics, the reports informed about the preparations of the international community to face the new "evil," the actions taken by NATO to secure the prompt support for the United States, and the changing landscape of the U.S. domestic terrains of freedom and privacy. In his article "Shoot Down the Passenger Planes," *Delo*'s foreign correspondent wrote of the slippery grounds for granting the U.S. Army the right to take down any suspicious civilian plane and the psychological effects the increasingly tightened belt over the basic principles of democracy and human rights were introduced to the American people. In other reports, however, *Delo* referred to terrorism as the "invisible enemy" and underlined the secrecy of measurements that were required to face it. This suggested a subtle agreement with the U.S. administration's redefining of the boundaries of civic liberties and citizens' rights.

As the time progressed and moved away from the tragic events of the 9/11, the focus in *Delo*'s reporting shifted toward anticipations of the war. Reports switched grounds between debating the role and the constitution of the anti-terrorist coalition and projecting the humanitarian crisis of unseen proportions. Appeals to reason and abandoning the desire to revenge were emphasized on the front page as well as inside the newspaper, most notably when the Pope made appeal to Western leaders not to be misled by the terrorist act. However, the headlines and photographs embarked on militaristic discourse. This included the use of "loaded language" in headlines (Lee and Solomon, 1990) such as "Declaration of War against Terrorists!" (13.09.2001), "The Empire will Strike Back" (13.09.2001), "The World Announces the War against Terrorism" (14.09.2001), "Bin Laden Alive or Dead" (19.09.2001), "Strenghtening of Coalition against Terrorism" (26.09.2001) "Global War Against Terrorism," "Terror United Former Enemies" (6.10.2001), and "Evidence Collected, the Attack Outlined" (3.10.2001). The newspaper also contained reports of U.S. army moves whereas visual and narrative exhibitions of its power preset a ground for anticipation of a grand spectacle. Given the quest for the reader's attention, the visual-narrative power of this spectacle made any critical appeals to abstain from the U.S. retaliation seem irrelevant.

The militant and ideologically laden front-page use of language was unreflected by the daily and deployed instead to maintain the dramatic level after the events on the 9/11 began to fade away. In contrast, the inside stories introduced analytic approaches that questioned the seemingly unproblematic course of events afterwards. Most notably, the international politics page gave room to other coalitions emerging in response to the U.S. one, such as the Arab coalition, and questioned the legal frameworks for the definitions of "war on terrorism ("Not the War and not the Crime," 29.9.2001:4). Articles illuminated the political and economical pre-texts that led to ideologically divided views of terrorism and Osama bin Laden (also characterized as an "Islamic Robin Hood"), including those who opposed the unjust divisions of global wealth and corporate exploitation (27.9.2001:4). The U.S. controversial role in "globalizing its national criminal law" (29.9.2001:4) was exposed, whereas the attempts to ascribe terrorism a definition that would be obligatory "for Uzbekistan, Mexico, the United States, Russia, Indonesia, Serbia, Israel, Sudan, Turkey, [...] intelligence and paramilitary units" (3.10.2001:1) were underlined.

Finally, *Delo*'s writer Mojca Drčar Murko wrote of the involvement of the West in the global trafficking with terror, a point that was not raised elsewhere. "Religious fanatics joined the dialogue offered by the secularized West via the money ... Behind the goal — whatever that might be — is a successful professional ... Does it come as a surprise that the people who had acquired a huge personal wealth now have been privatizing the war? ... Why these days, we don't hear much about the actions against dealers with weapons who are the core of the 'civilization of the good'?" (27.9.2001:5)

On the inside pages, *Delo*'s editorial politics included a presentation of views opposing the simplified narratives coming from the U.S. political leadership. The newspaper quoted Dominique Moisi, a director of the French Institute for the International Relations, warning against the U.S. isolationism in leading the world politics (27.9.2001:4). Similarly, a reprint of a *Le Monde* article about mass panic in the United States and a subsequent increase in the sale of gas masks also showed that the French were distancing themselves from the United States. The article said the French stayed "cool-headed" (29.9.2001:5). In another context, a foreign correspondent wrote of Checks behaving as "spiritual vassals" of the United States (29.9.2001:4); of British news media accelerating the support for the war by presenting images of poverty and hunger from Afghanistan and the unpopularity of the Taliban regime (28.9.2001:4); and of Italy, which, by joining the U.S. coalition, was on the brink of facing the same terrorist threat as its ally (6.10.2001:4).

Looking at the jigsaw puzzle of views, one could identify an emerging shared editorial politics of representation that we call the "European view": a political point of view inscribing both closeness and distance. The view was not one-dimensional and united but rather fractured and portioned in blocks of political identifications. Moreover, it was articulated and mobilized by the body Europe dividing within itself. Namely, *Delo* introduced two European views, the one aligned with the coalition led by the United States (Britain, Italy, Spain) and the other concerning the resisting, alternative body of European coalition (France, Germany). Combined with the front-page space given to the construction of the narrative in which the United States was given the prime voice, the editorial politics produced a contradictory meaning, divided between identification and distance; alignment and departure; reiteration and confrontation. Organized through the spatial structuring of the daily, the antagonistic politics of identification shifted between the front-page display of consent — "The Evidence Collected, the Attack Outlined" (3.10.2001:1) and "All the Roads Lead to Osama bin Laden," (4.10.2001:1) "Stability Against Terrorism" (6.10.2001:1) — and the inside-pages resistances: "How Much Solidarity with the United States Is Enough" (18.09.2001), "America Begins War for the Soviet Succession" (21.09.2001), "The Terrorists Want Their Share of Pie, too" (17.09.2001), and "When Fear Rules the World" (2.10.2001:1). In this contest of positions, both representations of 9/11 and the "European view" evolved as terrains of conflicts shot through with local political histories and ideological struggles.

The European view on which the daily relied was contaminated with its own political unconscious. Thus, Moisi argued against the use of the term the "crusade." "I believe that there are two significant differences between the Americans and the Europeans. The first one concerns the semantics. The Europeans feel uncomfortable at the religious culture of the Americans and the word 'crusade' for them sounds unnatural." When stating the reasons behind the discomfort, interestingly, he mentioned a clear separation of state and church and strong Muslim communities in Europe — but not the historical dominion of the "crusade" embedded in the European Christian past. The painful legacy, however, was pointed out by a high Slovene representative of the Roman Catholic Church, who reminded readers that "within Christianity there is still alive a memory of a painful historical experience of the crusade" (28.9.2001:5).

A *Der Standard* article reprinted by *Delo* went further, pointing out the ideological stakes involved in the Roman Catholic Church objections to using the historically burdened narratives of division between the two religious communities. The Pope's respect for Islam, pronounced in his public speech, which differentiated between the "authentic," "tolerant" Islam vs. the Muslim terrorists was "in fact so far the strongest expression of the civilization clash between the Roman Christianity and Islam." The clash, in the author's view, concerned the struggle over which side will re-gain the hegemony over moral values. Truly, Christianity envies the power of the Islam to rule over the masses, the power which is based on the intermingling together of the religion and the politics. This, the article sums up, is precisely the repressed desire of the Roman Catholic Church — namely, to regain its role in the politics and to take away from Islam the theme of "the rotten West" — which the Church knows all too well itself.

The European view, as articulated both in Europe and Slovenia, was a contested terrain of claiming the interpretive power over the past and present. By rejecting the notion of the "crusade," the European political and Catholic elites alike competed to redraw the historical memory as well as to open up on the refashioned map of public remembrance a new space of cultural hegemony for themselves. The ideological stakes were, as the *Der Standard* article suggested, high while the historical moment ripe with opportunities to re-colonize terrains of moral emptiness left by the 9/11. It was the Western egocentrism, the mufti of the Islamic community in Slovenia argued, which invented the West-East divide in the past and has resisted giving it up in the present. "There was 8 thousand Muslims killed in two days and one night in Bosnia and Herzegovina, yet nobody claimed that the Christians were criminals" (2.10.2001:2). In contrast, by differentiating the "authentic" from "terrorist," as *Der Standard* wrote, Muslims, the Pope and the Roman Catholic Church did precisely that. The best way to discredit Islam as a whole is indeed by rejecting insinuations that you yourself produce. "It goes like this: Well, the fact that Islam makes terrorists is not entirely true."

The representatives of the Roman Catholic Church in Slovenia reproduced a cultural divide in discourse and actions. When objecting to the term of the "crusade" and reviving the painful memory of the crusade in Europe, the above-quoted high representative of the Church in Slovenia went on to remind readers of the divide which followed as a consequence of the "crusade wars which went *awry"* ((28.9.2001:5; our emphasis). By a strange slippage, the project of the Catholic crusade itself appeared nonproblematic; the difficulties concerned its execution. In this light, the Roman Catholic Church's public mass for the New York Fire Brigades, which took place in Slovenia in the month of the attack, may be seen as a historic opportunity for the Church to set it right this time. Wanting its own piece of cake, however, Slovene sociologist Marjan Smrke wrote, the Roman Catholic Church reiterated the divide, offering once more the "Christianity as the signifier of the West" (2.10.2001:4).

The debates which were articulated on the pages of *Delo* illuminate ideological struggles in European and Slovene political and public spheres. Indeed, 9/11 not only shook the world politics and the boundaries of the mission to institute the "new world order" that was led by the United States; in Europe it also cut open the local body politics as well as unleashed ideological battles for the historical consciousness. The terms of "crusade" and the "clash of civilizations" were not simply dismissed as improper and derogatory — they provided potent grounds for the articulation of cultural distances and difference. By assuming a different, culturally and historically responsible deployment of semantics, Europe once again emerged in the image of a continent invested with power and agency, an image so deeply needed in times of Europe's own instable processes of integration and transformation. By joining the "European view," *Delo* reflected and reproduced the European ideology of political difference *qua* cultural distance. By marrying this ideology with the U.S. led coalition, however, it also accommodated Slovene political desires to secretly occupy both and, when suited, pragmatically switch between the two positions.

WEEKLY MLADINA: OPPOSITIONAL VIEWS

Mladina is one of the most influential political weekly magazines with a strong legacy of an alternative and critical publication. The magazine played a most vital historical role in the 1980s, when it opened up a space to the proponents of the civil society movements. With its commitment to independent and investigative journalism, it contributed to democratization and pluralization of the society and helped stimulate processes for political change. In its post-socialist, transition era, *Mladina* has continued its legacy of an alternative voice that has remained critical of the official politics and the emerging, post-socialist ideologies. Its circulation is about 20,000.

The oppositional political capital that has been built by the magazine over the past few decades has reflected in the editorial politics covering the 9/11 tragedy. In contrast to official political discourse and the governing "war on terrorism" theme, frequently uncritically recycled by the national media, *Mladina*'s reporting was marked by skepticism, analytic reflexivity and critical examinations of the *pre*-texts as well as *con*texts of the September attacks. The radical distance from the "official truth," distributed by global media (e.g, CNN), was inscribed in visual materials which — displayed on the cover page or inserted inside the magazine — ridiculed and parodied the U.S. government and its interpretive version of the event. The criticism, however, was most notably articulated by the ways the magazine chose to frame the tragic event.

In the analysis, three main thematic frames emerge which gave final shape to the magazine's politics of representing 9/11: terrorism as the product of global capitalism and the U.S. political domination in particular; the media's role in the production of the culture of fear; the constructedness of the enemy and the war of the civilizations paradigm. In their combined effect, the three frames deconstructed and reconstructed the global media narratives about 9/11 and shook the meaning of the event as it had emerged from the mainstream political and media discourse.

In its first issue published after the attack, *Mladina* already accentuated the interconnectedness of the event and the political and economic effects of globalization. The United States was exposed as the prime force behind globalization, but portrayed as incapable of reflecting its own involvement in the process. "The parole, 'We all are America — we all are globalization,' has faced a brutal criticism," Marcel Štefančič, Jr. wrote in his article (17.09.2001:19). The editorial in the same issue also emphasized the state of collective disbelief shared by Americans, and their inability to see the event as a statement of hate directed toward them. "How deep must be the hatred against 'America' […] Nobody in the U.S. has asked this question," the editorial asked on the first page of the magazine (17.09.2001: 2). Later on in the same issue in a commentary, Jurij Gustinčič similarly suggested that the success of the U.S. counter-action would depend on the United States and its capacity to abandon its "superior loneliness" (17.9.2001:25). The magazine expressed compassion with the families of the victims, but also underlined the need for the America to come to terms with the effects of its own politics. "The U.S., who had seen itself so far as an island free of violence and who had been observing the violence from a safe distance over the TV set, is now directly involved."

The magazine's journalists and commentators both pointed out the inter-relatedness of the U.S. foreign politics and the rise of terrorism embodied in the figure of Osama bin Laden. The link was the result of the U.S. direct involvement: "Afghanistan refugees as well as Arab volunteers, such as Osama bin Laden, had been financed, armed, trained and ideologically indoctrinated [by the U.S.], specifically — *they were reborn into guerilla, militant, fanatic, suicidal Islamic fundamentalist* (17.9.2001:20; italics original). The link was mediated by political, economic and military interests enveloped in a longer history of domination. The Twin Towers "represented the centre of virtual capitalism," according to Slavoj iek (24.9.2001:36). "America is in war," Marcel Štefančič, Jr. echoed him in an earlier issue. "[I]t has been in war since 1953 when it first directed putsch in Iran" (17.09.2001:20).

Many authors exposed the agonizing effects of global capitalism that have produced conditions for the upsurge of militarism and fundamentalisms of all sorts. They also pointed to the paradox that the violent models of resistance originated in the militant culture of the West. The symbolic maps of violence — including the spectacular targeting of the most vital and representative institutions and monuments of the country — have been culturally transmitted by global media and, by a stroke of irony, taken up by the deprived and oppressed worldwide. Terrorism has been a form of resistance by the oppressed and exploited by those who, culturally disenfranchised, "contemplate their condition most easily by a jigsaw puzzle of ideological stereotypes. This collage is produced in the U.S. by Hollywood and mass media which had played out scenarios of terrorist attacks prior to the actual ones." The same author went on to argue that "because the attentats are only a dreary effect of the ruling ideology, it is not surprising that the system recognized them instantly: they realized their formulae."

The media production and anticipation of terror has had an obscure effect on American psyche as well. The unintended, reciprocal effect of mass media construction of reality, caught between spectacle and horror, virtuality and historicity, has produced a condition in which people have lost a sense for the actual and the real. The explosion of reality TV and the culture of testing the borders of surviving more generally have displaced the human capacity to recognize the actual event as such. In contrast to Orson Welles' "War of the Worlds" radio scam from the early twentieth century, which brought out thousands on the street in panic, the early twentieth first century has experienced a different phenomenon altogether: while there was all the reason for the panic unfolding on the street, mass media did not transmit it because they did not believe it. "They are demolishing you, and you don't see it," Štefančič, Jr. wrote. "They did not see it. CNN did not even twitch. They did not grasp the scope. The commentators on CNN continued to calmly behave as if it were a car accident" (17.9.2001:19).

Last but not least, *Mladina* put a firm question mark on the seemingly consensual division between "us" and "them," between the "democratic," "civilized" and the "totalitarian," "barbarian" world. Instead, the magazine engaged in deconstructing the "making of the terrorist" and the notion of the war of civilizations. It outlined many aspects that were problematic in both respects which can be summed up in three groups: the implied cultural racism of the Huntingtonian paradigm; the transmission of the cultural racism into the political discourse; and the inability of local politics *and* media to distance itself from this version of "truth."

The thesis that the attacks on 9/11 and the reactions to them unfolded along the dividing line between two civilizations and deepened the cultural gap in the world, according to *Mladina*'s writers, carried ideologically burdened visions of supremacy and cultural differentiation that replaced earlier forms of racist politics and imagination. The differentiation had nothing to do with culture but involved political differences in conceptualizing the state, Rastko Močnik argued. The U.S invented its own version of state violence, privatized and politicized, with which it has operated successfully on the domestic (death penalty) and foreign terrains (Cuba, Iraq, Afghanistan). He continued: "With the kind of a disciplining violence ... sooner or later it [U.S.] has to find support in a Messianic ideology, begin a war under the slogan of "clash of civilizations." In another article, Slavoj i ek reiterated the problem of accepting the Huntington's theme. The clash of civilizations thesis needs to be categorically rejected, he wrote. What we witness are, rather, "clashes WITHIN civilizations" that concern social and political conditions and their consequences for the world order and human rights. In fact, he went on, looking at the history of Islam unveils a tolerance towards other religions that overpasses the attitudes conveyed by Christianity (24.09.2001:37). To enhance the point of ideologically driven project to construct the Other as different and alien, *Mladina* published an interview with anthropologist Jack Goody who discussed the meeting points between Protestantism and talibanism as well as articles which questioned the notion of a radically unbridgeable gap between two religious traditions. "Let's not forget that it was with the mediation of Islam that Europe came to meet its ancient roots in Greece," i ek (24.09.2001:37) wrote. By returning us to a different historical narrative, the author exposed forces that served the desire to perpetuate the conflict and the ideological attempts to repress stories of past cultural contacts and dialogues.

Mladina's most radical difference from the other two media in terms of representing and constructing the narrative of the 9/11, however, can be located in the magazine's continuous monitoring of the global and domestic media and their ideological service to the official foreign and domestic politics when uncritically recycling the theme of the "clash of civilizations." In *Delo*, we found two articles reflecting the news media reporting but both spoke of an emerging American media "monoculture" (1.10.2001:1) and media censorship (2.10.2001:4). In contrast, *Mladina* took a broader view. Jurij Gustinčič succinctly warned about uncritical adoption and translation of American vocabulary into the non-U.S. media language. The notions such as "crusade" and "revolution" carried different meanings than was the case in European cultural connotations. While "we" defended their vocabulary, "we" accepted it as ours, he wrote. But because the cultural and historical discrepancies in meaning obviously carried consequences for the linguistic construction of social reality, "we" ought to "think carefully before we let them join the media traffic" (15.10.2001: 26).

Whereas Gustinčič's critique of Slovene media was implicit, Rastko Močnik explicitly pointed to the censorship in reporting at work which helped to reproduce cultural racism. He first brought to attention the statement by French prime-minister Lionel Jospin, who rejected the political deployment of simplified divisions between cultures and spoke instead of the "enhancement of responsibility" of every state. Interestingly, whereas media exploited the Huntington's theme, his comment was left out of the reporting. Commenting on the title "The Beginning of the War Between Civilizations," published by daily *Delo*, Močnik further pointed to the journal's "playing of the American tune" with a "tastelessness, worthy of a Court of Honor, and with the precision of a blind-folded adept" (17.09.2001:35). *Mladina*'s editor Jani Sever similarly critiqued Slovene foreign minister and his endorsement of "one truth only," encouraging him publicly to accept some form of openness that he could learn from BBC (24.09.2001:5).

By analyzing other news media reporting and the official political discourse in the broader contexts of political and cultural histories of both West and Islam, *Mladina* complicated the neatness of the "official wisdom." In its editorial politics of representation, the events of the 9/11 were as much unfolding as a site of struggle for the reproduction of ideological, cultural and political dominance of the West as they were a stage to domestic, local national media and politics to construe their own, self-adored vision of a civilized, cultural superiority. It is this latter aspect which can be seen as the major contribution of the weekly *Mladina* as it powerfully illuminates the complicated relationship between, and mutual exploitation of, the global and the local in both news media and daily politics.

CONCLUSION

On Oct. 8, the main headline in *Delo* read: "The U.S. Attacked Afghanistan." The war was long anticipated and — from the moment the news corporations took up the "war on terrorism" theme — pre-staged by the global media. Considering the marching beat of headlines, it felt almost like a relief to finally see it happen — except the relief was not one *from* the spectacle but *of* the spectacle. Both Debordian spectacle and the Baudrillardian ecstasy of communication made their ways to global audiences. Behind this media landscape of fetishization of war and technology, the real suffering of people, both in New York and Afghanistan, was once again re-claimed by the civilized West.

Slovenia partook in the media staging of the war in its own, locally tainted way. A comparative look at three national news media, *TVS*, *Delo* and *Mladina* uncovers multiple and discrepant views that competed for the meaning of the 9/11 and its aftermath in ideologically oppositional views. Each source and its representation of the 9/11 that we looked at were preconditioned by the inherent logic of the medium to which it belonged. *TVS*, thus, relied heavily on dramaturgy of visual replay of the planes hitting the Twin Towers. The technological advantage of the electronic medium to reverse and replay the historic time in the unfolding frame of the present gave the televisual representation the interpretative power to accentuate the tragedy, granting in effect the legitimation for the war.

As a print medium, *Delo* constructed its dramatic layout by juxtaposing headlines with photographs in a way that identified the main "players": the United States, Osama bin Laden, the Afghans, the protesters, various diplomats and politicians. By placing them on the front or inside page, however, the daily also hierarchically ordered each of them, in effect ascribing them different levels of power to define the "truth," or, to use the words of U.S. Secretary of Defense Donald Rumsfeld, to "tell the truth." In this war for truth, the advantage was given to the Western coalition whereas other emerging coalitions, the Arab or the critical "European" were presented as "additional" views, imbedded in the interiority of the daily.

In contrast, in *Mladina* there was no discrepancy between the front page and the reports and/ or commentaries. Moreover, *Mladina* used different sources — not to multiply the editorial views but to strengthen its politics of representation which was based on critical analysis of terminology, media reports and political discourses that were circulating both globally and locally.

Consequently, the emerging narrative of the 9/11 construed by the three Slovene media was ridden with tension and conflict. Both *TVS*'s and *Delo*'s reporting can be described by a shared notion of what we call the "European view." In this view, the solidarity and compassion for the Americans combined with calls for reason and tolerance. The "noble" European pose, adopted by the two media, however, was itself problematic and burdened with its own political and ideological tensions. Most notably, the tensions erupted in the European rejection of the notions of crusade and the clash of civilizations, which was tainted with a difficult memory of Europe's own Christian colonial history. The vocabulary of crusade, deployed by a U.S. official, was not only culturally problematic for the Europe, it also traumatized the continent in a way that suggested a history of unresolved conflicts still lurking underneath its grandiouse discourses of tolerance and multiculturalism.

The Slovene identification with the "European" view was similarly orchestrated by local politics of *remembering* and *belonging*. Two processes running concurrently may be pointed to as they contributed to the formation of the local interpretive view at the 9/11. In 2001, Slovenia was in the waiting line for joining two major communities, the NATO and EU. For the first, the U.S. ruling was of the prime import. For the second, however, the sympathies went to "Europe" and its two pillars, Germany and France. It is, therefore, not surprising that in the two media, *TVS* and *Delo*, which in many ways reflected the daily politics, the United States was given support in military terms. Culturally, however, "we" allied ourselves with the European values and traditions, claiming our own "European" identity. The split map of identification, and the confirmation of the Slovene "European" identity, was evident in favourable reports about the Pope's appeals to Christian values; and in the distancing from the Italian and Spanish government's decision to join Bush's coalition.

When the "Vilinous group" and the Slovene foreign minister, who were waiting for the NATO's door to open for them, gave unconditional support to the United States, *Delo* followed the story with a similar tongue-in-cheek reporting. Whereas in the commentary, *Delo* openly wrote that after 9/11 the United States will measure the candidates for NATO with different measures, depending on their role in the U.S. coalition — which made the Slovene support to the United States questionable on many grounds (5.10.2001:1) — the critical statement was safely dissolved the next day by using the headline "Stability Against Terrorism" (6.10.2001:1).

To conclude, while the global media fed the local ones with selective and censored views at the 9/11 and suggested the main interpretive discourse to be taken up by the local news, the trafficking of information took its own course when hitting the local grounds. Although a seemingly shared view at the tragedy and the need to retaliate can be extrapolated from the two Slovene mainstream media, a closer inspection reveals that similar themes were given different contexts and interpretive tones. In Slovenia, the tones were governed by the local political unconscious. Split between the antagonistic romance with both the United States and Europe, mainstream political and public discourse created an uneasy relationship with 9/11, using it both as a terrain to demonstrate tolerance as well as willingness to look the other way when the local political interests were at stake. In fact, the responses to 9/11 and U.S. reactions uncovered deep internal divisions of the Slovene political body, with the president Kučan taking the "European" side and the foreign minister identifying the country (and himself) with the United States.

Moreover, the joining in the appeal to tolerance was a way of claiming a cultural superiority rather than a firm commitment to spread a new political culture. This proved true retroactively in both Europe and Slovenia. Whereas Europe tightened its tolerance with immigration laws that followed the 9/11, Slovenia added its own version of "European" tolerance with the political and public attempts to prevent the building of Muslim mosque in the capitol of Ljubljana, and the affair of the "erased" in which the state took away citizenship from a large group of people from ex-Yugoslavia. In this regard, global media reporting on the 9/11 was as much a battling field for the definition of shared values of democracy around the globe as it was a spectacular stage for the local political and public elites to portion the field for themselves.

CHAPTER ENDNOTES

[1] The authors want to thank Marjana Grčman for her help in collecting material for the analysis of the *TVS*'s reporting on the 11th September.

[2] Since we wrote this article, the major private owner, Pivovarna Laško, has increased its influence. This is reflected in the change of editors and editorial politics, which has shifted from center to right. Since the law passed in 2005, TVS, too, has come under greater influence of daily politics.

[3] Although worthy an examination of their own, for the purpose of relying on compatible materials we do not include caricatures in our analysis.

REFERENCES

Appadurai, A. (1990). "Disjuncture and Difference in the Global Cultural Economy," in Feathersone, M. (ed.), *Global Culture. Nationalism, Globalization and Modernity,* pp. 295-310. London: Sage.

Bagdikian, B. (1990). *The Media Monopoly,* Boston: Beacon Press.

Diamond, E. (1991). *The Media Show. The Changing Face of the News, 1985-1990.* Boston, Mass.: MIT.

Hall, J. R. (2004). "Apocalypse 9/11" in P. Lucas and T. Robbins (eds.), *New Religious Movements in the Twentieth-First Century: Political and Social Challenges in Global Perspective.* London: Routledge.

Hrvatin, S. B., et al. (2004). *Media Ownership. Impact on Media Independence and Pluralism in Slovenia and Other Post-Socialist European Countries.* Ljubljana: Peace Institute.

Lee, M. A. and Solomon, N. (1990). *Unreliable Sources, A Guide to Detecting Bias in News Media.* Lyle Stuart.

MacBride, S. and Roach, C. (2004). "The New International Information Order," in F. Lechner and J. Boli (eds.), *The Globalization Reader.* Blackwell Publishing, pp. 290-296.

Miller, D. (1992). "The Young and the Restless in Trinidad: A Case of the Local and the Global in Mass Consumption," in R. Silverstone and E. Hirsch (eds.), *Consuming Technologies: Media and Information in Domestic Spaces,* pp. 163-182, London: Verso.

Philo, G. and Berry, M. (2004). *Bad News from Israel.* London: Pluto.

Waters, M. (2001). *Globalization.* London: Routledge.

Chapter 10

SEPTEMBER 11 IN RUSSIAN MEDIA

Dmitry A. Ruschin

The initial Russian media reaction to the attacks on September 11, 2001, was to retransmit pictures and comments from CNN and other U.S. or British TV networks. Television stations in many cities canceled their regular programs and turned to CNN, the BBC or other networks for live coverage. In every major Russian city, the attacks dominated the front pages of newspapers and radio and television broadcasts.

RosBusinessConsulting (RBC), Russia's premier information media company, was one of the first Russian media outlets to report about the terrorist attacks. Throughout the entire day on 9/11, the www.rbc.ru site was one of few resources of Russia's Internet network that was not disrupted by a huge number of users and provided an uninterrupted flow of information about the American tragedy (RosBusinessConsulting, 2006).

Newspapers used their biggest type for headlines: "America Goes To War," "Terror in America," "War on the World," "Attack Against America," "War on America," "Armageddon," "Apocalypse Now," "Chronology of the Attacks," "Doomsday America," and "The Day that Changed the World."

The stories in Russian media covered the human drama, with quotes from witnesses, rescue workers, officials, portraits of victims, profiles of Osama bin Laden, and background pieces on Islam along with opinion and analyses that ranged from warm support of the United States to bitter attacks on its foreign policy. Few of the papers base foreign correspondents in the United States and, by necessity, had to rely heavily on wire services for news and photos.

Several days after the attacks, it was established that the planes had been hijacked by 19 suicide terrorists who had been trained by the Afghanistan-based al-Qaeda terrorist network headed by Osama bin Laden. The United States demanded that the Taliban, then in control of

Afghanistan, hand over bin Laden and his militants. The Taliban refused, and the United States carried out an anti-terrorist operation in Afghanistan. As a result, the Taliban and the largest part of al-Qaeda were eliminated. However, this did not spell the end of al-Qaeda.

According to RosBusinessConsulting (2006), 9/11 was a turning point in the history of the world. The attacks changed the alignment of forces on the planet. Russia's foreign policy turned toward the West sharply. Russian President Vladimir Putin was the first foreign leader to call U.S. President George Bush and offer condolences and support.

Russia played an important role in the anti-terrorist operation against the Taliban. Russia gave the United States access to military bases in Middle Asia, and NATO became the main striking force in the operation in Afghanistan. In response, the United States showed more tolerance to Russia's actions in Chechnya, conceding that Chechen separatists are international terrorists.

After the first days of coverage of the attacks in Manhattan and Washington, the story declined in prominence, but the bombing of Afghanistan and the search for bin Laden attracted new attention. In general, most Russian papers supported the strikes. In Moscow, *Izvestia* reacted to the bombing by reporting that Russia would provide humanitarian aid to Afghanistan together with European and American partners. And a front-page article said the air strikes seem to be more against those in Kabul who shelter bin Laden rather than against the terrorist himself. Overall, the Russian media has been supportive of the American response (Shuster, A., 2001).

REFERENCES

RosBusinessConsulting, (2006). September 11 tragedy: One year later.
Shuster, A. (2001, Fourth Quarter). The World Reacts. *IPI Global Journalist.*

Part II
ASIAN MEDIA

Chapter 11

The 9/11 Terrorist Attacks on America: Media Frames from the Far East

M. Zenaida Sarabia-Panol

T he terrorist attack on the building in New York that has "world" in its name is iconic in more sense than one. The first assault on the U.S. mainland since the War of 1812 and a tragedy of epic proportions, 9/11 deservedly occupied the headlines of the world's mass media. September 11 was a global news event. No story in recent memory has grabbed the attention of the international press the way the attacks did, and media coverage in the Far East was no exception to the rule.

Almost six years since the September tragedy, the "war on terror" is still on the media's agenda. Scholarly attention also has increased as the "war on terror" became a "war of ideas." Since the press reporting of events not only conveys the facts but also shapes perceptions of information received, it makes perfect sense to ask how the September atrocity was portrayed by the world's media.

This paper looks at how the newspapers in Asia covered the events of 9/11. Using content analysis, the study examines the news frames used by selected newspapers in seven Asian countries: China, India, Indonesia, Japan, Malaysia, Pakistan and the Philippines. The countries were chosen to reflect the diversity in the region in terms of the media system, political and economic structure, religion as well as each nation's relationship with the United States.

AGENDA-SETTING AND FRAMING

To explain the need and significance of investigating how the press in these Asian nations reported the American tragedy, it helps to recall the agenda-setting and framing theories of the mass media. Proposed by Walter Lippman in the early years of mass communication research and advanced by McCombs and Shaw in 1972, agenda-setting states that what the media choose to cover and how the information is presented set the agenda for the public. In other words, by selecting what to report, the media is telling us what is important to think about.

Using a national issue, Iyengar and Simon (1993), for instance, drew examples of agenda-setting by correlating the proportion of Persian Gulf War coverage with Gallup Poll rankings of the most important issues. Birkland's (1997) historical research of natural and accidental disaster coverage and relating it with corresponding Congressional and statistical data documented the impact of media reporting on public policy. Similarly, Atwater, Salwen and Anderson (1985) found a relationship between media coverage of environmental problems and the direction of government regulation.

While objectivity is a basic journalistic tenet, the processes through which reporters gather and select information about events lend itself to an assortment of frames that they use to interpret the world. According to Gitlin (1980), newsgathering methods are heavily tilted toward the status quo and tend to reflect the dominant, if not most accessible viewpoints. In a "dog-eat-dog," deadline-ridden work environment, a set of news frames, organizing ideas or themes emerge that "enable journalists to process large amounts of information quickly and package the information for efficient relay to their audiences" (Gitlin, 1980, p. 7). Therefore, this research asks: What sources and treatments were used by the media of selected Asian nations to report the events of 9/11?

Framing analysis as a way of understanding media coverage has evolved during the last 25 years from a cognitive strategy (Goffman, 1974), to distilling themes in news coverage (Entman, 1993), and to understanding possible message effects on audiences (Kahneman and Tversky, 1984). This study adopts Entman's (1993) definition of news frames as "aspects of a perceived reality made more salient in a communication text ... to promote a particular problem definition, causal interpretation, moral evaluation, and/or treatment recommendation" (p. 52). Of particular interest is the treatment of September 11 news stories and editorials by the media of some Asian countries.

Cottle (2002) noted that in "today's differentiated societies ... the extreme threats posed by terrorists aimed at Western governments and civil societies — are as likely to unleash a profusion of differing interpretive and prescriptive responses as to prompt a sense of "national identity." This is all the more so when the geopolitical resonance of the events in question extends beyond national boundaries" (p. 179).

Since the perpetrators of 9/11 came from foreign countries and the magnitude of the attacks "shook" the entire world, the tragedy prompts attention to U.S. foreign policy. Norris (1995) operationalized foreign policy as a nation's friends and enemies. A few studies have found that the state of diplomatic relations between countries affect media coverage (Peh and Melkote, 1991; Semetko and Valkenburg, 2000). In both the 1983 downing of a Korean jetliner by the Soviets and the 1988 shooting of an Iranian passenger plane by the American military; the Soviet Union, considered an enemy, was portrayed as evil while the United States, a friend, was depicted more favorably. The countries chosen for this study represent varying levels of diplomatic association with the United States.

In arguing that 9/11 was "an event of global proportions," Volkmer (2002) wrote that September "possessed the potential not only to create the basis for a new sense of global space, but also to help bring about an enhanced network of communication. Journalism, in this equation, was charged with the responsibility of contributing to the establishment of a worldwide discourse that would be sensitive to the different perspectives arising from local situations across the network society" (p. 236).

OVERVIEW OF SEVEN ASIAN COUNTRIES

Because it is important to explain rather than simply describe trends of world news coverage (Rosengren, 1974), scholars began to investigate the contextual predictors of international press coverage, such as population, trade relations, press freedom, political system, etc. Many of these extrinsic factors are considered in this study.

Several researchers have reported a positive relation between population size and volume of world news coverage (Chang, *et. al.*, 2000; Nnaemeka and Richstad, 1981). The group of countries examined in this study has two of the world's most populous: China and India. It also has the country with the largest Muslim population — Indonesia.

Geographic proximity was found by some studies to influence world news reporting (Adams, 1986; Rosengren, 1997). Two of the nations in our sample are from the eastern region of Asia (China and Japan), three from the southeast (Indonesia, Malaysia and the Philippines) and two from the south (India and Pakistan). Japan is the most urban and has the highest literacy and per capita GNP, the least restrictions on its press, and the highest newspaper circulation per 100 people.

Some political variables such as government system and press freedom were likewise shown to strongly predict international news coverage (Ahern,

1984; Robinson and Sparks, 1976). In terms of political system, one of the countries in the sample is communist with an increasingly capitalist-like economy (China), two are parliamentary (India with a predominantly Hindu population and Japan with Buddhist-Shinto religion); two are presidential (Indonesia and the Philippines which is predominantly Roman Catholic and is faced with a lingering Muslim insurgency in the south and a terrorist group, *Abu Sayyaf*, linked with Al Qaeda); one has a dominant party structure and has a substantial Muslim population (Malaysia) and another an authoritarian government with Islam as the dominant religion (Pakistan). The three Muslim nations in the sample represent the moderate branch of Islam.

China has the most restrictions on news media, followed by Malaysia, Pakistan and Indonesia. The Philippines has one of the freest press in Asia but the country suffered serious blows to press freedom during the Marcos regime and more recently during Estrada's short incumbency.

Trade volume and state of diplomatic relations also determine media coverage (Wu, 2000; Wall, 1997). U.S. relations with sample countries are mostly good with intermittent sore points for some. For example, U.S. diplomatic ties with India and Pakistan have been at times strained because of nuclear armament and the Kashmir issue. Pakistan and China share borders with Iraq and Afghanistan, core nations in the ongoing war on terror and, therefore, have a special interest about how 9/11 was reported.

Trade relations between the United States and China are strong, but overall, diplomatic relations are fragile because of China's human rights record. China also watches with concern any strengthening of U.S. relations with Japan in the same manner India does with Pakistan. A history of rivalry and aggression between the countries are at play.

The Philippines is the United States closest and longest ally. Since the end of World War II, relations with Japan have been friendly as well. Japan remains an important trading partner of the United States. And since India shed its socialist leanings and liberalized its industries, it has become America's vital information technology resource.

America enjoys healthy cooperation from Malaysia and Indonesia as a whole. However, the fight for independence of Indonesia's East Timor and anti-Western views held by Muslims in Malaysia and Indonesia have caused a large measure of unease in U.S. relations every now and then.

PROBLEM AND HYPOTHESES

The study seeks to answer the following questions: 1) How did newspapers of selected Asian countries report the September terrorist attacks? 2) What was the tone of the coverage? 3) What news sources were used?

It also was expected that the tone of coverage will vary with the nature or state of each country's relationship with the United States, the country's political ideology and certain demographic characteristics, such as the presence, influence or size of the Muslim population residing in the country.

METHOD

A content analysis of one English-language daily per country with back issues available on the Web was undertaken over a 19-day period (September 12-30, 2001). The newspapers with their corresponding city of origin are:

> China: *Zhongguo Ribao* or *China Daily* (Beijing) — circ. 150,000
> India: *Telegraph India* (Calcutta) — largest English daily in East India
> Indonesia: *Jakarta Post* (Jakarta) — largest of 3 English dailies
> Japan: *Mainichi Daily News* (Tokyo) — 3rd largest of 5 national papers
> Malaysia: *The New Straits Times* (Kuala Lumpur) — 4th largest of 7
> Pakistan: *Pakistan Press International* — news agency, Karachi
> Philippines: *Philippine Star* (Manila) — largest circulation

Because no English newspaper with back issues archived on the Internet was available for Pakistan, the author used stories obtained from the country's news agency. It was thought that Pakistan, an Islamic country with a common border with Afghanistan would be too important to leave out.

The total sample size is 400 (newspaper items). The dailies had an average of 57 news and opinion/editorial articles on 9/11. The unit of analysis was the entire story or opinion item. All newspaper articles were coded according to the following content categories: tone, news source, and topic or section of newspaper.

Tone was operationally defined as the manner or direction of the story, whether it was negative, positive or neutral. A negative tone means that the story blames the United States for the terrorist attack (for any given reason), the United States deserves to be punished, contains strong and several negative words or critical comments against the United States, its policies, what it stands for, etc. On the other hand, an article was coded as containing a positive tone if it contained a pro-American stance generally sympathetic to the United States or condemned the attack in strong, unequivocal terms. A newspaper item that expresses neither resentment or sympathy or contains a balance view is coded as having a neutral tone.

News source refers to people or organizations that are quoted or to whom information is attributed. News topic means the general subject

Table 11.1
Tone of Coverage in Asian Newspapers
(Percent of Stories)

	Tone of Coverage		
	Positive	Neutral	Negative
China	25.0%	75.0%	0.0%
India	9.0%	41.0%	50.0%
Indonesia	16.4%	43.3%	40.3%
Japan	19.6%	65.6%	14.8%
Malaysia	19.5%	39.0%	41.5%
Pakistan	20.0%	45.0%	35.0%
Philippines	34.4%	52.7%	12.9%

category (i.e. business, national, etc.). Basic descriptive statistics are used to present content analysis findings. To derive news themes, a textual, qualitative analysis was employed.

RESULTS

Table 11.1 gives the percentage of positive stories per country. Predictably, the Philippines had the highest proportion of positive articles (34.4%), followed by China (25%), Pakistan (20%) and Japan (19.6%).

India topped the negative chart, followed by Malaysia and Indonesia. Fully half of India's coverage was negative while 41.5 percent of Malaysia's and 40.3 percent of Indonesia's newspaper reporting was on the negative side.

With 75 percent of its newspaper items giving a balanced account of the events of September 11, China's *Zhongguo Ribao* came out as the most neutral. Japan with 65.6 percent and the Philippines with 52.7 percent occupied the second and third neutral slots. In short, the tone of the coverage generally reflects the status of relations between the United States and each of the countries.

Table 11.2 breaks out the tone of coverage over time. During the first

Table 11.2
Tone of Coverage Over Time
(Percent of Stories)

	Tone of Coverage							
	Positive				Negative			
	9/13-9/15	9/18-9/22	9/23-9/26	9/27-9/29	9/13-9/15	9/18-9/22	9/23-9/26	9/27-9/29
China	30.0%	20.0%	25.0%	0.0%	0.0%	0.0%	0.0%	0.0%
India	22.2%	0.0%	0.0%	11.1%	48.1%	56.5%	40.0%	55.6%
Indonesia	28.6%	11.1%	14.3%	14.3%	35.7%	55.5%	47.6%	14.3%
Japan	11.1%	21.4%	22.2%	14.3%	18.5%	14.3%	11.1%	14.3%
Malaysia	42.0%	0.0%	0.0%	0.0%	37.0%	37.5%	75.0%	57.2%
Pakistan	15.4%	25.0%	0.0%	50.0%	23.1%	33.0%	66.7%	16.7%
Philippines	45.9%	45.0%	18.8%	23.8%	13.5%	5.0%	31.2%	4.8%

three days of the attacks, all newspapers expressed sympathy for the United States and condemned the attacks. But the support began to decline as time passed, with Malaysia showing the most drastic drop, followed by India and Indonesia.

In terms of news sources, all of the newspapers used official sources, particularly national government officers as the top choice with the exception of the Pakistani news agency, which relied more on U.S. government sources (Table 11.3). The level of dependence on official sources ranged from 24.4 percent (India) to 62.5 percent (China). Indonesia, Malaysia and the Philippines had private individuals as their newspapers' second most-used news sources, while India and Pakistan relied on other foreign governments as their second reported news source. Only Malaysia (9.8%) and Pakistan (18.2%) attributed a relatively greater proportion of their stories to other sources, such as religious and local organizations. In fact, in the case of Pakistan, religious and local organizations comprised its second highest news source.

Three (Indonesia, Malaysia and the Philippines) of the seven newspapers treated the atrocities of September 11 as a national news agenda

Table 11.3
News Sources Quoted in Asian Newspapers
(Percent of Sources)

	Sources		
	National Officials	U.S. Government	Other
China	62.5%	9.3%	28.2%
India	24.4%	26.0%	49.6%
Indonesia	25.6%	11.0%	63.4%
Japan	35.1%	29.7%	35.2%
Malaysia	36.6%	9.8%	53.6%
Pakistan	6.8%	27.3%	65.9%
Philippines	30.6%	15.3%	54.1%

while four (China, Japan, Malaysia and Pakistan) relegated it to their international sections. India was the only one that had an equal proportion of its 9/11 stories appearing in *Telegraph India* 's national and international divisions.

Indonesia and the Philippines had significantly higher percentage of editorial or opinion articles compared with the newspapers of the other countries. In fact, op-ed materials in these two countries were the second highest type of newspaper item. All of the countries reported the September tragedy throughout the period studied. All of the papers provided local angles to their 9/11 reporting. News about citizens killed in the attacks and local reactions formed part of the coverage in all countries.

DISCUSSION

In general, the analysis supports the expectation that a newspaper's coverage of 9/11 reflects the nature of the political relationship between the United States and the newspaper's nation. In other words, the more positive the political relations, the more positive the coverage of 9/11. This was particularly the case for the Philippines. However, India and China were partial exceptions to the rule, and a qualitative analysis of the coverage suggests that certain unique features of the country may account for some of the differences in coverage.

Philippines

A democratic, Christian country like the Philippines with a relatively independent, free press and a long history of friendship with the United States reported the event in the most positive light. If the *Philippine Star* did not veer to the positive zone, it stayed neutral. As Table 1 shows, the Philippines had the third highest number of balanced articles.

Although the archipelago is beset by a persistent Muslim insurgency in Mindanao, the militancy of the minority Islamic population ebbs and flows with the government's response. As a result, while the reasons for the insurgency, legitimate or not, are gradually seeping into the mainstream media, the Muslim voice in this predominantly Roman Catholic nation is a small one.

The *Philippine Star* framed the 9/11 attacks as a "crime against humanity." "No cause, no faith justifies such mass murder. No condemnation is strong enough for this cowardly atrocity. Those responsible must be made to pay for their crime against humanity. The civilized world mourns with the American nation, with the victims and their families," the paper's Sept. 13, 2001, editorial stated.

Expressions of "horror, sadness and outrage" over the terrorist bombing and President Gloria Macapagal-Arroyo's support for a U.S.-led international coalition against terrorism found their way into the newspaper's pages. The *Star* also reported possible impact of the attacks on the nation's economy, raids of suspected local terrorist hideouts, and casualties/injuries among Filipino-Americans or Philippine overseas contract workers in New York (estimated at 10,000) and Washington, D.C. (about 4,000).

Because of the significant number of Filipino overseas workers in the Middle East, the *Star* mentioned the reviving of a six-year-old contingency evacuation plan called *Oplan Aguila* in the event of war in that region. On Sept. 26, a *Star* story also reported the suspension of deployment of overseas Filipino workers to Pakistan and Iran.

One other feature that distinguishes the *Star* coverage is the number of first-person accounts of the WTC carnage. The newspaper had the highest number of articles describing the experience of being in New York at that time as well as a high number of stories in which Filipino-Americans reaffirmed their faith in democratic ideals.

India

Coverage of 9/11 in the Indian newspaper, which registered the largest proportion of negative articles about America, is a mixed bag. At first glance, it defies conventional predictions because it is the world's biggest democracy with a vibrant, free press; yet its largest English regional paper broke ranks with the media in similarly situated nations and published the most negative accounts. The newspaper's coverage may have been affected by vestiges of its nation's support for the Soviet Union during the Cold War and its former socialist economy.

Moreover, with a volatile Islamic population that is a significant minority in the country and a government that has been trying to accommodate every minority group in an effort to preserve or enhance harmony among the Hindus, Sikhs, Christians and Muslims, the press seems to have placed a greater premium on internal conditions over those beyond its immediate borders. For India, endemic priorities might have trumped the generally good diplomatic and trade relations with the United States, especially with the two countries' growing reciprocity in the hi-tech sector.

News frames in *The Telegraph* might be characterized as a seesaw between India's offering of total cooperation with the United States in combating terrorism and the government's misgivings about America's aid and preferential treatment of Pakistan as well as concerns about the Kashmiri problem. In a Sept. 17 story, the *Telegraph* reported: "After raising a banner virtually proclaiming, 'We are all Americans now' for the first two days after the suicide strikes, the BJP is sounding disenchanted with the U.S., ostensibly because it is inching closer to Pakistan to trap Osama bin Laden" (Ramaseshan and Benedict, 2001).

India's Prime Minister Atal Bihari Vajpayee was also described as being "keen on dispelling the impression that India was ready to offer unconditional support to the U.S. in its offensive against Osama bin Laden and the Taliban. The Prime Minister had voiced his disappointment with the U.S.'s failure to take into account India's concerns while formulating its anti-terror strategy" (*Telegraph*, Sept. 21).

Noticeable presence of stories like these — in addition to reports of Muslims uniting against a U.S. attack ("War Cry Pierces Prayers on Either Side," Sept. 14), of Russia's cautioning India against offering bases to the U.S. armed forces if Washington chooses to go to war (Sharma, 2001), and of a Gallup poll in 31 countries suggesting that "international public opinion was mostly opposed to Washington's military plans" (Bakhtiar, 2001) — contributed to the overall negative tone of the *Telegraph*'s coverage.

Malaysia, Indonesia and Pakistan

The unfavorable tone of Malaysia's, Indonesia's and Pakistan's 9/11 reporting was expected considering the size of the Muslim presence and influence in these countries. Also, the press in these countries is known to have more restrictions compared with the rest in the sample. The United States has favorable diplomatic and economic relations with them but, like India, internal realities might have taken supremacy over other factors. Malaysia, for instance, is America's 10th largest trading partner, and the country enjoys the biggest trade volume with the United States among ASEAN nations (Sodhy, 2003).

Pakistan has an authoritarian government, although Malaysia and Indonesia, despite their dominant party or parliamentary system, have had their share of autocratic rulers. Not one is an Islamic state but many who are in powerful civil service positions are Muslims. The same may be said of other influential institutions such as the news media, business and educational organizations. A majority of the Muslims in these countries espouse the moderate kind of Islam, yet when an event with the scale of 9/11 happened, solidarity was shown as the tone of newspaper accounts revealed.

Malaysia's *The New Straits Times* carried official government condolences and condemnation of the WTC suicide bombing, which was called a "heinous crime." However, the news frames shifted later to analyses of what led to the attacks, criticisms against U.S. unilateral retaliation and calls to stay out of an imminent Afghanistan conflict. Ali's (2001) *Straits Times* article, for instance, reported that "suggestions that America's foreign policies and difficult relations in the Middle East had sown the seeds of hatred were given cursory attention" by the media. In "Defining Clearly What's Terrorism," Abdullah (2001) opined that "international law pertaining to terrorism is vague, so much so the U.S., the victim of today, was once the perpetrator of terrorism, at least on Afghanistan and Sudan and let off the hook."

Some of the headlines are illustrative: "Attack on Afghans will hit the innocent, says Gerakan" (*Straits Times*, Sept. 28) and "Blanket retaliation would be just as mad" (Samad, 2001). In the Sept. 28 story, "NGOs hand memo to U.S. Embassy," the *Times* mentioned an NGO president as saying, "Muslims had always been blamed for every terrorist attack, adding that some of the attacks could have been carried out by certain interest groups or American terrorists." These and similar sentiments that landed on the pages of the *Straits Times* rendered its coverage on the negative end of the continuum.

The *Times* also reported a hoax bomb threat of the Petronas Towers, the status of 23 Malaysians working at WTC, and government efforts to secure strategic locations. This newspaper framed "global peace" as contingent on the United States' nonuse of "violence against violence" and a UN-led global war against terrorism.

Similar framing patterns are discernible in Indonesia's *Jakarta Post*. While coverage began with President Megawati Soekarnoputri's declaration of "great shock" over the "barbaric and indiscriminate" terrorist attacks, a crescendo of negative voices, mostly from the Muslim community, appeared in the *Post*. Some examples are: "U.S. warned against blaming Islamic groups for attacks" (Sept. 13. 2001); "Terror will only produce terror" (Sept. 22); "Muslim groups hunt for Americans" (Sept. 24); and "MUI slams attacks on U.S.' planned Afghanistan strike" (Sept. 26).

At least three stories reported that hundreds of members of radical Muslim groups scoured five-star hotels to tell Americans to leave Indonesia if the U.S. strikes at Afghanistan. One article said that the police hesitated to prevent these militants from carrying out their intimidation campaign.

The overarching theme of *Jakarta Post*'s coverage is best summarized by the following statements in the news stories: "The Indonesian Ulemas Council called on Muslims all over the world to wage a *jihad* should the U.S. and its allies go ahead with their planned aggression toward Afghanistan" (Sept. 26); "Local observers said that the American habit of attributing terrorism to particular religious or ethnic groups was dangerous because it unfairly stigmatized Islam and the Middle East" (Sept. 13); and "Conflicts between the West and the Muslim world are largely due to the inconsistent policy of the U.S. which has supported corrupt, repressive "friendly tyrants" in the Islamic world through its long history of economic and military intervention" (Perwita, 2001).

Articles from Pakistan's news agency, PPI, echoed identical frames found in the Indonesian and Malaysian newspapers with three salient distinctions: at least five news items alluded to an Israeli conspiracy; two articles urged the United States to take notice of "state terrorism of India against innocent people of Jammu and Kashmir" (Sept. 19); and a number of stories cited protests against Musharaf's decision to support the U.S stating that Muslims will support a *jihad* if Afghanistan is attacked.

For instance, an interview attributed the following to a Pakistani former chief justice: "Terrorist attacks on America were condemnable but the absence of 4,000 Jews working in (the) World Trade Center on the day the calamity hit the building and cancellation of Israeli Prime Minister's scheduled visit to New York in the eleventh hour, indicated to some other direction" (Sept. 25). Another article alluded to "involvement of the Israeli intelligence agency, Mosad" (Sept. 18).

September 11 also became a platform to dramatize the rift between India and Pakistan over Jammu and Kashmir. PPI carried items calling India, a "terrorist state." In opposing the Pakistani government's support of U.S.' action against Afghanistan, some PPI articles quoted a Taliban leader in Afghanistan saying "it is not because of Osama. This is the demonization of Islam" (Sept. 15). In assigning blame for the attacks, stories referred to "America's interference in other poor nations' affairs" (Sept. 14) and "part of conspiracy of the Jews who wanted to create a difference between the Muslims and the government of the United States" (Sept. 24). Elements of Huntington's (1996) "clash of civilizations" are operative here.

China

Somewhat surprising is the fact that China's newspaper had the second biggest percentage of positive stories. Its communist system is the antithesis of democracy. It also has the most controlled press among the sample countries and its relationship with the United States has been mired by incidents epitomized in Tianamen. Given these, a more negative reportage might have been expected. However, with China's exceptionally strong export trade with the United States soon after the country shifted to a free market-like economy, it is easier to understand why its highly controlled press would tout the government line and report a balanced, if not a sympathetic, account of the terrorist attack.

The Chinese government's reaction to September 11 clearly has been supportive of the United States — it backed the use of force against terrorism and strengthened border security with Afghanistan and froze assets of suspected terrorist groups (Gill, 2003). It must be noted that among the countries in the study, the Chinese newspaper attributed 63 percent of 9/11 stories to national government officials.

More significant, the *Zhongguo Ribao* or *China Daily* had zero negative articles. It appears that the country and its media did not want to be on the opposite aisle from its major trading partner and, in fact, saw the attacks as an opportunity to shore up constructive relations with the United States. The nation's dominant religions, Buddhism and Confucianism, with their dogma of nonviolence, may have played also a role in the otherwise positive tone of the coverage.

The *China Daily's* principal frames include the country's opposition to terrorism and its sympathy with the United States; the importance of international cooperation in anti-terrorist efforts, particularly emphasizing the dominant role the United Nations should play; and its confidence in the resilience of the U.S. economy and political system. The following quotes from Chinese government officials represent the various themes: "Momentum for the improvement of ties between China and the United States continued on Friday as the two countries agreed to enhance their consultations and cooperation in the fight against terrorism" (Zongwei, 2001) and "that the eradication of terrorism as a major menace to the international community can only be achieved with global cooperation, making such effort both pressing and necessary." President Jiang Zemin continued: "It is necessary for the U.N. Security Council to play its due role and that all actions should help maintain the long-term interests of world peace and development" (Min, 2001).

Referring to comments by China's business leaders and economic and world trade ministers, Daozu (2001) wrote: "Now the crashes, which are expected to bring new difficulties to the U.S. economy, may influence U.S.-related transactions and plans ranging from trade and investment to Chinese companies. But many also think that the impact would be insignificant in the long-term since the impact of the crashes on the U.S. economy, which is still based on strong fundamentals, would be short lived."

Understandably, the *China Daily* devoted substantial space to the economic effects of the 9/11 attacks. The tone of these articles was upbeat and optimistic: "The nation's oil imports and exports are not likely to be greatly affected by the United States' possible attack on Afghanistan," (Ye, 2001). A Foreign Ministry official was also quoted saying that "China's commitment to join the global front against terrorism embraces the issue of checking and blocking the money channels linked with the terror attacks" (Min, 2001).

Interestingly, the head of the mission of the Pudong New Area in Shanghai who participated in the design of Shanghai's Jinmao Tower, China's tallest skyscraper, told the *China Daily*: "The World Trade Center towers were the sister towers of the Jinmao Tower in Pudong, and we had close relations with the WTC in New York while designing, building and working out plans to manage the Jinmao Tower. We feel we've lost a sister and, above all, we believe that terrorist activities pose grave threats not only to the United States but to the countries which have skyscrapers as well as all the countries on Earth" (Xing, 2001).

Japan

Next to China, Japan posted the second largest percentage of neutral stories and the second smallest proportion of negative articles. This result is expected, because Japan is a politically stable, prosperous and democratic country with a relatively free press. It is noteworthy that The *Mainichi Shimbun* is considered "liberal, left-leaning ... and favored by intellectuals" (Sakai, 2003). The daily presented various sides of the story, including the opinions of Muslims and scholarly Islamic studies. Its editorials expressed pacifism, finding of other ways to combat terrorism and avoiding a "clash of civilizations." In contrast, the conservative press underscored Japan's alliance with the United States and its role in the global community. It supported the call to arms against terrorism as a means of preserving world peace (Sakai, 2003).

Indeed, Japan joined the international unison denouncing terrorism and supporting the United States. Several of the *Mainichi Shimbun's* articles dealt with internal discourse over introducing constitutional changes removing restrictions on the Self-Defense Force, thereby allowing Japan to aid U.S. military action against terrorists. The following headlines tell the story: 'Government favors loosening SDF troops triggers" (Sept. 27); "90 percent of Japanese favor support for U.S. retaliatory strikes" (Sept. 25); "Koizumi tells Bush Japan is with you" (Sept. 13); Public divided over how to assist U.S. (Sept. 18); and "Don't' rush to send in the SDF" (Sept. 22).

The *Mainichi* also published stories about 24 Japanese casualties at WTC; the country's increased security and the "choking off funding for terrorists" (Sept. 24).

Conclusion

Although all of the Asian countries and their print media in this study initially and unequivocally declared kinship with America right after 9/11 and condemned the heinous murder of innocent victims, support for the United States began to fade as time passed. Critics from the Islamic population of India, Malaysia, Indonesia and Pakistan expressed concern over the use of armed reprisal against the "core terrorist" nations. So while the governments of these countries officially declared "zero tolerance for terrorism," they were critical of waging war against Afghanistan.

Among the nations with large Muslim populations, Pakistan was somewhat unique. Its news agency started with a low volume of positive coverage that dramatically spiked during the latter part of the study. This improvement over time may be partly due to intensifying U.S. and Pakistani government cooperation in the search of bin Laden and in rooting terrorists that fled from Afghanistan into Pakistan.

What this study shows is the interplay of both intrinsic journalistic and external variables that created the variety of perspectives and frames used by the Asian news media in their reporting of 9/11. Reporters' routine practices of finding local angles as well as factors such as political ideology, religion, press freedom, trade and diplomatic relations with the United States appear to have influenced what was said or unsaid in the newspaper accounts of the September 11 events.

Since the research did not establish direct empirical causality and was focused on message content only, all of the probable determinants of the reporting are simply implied. What is indisputable, though, is that the international press represented in this study by the Asian newspapers made 9/11 a priority agenda.

REFERENCES

Abdullah, A. (2001). Defining Clearly What's Terrorism. *The New Straits Times.* Sept. 19, 2001.

Adams, W. C. (1986). Whose Lives Count? TV Coverage of Natural Disaster. *Journal of Communication.* 36. pp. 113-122.

Ahern, T. J. (1984). Determinants of Foreign Coverage in U.S. Newspapers. In R.L. Stevenson and D. L. Shaw (eds.). *Foreign News and the New World Information Order.* Ames: Iowa State University Press. pp. 217-236.

Ali, A. (2001). So Why Did It Happen? *The New Straits Times.* Sept. 27, 2001.

Atwater, T., Salwen, M. and Anderson, R. (1985). Media Agenda-setting with Environmental Issues. *Journalism Quarterly.* 62(2), 393-397.

Bakhtiar, I. (2001). US Loads Gun, Taliban Fire Up Faith. *The Telegraph.* Sept. 21, 2001.

Birkland, T. (1997). *After Disaster: Agenda-setting, Public Policy, and Focusing Events.* Washington, D.C.: Georgetown University Press.

Chang, K., Lau, T and Hao, S. (2000). From the United States with News and More. *Gazette.* 62(6). pp. 505-522.

Cottle, S. (2002). Television Agora and Agoraphobia Post-September 11. *Journalism after September 11.* Barbie Zeliger and Stuart Allan (eds). London and New York: Routledge. pp. 178-198.

Daozu, B. (2001). "Blasts Cause Mixed Reactions. *China Daily.* Sept. 13.

Entman, R. (1993). Framing: Toward Clarification of a Fractured Paradigm. *Journal of Communication.* 43. pp. 51-58.

Gill, B. (2003). Sptember 11 and Northeast Asia: Change and Uncertainty in Regional Security. (The Shock Wave Abroad). *Brookings Review.* 20(3). pp. 43-47.

Gitlin, T. (1980). *The Whole World is Watching: Mass Media in the Making and Unmaking of the News Left.* Berkeley: University of California Press.

Goffman, E. (1974). *Framing Analysis: An Essay on the Organization of Experience.* New York: Harper & Row.

Hungtington, S. (1996). *The Clash of Civilizations and the Remaking of a New World Order.* New York: Simon & Schuster.

Iyengar, S. and Simon, A. (1993). News Coverage of the Gulf Crisis and Public Opinion: A Study of Agenda-setting, Priming, and Framing. *Communication Research*. 20. pp. 365-383.

Kahneman, D. and Tversky, A. (1984). Choice, Values, and Frames. *American Psychologist*. 39, 341-350.

McCombs, M. E. and Shaw, D. L. (1972). The Agenda-setting Function of Mass Media. *Public Opinion Quarterly*. 36(2). pp. 176-187.

Min, Z. (2001). Leaders Talk as Tension Increases. *China Daily*. Sept. 19.

Min, Z. (2001). Economic Issue to Top Agenda of Summit. *China Daily*. Sept. 26.

Nnaemeka, T. and Richstad, J. (1981). Structured Relations and Foreign News Flow in the Pacific Region. *Gazette*. 26. pp. 235-258.

Norris, P. (1995). The Restless Research: Network News Framing of the Post-Cold War World. *Political Communication*. 12. pp. 357-370.

Peh, D. and Melkote, S. (1991). Bias in Newspaper Reporting: A Content Analysis of the Coverage of Korean Airlines and Iran Airbus Shooting in the U.S. Elite Press. *Gazette*. 47, 59-78.

Perwita, A. (2001). Misconceptions all around. *Jakarta Post*. Sept. 22, 2001.

Ramaseshan, R. and Benedict, K. (2001).US Pak Tilt Bothers Sheepish BJP. *The Telegrap*. , Sept. 17, 2001.

Robinson, G. and Sparks, V. (1976). International News in the Canadian and American Press: Comparative News Flow Study. *Gazette*. 22, pp. 203-218.

Rosengren, K. E. (1974). International News: Methods, Data and Theory. *Journal of Peace Research*. 11, 145-156.

Semetko, H. and Valkenburg, P. (2000). Framing European Politics: A Content Analysis of Press and Television News. *Journal of Communication*. 2. pp. 93-109.

Sakai, K. (2003). 11 September and the Clash of Civilizations: The Role of the Japanese Media and Public Discourse. *Arab Studies Quarterly*. 25(2). pp. 159-179.

Samad, N. (2001). Blanket Retaliation Would be Just as Mad. *z*. Sept. 15, 2001.

Sharma, P. (2001). Moscow Gives Go-Slow Advice to Delhi. *The Telegraph*. Sept.18.

Sodhy, P. (2003). U.S.-Malaysian Relations during the Bush Administration: The Political, Economic, and Security Aspects. *Contemporary Southeast Asia*. 25(3). pp. 363-387.

Volkmer, I. (2002). Journalism and Political Crises in the Global Network Society. In *Journalism After September 11*. Barbie Zeliger and Stuart Allan (eds). London and New York: Routledge. pp. 235-245.

Wall, M. (1997). The Rwanda Crisis: An Analysis of News Magazine Coverage. *Gazette*. 59. pp. 121-134.

Wu, H. D. (2000). Systematic Determinants of International News Coverage: A Comparison of 38 Countries. *Journal of Communication*. 50(2). pp. 110-130.

Xing, L. (2001). Activities Aim to Deepen Understandings. *China Daily*. Sept. 15.

Ye, X. (2001). Oil Policy Unaffected. *China Daily*. Sept. 19.

Zongwei, S. (2001). The Momentum Continues. *China Daily*. Sept. 24.

Chapter 12

CHINESE PRINT MEDIA COVERAGE OF 9/11 SINCE 2001

Mobo C. F. Gao, with Ming Liang

This chapter examines coverage of 9/11 in Chinese print media. We focus on print media and divide that coverage into three categories: official, semi-official and the unofficial.

For the official media, we selected *renmin ribao* (*People's Daily*) which is the mouthpiece of the Communist Party of China (CCP) and the Chinese government. For the semi-official media, we selected *nanfang zhoumo* (the *Southern Weekend*). And for the unofficial media, we selected e-media (i.e., various Web sites), which are not confined geographically to China. In fact, much of the e-media discussion takes place on sites that are hosted outside of China but include contributions from people inside of China, Chinese citizens, or dissidents living outside of China.

We examine coverage from the first month after September 11, 2001. After that, from 2002 to 2004, we selected only coverage on the anniversary of 9/11. The rationale for this sampling is a pragmatic one: We did not have enough resources to examine everything. Our method is basically a content analysis to see whether and how the three categories of media may differ in terms of narratives and messages.

THE CHINESE OFFICIAL REPORTING

Like other media around the world, the *People's Daily* published many stories about the deaths and casualties from 9/11. They also covered the effect of 9/11 on the U.S. and world stock markets, the airlines and tourist industries, and the U.S. economy. The newspaper also reported, quite neutrally, the various U.S. and U.N. resolutions and announcements. And it gave significant coverage to how the United States and United Kingdom were building up their resources for the war in Afghanistan.

People's Daily coverage also stressed that China "had always been" (*yi guan*) opposed to "any and every form of terrorist violent activities" (*yi qie xingshi de kongbu zhuyi baoli huodong*). This was expressed in the Foreign Ministry Spokesperson news brief on the Sept. 12, 2001, and it also expressed by Qian Qichen, a veteran Chinese diplomat and vice-premier of the State Council, who spoke by telephone with Colin Powell on Sept. 14 (as well as by Jia Chun Wang the Public Security Minister on Sept. 18). On Sept. 12, Jiang Zemin, the president of the PRC, sent a message of condolence to President George Bush. On Sept. 13, the newspaper reported that Zemin spoke with Bush to offer his condolences and to condemn terrorism. It also reported that the Chinese State Tourist Bureau was helping American tourists in China who might have difficulties in returning home immediately after 9/11.

When reporting the impeding war in Afghanistan, the paper used its reporting of Chinese leaders' exchange with foreign leaders to push the Chinese official opposition to the war and its advocacy of working through international organizations and international laws and treaties to fight terrorism. The paper reported that Jiang Zemin, in his telephone conversation with the British Prime Minister Tony Blair, pointed out that war against terrorism had to be conducted according to international law and along the lines of the commonly accepted international principles. The paper also reported that during his telephone conversation with Russian President Vladamir Putin, Jiang expressed his wish that China and Russia work together to strengthen the international mechanism for dealing with terrorism. And the newspaper also reported Jiang's telephone conversation with French President Jacques Chirac, during which he stressed the importance of international cooperation in combating terrorism.

The *People's Daily* reported that the Taliban condemned the U.S. and U.K. war against Afghanistan and accused it as an act of terrorism. To show that the Taliban regime was reasonable, the paper explained that the Taliban was willing to arrest and put bin Laden on trial if the United States could present evidence of his crime. It also reported the Taliban's firm stand that it would not hand in bin Laden unless evidence was presented. In expressing its position against the war in Afghanistan, the paper used its correspondent's interviews with the locals in the country to appeal for peace under the headline: "We Need Peace."

In further developing the thesis of opposing "all forms of terrorism," the paper reported that the Palestine leader Yassir Arafat's plea that the world should not forget Israel's state terrorism simply because the United States was attacked. It also reported that Cuba held an anniversary to commemorate the 10/06 Incident in which a bomb exploded and killed 73 passengers aboard a Cuban airline on October 6, 1976. The report quoted President Fidel Castro, who expressed sympathy for the American people and requested that other countries stop terrorist activities against Cuba. The paper also reported various government announcements and people protests all over the world against the US-led war in Afghanistan.

For the first anniversary of 9/11, the *People's Daily* had a mixture of new themes. One was that the anti-terrorist war activities by the United States had made the world less safe and more worrisome. From its correspondents in the United States, the paper reported that the Americans were still recovering from the fact that their country was vulnerable to attack. It reported that one of the most obvious consequences of this was that Americans were much more nationalistic.

Its correspondent from France told of an interviewee's argument that the terrorist attack on the United States stemmed from its support of Israel. Its correspondent from Russia reported on some Russian resentment that, although Putin was one of the first to send message of sympathy to the United States after 9/11, the United States had no sympathy for the Russians when they were attacked by terrorists. Its correspondent from Pakistan reported that, according to one survey, 60 percent of the people there resented the United States and felt less safe, believed their freedoms were more restricted and that their country's income had declined as a result of the decline of tourism. The newspaper's correspondent from Syria stated that the Syrians had changed from having sympathy for the United States to resentment and anger. The people interviewed indicated that there had been movements to boycott U.S. products. Finally it reported that four out of the five Central Asian states had military contracts with the United States as a result of war against terrorism. The correspondent reported that some of the people interviewed were convinced these countries were to be de-stablized as a result of Western democratic values and U.S. lifestyle values.

Another theme in the second anniversary coverage of 9/11 in the *People's Daily* was U.S. unilateralism. In an article that reflected on the past and future of terrorism, the paper stated that terrorism and anti-terrorism were not something that occurred after the 9/11. Since 1962, the United Nations had passed 12 resolutions and regulations in its efforts against international terrorism. The story argued that the U.S. war in Iraq had nothing to do with terrorism. Instead, it harmed the UN efforts against terrorism because the United States had marginalized the UN. The war on terrorism will succeed only if all nations act and work together, the article stated. In another article titled, "the trap of unilateralism," the newspaper argued that U.S. accusations about "rogue states" and "Axes of Evil" reminded people of Cold War propaganda.

In its second anniversary coverage, the paper asserted that the U.S. wars in Afghanistan and Iraq essentially were the same as the 9/11 attacks, in that both wanted to deter the enemy and shock them to the core. But both failed to fulfill their aims. Since the United States acted alone (yi jia shuo le suan), it cannot expect others to help it now when it is in a mess. The paper asserted that the past two years seem to show that the "theory of clashes of civilizations" is correct. But the civilizations, the South and North, are not equal. Only when this inequality is addressed will the final solution found for the problem of terrorism, the paper concludes.

The third anniversary of the 9/11 was almost a nonevent. There is only one short report from the United States. It was a photo showing someone placing a concrete road block on the pavement near the U.S. House of Representatives as a measure to prevent terrorism. The headline was "anti-terrorism road block," which could have been interpreted as meaning either a road block to prevent terrorism or the road is blocked for anti-terrorism. The report states that people in the United States still do not feel safe.

SEMI-OFFICIAL COVERAGE

Until the reforms of the 1990s, the Chinese print media was not only tightly controlled but also neatly categorized. There are central papers such as the *People's Daily*, sectorial papers such as the *Chinese Youth*, and *Guangming Ribao* (the *Guangming Daily*) which is meant for the Chinese intellectuals, *Jiefangjun bao* (*The People's Liberation Army* paper) and provincial papers and local such as *Guangdong ribao* (*Guangdong Daily*). The central papers are distributed nationally, whereas provincial and local papers are not available outside their own location except in libraries. However, since the reforms some new papers have emerged that challenge this categorization and also are more cosmopolitan in content.

Nanfang zhoumo is one of the new papers. It is located in Guangdong Province but is widely distributed all over China. It is not sectorial and it is not provincial. It often carries coverage that is critical of local governments and highlights topics of the day. It is rumored that some provincial bureaucrats complained to the CCP central authorities that *Nanfang zhoumo* had no right to interfere internal affairs of other provinces since it is not a government central paper. An example of how the paper sets the agenda is its reportage of Li Changping and his exposure of rural situation in China.[1] The paper is, therefore, also controversial. Leftists accuse it of being pro-capitalism and pro-globalization. It also is accused of ignoring the horrendous migrant working conditions in Guangdong and supporting the continuation of bank accounts opened in pseudo-names.

As the paper only publishes on weekends, its first coverage of 9/11 appeared two days later, on Sept. 13. The first four pages of the paper were devoted to 9/11. The first page carried a headline in big and black characters *meiguo yu xi ji hou de shijie* ("the world after the American attack"). The whole page, which quoted world leaders and U.S. officials, is divided into three sections. The first is *beitong yu qianze* (pain and condemnation), the second is *meiguo hui bu hui baofu* (will the US revenge?) and the third *shijie jingji xue shang jia shuang* (snow on top of frost on the world economy). The headline on the second page is "Black Tuesday, Black USA." On this page it also carried photos of the scenes that we saw in the Western media, such as the collapsing of the two towers amid smoke, people escaping from the attack covered by dust rain and the unbelievable horror on the faces of these who were watching what was happening.

In describing the event, the paper has four subheadings. The first is "misfortune fell from the sky"; the second, "Manhathan, a shocking 120 minutes"; the third, "Washington: everywhere on fire"; and the fourth, "speedy reaction." Page three was devoted to the brief introduction of the World Trade Towers, the Pentagon and U.S. anti-air attack institutions and technology. Finally the headline on page four was "Apart from 'God bless you.'" Under this headline there are remarks about 9/11 from different people. U.S. officials' and Tony Blair's responses are categorized as "The will of the U.S. is being tested." The responses from Arafat and the U.N. Secretary-General are categorized as "Terrorism will not promote any cause of justice," while the responses from Chirac, Putin and Israel's Shalon belong to the same category of "This is a challenge to all humanity." The responses from the Taliban, Libya and bin Laden (who denied that he had anything to do with it) are categorized as "This may be a plot by certain government."

The second weekend after 9/11 was Sept. 20 and *Nanfang zhoumo* again had four-page coverage. It first carried a report attempting to analyze the connection between bin Laden and the Taliban. The reporter, named Fu An, mostly quotes U.S. sources and only at the end adds that financial and military support of bin Laden actually came from the United States when it wanted him to fight the Soviet troops in Afghanistan. It then published an opinion piece by Zhang Guoqing of the Institute of American Studies of the Chinese Academy of Social Sciences. Zhang argues that 9/11 presented Bush with four opportunities: 1) to unite his people, 2) to rectify domestic politics involving issues such as ethnicity, class and violence, 3) to re-shape foreign policies and 4) to reduce trade obstacles and to speed up globalization. Not surprisingly in the last "opportunity." Zhang mentions China's WTO membership issue.

On the same page, three military specialists introduce technical specifications of the B-2 Stealth Bomber that the United States is likely to use to "revenge" 9/11. Another page of this weekend issue was devoted to the introduction of the Taliban, with a grotesque picture of a smiling Taliban soldier holding a Stinger Missile in front of a man being hanged. However, the reportage under the name of Fu An from Beijing attempts to show that the Taliban has done some very positive things in Afghanistan within seven years in power, including suppressing the war lords and restoring peace in the country, delivering free food to the poor, reducing taxes and prohibiting the production of drug crops. Fu further argues that the American sanction and international isolation not only made the people in the country suffer but also pushed the Taliban to the extreme version of Islam state.

On page three of the same issue, the paper, while carrying a briefing of the elite anti-terrorist military units in the world (USA, Germany, Russia, France and UK), published an opinion piece by Wang Fuchun of the Beijing Institute of International Relations. Wang argues that although terrorism may be more cruel, more violent and less rule-binding than normal warfare, it is nevertheless a war, and asymmetry warfare of the weak against the strong may be very effective. Therefore, to use violence to fight terrorism would not work but would actually reduce the moral strength of those who suffer from terrorism.

The newspaper printed only one story on the weekend of Sept. 27. This focused on the possible energy crisis as a consequence of 9/11 and what China should do to cope with the situation. The paper invites four academics to discuss the issue. Hu Angang of Qinghua University and the Chinese Academy of Social Sciences asserts China is facing an energy crisis. Chen Xinhua of the International Energy Organization suggests that China should take five measures to cope with the situation: 1) strategic storage of oil, 2) diversification of import sources, 3) more efficiency in consumption, 4) insurance of transportation channel of energy and 5) an energy emergence organization. While Chen Hui of the State Council Development Centre thinks China should use the international market to buy and sell oil to its advantage. And Wu Yuanwei thinks in the next 30 years coal should still be main energy source for China.

On Oct. 4, the paper devoted one page to a discussion of how to prevent terrorism from the point of science and technology, such as airport security check. On Oct. 18 the paper published two articles on page three covering 9/11. One was written by Liu Xiaobiao of the China International Broadcasting Station and the other by Liu Ying of the Beijing Institute of Communication, both of whom discuss whether 9/11 indicates clashes of civilization, since some Muslims became the innocent victims of the war on terror and since five of the seven "rogue states" named by the United States are Islamic countries. Finally an opinion piece by Tong Zhongying of Qinghua University argues that 9/11 shows that globalization brings freedom. But if there is no international order, freedom is in danger. On page 27, an author named Feng Duan discusses what has effects 9/11 had the Internet and e-media.

The first anniversary came with a reporting of how the families of several U.S. victims of on the 9/11 event commemorate the event. The reportage summarizes the activities of these families, saying that they commemorated the anniversary by working, being quiet, enjoying life, expressing friendship, affection and love. In a word, their commemoration was expressed through hope. One opinion piece by Xu Tianqing of Zhongshan University comments on the effect of 9/11 on the U.S. economy. Xu argues that the U.S. economy started its path on depression before 9/11, and the attacks sent a damaging message to consumer confidence. The United States should take measures to restore confidence; but instead, the United States took the opportunity to exercise hegemony behavior and to list some countries as "rogue states." He also pointed out that the United States increased military spending to an unprecedented level and, thus, further accelerates the economic downturn.

Another commentator expresses a similar view. Quoting *New York Times* columnist Paul Krugman, He Fan of the Chinese Academy of Social Sciences argues that the Enron collapse is responsible for changing the prospects of the U.S. economy. In criticizing a widely accepted view that 9/11 was an act of anti-globalization, He Fan argues that 9/11 could only be carried out by people who benefited from globalization. The bin Ladens were not peasants. They were educated in the best education institutions in the United States and Europe, they learned piloting skills in these countries and they were carrying U.S. dollars. Surely they had more in common with Bush than they had with a peasant in Afghanistan or Western China, He Fan concludes.

One correspondent sent a report titled, "U.S., Are You Still Safe?", accompanied with a picture of armed police guarding the British Embassy in Washington. On the same page of the paper, there is an old question and new answer section in which three questions are asked. Why is it necessary to combat terrorism? And the answer is provided by Pan Wei, a professor of international relations at Beijing University. Basically he says that international terrorism has to be suppressed because it is "uncivilized." It is uncivilized because it does not obey the rules of engagement. On the other hand, state terrorism is "civilized" because it obeys rules and is sensitive to all kinds of international factors. The second question is "Why had 9/11 made the US so nervous?" The answer is given by Ni Luoxiong, director of the Institute of War and Culture at East China University of Technology, who said that 9/11 shows that terrorism renders U.S. military power, however awesome and however powerfully the best in the world, impotent. In addition, 9/11 shows made the United States realize that it can also be vulnerable. The third question: "How did 9/11 benefit the U.S. military?" The answer is given by Xue Pan, a Ph.D. candidate at Yale University. Xue Pan uses the example of how the U.S. military now could use Yale's Career Service to recruit its students, something that was never allowed before. Yale has to give in to this demand because the U.S. government threatens to withdraw its financial support of $328 million, which is 16 percent of Yale's operating costs, if Yale does not comply with the military demand.

In interviews with three Americans from three different states, Chen Xiaowei wants to find out how Americans answer two questions. The first question concerns a survey which shows that more than half of the Europeans think that U.S. foreign policies are partially responsible for the 9/11 attacks. The second question is to ask whether they think the United States should attack Iraq. All three interviewees deny that the U.S. foreign policy had anything to do with 9/11, and only one of the three thinks that the United States should not launch a war with Iraq. The paper also published an article by Lu Hongbing that presented a picture of how modern technology provides new opportunity for reporting 9/11. The article discusses the Web sites of 9/11, the DIY journalists working on 9/11 and the role of the blogs. It then lists several Web sites as example, including www.sept11photo.org, www.sept11thememorial.com and www.msnbc.com/news/msnsp-"9.11"_front.asp.

A commentary by Wang Shuangyan thinks that 9/11 has pushed humanity to a crossroad where people have to choose between violence against violence or appeasement (he jie) measures to stop the bottle neck of terrorism. Although many people assume that terrorist attack on the United States is an attack on U.S. freedom, anyone who takes a rational analysis will realize that terrorism against the United States indicates clearly that the U.S.-centered approach to its own interests and power has offended come countries and some people's feelings. The commentator continues to assert that 9/11 was a watershed event for the United States, for it has not only provided an opportunity to control its hegemonic behavior but also gives it a seduction to continue its hegemonic action. Whatever direction the Unites States takes will decide the future of the world in the next 50 years at least. The most positive aspect for China is that 9/11 provides an opportunity for it to work together with the United States.

A much longer and sophisticated commentary by Wang Yikui, an academic from the Institute of American Studies of Fudan University, also appeared during the second anniversary. The author quotes Western sources to demonstrate that the Unites States has moved to a more closed society, and, therefore, it has abandoned some of the very values that it was proud of. It is also a sad fact that the United States has withdrawn from consensus actions with other nations in combating environmental degradation and in a fairer world trade arrangement. He argues that "we" ought to condemn 9/11 for its killing of the innocent civilians but also condemn it for the opportunity that it gave the United States to embark on its road to a New Empire. And the latter is the real tragedy. The commentary then argues that the wars in Afghanistan and Iraq were just excuses for such an ambition, for no evidence has been found that al-Qaeda had planned the 9/11 attacks or that there were weapons of mass destruction in Iraq. WangYikui further argues that United States is an exceptional country only in the sense that, unlike other nations, it does not have an ethnic identity. Therefore, it has been seeking enemies to build up its identity. During the Cold War, the U.S. enemy was communism, and at the end of the Cold War the enemy was to be other civilizations (clashes of civilizations) and China (the China threat). September 11 diverted its attention to identify terrorists as enemies and the list of these enemies became longer and longer. But the United States is still looking for the "smoking gun." The Iraqi War has already exposed the lie of justice and the Emperor's New Clothes. It is clear now that be they terrorists or North Korea — their actions are all reactive to the U.S. behavior and very often are desperate actions out of no choice. The rules of international affairs and the world are unchanged. There is nothing new and the announcement that "everything has changed since 9/11" is nothing but a real lie, Wang Yikui concludes.

By the time the third anniversary arrived, the paper took a quite detached but sober attitude. There were two commentaries on the issue of 9/11. Accompanying one commentary authored by Song Wei was a picture of flowers and a huge teddy bear placed where Russian school children were killed in a Russian terrorist incident that occurred just few days previously. Beside the picture there is a poem commemorating those who died in the incident.

The commentary by Song Wei also mentions the train station explosion in the Madrid that killed 202 people. The commentary asserts that terrorism is a phenomenon since ancient times but has reached an unprecedented scale recently. By using the ancient Chinese Daoist philosophical idea that whatever rises will also decline, Song Wei declares that the end of terrorism is not far away. The reason offered for this is that terrorism today in its ends and means it has lost its legitimacy. The kind of terrorism that took place under the circumstances of colonialism was legitimate. But terrorism took a new form since the end of colonialism and that was in the name of religion and extreme nationalism, which reached its height after the end of the Cold War. For Song Wei, the terrorism has come to its dead end because of its stupidity of confronting every one in every direction. The United States supported terrorism in certain countries for a long time during the Cold War. So did the former Soviet Union. But now terrorists can find new backers.

In a longer commentary, Ma Jian has a far more complicated picture of terrorism. First it points out that the UN listed more than 40 organizations as terrorist, while the U.S. list includes 77 organizations in 2004 — 16 more than what was included in its own 2003 list. Second, the commentator admits that evidence seems to suggest that most terrorist activities, with the exception of those that took place in Israel and Chechnya, are not only religious nature but also have connection with the al-Qaeda. The commentary then lists all terrorist activities since 2001, including those in the Philippines, Spain, and Russia. But curiously, the commentator does not include the Uigour separatist activities. Contrary to Song Wei, Ma Jian concludes that despite of all the efforts and success in combating terrorism all over the world, anti-terrorism has a long long way to go and the reason is that nations of the world cannot unite together in its fighting against terrorism. They cannot unite because they cannot have a unified definition of what terrorism is and, therefore, cannot identify who is a terrorist.

UNOFFICIAL COVERAGE

By unofficial coverage, we mean the coverage in electronic media and on Web sites, such BBS and blogs. Some of the e-discussions are taken from a Web site by *da ji yuan*, which is the mouthpiece of Falungong. This decision is taken not because we think Falungon is more reliable but because it seems to have the best archive system. Some of the Web sites are located in China and some are located outside of China but accessible to participants inside China. Because of the very nature of the e-media, the definition of what is Chinese media cannot be assumed to be within the Chinese national boundaries. Some of the participants of the e-media contribution may not reside in China or may not even be Chinese citizens. They are considered part of the Chinese unofficial media because, first, they are in Chinese language; second, they are of ethnic Chinese origin; and third, and more importantly, they do not only either respond to or address Chinese policies and attitudes but also are engaged with Chinese inside China by debating with them. Therefore, in this section what is meant by "coverage" is less of news reporting and more of opinions expressed in the debates between what are usually referred to as Chinese nationalists/leftists and Chinese liberals/dissidents.

When news of the 9/11 attacks reached Chinese people, there were two contrasting unofficial reactions and responses. One was blatant jubilation and the other was condemnation, not only of the 9/11 attacks but also the Chinese who thought the Americans deserved the attacks. Soon after 9/11, democratic dissidents called for a meeting in Washington. At the meeting titled "China's past, present and future: from the perspective of 9/11," well-known dissident Wei Jingsheng condemned some Chinese who were happy that America was attacked and those who even lit firecrackers to celebrate. He implied that the Chinese government used the occasion to arouse anti-Americanism in China (Da Can Kao, 2001).

One unnamed person said the response in the streets of Beijing was that United States deserved it (Si xiang ping lu 2001). Some e-media debate participants openly expressed their support for the attack and hailed those who took part in the attack as heroes (Du Daobing, 2003). On the other hand, Chinese dissidents not only expressed sympathy and support for the U.S. government, they also actually identified themselves with the United States. Ren Bumei, a well-known dissident, declared that he felt ashamed of many of the Chinese responses expressed in BBS (Ren Bumei, 2001). Yu Jie, another well-known dissident residing in China, described how he was crying in front of the TV with an American missionary friend (who brings the Gospel to the Chinese, Yu adds) and accused Yan Xuetong, a professor of Qinghua University, of being an animal — evil and Satanic, because the latter stated that the United States was only harvesting what it had sewed (Yu Jie, 2001). Another democracy activist, Zhao Dagong, declared that the United States is the symbol of human civilization, democracy and freedom — a country that embraces justice and peace and a country that represents the future of humanity. Zhao said that he wanted to hide his ethnic identity after knowing how the Chinese expressed delight at seeing the United States got punished (Zhao Dagong, 2001).

Chinese dissidents, many of whom want to move to the United States, have a very positive attitude toward the country. Part of the reason for this is that U.S. government actively encourages Chinese dissidents by providing protection, scholarship, visa and other means of political and financial support. It has been providing millions of dollars to support Chinese dissident activities. For instance the well-known dissident Yu Jie was invited by the Bureau of Educational and Cultural Affairs, U.S. Department of State, to visit Washington, New York, Boston and other places for two months to give talks on China (Li Hongkuan, 2003).

The Chinese dissidents are usually referred to as *minyun fenzi* (democracy activists), because their main criticism of China is that it is not a democratic country that respects human rights. However, increasingly on the e-media, the Chinese dissidents are referred to as *fen shi pai* (whateverists).[2] One of the first expressions of support and sympathy for the United States came from the Chinese Democratic Movement Alliances Overseas. In its declaration, the Alliances assert that the root of terrorism is communism (Da ji yuan, 2001).

Some of these dissidents openly declare that they worship (*cong bei*) America (An Qi, 1998). One well-known dissident declares that he would rather be an animal of foreign country than a Chinese person (Zheng Yi, 2004). When the Iraqi invasion started, one dissident academic in Hong Kong said in an e-message that he envied the Iraqis, because people all over the world went to the street to protest against the U.S. invasion and protest against the death of innocent people. Why is there not any one protesting against the death of people in China, as a result of accidents and SARS for instance? (Wu Guoguang 2003).

Immediately after 9/11, dissident Liu Xiaobo drafted an open letter to President Bush and the Americans on cyberspace and sought signatures. In this letter, co-drafted with Bao Junxin, Liu declares that attacks have nothing to do with race, nationality; they are, instead, challenge to life, freedom and peace by evil forces. September 11 is a tragedy of all humanity and a super sacrifice by the Americans for global freedom. The letter ends with "tonight we are all Americans" (Bao Junxin and Liu Xiaobo 2001). His tone and words were much stronger and emotional than these those in the French *Le Mond*, so much so that Liu and others who signed the letter were referred by their opponents as "a one night stand Americans"(Qing Zheng, 2002). The letter collected 1,015 signatures through October 14, 2001. Before drafting the letter, Liu wrote a self-declaration piece to swear that he wanted to sacrifice his life to rescue the people in the towers and wished that he was a rock that fell together with the building (Liu Xiaobo, 2001).

The Iraqi War, as expected, further accelerated the fight between the democratic dissidents and Chinese nationalists and leftists. Yu Jie, one of the principal signatures of the open letter in 2001, initiated the letter of *zhong guo zhi shi fen zi guan yu sheng yuan mei guo cui hui sa da mu du cai zheng quan de sheng ming* (A declaration by Chinese intellectuals in supporting U.S. government's destruction of Saddam's dictatorial regime) in 2003. In the letter, Yu says that Mao is the predecessor of Saddam, that human rights take priority over national sovereignty, and that the United States did not act unilaterally because U.S. values of democracy and human rights are universal (Yu Jie, 2003)

Liu Xiaobo, who once openly declared that China could only be saved by being colonized for 200 or 300 hundred years (Cheng Dan 2003), argues that even though the U.S. invasion was self-motivated, the war was good for human kind, as all other wars that the US participated with sole exception of the Vietnam War (Liu Xiaobo, 2003). In a poem titled "To the American Soldiers," Jiao Guobiao, a professor of Beijing University, expresses his extreme worries and ache for the American soldiers in Iraq. Guobiao (2003), in very poetic language, says the uniform of the U.S. soldiers symbolizes green hope in the Arabic desert — that the camels need to be replaced by U.S. soldiers (the following extract of the poem is our translation).

> Ah American soldier!
> You willingly go to Hell to fight evil.
> If you die, humanity will lose its backbone of justice.
> If the U.S. loses the war, humanity will return to the dark ages of the Middle Ages
> If not this life I want to be an American soldier in my next life.
> I would like to join and I wish to die.
> Shoot me! Shoot me!

The pro-American stand by the Chinese dissidents were so blatant that even a BBC correspondent, when commenting on the electronic media debate by the Chinese on the Iraqi war, has to admit that these Chinese love America and are pro-Bush more than the Americans themselves (Wei Cheng 2003).

Judging by the figures of Internet signatures, however, those who were against the war far outnumbered those liberals/dissidents who supported it. Headed by Han Deqiang, Kuang Xinnian and Tong Xiaoxi, a letter titled *zhong guo ge jie fan dui meiguo zhengfu dui yilake zhenzheng jihua de shengming* (A Declaration against the US War Plan in Iraq Signed by Chinese of Various Circles) was published on *shi ji sha long* (http://forum.cc.org.cn/luntan/china) on Feb. 10, 2003. The letter soon attracted fierce attacks from the dissidents. One scholar of Chinese ethnic origin who signed his name argues that there has never been such fierce attack on any Internet declaration or petition before. The reasons, he argues, are because, first, during the 1990s China was dominated by liberal discourse and, second, because this time, unlike previous occasions, it was an opposition to the United States and that was something that the liberals could not accept (Bing Lang, 2003).

Some accused those who signed the declaration against the war as being on the side of terrorists (Dong hai yi wu, 2003). Dong hai yi wu is clearly a pseudo name, of a well-known active e-media participant. Zhu Xueqin is a well known liberal scholar in China, and he accuses those who signed the declaration of violating two important principles. The first is that one cannot use the anti-war stand as an excuse for being anti-American. The second is that sympathy should be not given to the Iraqi dictator (Zhu, 2003)

The anti-war participants fought back. A participant based in Japan, in his rebuttal of Liu Xiaobo's assertion that the United Kingdom and United States are the mainstream of human civilization and that the former is the mother of modern civilization and the latter crystallization of modern civilisations, Cheng Dan questions whether Liu was paid by the United States to work in China (Cheng Dan, 2003).

CONCLUSION

Our examination of the three categories of print media coverage of 9/11 shows that the official media clearly is still the mouthpiece of the CCP and the Chinese government. Its coverage does not step away from official Chinese government positions. Three of these positions are clearly stressed: 1) We "have always" opposed terrorism, 2) We oppose terrorism of "all forms," and 3) The war against terrorism should be conducted within the existing international framework. The three positions carry forward three messages: 1) We are not brutal regime that violates human rights, 2) There are terrorists in China, and 3) The role of the UN should be maintained and so should be the legitimacy of national sovereignty.

Coverage of 9/11 in the semi-official media, on the other hand, was much broader, from international relations to economic consequences. It sought opinions from academics and also tried to get some sense of how people around the world felt about 9/11. It acknowledged that the attacks were terrorist acts and that they should be condemned, if not for anything else than for the loss of innocent civilian lives. But the coverage in semi-official media tended to have a much more nuanced analysis of the causes of 9/11.

Finally, cyberspace brought a much more emotional and more disputed picture of 9/11. There were debates on the causes and the reactions to 9/11. There also were debates on the U.S.-U.K. war in Iraq. The thematic debates revolved around different value and belief systems about the United States and freedom, democracy, God (may dissidents are Christians), human rights, and indeed the meaning of life. There is a clear division between the two fractions in terms of how to evaluate not only what is happening in the United States but also in China, and not only what has happened in the past but also what should be the future direction of China.

CHAPTER ENDNOTES

[1] Li Changping was a CCP Party Secretary of a township in Henan Province. After his failed attempt to rectify the serious levy and tax problems on the peasantry in the township under his leadership, he wrote a letter to then Premier Zhu Rongji to report the seriousness of the situation. Zhu was actually very sympathetic and supportive of Li's efforts of reform. After the failure in his second attempt of reform, even with the support of the Premier from Beijing, Li resigned from his post and wrote a book about the situation. For a review of the affair and Li's book, see Mobo Gao, "Li Changping, Wo xiang zongli shuo shihua [I Told the Truth to the Premier], *The China Journal*, No. 48 (July) 2002, pp. 175-177.

[2] The term *fan shi pai* here means whatever the United States does is good and whatever China does is wrong. The term was used by Deng Xiaoping and his followers to attack those who wanted to follow Mao's policies after the chairman was dead: whatever Mao said must be followed and whatever Mao did is correct. The phrase originated in the early 1980s, when Deng Xiaoping and the reformists used it to knock down these inside the CCP who wanted to adhere to Mao's policies.

REFERENCES

Named sources

An Qi, "bu pa gu li cai you du li — zhuan fang zi you zhuan gao ren Cao Changqing" (Independence can only come from non-fear of isolation — exclusive interview with free lance writer Cao Changqing, *Can Sao*, No. 5 1998, WWW.caochanbgqing.com, accessed on the 13th May 2004.

Bao Junxin and Liu Xiaobo, "zhi Bushi zongtong he Meiguo renmin de gongkai xin," (Open Letter to President Bush and the American People), http://www.dajiyuan.com, 12th September 2001, accessed on the 19th April 2005.

Bing Lang, "cong wang luo qian ming shuo dao xixiang de fen hua," (On Internet Signatures and fractions of ideologies), *Shi ji sha long lun tan*, http://forum/cc.org.cn/luntan/china/showcontent, accessed on 17th February 2003.

Cheng Dan, ""Liu Xiaobo shi duli xuezhe haishi mei di guyong?" (Is Liu Xiaobo an Independent Scholar or An American Mercenary?), *riben jiu ge wang* http://www.danielviolins.com/jg/, accessed on the 21st march 2003.

Cheng dan, "Liu Xiaobo shuo: mei guo zhi min di 200 nian shi zhong guo de wei yi xi wang," (Lix Xiaobo says: China's only hope is for the US colonization for 200 years), *Wan wei lun tan* www.creaders.org/forums/politics/messages/466937.html, accessed on the 24th February 2003.

Center for Public Integrity, http://www.publicintergrity.org/wow/report.aspx?aid=75

Christoffersen, Gayer, "Constituting the Urgur in U.S.-Chian ?Relations: The Geopolitics of Identity Formation in the War on Terrorism," *Strategic Insight*, 2nd September 2002, the Center for Contemporary Conflict (CCC). http://www.ccc.npa.navy.mil/resepResources/si/sept02/eastAsia.aso, accessed on 25th October, 2002.

Da Can Kao Daily News, "hua fu zhao kai 9.11 kong bu xi ji shi jian hou kan zhong guo hui yi" (a meeting to look at China after the 9/11 terrorist attack), http://www.bignews.org/, accessed on the 16th October 2001.

Dong hai yi wu, "zuo xiu gao shao Han Deqiang," (Smart Actor Han Deqiang), *Xin shiji (New Century Net)*, http://www.ncn.org/zwgInfo/da KAY.asp?ID=21948&d=3/1/2003, accessed on the 7th February, 2003.

Du Daobing, "qizhi xiamming de zhan zai Liu Xiaobo yi bian," (Resolutely and clearly stand by the side of Liu Xiaobo), *Xin shi ji (New Century Net)*, http://www.ncn.org/zwgInfo/da-KAY.asp?ID=21948&d=2/27/2003, accessed on the 7th February, 2003.

Gao, Mobo, C. F., "Sino-US Love and Hate Relations." *Journal of Contemporary Asia*, Vol.30: 4 (Oct.) 2000: 547-561.

Gao, Mobo, C. F., Stephanie Hermelryk Donald and (Eric) Shaoquan Zhang, "National Sovereignty versus Moral Sovereignty: the Case of Australian Press Reporting of Taiwan," with Stephanie Donald and Eric Zhang, *Asia Media*, Vol. 30, No. 1, (2003): 22-30.

Gladney, Dru. *Muslim Chinese, Ethnic Nationalism in the People's Republic of China*, Cambridge, Mass., Harvard University Press, 1991.

Gladney, Dru, ed., *Making Majorities: Constituting the Nation in Japan, Korea, China, Malaysia, Fiji, Turkey, and the United States*, Stanford California: Stanford University Press, 1998.

Gladney, Dru, "Clashed Civilizations? Muslim and Chinese Identities in the PRC," in Dru C Gladney ed., 1998: 106-134.

Jiao Guobiao, "Zhi meiguo bing," (To American soldiers), accessed from http://www.readers.org, on 2nd June, 2004.

Li Hongkuan, "zhongguo ziyou zuojia ying yao fang mei," (Being Invited, Liberal Author Yu Jie visits the US) *da can kao*, http://www.bignews.org/20030605.txt, accessed on 6th June, 2003.

Liu Xiaobo, "mei guo gong yi zhu guan wei zi yi ke guan wei ren lei," (American attack on Iraq: subjectively for self-interest but objective for the good of human kind), *Shi ji sha long lun tan*, http://forum.cc.org.cn/luntan/china/showcontent1.phb3?eb=I&id=107705&id1-35816, accessed on 3rd March 2003.

Liu Xiaobo, "we xiang wei henwei shengming, ziyou yu heping er zhan—xian gei da zainan zhong de xun nan zhe," (I want to fight for the defence of life, freedom and peace—to those who sacrificed themselves in the big disaster), http://www.dajiyuan.com 11th September 2001, accessed on the 19th April 2005.

Luard, Tim, "China's Changing Views of Terrorism," *BBC* original link 16th December 2003, accessed on the 17th December 2003, via http://www.Chinastudygroup. org/newsarchive.php?id=4006.

Qing Zheng, "'cong jin ye women shi meiguo ren' dao 'bu xu yi women de ming yi',"(From "Tonight we are Americans" to "Not in Our Names), internet correspondence, WSG wangshaoguagn@cuhk.edu.hk, accessed on the 6th November 2002.

Ren Bumei, "quan ren lei zai kuxi," (All the humanity is crying), appeared on *qing nian lun tan* and re-publicized on http://www.dajiyuan.com, 12th September 2001, accessed on the 19th April 2005.

Wei Cheng, "Zhong wen wang shang xiao yan nong," (the smoke is thick on the Chinese Debate on the web), *Wan wei lun tan* www.creaders.org/forums/politics/messages/467501.html, accessed on the 25th February 2003.

Wu Guoguang, "xian mo yi la ke ren," (I envy the Iraqis) www.creaders.org/forums/politics/messages/494794.html, accessed on 3rd April 2003.

Yu Jie, zhong guo zhi shi fen zi yu yi la ke wei ji (Chinese intellectuals and the Iraqi crisis), interview with Yu Jie by Ren Bumei, *Shi ji sha long lun tan*, http://forum/cc.org.cn/luntan/china/showcontent1.phb3?eb=I&id=1077 05&id1 -35901, accessed on 3rd March 2003.

Yu Jie and Xu Jinru, "*zhong guo zhi shi fen zi guan yu sheng yuan mei guo cui hui sa da mu du cai zheng quan de sheng ming,*" Shi ji sha long lun tan, http://forum/cc.org.cn/luntan/china/showcontent1.phb3?eb=I&id=1008 56&id1-3469, accessed on 21st February 2003.

Yu Jie, Songzhong wei shui er ming," (For whom the bell tolls), first appeared on *minzhu lun tan*(democracy forum) http://asiademo.org/ and re-publicized on http://www.dajiyuan.com, 20th September, 2001.

Zhao Dagong, "shen wei zhongguo ren zhen de wu di zi rong," (Being a Chinese I really cannot bear being seen), http://www.dajiyuan.com, 19th September, 2001, accessed on the 19th April 2005.

Zheng Yi, "Ning wei wai guo chou bu zuo zhong guo ren," (rather be a foreign animal than a China person), www.readers.org/forums/politics/messages/710505.html, accessed on the 13th May 2004.

Zhu Xueqin, "min jian lun Zheng di yi bo," (The first wave of Popular Politics), *Shi ji sha long lun tan*, http://forum/cc.org.cn/luntan/china/ showcontent1.phb3?eb=I&id=106003&id1 =35555, accessed on 28th February, 2003.

The People's Daily (electronic version)

"Jia Chuwang qiang diao fan dui yi qie xingshi de kongbu zhuyi" 18th September 2001.

"Qian Qichen yiyue yu Baoweier tong hua," 14th September 2001.
"Waijiaobu fabu gonggao tanhua," 12th September 2001.
"Jiang Zemin zhi dian Bushi," 12th September 2001.
"Zhushi qianze," 12th September 2001.
"Ge fang qianze gongbu fenzi yiji meiguo," 13th September 2001.
"guojia luyou ju fabiao gonggao, jiang wei bun eng jishi hui guo de meiguo you ke ti
    gong bangzhu" 13th September 2001.
"Jiang yu Bushi tong dianhua: zhongguo qianze gongbu zhuyi," 13th September 2001.
"Jiang Zemin yu Bulaier tong dianhua," 19th September 2001.
Jiang Zemin yu Pujing tong dianhau," 19th September 2001.
"Jiang Zemin you faguo zongtong tong dianhua," 19th September 2001.
"Taliban qianze meiying dui a dong wu," 8th October 2001.
"women xuyao heping," 2nd October 2001.
"Alafate jinchi baowei lingtu." 3rd October 2001.
"Guba jinian 10.6 shijian 25 zhounian," 8th October 2001.
"shijie ge di zhongfu fa yan he chunzhong yaoqiu meiguo bun eng yinwei fan gong
    er shang wu gu," 1st October 2001.
"Qiang guo ye yi shou shang hai" 11th September 2002.
"an quan fang fan shi guanjian," 11th September 2002.
"Eluosi bai gan jiaoji hua fangong" 11th September 2002.
"Bajisitan dongdang bu an kun an yan," 11th September 2002.
"Zhongdong dui mei tongqing ye bu man" 11th September 2002.
Zhongya baixing rizi bu xiaoting," 11th September 2002.
"Guoji fangong qian lu man man," 11th September 2003.
"Dianbian zhuyi de kunjing," 11th September 2003.
"Liang zhou nian nian xu," 11th September 2003.
"fang gong lu zhang" 11th September 2004.

Nanfang zhoumo (hard copies)

Fu an, "Laden you Taliban shenme guanxi" (What is the connection between Bin
    Laden and Taliban), *Nanfang zhoumo*, 20th September 2001, p 1.

Zhang Qingguo, "Bushi de si ge jihui" (Bush's four opportunities), *Nanfang zhoumo*,
    20th September 2001, p 3.

Fu An, "jiduan de taliban, duo zai de afuhan" (The extremist Taliban, the
    Afghanistan that has so many misfortunes), *Nanfang zhoumo*, 20th September
    2001, p 2.

Mo Mo, "fan kongbu: quanxin de zhanzheng," (Anti-terrorism: a complete new war),
    Nanfang zhoumo, 20th September 2001, p 3.

Wang Fuchun, "kongbu zhuyi yu fei duicheng zhanlue" (terrorism and asymmetry
    war strategy), *Nanfang zhoumo*, 20th September 2001, p 4.

Ma Ke, "nengyuan weiji: jianyi yu fenqi" (energy crisis: suggestions and differences),
    Nanfang zhoumo, 27th September 2001, p 10.

Li Hujun, "women ruhe duifu kongbu zhuyi" (how do we cope with terrorism),
    Nanfang zhoumo, 4th October 2001, p 9.

Liu Xiaobiao and Liu Ying, "zhe shi wenming de chongtuo ma?" (is this clashes of civilization?), *Nanfang zhoumo,* 18th October 2001, p 3.

Tong Zhongying, "quanqiuhua, 9/11 shijian yu shijie cixu chongjian" (globalization, the 9/11 Incident and the rebuilding of the world order), *Nanfang zhoumo,* 18th October 2001, p 3.

Feng Duan, "9/11 zhihou de eang lue (the internet after 9/11), *Nanfang zhoumo,* 18th October 2001, p 27.

Xu Tianqing, "9.11 yu meiguo jingji xing shuai," (9/11 and the rise and fall of the US economy), *Nanfang zhoumo,* 12th September 2002, p. B14.

He Fan, "women gai ruhe jinian 9.11," (How should we commemorate 9/11?) *Nanfang zhoumo,* 5th September 2002, p. B14.

Shao Hongyan, "zui gai jinian 9.11 de ren ruhe jinian 9.11," (how do the people who mostly ought to commemorate 9/11 commemorate 9/11), *Nanfang zhoumo*12th September 2002, p. A10.

Mo Yu, "meiguo, ni hai anquan ma?" (US, Are You Still Safe?), *Nanfang zhoumo,* 12th September 2002, p. A10.

Wang Shuangyan, "9.11 bu zhi shi meiguo de zuobiao," (9/11 is not only the zuobiao for the US), *Nanfang zhoumo,* 12th September 2002.

"jiu wen xin da," (old questions and new answers), *Nanfang zhoumo,* 12th September 2002, p. A10.

Chen Xiaowei, "Meiguo ren zai xiang shenme?" (What are the Americans thinking?), *Nanfang zhoumo,* 12th September 2002, p. A9.

Lu Hongbing, "DIY xinen ren jilu 9.11," (DIY Journalists record 9/11), *Nanfang zhoumo,* 12th September 2002, p. D31.

Wang Yikui, "9.11: beiju you xi kaishi," (9/11: tragedy has begun since), *Nanfang zhoumo,* 18th September 2003, p. A8.

Song Wei, " zou xiang qiong tu mo lu de kongbu zhuyi," (the terrorism that reached its dead end), *Nanfang zhoumo,* 9th September 2004, p. A8.

Ma Jian, "fan kong, zai 9.11 shidai," (anti-terrorism during the post-9/11 period), *Nanfang zhoumo* , 9th September 2004, p. A8.

Un-Named Sources

Si xiang ping lun, re-publicized on http://www.dajiyuan.com , 12th September 2001, accessed on 19th April 2005.

Da ji yuan,)zhongguo minzhu yundong haiwai lianxi huiyi helan lian luo chu sheng ming," (Declaration by the Holland Office of the Chinese Democratic Movement Alliances Overseas), http://www.dajiyuan.com, 11th September 2001, accessed on the 19th April 2005.

"Meiguo yu xi zhihou de shijie" (The world after the attacks on the US), *Nanfang zhoumo,* 13th September 2001, p. 3.

"Heise xingqi er, heise meilijian" (Black Tuesday, black USA), *Nanfang zhoumo,* 13th September 2002, p. 2.

"Shimou zhongxin, bei mei fang kong tixi jiqi ta" (The World Trade Center, anti-air attack systems in North America and so on), *Nanfang zhoumo*, 13th September 2001, p 3.

"Chu le "shangdi baoyou…" (Apart from "God bless you"…), *Nanfang zhoumo*, 13th September 2001, p 4.

Chapter 13

OFF THE AXIS: MEDIA IN
JAPAN AND CHINA

Yoichi Shimatsu

For media commentators in Japan and China, the
principal concern arising from the 9/11 crisis was its potential effect on the
U.S. security role in the East Asia region. The war on terrorism, since its
inception in the wake of the 9/11 attacks, was viewed in the Japanese and
Chinese media as alternately a steppingstone and impediment to their own
nation's geopolitical aims in East Asia. American retribution against Islamic
militants for the World Trade Center attack was perceived as an objective of
short duration and less significance than the looming collision between an
increasingly hawkish U.S.-Japan military establishment and China, with its
expanding economy and defense muscle.

Throughout his first eight months in office, President George Bush had
promised to confront the "axis of evil," which included Iraq, Iran and North
Korea, and Asians were expecting an imminent showdown with Pyongyang,
the sole possessor of nuclear weapons among the targeted trio. Centrist
opponents of the Pentagon neoconservatives, concentrated mainly in the
State Department and Japan's Foreign Ministry, were then still influential
enough to avert an open rupture with Beijing over provocative actions in
support of Taiwan independence, such as high-tech weapons sales. Ending
this period of division in the White House, the counter-terrorism strategy
took U.S. foreign policy far astray of its earlier focus on North Korea and its
crucial ally, China. In hindsight, it is safe to say that the military occupation
of Afghanistan and Iraq shifted U.S. funding, military resources and valuable
time from the flashpoints of North Korea and Taiwan.

While American forces were diverted by the hunt for Osama bin Laden
and Saddam Hussein, Japan and China rushed to fill the strategic power
vacuum in East Asia. Disputes over offshore islets and protests against
textbooks quickly led to a breakdown in diplomatic exchanges between
Beijing and Tokyo. Bilateral tensions prevented the cooperative action that

both Japan and China, as the largest investors in U.S. treasury notes, required to stem the steep slide of the U.S. dollar.

In hindsight, the destruction of the World Trade Center can be seen as the symbolic start of the dollar's historic plunge from its lofty position as the world's money. Today, at exchange counters across Asia, the Hong Kong dollar — the surrogate for the Chinese yuan — has quietly replaced the greenback as the currency of choice. This reversal of fortunes could well be the broadest ripple from the shocks of 9/11.

From a broader perspective, the Chinese and Japanese media reactions to 9/11 heralded a new reliance on the nation-state amid a weakening of global institutions and regional structures. Commentators have alternatively interpreted the nation-state revival as a step backward from international cooperation or as a return to realism in an anxious world.

ONE NIGHT IN BANGKOK

At dusk on September 12, I had just landed in Bangkok after a two-week journey through Pakistan, from Karachi to the Line of Control in Kashmir. Over a long-missed bottle of wine with some Japanese friends, I picked up whispers inside an Italian restaurant indicating something terrible had just happened in New York. Outside on the pavement, the crowds were in a commotion over televised images of jetliners crashing into the World Trade Center. In the following days, I crisscrossed from Bangkok to Hong Kong, Tokyo and Beijing to deal with the many demands of the Asian media for news sources in Pakistan and to negotiate freelance assignments. Luckily for my team, the Asian media were eager for some first-hand reporting independent of the Western media.

Within a week of leaving Pakistan, I had returned to report inside Pashtun tribal areas along the Afghan border for a Japanese photojournalism magazine. The Afghan conflict was a significant advance for the Chinese media because it was their first time to send dozens of reporters into a foreign theater independent of government supervision. The increased size of the Chinese press corps was due to two factors: first, in the Kosovo conflict, China's thin news-gathering ability was crippled by the deaths of three Serb-speaking journalists in the U.S. bombing of the Chinese Embassy in Belgrade; and second, Beijing was experimenting with greater press freedom for reporters and editors.

Many of the Chinese reporters told me that they felt lost in a strange country, and their reports suggested that they could not handle intricacies of issues such as the U.S. military downplaying of the civilian deaths caused by

American bombing. In contrast to the Chinese exuberance and naivete, Japanese editors were single-mindedly focused on penetrating behind Taliban lines. I discovered that something other than scooping the competition was involved in this fascination when I attempted to make a freelance sale to two Tokyo-based television networks.

Helped by local contracts from my earlier visit to Pakistan, I sent two digital videocams with Taliban supporters into Jalalabad and Kabul. The videotape showed the orderly evacuation of these cities and other interesting scenes, such as the barrels of anti-aircraft artillery poking out of a mosque compound. In addition, I obtained photos of a meeting of Taliban chieftains agonizing over whether to detain Osama bin Laden. That outdoor debate turned out to be fatal for many of the delegates, who were hit with bombs that evening in the first wave of U.S. air strikes.

I offered the video and photos to producers with rival Tokyo networks. Both eagerly studied the tapes, and forwarded copies to their Tokyo headquarters. Payment, however, was never made because Tokyo wanted "images of military value," such as missile batteries and heavy artillery emplacements. The reply was disappointing, and it confirmed my suspicions that many in the Western and Japanese media were serving as forward observers and intelligence gatherers for the Pentagon.

Earlier that week, I had met Afghan refugees in Peshawar who were handed wads of dollar bills from producers with two American news networks in exchange for their family photos taken inside Afghanistan as well as documents and diaries. These materials were never shown in news broadcasts but simply vanished, presumably into the hands of the hidden paymasters.

Certainly there was no shortage of journalists willing to play an espionage role either on contract or as eager volunteers. On arrival with other journalists at Islamabad airport, one veteran Japanese photographer grilled me about trekking into remote parts of Afghanistan. Other Japanese journalists told me that this individual had gained notoriety and a hefty sum for his behind-the-lines espionage in Kosovo for a U.S. intelligence agency. What was striking about all these media warriors was their total lack of interest in the deeper issues — for example, the Taliban's work to prevent child prostitution and the secret cooperation between bin Laden's Sunni militia and U.S. covert operatives against the Soviet occupiers in Afghanistan and later against Shiite Iran.

Despite the best efforts of Asian journalists on the ground, the media in East Asia remained heavily dependent on CNN, BBC, AP and the AFP. Our initial Japanese sponsor soon stopped publishing independent reports due to "orders from outside and above," according to the assignment editor in Tokyo. Disconnected from our main reporting contract and funding source, my tiny team had to track the story angles set by other publications in Tokyo in hopes of making a sale. Fortunately, many editorials and commentaries of the time were available over the Internet and have since been preserved by institutions such as the Japan Press Center and international-oriented magazines, notably *Japan Echo*. *Yazhou Zhoukan*, a Chinese-language newsweekly, agreed to purchase articles and photos, and these turned out to be quite influential in China, where that magazine was read widely despite a ban against its sale.

AN AMERICAN NIGHTMARE

The spectacular collapse of the World Trade Center had triggered a welter of astonishment and relief among Asians in contrast to the rampaging fear and anger felt inside the United States. The televised scenes of helpless victims in Lower Manhattan contrasted sharply with the preconceived notion that Americans are immune to the misery suffered by the rest of humanity. Only Americans had the casual confidence to wear on their chests: "I (heart) NY." Now, for the first time in their lives, Asians were thankful for not being lucky enough to be in New York.

The contrast between living inside the American Dream versus the seemingly unreal images from a fearsome world outside was a theme delineated in the first editorial in *The Japan Times*, Tokyo's English-language daily, which follows the lead of the Cabinet and Foreign Ministry. "The enormity of Tuesday's events will take a long time to sink in, but it is probably true that, as commentators said in the wake of the shocking terrorist attacks, Americans' lives will never be quite the same again. The stuff of nightmares briefly broke through into the real world, and will cause profound and lasting anxiety."

The Japanese, unlike the Americans, were accustomed to large-scale tragedies and terrorist attacks at home. Six years earlier, the Hanshin Earthquake leveled much of Kobe and the Tokyo subways were gassed at rush hour. September 11 still had the power to shock the Japanese because of the suicidal determination of the perpetrators and the ensuing panic that engulfed America. The Japanese viewers were aghast at what came next.

"Former Republican House Speaker Newt Gingrich invoked memories of Japan's attack on Pearl Harbor when he declared Tuesday 'a day of infamy.' ... in fact the Pearl Harbor analogy is off the mark. In that case, the perpetrator and its goals — specific military goals — were known; in this case, nothing comparable is known. There are only suspects and speculation.

It is hardly feasible to declare war on a 'possible enemy.'" (The Japan Times, Sept. 13, 2001)

Americans were ready to lash out at still unknown assailants, and the first mental picture of a hated enemy to surface was of the Japanese. At the depths of national trauma, Pearl Harbor emerged as the primal image of fear and loathing in the American public mind, just as Hiroshima holds lasting meaning for the Japanese. This moment of truth, exposing the persistence of distrust, did not bode well for the future of the Japan-U.S. security alliance.

CROSSROADS FOR POSTWAR JAPAN

Japanese media commentators were divided over the type and extent of official support for America's war on terrorism. Previous dispatches of the Self-Defense Forces (SDF) were limited to United Nations peacekeeping missions, and even those few occasions, such as the Cambodia and Rwanda interventions, were controversial in their time. The 9/11 crisis was a different matter. In reaction to a direct hit on an ally, the Koizumi government could invoke the Japan-U.S. Security Treaty. His dilemma was that participation of Japanese personnel in combat operations would violate the postwar "peace" Constitution, which forbids war-making activities.

Through the late night of Sept. 19, Prime Minister Junichiro Koizumi met with his national security team to issue an anti-terrorism response plan. The keystone of the seven-point plan was a proposal for the SDF to provide rear-guard support for an American-led retaliatory strike. In their Sept. 21 editions, all the major newspapers favored some form of Japanese support for the counterterrorism campaign, but the media were seriously split on the issue of a combat role because it would require a revision of the Constitution.

The liberal *Asahi Shimbun*, editorially aligned with *The New York Times*, urged prudence in enacting legislation to provide rear-guard support. "We would like to consider providing support as long as it is not linked to the use of military force and is permissible under the Constitution." The *Mainichi Shimbun*, also of liberal persuasion, advocated that any military intervention should have prior approval from the United Nations. "We should think carefully about dispatching the SDF for any activity on the basis of the consensus among the international community."

The conservative *Yomiuri Shimbun* and ultra-right *Sankei Shimbun* demanded swift approval of the Cabinet's action plan and de facto preparations for military action. "The government of Japan has decided on a seven-point plan, but it was too late in coming," stated a *Yomiuri* editorial.

"Japan must carry out its international responsibility to join other countries on the frontline in the fight against terrorism."

The 9/11 attacks provided a convenient tool for Japan's conservatives to push for a revision of the Constitution and re-designate the Self-Defense Forces as a national military with the right and duty to fight wars against foreign enemies. For these drastic changes to be implemented, Washington would first have to lay blame on an enemy state rather than a shadowy network — and the targets of intervention and occupation turned out to be Taliban-controlled Afghanistan and later Iraq. Before the start of the Afghan air strikes, the SDF flew aircraft into Pakistan to evacuate Japanese, and the Embassy ordered the registration of its nationals such as members of my news team. The conservative press bristled at the gap between the government's strong words against terrorism and its typical timidity on the ground.

In *Voice* magazine, Kyoto University Professor Terumasa Nakanishi "ascribes the dithering in Japanese domestic discussion of the attacks to the fact that no coordinates have been fixed and he proposes three bearings: first, a common recognition that such attacks must never be repeated; second, the recognition that the victim of the attacks was America, an important friend and ally of Japan; and third, the cold reality that in the 21st century countries have no choice but to protect themselves." ("Now is the Time to Change the Constitution," *Voice*, November 2001),

The conservation calls for remilitarization were a double-edged sword since the objective was to sever the antiwar shackles of Article 9 imposed by the Americans who ghostwrote the Constitution of 1952. The sneak attack on the World Trade Center was the very tool needed to undo the Constitution that was intended to prevent another Pearl Harbor. The conservatives and Japan's defense establishment had some real grounds for distrust of American promises of protection. Several years earlier, the State Department withheld data from the Japanese government indicating that North Korea was preparing a missile test. President Bill Clinton had also pursued a policy of "bypassing" Tokyo with bilateral talks with Beijing, disrupting the spirit of the security treaty.

The 9/11 events exposed the lack of preparedness against the asymmetric tactics of suicide pilots and anthrax letters. Though the guarantor of postwar Japan's security, the U.S. military felt itself suddenly at risk and had no clear idea of the enemy's identity or motive. The giant U.S. Navy base at Yokosuka was put on high alert, and the American Embassy closed its doors in fear of a second round of attacks. For an anxious moment, Japan — its armed forces limited to non-nuclear self-defense — was momentarily stripped of the American umbrella under the provisions of the U.S.-Japan security treaty. If, just if, Pyongyang had unloosed its nuclear-tipped missiles on Tokyo at that vulnerable instant, the result would have been a terminal nightmare for the alliance. Fortunately, the axis was not quite as evil as portrayed by the Bush administration's rhetoric.

The conservative drive for constitutional revision, however, lacked sufficient support within the Diet, especially from opposition members of parliament who aim to restrain the authority of the Cabinet. In a commentary in *Voice* magazine (November 2001), Seiji Maehara, a politician with the opposition Democratic Party, criticized the Koizumi administration for failing to clarify the government's interpretation of the right to collective self-defense under the Constitution, arguing that such headlong action "undermines the rule of law and threatens to alienate even those Japanese who appreciate the need for Japan to cooperate with the United States." In the heated regional disputes since 2001, the peace Constitution has showed its practical value in denying grounds for China and the Koreas to take military action over the disputed islets.

THE VIEW FROM BEIJING

In response to the 9/11 attack, Beijing suspected that the Pentagon would try to use terrorism as a pretext to advance its forward lines against China.. The first editorials from *People's Daily* called for international consultation, a code word for a U.N. Security Council discussion, in counterterrorism policy and warned the Bush administration against using the World Trade Center attack to promote funding for a National Missile Defense system.

On Sept. 13, *People's Daily* reported the remarks of Vice Foreign Minister Wang Guangya in reaction to NATO's decision to support U.S. reprisals anywhere in the world. Wang asserted that the United Nations was the sole international body authorized to make such decisions, especially in regions outside of Europe. "NATO is a regional military organization within Europe, so if action is taken beyond Europe, it will have implications," Wang said. "So that's why I think consultation is needed."

Beijing was still smarting from the bombing of the Chinese Embassy in Belgrade and the Balkans wars. Since the dismemberment of its socialist ally Yugoslavia, China had been wary of the eastward expansion of NATO. Its fears came to be realized with the U.S. invasion of Afghanistan, which positioned American troops on China's borders for the first time since the Laotian phase of the Vietnam War.

For several months, the Chinese leadership was divided over whether to send Chinese troops into the Afghan conflict. Beijing had its own reasons for wanting to crush Islamic insurgencies, since exiled Uyghur separatists from its westernmost province of Xinjiang were inside Afghanistan. For Beijing, there was little to gain from joining the U.S. counterterrorism campaign because the Bush administration was showing no enthusiasm for involving Beijing in the planned invasion of Afghanistan.

A heated exchange erupted when Bill Gertz, columnist for the conservative *Washington Times*, leaked an intelligence report that China had upgraded the Taliban's anti-aircraft artillery system. Beijing briskly denied the charge. In conformity with its even-handed foreign-donor policy, China had installed an optic-fiber telephone network in Afghanistan. The phone system was one of the first targets of the U.S. bombing campaign.

As the only Asian journalist highly critical of the U.S. intervention in Afghanistan, I was invited in mid-November 2001 to speak at Tsinghua University's newly founded School of Journalism and Communications on the Afghan situation on my return from Pakistan. The topic was the relationship between the Afghan war and the Caspian Basin oil strategy promoted by key member of the Bush Cabinet, including Vice President Dick Cheney and national security adviser Condaleesa Rice. My interviews at the Petroleum Ministry in Islamabad had uncovered long-standing U.S. plans to lay an oil and gas pipeline from Karshi, Uzbekistan, down western Afghanistan and to the Pakistani port of Gwadar. Under the Cheney energy strategy, the Afghan pipeline was to circumvent Russia and OPEC member Iran as well as to divert oil that might otherwise be sold to China. A map of the Central Asian pipeline network showed the gathering of Chinese journalists that the Afghan intervention was not merely a punitive expedition against Osama bin Laden but the linchpin in a strategic plan to outflank Iran, Russia and China.

What began as scattershot coverage of distant 9/11 events began to pull together into the focus of geopolitical contest centered in Central Asia, of vital strategic importance to Beijing. On the first anniversary of 9/11, *People's Daily* ran these comments from an unnamed analyst. "Taking advantage of the unprecedented moral support extended to the United States by the international community, America has successfully organized an international counter-terrorist alliance, and has gained political dominant power; it has strengthened its relations with its allies, at the same time it has pushed forward its ties with other big powers, particularly U.S.-Russian relations; US troops have entered Central Asia, gone deep into South Asia and returned to Southeast Asia, and further enhanced the superiority of its global strategy. In the anti-terrorist war, it has put into practice its theory of revolution in military affairs, and displayed and consolidated its military superiority. Generally speaking, the U.S. status as the superpower has become more prominent after September 11."

FINANCIAL MELTDOWN PREVENTED

The impression of colossal U.S. military power that came out of the Afghan theatre was magnified by the relative weakness of the Taliban militia, which hastily retreated to the rugged mountains with their Soviet-era AK-47s and grenade launchers. The shutdown of shares trading in New York on 9/11 showed that the military colossus had feet of clay.

On news of the New York attack, the Nikkei index of leading companies listed on the Tokyo Stock Exchange fell through the psychological 10,000-point barrier for the first time in 17 years. The Tokyo market suffered the steepest drop of any other bourse in the world since it was the first to open after New York and Chicago. Western finance ministers had not yet imposed emergency interventions to prevent what one Wall Street analyst told me was "the real possibility of a market meltdown." The market rescue operation remains one of the unreported stories of 9/11.

Haruna Mikio, a commentator for Kyodo News, the Japanese equivalent of Associated Press, wrote on the same day, "The threat of terrorism has been magnified by the fact that economic activities in New York, including stock trading on Wall Street, were paralyzed. ... America, the most open society in the world, has proved incredibly vulnerable to terrorist onslaughts."

Other than such passing references, the Asian media put the best face forward and avoided mention of the full extent of financial damage sustained by banks and brokerages. According to a Foreign Ministry tally reported in the *People's Daily*, 18 Chinese companies were housed in the World Trade Center and six other Chinese financial institutions were in the vicinity. These official institutions tended to handle letters of credit, interbank transactions and Treasury bond purchases. Much more money from China was handled in the opaque realm of hedge funds and private banking services.

In Beijing, I had learned that Western hedge funds and even some brokerages took advantage of the destruction of computers inside the World Trade Center to simply deny the existence of accounts held by Chinese investors. Many of these missing funds were technically illegal, as they were part of the capital flight out of China. Fortunes were lost and fortunes were made on 9/11, and not all due to the collapse of the Twin Towers. Whatever actual harm 9/11 events inflicted upon Japanese and Chinese finance houses, it has since been eclipsed by the subsequent decline of the U.S. dollar.

Despite their war of words and skirmishes over islets, China and Japan have managed to avoid armed clashes, and neither side has made significant territorial gains or military advantages over the other. It appears that the stalemate is promoting regional relationships based on a balance of power that does not require a strong U.S. military presence. In this perspective, East Asia has evolved on its own beyond the Cold War standoff toward a relatively stable era of self-containment.

THE HARDENING OF SOFT POWER

Taliban-controlled Afghanistan was a convenient outlet for American rage, since the radical Islamic government was providing shelter to Osama bin Laden. The U.S. domestic demand for military reprisal was so compelling that the secret negotiations with the Taliban to expel bin Laden were scuttled in favor of air strikes. Directing American and British wrath against the Kabul regime was popular in any case due to the prior Afghan coverage by the Western media. Aid agencies and even U.N. staff were frustrated with the intransigence of the mullah-influenced government on human rights and women's issues. The Western press, following the lead of India's foreign policy, tended to demonize the Taliban and lionize the rebel Tadjik and Uzbek forces, who were also responsible for the ongoing destruction and poverty. One important issue that was ignored by the entire world media was the Taliban effort to stop the sexual exploitation of children, a common practice under warlord rule that has since revived under U.S. occupation. An NHK news producer who reported on the making of the film "Osama" agreed with me that pedophilia was a subtext that was glossed over in that movie.

To their credit, many Japanese commentators and reporters provided a more balanced appraisal of Taliban rule, taking into account its efforts to stop violent crime and suppress drug trafficking as well as its faults of extremism. Yoshio Endo, a Takushoku University scholar who had spent a year in Taliban-ruled Afghanistan, stated in "Averting a Worst-case Scenario" (Ushio magazine, November 2001): "The United States and the international community abandoned Afghanistan in the aftermath of the 1979-89 war, paying scant attention to such tasks as setting up a new government and postwar reconstruction. The Taliban regime, which was welcomed by the people when it captured Kabul in 1996 and put an end to a four-year civil war and put an end to a four-year civil war that had claimed almost 30,000 lives, has since lost the support of the people because of its extreme suppression of human rights and lack of will to improve living standards. ...

Unable to muster a supply of new troops, it effectively became a coalition of Pashtun, Arabs belonging to Al Qaeda, and recruits from Pakistan."

Endo, like many other Japanese writers, urged Japan to use its soft power rather than military force to aid the people of Afghanistan. Heeding such appeals, the Japanese government organized the Afghanistan reconstruction conference in Tokyo in January 2002. The donor meeting turned out to be a showcase for Secretary of State Colin Powell, and the Foreign Ministry made no attempt to distance Japan's policies from American firepower. Soft power served as an adjunct to military occupation, and the Tokyo conference became a sales tool to assuage potential critics of the newly installed pro-U.S. regime in Kabul. The news conference, like the ones in Islamabad, was stage-managed to take friendly questions from pro-U.S. correspondents and deny the floor to critical journalists. What the mass media failed to understand was that blanket censorship and self-censorship in Tokyo or Washington is far more insidious to democratic societies than Taliban restrictions on press coverage.

While most of the U.S. media presented 9/11 as a barbarous violation of civilized norms, Japanese commentators have suggested that Americans were not quite the innocent victims as presented by the Western media. Literary critic Kazuya Fukuda in an essay for *Seiron* magazine, put the civilization vs. barbarism formulation into a grand historical schema. Fukuda argued that "the (first) Gulf War clearly etched the outlines of the U.S. version of civilization. Once those lines were drawn the forces outside them were defined as barbarian; it became inevitable that civilization would have to fight against them and in doing so become barbaric itself." ("American Hegemony: The Beginning of the End," *Seiron* magazine, November 2001)

Chapter 14

ALTERNATIVE VIEWPOINTS: THE INDIAN MEDIA PERSPECTIVE ON THE 9/11 ATTACKS

Janet Fine

India has always had an ambivalent relationship to America. It respects its riches and power but is wary of embracing its political and moral values. Yet the ultimate dream of immigrating to the United States has long permeated Indian sensibilities, fueled by success stories of the Non Resident Indian (NRI). The British Raj has long since concluded its post-colonial influence with an increasing number of Indian students opting to study in the United States to pursue the "American dream." But after Indian media reported on the Indians who were killed in the 9/11 attack, many Indians returned to India. The Indian media reacted to the 9/11 attacks by voicing a collective uneasiness of what action President George Bush would take in the subcontinent region and what revenge, if any, would be taken against foreigners in the United States (one turbaned Sikh Indian was killed in Arizona).

There phrase, "Since 9/11," seems to be universal and, especially in India, seems to apply to everything, including the long passport "queue" outside the American Consulate in Mumbai, heightened airport security, and rising prices. The 9/11 attack also is used to explain why journalists can't interview American diplomats in Indian newspapers without intricate clearance or why Americans and foreign nationals in India were asked by the then Secretary of State Colin Powell to leave India in 2003 for fear of a "nuclear attack" by Pakistan, and many complied for a few months.

INDIA MORE CONNECTED TO NEWS NOW

Looming fear and terror has fueled a seemingly insatiable appetite of India for news, and "since 9/11" the growth of Indian TV news channels has been considerable and accompanied with diminished domination of the government-run Doordarshan channel (whose news coverage has correspondingly also grown in each Indian state). Print media are also booming; for example, three major national newspapers have emerged in Mumbai since 9/11 (*Asian Age, The Hindustan Times and DNA*), along with a plethora of magazines and international newspapers (like the *International Herald Tribune*), which help contribute to wide-ranging viewpoints. News reporting, although occasionally censored by the Indian government, has transformed the media arena. Satellite news channels are growing steadily and, in 2003, more than six news channels started up (including NDTV 24/7 in English and Hindi).

Indian viewers previously depended on CNN and BBC for foreign news. But these Western channels are reportedly losing viewership, in part because of their Iraq war coverage, which many Indians saw as pro-Western and as filled with "propaganda." There is an increased desire for Indian news to find its own "voice."

INDIA'S 9/11 FOCUS

Ironically, many network critics were subsequently fired, which has further diminished CNN, CBC and BBC's ratings to only 2 percent of Indian viewership compared with 38% for the Hindi news channel Aaj Tak (India Today News), according to an AC Nielsen Tam Media 2003 survey. But TV-connected households provide fertile ground for one billion Indians. About 109 million households had a television in 2005, and cable penetration is surging at 56 percent of those households (61 million homes).

"My perspective on Indian media coverage of 9/11 was that reports were by and large sourced from American media since that is all what we had in those days," said Mani Subramanium, a Mumbai wire service editor now at *Kaleej Times* in Dubai. He added:

> The focus of Indian media was primarily on how Indian families were
> affected by death of near and dear ones and how tightening of security
> measures at airports in the United States would affect Indian travelers.
> There were the usual eye witness accounts of how the aircraft crashed
> into the twin towers used by Indian television channels and pictures
> displayed by Indian newspapers were lifted from U.S. media forces like

CNN and NBC or published by arrangement with Western media.

We felt that BBC gave a more balanced coverage even as American media rallied around President Bush. Indian newspapers carried cartoons of Osama bin Laden together with Bush. Indian media also assessed the threats from terrorists on Indian soil and there were calls for more Indo-U.S. cooperation in the war against terrorism."

Unlike the almost universal pro-U.S. government support in the Western press, Indian journalists were not afraid of being fired for expressing raw emotions that spanned "the sorrow and the pity" to simmering anguish.

ANGER AND ANGST

"Today, I find anger at myself and at others," wrote Hari Sreenivasan in the Indian Rediff Internet Web site in an essay titled, "The Indian Media Reaction To The 9/11 Attacks."

I'm angry at myself because I am a member of the media, and I saw, along with an unprecedented amount of cooperation between the major networks in sharing video, some absolutely irresponsible coverage that today has caused me to be angry with others.

Let us see if you can figure why. While waiting for a washing machine at the Laundromat this morning, a couple of young men walked near me, having a rather loud conversation on what we as a country could and should do with the living body of Osama bin Laden, and frankly anyone that can even pronounce his name correctly. Trying to mind my own business, I sat on the bench, staring at remnants of the news in the local paper, wondering whether, with emotions running this high, the president could launch a nuclear response on Afghanistan.

At seeing me ignore their conversation, their pitches changed, they came closer and were speaking at me, every once in a while, looking back at one another when I looked up at them I could see by now that these two young men had every interest in engaging me in some way, whether it be conversation or otherwise, and I was torn between becoming defiant and challenging them, or quiet in some Gandhian way. I thought in my head whether I should point out that I'm not even from the Middle East, that I'm Indian, I'm not even Muslim, I'm Hindu, but then I realized how cowardly that would be, and that ultimately it didn't make a damn bit of difference to these closed minded men where I was from. I was brown, that's all that mattered.

Sreeni Sreenivasan, president and co-founder of the South Asian Journalists Association (SAJA) in New York and the Dean of Students at

Columbia University Graduate School of Journalism, said he focused the media organization's concern to first covering the tragedy of the 9/11 attack and then to another tragedy unfolding — reprisal attacks against South Asian journalists and other South Asians across the United States and Canada, perhaps because of the "brown" color now odious in post-9/11 America. In addition to tracking the Indians lost in the World Trade Center collapse, SAJA had to deal with a different kind of attack against Indian media, according to Sreenivasan:

> By Saturday afternoon, SAJA had received 37 death threats from within the U.S. and from around the world; one Sikh had been killed in Arizona and others injured, obviously in what was a clear case of mistaken identity ... While the press has done a good job of covering the dangers posed to Arab Americans and Arabs living in the United States by media stereotyping, we feel there still was not enough awareness of the bias crimes against South Asians and how they were coping with it.

Sreenivasan also saw that in "the aftermath of the disaster, attitudes in the media were also changing ... the U.S. and the Americans have been looking inward. They should look beyond the shorelines of the United States. They need to know what's going on in the rest of the world." He cited a New York editor who said that he would now deploy more journalists to India and Pakistan. SAJA mobilized with a media guide and Web site guiding reporters on 9/11 coverage and conducted an outreach meeting, "Covering the WTC Attacks and the Aftermath" opened to the public. Senior journalists discussed the coverage of the attacks and its backlash. Sreenivasan wrote:

> It was the first large-scale community gathering after the terrorist attacks and it became a cathartic experience to see other brown faces. People spoke what they had been going through in the past few days and those who still had not managed to trace their loved ones after the terrorist attacks talked about them. As we finished with the meeting, we saw a Sikh man being interviewed by a television crew. As he spoke, a white American who was passing by shouted, 'You Islamic mosquitoes should be killed.'
>
> THIS is what we are facing. A friend of mine, who is a senior journalist here and who doesn't want to be identified, faced a similar situation on the night of the terrorist attack. He was at a bar when two men in army clothes asked him if he was Middle Eastern. They posed several uncomfortable questions and it got nasty.

The perspective of also being a target impacted the writings of many in the Indian media. For example, here's an excerpt from Sevanti Ninan's "Coping with Calamity," which was published in the Rediff series immediately after the 9/11 attack:

> It is easy to acquire and bandy about a breezy prejudice against an entire community. The media does play a role in this. On Tuesday, millions of children and adults around the world watched the instantaneous destruction of what could be at least 20,000 lives. And several times in a space of a few hours they were shown people dancing, celebrating and making V-for-victory signs in the Arab quarters of Jerusalem.
>
> On one hand you had TV anchors groping for adjectives to encompass the enormity of what had happened — an attack to rival Pearl Harbor, the worst terrorist attack in the history of mankind, a crime against civilization — and on the other you had these scenes of celebration presented with little or no conceptualization ... For every innocent American that died yesterday, 1,000 Arabs have met with the same fate over the years, some of them, I suspect, directly related to the "crazy" highjackers. Why? Because of the U.S.'s oil thirsty foreign policy. Oh, and before you all jump to any conclusions, I am, and have always been, Christian.

Ninan brought up the conflict of religion, always an issue in India, which has the world's third largest Muslim population:

> When the projected villain is Islamic fundamentalism, the Muslim community worldwide, as innocent as the victims of terrorist attacks, ends up bearing the brunt. On the first day of the attacks in the U.S. there were occasional references on television to the disappearance of New York cab drivers who are substantially West Asian in origin. Eight million Muslims in the U.S. would have instantly begun to feel vulnerable. So what can the media do about it?
>
> Recognizing that attacks on U.S. embassies in Africa and counter-attacks by the U.S. rekindled prejudices against American Arabs and Muslims, *The Detroit Free Press* for example on the eve of the release of "Siege," the movie featuring bombings by Arabic Muslims in New York, organised for its staffers to hear from Detroit-area Muslims. They were invited to come and talk to the newspaper. One complaint voiced was that every time there was a terrorist attack, journalists asked Detroit area Muslims for their opinion. Every time there is violence in Northern Ireland, Muslim community leaders asked, did the media ask local

Catholics what they thought? Was the media failing to see a separation between a community and the terrorists belonging to that community?

PAKISTAN AND INDIAN PERSPECTIVES

Many professionals in Indian media pointed out that Western media were not as familiar with the specter of terrorist attacks at home that India has experienced, especially in Kashmir (from Pakistan-trained guerillas). This perhaps gave a more independent viewpoint of the 9/11 attack, with articles questioning President Bush and criticizing American media's often "hysterical" reaction to a profound tragedy. Many Indian journalists predicted (on the mark) that the hysteria and "hunt" for the proclaimed perpetrators of the attack would lead to a war in the subcontinent or Middle East region and the marginalization of India's influence.

On Oct. 18, 2001, K. K. Katyal wrote in India's influential South Indian newspaper, *The Hindu* ("Loss of leverage for India"):

> It was a painful experience — during a recent visit abroad, especially the four weeks in the U.K. after September 11 — to find India almost completely missing in the media focus on terrorism or the debates on diverse issues arising out of it ... . The sweep of the media coverage and the intensity of the discussions was not a surprise. What was a matter of surprise was that India did not figure or was insignificantly mentioned.
>
> Distressing indeed, because India had been the victim of trans-border terrorism for years, with heavy loss of innocent lives ... and had been persistently drawing attention to this menace with all the while, regarding itself — and for good reasons — in the forefront of the struggle against terrorism. But now it was conspicuously absent — so it seemed from London and, perhaps most other European capitals — in the global discourse on terrorism. "It seems India does not exist on the globe," remarked an irate NRI in an informal conversation in what seemed a representative comment.

Some Indian journalists like Kayal wrote there were more stories being covered by Western journalists from Pakistan (such as Pakistan's concerted decision to back the U.S. "war on terror" and distance itself from Muslim fundamentalists and Pakistan-trained Taliban terrorists). Some Indian journalists pointed out that Pakistan President Gen. Pervez Musharraf's statements on the 9/11 attack were heavily covered in Western media compared to Indian Prime Minister Atul Bihari Vajpayee's statements.

"Pakistan was projected as the standard-bearer of the fight against terrorism. Could the irony be more acute?" wrote Kayal, adding that "the

Pakistan media coverage, however, was not all positive to this pro-West position. There was the negative side as well, with graphic visuals of the rallies and demonstrations by angry pro-Taliban groups."

Many Indian media tried to analyze why India was not factored into the subcontinent's fight against terrorism. But they reasoned that the American government might be promoting Pakistan's role in capturing Osama bin Laden and the al-Qaeda residing near its borders. And they also pointed to the "irony of a democratic country like India superseded by a dictatorship like Pakistan fighting a war for democracy."

IRAQ WAR SIGNS

In a Sept. 29, 2001, essay published in The Guardian of London, Booker Award-winning author Arundhati Roy ("The God of Small Things") wrote one of the more unique Indian media interpretations of the 9/11 attacks. She predicts the American reaction would be war.

> The trouble is that once America goes off to war, it can't very well return without having fought one. If it doesn't find its enemy, for the sake of the enraged folks back home, it will have to manufacture one. Once war begins, it will develop a momentum, a logic and a justification of its own, and we'll lose sight of why it's being fought in the first place.

Like many intellectuals, Roy's definition of "freedom" differs from that of President George Bush, and she tried to comprehend why Americans became a terrorist target while joining many Indian journalists in stepping away from the patriotic fervor that has become emblematic of the post 9/11-rhetoric.

> American people ought to know that it is not them but their government's policies that are so hated. America's grief at what happened has been immense and immensely public. It would be grotesque to expect it to calibrate or modulate its anguish. However, it will be a pity if, instead of using this as an opportunity to try to understand why September 11 happened, Americans use it as an opportunity to usurp the whole world's sorrow to mourn and avenge only their own. ...

> The world will probably never know what motivated those particular hijackers who flew planes into those particular American buildings. They were not glory boys. They left no suicide notes, no political messages; no organization has claimed credit for the attacks. All we know is that

their belief in what they were doing outstripped the natural human instinct for survival, or any desire to be remembered. It's almost as though they could not scale down the enormity of their rage to anything smaller than their deeds. And what they did has blown a hole in the world as we knew it ... But war is looming large ... for America in its almost godlike mission.

Some Indian writers like London-based writer Salil Tripathi disagreed with Roy, writing in Oct. 5 issue of *The Guardian* that "some readers will take Ms. Roy's analysis as facts such as that if Osama bin Laden did not exist, America would have invented him. This is careless."

But the writings of Roy and other Indian media reactions to the 9/11 have provided a window into India's continuing independent position in the region, with journalists having less pressure to be coerced by an American censor. Perhaps that is why, after mourning a tragic loss, there is a degree of perceptive reasoning that somehow explains the current Iraq-American quagmire of continuing loss of lives started by the tragic 9/11 attacks.

"Now Bush and bin Laden have even begun to borrow each other's rhetoric," wrote Roy in *The Guardian*. "Each refers to the other as 'the head of the snake.' Both invoke God and use the loose millenarian currency of good and evil as their terms of reference. Both are dangerously armed — one with the nuclear arsenal of the obscenely powerful, the other with the incandescent, destructive power of the utterly hopeless. The fireball and the ice pick. The bludgeon and the axe. The important thing to keep in mind is that neither is an acceptable alternative to the other."

Perhaps the overall Indian media reaction to the 9/11 attacks can be considered as providing an acceptable alternative viewpoint.

Part III

ARAB/MIDDLE EASTERN MEDIA

Chapter 15

IMPACT OF 9/11
ON THE MIDDLE EAST:
PERSONAL REFLECTIONS

Ralph D. Berenger

After 9/11, the Arab World struggled to put the attacks on the United States in context. On the one hand nearly two generations had grown up believing the United States was "The Great Satan," since America emerged as the leader of the Western World following World War II. On the other hand, they saw America as a land of opportunity, wealth, freedom, and rule of law — most of which does not exist for the vast majority of Middle Easterners in their own societies.

Egyptian reaction was mixed to the terrorist attack. Except from some individuals with close ties to American companies, organizations or institutions, the Arab street response in places like Palestine, Jordan and Egypt initially appeared supportive of the attack that killed thousands of U.S. citizens and nationals from other countries. In some places, Egyptian and Palestinian reaction was as jubilant, as if Egypt had just won had won the World Cup.

"Mabruk! Mabruk! (congratulations)," several Egyptians shouted from the street as they watched television news reports at a corner appliance store on Tahrir and Falaki streets. "This is a proud day. A blow has been struck against the Great Satan. Allah ahkbar! (God is great)."

Gawish Abdel Karim, who drives a car for an Asian Embassy, told a French reporter: "Americans have forgotten that God exists. They have us by the throat and now they find themselves in a science fiction scenario — this time Rambo's not there to save the White House." (John Rambo was a large-than-life fictional Vietnam veteran character played by Sylvester Stallone in two motion pictures.)

Abdel Karim, a student watching the news from the curb, compared the attack on Washington and New York with the temporary Sixth of

October victory in 1973 of Egyptians over Israelis, who were occupying the Sinai Peninsula since the Six Day War in 1967. Egyptians are proud of the victory (a bridge, a university and a city have been named after it). Six years later Egypt was returned the Sinai under the Camp David Agreement. "This is a glorious victory like that," Karim said.

Most heads of state in the Middle East, including Egyptian President Hosni Mubarak and King Abdallah Hussein of Jordan, expressed shock and condemnation over the terrorist attack and officially offered condolences. While saying U.S. policies "against the weaker people of the world" were to blame for the aircraft attacks, Israel resistance group Hamas leader Sheik Ahmed Yassin regretted the loss of innocent lives. In March 2004, Israel killed the wheelchair-bound sheik with a targeted missile. Even arch-nemsis Moamar Khadafy of neighboring Libya, which the U.S. bombed during the Reagan administration to send a strong anti-terrorism message, expressed official regret. Libya has since renounced terrorism, and relations are gradually warming with the West.

Hojjatoleslam Hassan Rowhani, secretary of the Supreme National Security Council, in Afghanistan, where the Sunni led Taliban was sheltering Osama bin Laden at the time, also expressed official regret. Rowhani said: "From the Islamic point of view, we condemn terrorist acts and killing of defenseless human beings and regard it as an ugly and inhuman action." However, the United States should take the attacks as a warning, he said, suggesting America mend its cultural ways. Rowhani said he did not believe the indicted terrorist could have orchestrated the attack, because he had no telephone, fax, Internet access or other means of communications.

"This is very sad," said Maher Melagy, a university employee, shaking his head slowly. "All those poor people, and all those children who lost their mothers or fathers. This is very sad."

Some Egyptians doubted a connection to the Middle East as all.

In Cairo, one is never really sure what century he or she lives in. Walking by modern, albeit dusty, buildings one feels comfortably at home in the middle of the 20th Century, but turn a corner and the feel is medieval with narrow, twisting streets, overhanging balconies, and heavy Arabesque carved wooden doors, and windows covered by decorative mashabaya, lending a harem-like mystique to ordinary buildings. Donkey carts and Mercedes share the same roadway. Men in Italian cut suits mingle with country people in traditional galabayas. Throughout Cairo on any given day the visitor is hard pressed to see a woman on the street without a veil (hijab) or who is fully covered by a nihab. Rich and poor alike interrupt their day at least five times to answer the call to prayer over loudspeakers from the thousands of minarets the poke into the dusty, polluted air. Within this context, the era of instant global communication is confounding.

While an estimated 30 percent of Careines watched the WTC and Washington plane bombings unfold on television that Tuesday night, others got their information from sparse radio reports, and a sliver of the population followed it over the Internet, evidence of a shrunken world of communications. Young men on the crowded Metro hawked the morning editions of *Al Ahram, Al Akhbar* or *Al Gomhuriya* — the city's top circulated daily newspapers — all government controlled. The front pages all had bold headlines and large pictures of the 9/11 attacks, and they were greedily snapped up by passengers to the delight of the newsboys. Every news stand developed a crowd to read the front pages for free and offer their opinions about who was responsible.

My taxi driver asked me bluntly in Arabic if I was from *Amrika* shortly after I climbed aboard for the last leg to my house in a Cairo suburb. Yes, yes, I was, I answered nervously, not knowing what the taxi driver had in mind. "Sorry. Sorry," the driver said in heavily accented English. "Very bad. Bad. Sorry."

The news of the terrorist attack on New York flashed through the American University in Cairo's campus with the speed of electrons. Within 10 minutes of the initial CNN broadcast, most students outside of classes had heard about it. Within a half hour, crowds had gathered outside televisions in the appliance store windows. In a mixture of English and Arabic students, cab drivers and shop clerks were buzzing with the latest tidbits of information of the shocking news that had occurred seven time zones away. While reaction of students attending the American university was subdued, the reaction in the street was at times jubilant. In the computer labs and the few offices that remained open, computers clicked on CNN.com, the drudgereport.com and newspaper Web pages to find out the latest information. In near real time, they learned a second plane had crashed into the second tower, and a half hour later, at 4:50, news flashed that an airplane in what was the worst terrorist attack anywhere, ever, had also hit the Pentagon.

An American professor, wondering whether it would be safe to venture out into the evening street and make his way home for the evening was counseled by one staff member. "Yes, yes. Perfectly safe. No one will bother you. But if someone asks if you are an American, say you're from Cyprus. You look like you're from Cyprus."

A shell-shocked group of American University faculty members walked over to the apartment of another faculty, who lived nearby to watch the event on CNN. Others without TV watched the streaming broadcast from CNN, BBC, MSNBC or ABC over the Internet. My Arabic-speaking colleagues followed the events on the upstart Al-Jazeera. No other major news event in history had diffused so rapidly around the world as did the terrorist attack on the Twin Towers. Of course it was an event designed by the masterminds to generate this kind of publicity, the ultimate "propaganda of the event" (Scotton & Hachten, 2002).

Around midnight some of us walked to a nearby Metro along dark, nearly deserted streets. Uneasiness about the unknown was in the air, and for the first time after arriving in Cairo a year earlier, I was nervous about the reaction I, an American, would receive from Arabs, who before 9/11 were touchy about the linkage of terrorism to their ethnicity. I was sensitive, perhaps overly so, about every glance thrown my way by askaris on the corners. I did note how little traffic there was on the dark, Cairo streets, which usually bustle each night until early in the morning. People were home watching TV news, I deduced.

Cairo (population 13 million) has access to satellite and cable television and the Internet and is one of the regional leaders in satellite technology It also has an active press. Colored photos appeared in the morning editions of the Arabic media, which carried news service versions of the story. Young men on the Metro pointed to the photos of the burning Trade Center, grinned and laughed, before sharing it with others. Some read the stories and sat in stunned silence.

The U.S. Embassy in Cairo and the Consulate in Alexandria were both in a heightened state of alert for the week following the attacks in New York and Washington. Classes at the American school and university were canceled for the rest of the week, but Egyptian schools continued unaffected.

CHARACTERISTICS OF AUDIENCES IN THE MIDDLE EAST

One cannot discuss reaction in the Middle East without a brief analysis of the characteristics of the Arab audience in September 2001.

The most startling statistic is that increasingly younger audiences populate the Middle East. According to the United Nations Arab Human Development Reports in 2002 and 2003, young Arabs under the age of thirty comprise nearly a 70% of the total population, a demographic at odds with global figures. Islam is the region's dominant religion, although measurable percentages of Christians and Jews can be found in most populations, sometimes as the majority, such as in some of the locations in Lebanon.

There is a general distrust of the West, with some historical justification, and Western media products, which are selectively censored. Western news critical of the region is personalized and generally discounted as propaganda. Such a view is often fueled by media critics in the West (Nacos, 2002; Schlechter, 2003).

Because of high illiteracy rates, broadcast rather than print messages have greater population penetration, but the number of radio and television receivers still lags behind the developed world. FM stations dominate AM as the preferred medium. Until recently, governments controlled the content of radio broadcasts, and, through licensing of journalists, most governments still have influence over what is written or broadcast.

Countries in the region have low levels of formal education, averaging fewer than two years in Somalia and Sudan, perhaps because of protracted conflict, to around six years in the rest of the 22-country region. By contrast, Israel has 9.23 years and the United States 12.25 years.

The academic output in scholarly journals in 2001 was negligible, and the number of books published in the entire region was less than the annual output of Portugal. Each country has suffered a "brain drain," particularly of scientists and technicians, lured to the West by quality education, higher salaries and intellectual freedom.

Despite the majority of the population living at or below the United Nation's recommended minimum of $2 a day, media are playing an increasingly important role in the lives of Arabs. However, some elite families are among the world's richest, and they are avid players in owning or bankrolling Middle East media.

Transnational channels in Arabic such as Al-Jazeera, Al Arabiya, Al Manar and dozens of others are now broadcast from Morocco to Afghanistan, with all points in between. The transnational broadcasters enjoy a freedom to report unparalleled in the region's history, and early indications are these broadcasters are gaining credibility among viewers (Al Jabar, 2004). Satellite television has made its presence felt in the region (Sakr, 2001), and Al-Jazeera has been at the front of the band (El Nawawy & Iskander, 2003).

Former Yemen Ambassador William Rugh's 2003 book, *Arab Mass Media*, says the traditional taxonomy of authoritarian media fails to take into account varying shades of government control. Although some media systems in the region are owned and operated by government, others are not, and yet they toe the official line closely. Increasingly, Rugh asserts, the strictly controlled press, which he calls the mobilization press, is giving way to a diverse press that is starting to show criticism of the regimes in power. While a far cry away from a liberal-democratic press, there has been progress since 9/11 toward freedom of the press in the region. No small credit can be given to Al-Jazeera, which broadcasts from tiny, albeit oil-rich, Qatar in the Persian

Gulf.

Noha Mellor (2005) studied how Arab news differs from the West and came to the conclusion that its form and style evolved over centuries of storytelling, a favorite pastime since antiquity. Even today professional storytellers are in high demand. From this storytelling tradition emerged a style of journalism that is investigative and analytical rather than narrative and descriptive.

According to Majid Tehranian (1999), when it comes to Middle East relations with the West, four misunderstandings must be overcome. First, the West does not understand the Middle East; the Middle East does not understand the West; the West does not fully understand the West, and the Middle East fully does not understand the Middle East. This negative matrix mitigates against a clear picture of each other and themselves, and nothing demonstrated these facts better than the reaction to 9/11, and the resulting thesis that the United States is disliked intensely around the world.

CHARACTERISTICS OF THE ARAB STREET

Public opinion thrives in the Arab World and in the mythical Arab Street, where mostly men visit their favorite coffee shops and sit around tiny round tables and drink either demitasses of thick, bitter Turkish style coffee or clear glasses of tea, both heavily sugared. The patrons often draw on a coal-fired bowl of flavored sheesha through their hubbly-bubbly water pipes as they discuss everything from religion and politics to their humdrum lives. Small screen television sets, mounted near the ceilings, are tuned variously to soccer games or Al-Jazeera, the TV satellite news channel.

Those who can read newspapers discuss with anyone within ear shot their understanding of the paper's analysis of the news. Arguments commonly erupt between differing viewpoints on a given subject. Consensus, it seems, it not the ultimate goal of these street cafe dramas; the mere act of expressing opinions is what matters in a culture where governments try to manage news, ideas and their image abroad. What is lacking throughout the Arab World is adequate measurements of public opinion, a process scorned by authoritarian regimes throughout the region's 22 countries.

Coffee shops, such as the Café Rich downtown, traditionally have been places where intellectuals, such as Nobel laureate Naguib Mafouz, would meet and discuss their ideas of what the Middle East ought to be. Gamal Abdel Nasser, as a young Army colonel in 1952, outlined the goals of the Free Officers Association before they overthrew King Farouk. Shortly after assuming power himself, Nasser shut down the larger cafes (Bieber-Roberts & Pierandrei, 2002, p. 7).

Arab Street reaction is watched closely — and monitored — by governments that do not take lightly to criticism from their populations. Prisons from Rabaat to Tehran are swelled with the ranks of the discontented. For example, Dr. Saad Eddin Ibrahim, a political sociology professor at the American University in Cairo, spent nine months in jail on trumped-up charges before international pressures were brought to bear on President Hosni Mubarak. His widely acknowledged sin? A suggestion made by Ibrahim that the Mubarak was engineering a dynastic succession to the presidential office by a son, Gamal. Reporters who speculated about the succession were disciplined, threatened or lost their jobs under the Egypt's state-controlled media.

In the Middle East, one can count on one finger the number of governments that allow rigorous — sometimes-vicious — dissent and criticism of government in the street and press. That turns out to be the regional scapegoat, Israel. Arab World governments often encourage anti-Israel/anti-American protests as a safety value for dissent, creating the climate to crystallize public opinion in the Arab Street. Arabs are no fools. They know what is safe to talk about, and what could be extremely uncomfortable for them if their conversations fall on the wrong ears. Pro-American statements fall into the latter category. Elisabeth Noelle-Neumann called it a "spiral of silence." Few places in the world, like the Middle East, so rigorously support her theory that people have a sixth sense that discerns whether if they are out of step with majority opinion, and fearing isolation they prefer to remain silent or mouth the majority view (Griffin, 1997).

Arab governments, however, find mobilization of the Arab Street to their advantage. For a few dollars, truckloads of poor, unemployed country people in Egypt, for example, can be bused to Tahrir Square, in the shadow of the huge Soviet-looking main bureaucratic office building, the Mogamma, in the heart of the city. Staged demonstrations almost always are well-covered in the government press and almost always treated as a spontaneous event. When other groups try similar protests, especially around the parliamentary elections, hundreds of riot police with sticks surround the demonstrators. And at the appointed time, the crowds are dispersed, sometimes resulting in a few cracked heads.

On September 11 and the days that followed, Arab Street reaction and the facts as presented by the Western media about who was responsible elicited four major reactions: disbelief, denial, deflection, dissociation, and dislike of U.S. foreign policy.

Disbelief

The first response on the Arab Street was that Arabs could not have been involved, as CNN and BBC were reporting. "This event was too well planned and coordinated," one of my students told me. "Arabs are incapable of that kind of planning." There is no small measure of self-doubt in the Arab World. But Israelis? Well, yes, Israelis were that smart, everyone knows about that "evil."

The initial stories about Al Qaeda's involvement in 9/11 were discounted on the Arab Street. How could one man, even a rich man like Osama bin Laden, an Arab, possibly carry off such a daring and logistically complicated plan? A public opinion poll conducted by the George Gallup organization of 9,924 adults in nine Muslim countries supported this disbelief. Sixty-one percent of those polled labeled untrue reports that Arabs were involved, only 18% believed the media reports (USA Today, 27 February 2002).

Denial

As the evidence seemed to mount that 19 Arabs were actually involved, the Arab Street slowly came around to the realization that Al Qaeda was involved and that Osama bin Laden was the hidden hand guiding the three airplanes into New York, Washington and a field in Pennsylvania. Bin Laden appeared on Al-Jazeera in October, 2001, and gleefully praised the attackers as martyrs for jihad. His admission, though less forthright than it could have been, was widely interpreted in the Arab Street as taking responsibility for the skyjackers of September 11.

Palestinian authorities, always cognizant of world opinion, confiscated Associated Press camera equipment after a field reporting team photographed celebrating Arabs. Later, spokesmen for the Palestinian Authority denied that any celebration had taken place, and that video footage shown on CNN was from the network's news archive of a different event entirely. That theme gained credence in the Arab World on a false report that a Brazilian mass communication professor produced the exact same footage for his class. The story spread rapidly over the Internet, forcing the Brazilian professor to issue a denial and acknowledge that CNN's footage was new.

"This is just like that Oklahoma (City Federal Building) bombing. How do they know Arabs were involved?" Sadek Samir asked between puffs of apple-flavored sheesha through a gurgling water pipe, his head craned upward to the fuzzy 13-inch black and white television on the wall of a narrow coffee shop along Mohammed Mahmoud Street. "Those (in

Oklahoma City) were Americans killing other Americans; this is the same. Maybe this was a conspiracy of air traffic controllers," he said without cracking a smile.

"They always blame Arabs first," his friend, Tarek said, sipping hot tea from a glass. "Maybe it was the Zionists?" He, too, did not smile.

Deflection

So, in the logic of Middle East Arabs, it must have been the Israelis or even the Americans themselves. Fueled by a report from the Hamas channel in Lebanon, Middle Easterners were quick to blame the Israelis. The evidence, according to the television news show, was that 4,000 Jews did not show up for work at the Twin Towers and, thus, were spared the coming carnage. They must have had advanced knowledge of the incident.

That conspiracy theory fit well into the schema of Arabs who had tried unsuccessfully to militarily destroy the Jewish state of Israel in 1948, 1967 and 1973 — before supporting financially and with materiel two uprisings in Palestine, which most felt they could have done without the interference and threat of U.S. military might (Abu-Odeh, 1999). Reported in newspapers in the Middle East, the story of absent Jews from the Trade Center was never corrected. In fact, another false story — which alleged that five Israelis were arrested on top of an apartment building after rejoicing about their victory in guiding the airplanes into the Twin Towers — was widely circulated on the Internet convinced them that Arabs were not involved. In part these stories are believed because they fit nicely into the schema that the creation of the State of Israel is the root of all evil in the Middle East, which includes beliefs that the secret intelligence agency Mosad has infiltrated the intelligence agencies around the world to do the bidding of their masters in Tel Aviv and that ethically weak-minded Americans in power are unduly influenced by Israel's IPAC, a political action committee that funded political campaigns in the United States.

The father of the Egyptian leader of the 9/11 attack in New York, Mohammed Atta, held a widely publicized news conference a few weeks after 9/11 in which he alleged he had spoken on the telephone to his son after 9/11 and that he proclaimed his innocence. He repeated at the news conference the widely circulated stories above as evidence that the Mosad was behind 9/11, and "the fact" that five Israelis were arrested after rejoicing in the attacks from a rooftop with a view of the Twin Towers. The elder Atta's comments were widely covered in the Egyptian press. Middle East media indulged in a sense of blame shifting for what happened on 9/11 and who was responsible. Arabs were quick to point out that their ethnic group had been blamed initially for the Federal Building bombing in Oklahoma City in 1995, for which an American, Timothy McVey, was ultimately executed. There was never a mention in the media that the Oklahoma City bombing resembled closely the first attempt on the Twin Towers in New York in 1993 for which a cell of militant Islamacists was found responsible and several, including a blind Egyptian sheik, are currently serving time in prison for their involvement.

Dissociation

Arab media seemed dissociated with what happened during 9/11. Here was an unprecedented disaster with long-term reverberations for the region, but the government-controlled press was unable to localize the story to reflect what their readers and viewers actually thought about the event.

In keeping with the closed societies in which many media functioned, sympathy for the victims of the terrorist attacks rang perfunctory and, usually, without taking a collective breath — a standard anti-U.S. response was woven through the rhetoric. As with most things in a region, where circular reasoning dominates, there was a disconnect between the near-pride some Egyptians felt that an Arab could have pulled off such a technically complex and well-coordinated attack, while at the same time decrying loss of innocent life.

A Muslim bag salesman the day after the terrorist attack, noticing his customer was a Christian by the "hanging cross" she wore, handed her a plastic bag with candles inside and asked her to burn them in her church in thanksgiving for the attack on America. To avoid an unnecessary confrontation, the woman said later that she took the candles but refused to light them in her church (Hulsman, personal interview, 13 September 2001).

"I don't understand this celebration of death," said Kees Hulsman, a Dutch journalist with connections to the Coptic community in Cairo for a quarter of a century who writes extensively about social matters in Egypt. "Imagine, governments offer condolences and simple people on the street express their joy over the deaths of others," he said, shaking his head sadly (Hulsman, personal interview, 13 September 2001).

Disenchantment with U.S. Foreign Policy

A common refrain is that the Arab World hates America and what it stands for, and some research seems to bear that out as part of an international trend. Surveys of high school students around the world and other research shows that foreigners believe Americans are self-centered, greedy, unqualified and uncritical backers of Israel, supportive of the regimes that repress them, unholy in their belief systems, and a mixture of either evil geniuses bent on corporate world domination or idiot savants who have lucked into everything they have (DeFleur & DeFleur, 2003; Napoli, 2004).

Nevertheless, Egyptians are curious about and mostly friendly to individual Americans. Their anger — bordering for some on hatred — is specific: the U.S. government's support of Israel. That issue has "poisoned the air" (Hulsman, personal interview, 13 September 2001).

There is no small measure of intellectual dishonesty in the jerk-knee anti-Americanism, most of the tens of thousands of American expatriates in the region say privately. After all, it was the United States, not Europe, who came to the rescue of Muslims in Kosovo under genocidal attacks from Serbs. It was America who is one of the first to pour aid into places like Bangledash, Indonesia and even Turkey — all Muslim countries — when disaster strikes, and to send troops to Somalia to keep Muslims from killing other Muslims, and even to Afghanistan to stop Muslim-on-Muslim murders. Hundreds of thousands more Iraqi Muslims died at the hand of Saddam Hussein than allied forces sent to remove him from office. Even suicide bombers — called martyrs in some Arab media — kill more Muslims than non-Muslims in their attacks throughout the Middle East. To say that the United States is anti-Muslim rings hollow in the face of evidence, yet many in the Arab World believe America is practicing genocide against them. They are misunderstood around the world, Arabs say, a permanent "Other" (Kempf &Luostarinen, 2003).

Anti-American sentiment had been simmering in Cairo for nearly a year since the second *intifada* (uprising) in the Palestinian area in 2000. Many Palestinians attend university or live in exile in Egypt.

The United States is seen, curiously, as a puppet of Israel. Widely held views are that Jews control the U.S. news media and the U.S. Foreign Service. It did not help public perception that the U.S. Ambassador to Cairo at the time, Daniel C. Kurtzer, was Jewish. He is the current ambassador to Israel.

On Sept. 10, a day before the terrorist attack, an anti-U.S. rally was authorized in the huge Tahrir Square by the Egyptian government in front of The American University in Cairo, a lightening rod lately for anti-U.S. sentiment. After shouting slogans, waving banners and denouncing the U.S. and Israel, the crowd, estimated at 500, was blocked by flak-jacketed and helmeted security forces, who vastly outnumbered the protestors, from moving toward either toward AUC or to the nearby U.S. Embassy and soon broke up.

American professors and residents often support pro-Palestinian rallies. The year before 9/11, anti-Israel and U.S. rallies took place at all the city's colleges, including the heavily American-influenced American University in Cairo. Again, well-armed security forces in large number made sure the crowds were contained and behaved properly — meaning that they criticized Israel and what they consider its sponsor, the United States of America.

Anti-Israeli/anti-American sentiment had been growing up to and through 9/11 in the Arab Street and media. A particular target was President George Bush since his election in 2000. One would be hard pressed to find a single, positive cartoon or a sustained or positive editorial on the Bush presidency. Even after 9/11 the criticism of his administration went unabated and only intensified to the buildup to the Iraq war. The CNN/Gallup Poll conducted several months after 9/11 found that 58 percent of the nearly 10,000 Arabs in the sample disliked George W. Bush, who had been in office for just over one year when the poll was taken. The dislike of America was only slightly lower but still a majority opinion among the respondants. Fifty-three percent of the Arab World respondents held unfavorable views of United States, while only one in five thought of the United States in positive terms.

The governments allow this criticism in their controlled media and on the Arab Street because it deflects attention to problems closer to home. Such anti-West/anti-Israel media policies are an artifact of the Gamal Abdul Nasser era. The effect of this persistently negative interpretation of U.S. foreign policy has contributed to building the anti-American schema in the Arab psyche, which might be interpreted as an application of Gerbner's cultivation theory of media that extends beyond television as the main media of schema creation. In short, Arabs' negative views of America have been cultivated — across print and broadcast mediums — for more than half a century in a region where up to 70 percent of the population is under 30 years of age and increasingly turns to media to develop their worldview.

CONCLUSION

Some Arab political leaders understood from the start that the attacks of 9/11 would rock their world, and how much it quaked would depend on their immediate expression of sympathy that such a thing had happened at the hands of their countrymen and fellow members of the Islamic *ummah* (community). Many of these same leaders have themselves been threatened or lost relatives to assassination and are more aware than Westerners that they ride the backs of tigers. They know the hands waving at their motorcades can just as easily be throwing grenades. These leaders are betting on the power of the world's lone hegemon to keep order in the region, regardless of their public rhetoric, which is often critical of U.S. foreign policy.

While the United States preaches increased democracy, open elections, free presses, and market economies, there are few Pollyanna's in Washington who think these things will actually result anytime soon in the Middle East. There is too much ground to make up, and technology in other parts of the world has sped up the clock. The lesson of 9/11 on Middle East leaders was clear. If a country as powerful as the United States could be fought to a standstill in the war on terrorism, what chance do they have?

Terrorism has increased, not decreased, since 9/11 in the Arab World. Innocent civilians, once a protected class by would-be suicide bombers, are now the targets of opportunity in previously safe places like Saudi Arabia, Iraq, Jordan, Egypt, and Lebanon, and in non-Arab Muslim countries like Pakistan, India, Indonesia, The Philippines and Thailand. Terrorists have also struck at London, Spain, Russia, Holland, Denmark, Germany and France. The attacks of 9/11 have spawned a global, sometimes ill-defined reaction of violence, and there are no signs of it abating soon. The whispered truth is that terrorism works in the unintended consequences of fighting it — a truth all-too-well understood by iron-fisted Middle East regimes struggling to join a world community of development while trying to survive

REFERENCES

Abu-Odeh, A. (1999). *Jordanians, Palestinians and the Hashemite Kingdom in the Middle East peace process.* Washington: U.S. Institute of Peace Press.

Al-Jaber, K. (2004). *The credibility of Arab broadcasting: The case of Al Jazeera.* Doah, Qatar: National Council for Culture, Arts and Heritage.Barber, B.R. (1996). *Jihad vs. McWorld: How globalism and tribalism are reshaping the world.* New York: Ballantine Books.

Berenger, R. D. (2006). Media in the Middle East and North Africa. In McPhail, T.L., Global communication: Theories, stakeholders, and trends. (2nd Ed.), pp. 192-225. Cresskill, NJ: Blackwell.

Bieber-Roberts, P., & Pierandrei, E. (2002, July 22). Café Riche: Memory in the formation of Egyptian national identity. Paper presented at the 2002 International Association for Mass Communication Research, Barcelona. [online]. Accessed November 22, 2005, at http://www.portalcomunicacion. com/bcn2002/n_eng/programme/prog_ind/papers/b/pdf/b005_biebe.pdf

DeFleur, M. L., & DeFleur, M. H. (2003). Learning to hate Americans: How U.S. media shape negative attitudes among teenagers in twelve countries. Spokane: Marquette Books.

El Nawawy, M., & Iskandar, A. (2003). *Al Jazeera: The story of the network that is rattling governments and redfining modern journalism.* New York: Westview/Perseus.

Gewen, B. (2003, March 30). The global villain (review of *Being America*). *New York Times Review of Books,* p. 7.

Griffin, E. (1997). Chapter 30: The Spiral of Silence of Elisabeth Noelle-Newmann in A first look at communication theory. 3RD Ed. New York: McGraw-Hill.

Hulsman, C. (2001 September 13). Personal interview with author. Cairo, Egypt.

Kempf, W., & Luostarinen, H.. (Eds). (2003). Journalism and the New World Order: Studying war and the media. Vol. 2. Göteborg, Sweden: Nordicom.

McPhail, T .L. (2002). Global communication: Theories, stakeholders, and trends. Boston: Allyn and Bacon.

Mellor, N. (2005). *The Making of Arab News.* London: Rowman & Littlefield.

Nacos, B.L. (2002). *Mass-mediated terrorism: The central role of the media in terrorism and counterterrorism.* Oxford: Rowman & Littlefield.

Napoli, J. J. (2004). Hating America: The press in Egypt and France. In R.D. Berenger (Ed.) *Global media go to war: Role of news and entertainment media during the 2003 Iraq war*, pp. 3-13. Spokane: Marquette Books.

Schechter, D. (2003). *Media wars: News at a time of terror.* Lanham, Md: Rowman & Littlefield.

Scotton, J. F. & Hachten, W.A. (2002). *The world news prism: Global media in era of terrorism.* Ames, IO: Iowa State University Press.

Rugh, W. A. (2003). *Arab mass media: Newspapers, radio and television in Arab politics.* Westport, CT: Praeger.

Sakr, N. (2001). *Satellite Realms: Transnational Television, Globalization & the Middle East.* London: I.B. Tauris.

Tehranian, M. (1999). *Global communication and world politics: Domination, development, and discourse.* Denver: Lynne Rienner Publishers

United Nations Development Programme. *Arab Human Development Report 2002: Creating opportuities for future generations.* New York: United Nations, 2002.

United Nations Development Programme. *Arab Human Development Report 2003: Building a knowledge society.* New York: United Nations, 2003.

USA Today (27 February 2002). Gallup Poll: Anti-U.S. sentiment in Arab world. [online] Accessed 23 November 2005 at www.usatoday.com/news/sept11/2002/02/27/usat-poll.htm

Zogby, J. J. (2002 September) What Arabs think: Values, beliefs and concerns. A report of Zogby International. Beirut: Arab Thought Foundation.

Chapter 16

A SEMIOTIC ANALYSIS OF 9/11 IN THE PALESTINIAN PRESS

Qustandi Shomali

This paper presents a formal analysis of the image of the 9/11 attacks in the Palestinian press using semiotics. It is not a political analysis of news reports or opinion articles, but rather how political thoughts and opinions are expressed through text and graphics. In fact, news and articles draw their meaning and significance from the way they interact with each other and with other forms of expressions in the same newspaper. We cannot fully understand any of them until we have looked at how they make meaning together, multimodally, with one another.

Consequently, the image of the 9/11 attacks is defined in terms of contrast and similarity of different forms of expression in the same context. A selection of opinion articles, news reports, political caricature and pictures from the Palestinian press are analyzed. Their meaning and significance are defined not only by their content, but also by contrast and relations among different forms in the same newspaper.

This study focuses on the printed press. In fact, Palestinian media is mainly a printed one, and it is the most appropriate tool to portray the image of 9/11 attacks. The Israeli occupation authorities did not allow television, radio and other forms of electronic media to operate until the arrival of the Palestinian Authority in 1996. These resources are still in development and depend to a large scale on resources from Arab and foreign media.

The material examined will be taken from two of the three main local newspapers in the Palestinian Territories, *al-Quds* and *al-Hayat al-Jadidah*. The first is an independent newspaper and the most important newspaper. The second is a semi-official newspaper. The collected material covers a period of four months extending from Sept. 12, 2001, to Dec. 31, 2001. This represents 110 media coverage days.

POLITICAL TRENDS AND EVALUATIVE MEANING

Content from the two newspapers — which includes news reports, opinion articles, pictures and political caricatures related to the 9/11 attacks directly or indirectly — are subjected to a semiotic reading and are divided into four different semantic classes that account for the articulations of four different viewpoints of the 9/11 attacks within the Palestinian newspapers.

> 1-Forms expressing support for the United States and opposing the 9/11 Attacks
> 2-Forms expressing opposition to the United States and supporting the 9/11 Attacks
> 3-Forms that rationalize the 9/11 Attacks and present justifications for it.
> 4-Forms that irrationalize the 9/11 Attacks and portray a negative image of American policy in the Middle East

A. J. Greimas, in his book *Structural Semantics* (1966), suggests a formal procedure for the perception of meaning in a discourse and provides a semiotic model designed to account for the articulations of meaning within a semantic universe. According to Greimas's model, the fundamental structure of the 9/11 attacks in the Palestinian media is a pair of semantic classes which in their opposition to one another are correlated with another pair of classes so as to produce a thematic interdependence.

1. EXPRESSING SUPPORT TO THE UNITED STATES:

Most of the material in this semantic class is represented by textual forms, news and news reports. Very few pictures or caricatures represent this trend.

The reading of the following titles shows that the 9/11 attacks were strongly condemned by all the Palestinian political organizations, unions and committees, and Human Right organizations. The President of the Palestinian Authority sent a letter of condolences to President George Bush and began a blood donation drive. The Palestine Legislative Council condemned the terrorist attack on the United States and sent an urgent letter of condolences to Speaker of the House of Representatives. Almost most of the important figures in the Palestinian authority expressed grief and outrage, fully expressing sympathy with the Americans who lost loved ones.

Palestinians in East Jerusalem held a candle-light vigil to express their grief and solidarity with the American families struck by this tragedy. The one million Palestinian students in the Palestinian Territory stood five minutes in silence to express their solidarity with the hundreds of American children who have been struck by this tragedy, which resembles in its shocking effects their daily sufferings. Students and professors went to hospitals in order to donate blood for the American victims. The following is a list of headlines of news reports that represent this viewpoint:

1- The Legislative Council Condemned the Terrorist Attacks against the United States and warned Israel against Using the Attacks as a Pretext to Escalate Attacks on Palestinians. *al-Quds* 16-9-2001

2- Children of Palestine Observe One Minute of Silence for the Innocent Victims in the United States. *al-Quds* 13-9-2001

3- Children Carried Flowers and Candles Expressing their Sorrow. A Palestinian Demonstration in front of the American Consulate in Jerusalem to Condemn the Attacks on New York and Washington. *al-Quds* 13-9-2001

4- Premier Qurie Presents his Condolences for the Victims of the 9/11 Attacks in the United States. *al-Quds* 13-9-2001

5- President Arafat Opens a Campaign to Donate Blood for the American Victims. *al-Quds* 16-9-2001

6- Special Prayer for the Memory of the Victims of the Tragedy of New York and Washington. *al-Quds* 16-9-2001

7- A Letter of Condolences from Arafat to Bush. *al-Quds* 12-9-2001

8- Arab and Muslim Religious Leaders Condemn Terrorism in Friday Sermon Prayers. Islam Calls for Love not for Killing. *al-Hayat al-Jadidah* 15-9-2001

9- Intellectuals and Journalists in Ramallah Condemn the Attacks on the United States. *al-Hayat al-Jadidah* 9-2001

10- NGOs in Gaza Condemn the Attack on the People of the United States and Call for War on Terrorism. *al-Hayat al-Jadidah* 9-2001

11- Health Ministry Calls on the Citizens in Nablus to Donate Blood to the Victims in the United States. *al-Hayat al-Jadidah* 9-2001

12- Palestinians Express Solidarity with the American People and Condemn the Attacks on Washington and New York. They Donate Blood and Announce Mourning in Schools. *al-Hayat al-Jadidah* 14-9-2001

13- The Political Parties Condemn the terrorist Attacks and Present their Condolences. They Warns Against the Use of the Attacks to Disgrace the Palestinian Struggle. *al-Hayat al-Jadidah* September 2001

14- The Legislative Council Expresses its Deep Sorrow for the Tragedy on the American People. It warns Against the Escalation of Violence against the Palestinian People and the equity of its Struggle for Ending Occupation with Terrorism. *al-Hayat al-Jadidah* September 2001

15- Special Meeting Held to Discuss the 9/11 Attacks on Washington and New York. Islamic and National Forces Affirm their Support for the American People. *al-Hayat al-Jadidah* 16-9-2001

The two newspapers published many pictures showing the destruction and human suffering of the victims. Most of these pictures are taken from different media sources around the world. Very few pictures showed expressions of grief and sympathy in the Arab and Muslim world. At the same time, few opinion articles and political caricatures expressed support for the United States and they condemned the attacks, as it will be shown down in the table at the end of this paper.

2. Expressing Opposition to the Policies of the United States

The second class of news reports and opinion articles represent direct and indirect accusations that the United States is supporting injustice and perpetrating terrorism throughout the world, including bombings. Most of the columnists in the two newspapers argue that the actions of the United States and its support for Israel are the main reason for the 9/11 terrorist attacks. Osama bin Laden ordered the attacks because the United States favors Israel in the Middle East conflict. There are 11 news reports and 19 opinion articles expressing this trend. The following are the headlines of the news reports and quotations from the opinion articles:

1- Bin Laden Calls on Muslims in Pakistan to Fight the Crusaders. Al-Hayat 11-2001
2- Rice in her Response to leaders from Arab and Muslim Countries: America Cannot Stop Attacks during Ramadan. Hayat 11-2001
3- The American Position is Against Arabs and Muslims. al-Hayat al-Jadid 12-9-2001
4- The American Media are Portraying Bad Images of Arabs, Muslims, and Palestinians. *al-Quds* 10-2001
5- Egypt and Saudi Arabia are Under Violent Attack from the American Media and Congress. *al-Quds* 13-10-2001
6- American Attacks Increase the Popularity of Bin Laden *al-Quds* 13-10-01
7- Admiration for Bin Laden is Widespread among young men in the Gulf. *al-Quds* 29-10=01
8- Hate to America will increase in the Arab and Muslim World if the Attack Continues in Ramadan. *al-Quds* 13-11-01
9- Arab Americans Complain from Discrimination after 9/11. *al-Quds* 2-11-01

10-Arab Students Leave the United States fearing Discrimination. *al-Quds* 6-11-01

11-Bin Laden is the New Saladin. Bush Increased his Popularity in the Gulf. *al-Hayat al-Jadidah* 24-9-2001

Most of the material expressing opposition to the Untied States was in the form of opinion articles. Provided below is a sampling of the wording from some of these articles.

1-"Ask the people who stand behind these terrorist attack to announce clearly who they are and what they want so that the Palestinians will not be suspected." Adli Sadek, *al-Hayat al-Jadidah*, September 14, 2001

2-"Palestinians condemn the attacks and consider these actions unacceptable because they suffer from the attacks by those who consider themselves the only victims of the West." Baker Abu Bader, *al-Hayat al-Jadidah* 28-9-2001

3-"The American administration embarrassed in front of the American public for the lack of the security measures, channeled the emotions resulting from the terrible scenes of destruction and death toward an external source, mainly owned or manipulated by the Zionist lobby in the United States defined that source in the Islamic world." Nahid Munir al- Riess, *al-Hayat al-Jadidah*, 17-9-2001

4-Despite thousands of condemnations by official, political and popular representatives on all levels across the Arab World and despite all signs of sympathy and manifestation by Palestinian children, the media chose only the march of few children expressing victory. These children according to the governor of Nablus were demonstrating against the occupation. The emphasis of the Media on this marginal event aims at the creating an image of Arabs and Muslims in the Western imagination connected with terrorism. The diffusion of the same image frequently is a method used by media to promote a political ad social content which is the defense of Israel. Fayez Rashid, *al-Hayat al-Jadidah*, 19-9-2001

5-Questions need to be answered on the Black Tuesday:" Where were the CIA and the FBI during the preparations for these attacks?" Where is the Mossad which works for both Israeli and American security and pretends to be the most powerful secret service? Ahmad Sidki Dajani, *al-Hayat al-Jadidah*, 17 -9-2001

6-"The images of a few Palestinian youths after the tragedy have been played over and over again on CNN, thus reinforcing the myth that somehow the whole Palestinian people rejoices at that painful tragedy. A closer examination has revealed that that celebration was in fact a very limited phenomenon; limited to a few Palestinian villages…The Palestinian people is presented as a supporter of the attacks on the United States. The picture presents twenty to forty people mostly children who react in the same way in the presence of foreign media. They gather and smile for the camera and raise the victory sign which became a symbol since the beginning of the Intifada. This is a natural reaction in front of any cameraman who visits the Palestinian territories. Nigel Parry, *al-Hayat al-Jadidah*, September 2001

7-What is Washington expecting from Arab writers and public opinion when it uses fragmented bombs against civilians or military targets. What does it expect when it bombs the Red Cross buildings housing food and medicine or even bombs neighborhoods in cities? What do you expect from writers or analysts who were known for their stand against terrorism and their support to the American people but do not know now what the aims of the American military operations are. Jamil Mattar, *al-Hayat al-Jadidah*, 12-11-200

8-Why Arabs and Muslims only and immediately. Ra'id Abdelrazak, *al-Quds*, 2-9-2001

9-Why do many have no sympathy for the United States? The United States should understand that hatred of its policies is a result of its actions and the double standard in dealing with peoples, helping the oppressor against the oppressed. This hatred will result in more hate and violence and terror. Fighting terror is done by dealing with its causes and supporting justice for all peoples without discrimination. Hatem abu Sha'ban, *al-Quds* 10-11-01

10-The War is on Islam not on Terrorism:" President Bush in front of TV cameras said clearly that this war is a crusade." Jaber Bitawi, al Quds, 1-12-01

11-"All these fierce American campaigns against Islam will not extinguish its light. Islam will stay strong and will blind those who try to extinguish it. All the efforts and resources of the United States on fighting Islam will wither with the wind. Yusuf Quteneh, *al-Quds*, 28-12-01

12-Is there a relationship between Black Tuesday and the American policy? I think that the rapidity in which the United States declared war on unknown enemy is anal-Hayat al-Jadidahexpression ofal-Hayat al-Jadidahprevious intentionsal-Hayat al-Jadidahtowards a number of countries and organizationsal-Hayat al-Jadidaharound the world that oppose its policies. Khalid Hilu, *al-Quds*, 24-9-2001

13-Who is responsible for the Attacks on America?If the United States wants to understand better the reasons behind the increase of this radicalal-Hayat al-Jadidahenmity to its policies in the world, it has to undertake a critical analysis of its policies in the world,al-Hayat al-Jadidahspecially inal-Hayat al-Jadidahthe Middle East mainly,al-Hayat al-Jadidahthe Palestinian problem and theal-Hayat al-Jadidahsiege imposed on the Iraqi people. Tawfiq Madani, *al-Quds*, 3-11-01

14-Palestine and the Arabs in the Age of Terrorism. The first results of the war will affect the Arab societies under the pretext that they foster terrorism and they need to eliminate it. This waral-Hayat al-Jadidahmight reach alsoal-Hayat al-Jadidahhundred of billions of dollars in the Western banks under the pretext of liquidation ofal-Hayat al-Jadidahthe financial sources of terrorism… all of this is done in order to be able to draw a new map of the Middle East. Diab Nasser, *al-Quds*, 28-11-01

15-Questions after the Black Tuesday Tragedy. There is a gap between how the United States sees itself in the world and how other peoples see this Super Power. Washington should heed of this gap in vision. The results of unintended decision in the foreign policy are not less that an intended decision. Umar Adassal-Hayat al-JadidahWissan Assadi,al-Hayat al-Jadidah*al-Quds* 1-10-01

16-We and the American Tragedy. The United States has practiced so far a self-interest policy toward peoples and their wealth. The result was this catastrophe on its policies and its people. If it is really interested in the elimination of terrorism it should look for its causes and motives. They lie without doubt in the oppression of peoples and the double standard. This is represented in its position towards the Palestinian problem. We hope that this tragedy will change the policy of the United States and bring peace and security to the peoples of the world and the people of the United States. Lutfi Zaghlul, *al-Quds*, 9-2001

17-Will the United States understands the lesson of 9/11?Solvingal-Hayat al-Jadidahinternational disputes, lifting the embargo on Iraq, holding an international conference to solve the Arab Israeli conflict based on justice not power that suits the Israeli side and a Marshal project for the development of the Middle East …all are indications that will show that Washington understood the lesson of 9/11. *al-Quds* Afeef al-akhdar

3. RATIONALIZE THE ATTACKS, INTERNATIONAL LAW

Many writers expressed their views by presenting a rational analysis of what happened. They emphasize that the best defense against terrorism is promoting justice, peace and respect for the international law and human rights in the Middle East. Only American commitment to solving the Palestinian question will halt terrorism in the world. Many writers tried to explain that the conflict between Israel and Palestinian is not part of the war on terrorism, as the Israelis claim. For all those reasons, it is very important that people solve the Arab-Israel conflict, they argued. That doesn't mean people shouldn't be looking at and addressing other problems while trying to solve that conflict. The following are news reports, headlines and quotations from opinion articles reflecting this position.

1-A conference held in al-Azhar shows the reasons for terrorism in the world: Injustice, atheism and double standards. *al-Hayat al-Jadidah* November 2001

2-American policy has an important role in the 9/11 attacks. *Al-Hayat al-Jadidah* 12-2001

3-*al-Hayat al-Jadidah* organizes a debate in Gaza on the effect of the 9/11 attacks on the Palestinian cause. Al- Hayat 26-12-2001

4-Attack on America: Arabs are Afraid to be accused. *al-Quds* 9-2001

5-The United States Should Pay More Attention to the Palestinian Problem. The Attacks Should Push the US to reverse its Stances toward the Problems of Peoples. *al-Quds* 16-9-2001

6-Bin Laden did not mention the Palestinians before the Attacks on the World Trade Center. 22-10-01

7-Bin Laden Uses the Palestinian Cause. *al-Quds* 12-10-01

8-Oppression and Suppression in the Arab World fostered Hate towards America and the West. *al-Quds* 6-11-01

9-Rojoub: The Attacks on America Make the Palestinian Revise their Strategy. *al-Quds*, 10-01

10-Mubarak: A Solution to the Conflict in the Middle East is the Only Way to End International terrorism. *al-Hayat al-Jadidah* September 2001

The majority of the Palestinians writers argued that U.S. commitment to a fair resolution of the Palestinians Israeli conflict is important in the fight against terrorism and in order to promote moderation, tolerance, and human rights. If America wants the cooperation of the Arab countries to fight terrorism and fundamentalism, it must uphold international justice. Most of the articles in this class agreed that Americans need to increase their awareness of the history of the conflict, geography and the culture of Palestinians.

1-Are Americans required to pay for the price of the support of their government to Israel twice? Once from taxpayers (Total of 192 billion until today according to Edward Said) and the second by their blood as it happened in the last tragedy 7000 lives). Fahmi Huwaidi, *al-Hayat al-Jadidah* sept 2001

2-Why America lost Security? The security in the West will not be realized at the cost of week peoples. The support of the West to Israel will not provide it with security. Justice and respect for humanity are the only way to bring security to all. Abdel Aziz Rantissi, *al-Hayat al-Jadidah* 9-2001

3-The Catastrophe of Manhattan does not make the United States a Guardian of world ethics Showing sympathy with the victims of the United States in this tragedy does not mean a support for its previous or future policies and does not mean a green light to all the plans that are in the drawers of the White House, the Pentagon or the State Department. Salman Natour, *al-Hayat al-Jadidah* 22-9-2001

4-After Black Tuesday Attacks a new obligation on Arab Elite to refuse the acts of those who disfigure the image of Arabs in the world. Arab intellectuals should launch a new battle to confront the new moral danger and fight the distortion of their image in the world. *al-Quds*, Abbas Rida, 15-9-2001

5-Why Muslims Became an Easy Target?! We have no right to justify these acts as a clash of civilizations or as a result of historical heritage of hate, religious wars and cultural differences. We must look for solutions from within ourselves and not from outside. God will not change a people until they change themselves. Salameh Ahmad Salameh, *al- Quds*, 3-11-01

6-If there is need for a change in the Arab World, it should beal-Hayat al-Jadidahdone from inside according to an Arab vision which includes all the forces in the society: active, moderate , enlightened so that it will not lead to internal fights, but to respect human rights and believe in the political and civil freedom, accept democracy and accountability to be and able to absorb the new changes in the world and choose the best of the Arab and Islamic heritage which will suit the spirit and realities of our time. Without this vision, the Arab world and nation will stay in a permanent state of division, backwardness, extremism and conflict with others. AbdulKhalik Abdullah, *al-Quds* 10-11-01

7-Terrorism and Islam. Atieh Jabarin, *al-Quds*, 22-12-01

8-Terrorism and Armed Resistance. Fadi Abu Sa'da, *al-Quds*, 22-12-01

4. IRRATIONAL REPRESENTATION OF THE ATTACKS

Most of the material in this class is represented by political caricatures or cartoons. Most of the newspapers publish caricatures daily. It became popular with the use of color in the Palestinian newspapers. Caricatures are actually in higher demand than photographs, because they are simple and based on cultural and social realities.

The message in each caricature is clear in the satirical comment in each captions and dialogue with different degrees of emphasis. They criticize the United States and Israel and express the political concerns of the Palestinians, Arabs and Muslims. They communicate a call for change and seek to change the alienated position of the United States. The different caricatures in the two newspapers show the way how Palestinians view, think and reason the USA. At the same time they are very successful in helping the reader to understand the policy of the United States and to make judgments about complex issues in international politics. A sampling of the caricatures is shown on the next three pages.

Structurally, caricature represents a relation between things that seem real and true, and uses wild imagination, exaggeration and humor, in order to give a powerful message in a pleasant way. The published caricatures represent the irrational trend in the two newspapers. Both newspapers published strongly offensive caricatures of American and Israeli leaders. In most of the images, the names of President George W. Bush and Prime Minister Ariel Sharon were intertwined. Many caricatures also suggested that Israel reaped political and financial gains as a result of the 9/11 attacks and war on terrorism. Other images suggest that Israel either profited from or helped orchestrate this war, which is another idea widely accepted as truth in the Arab world (also see Chapter 15 in this book). This group of caricatures shows that the United States is demonized in the Palestinian media.

CONCLUSIONS

Overall, the findings show that Palestinian newspapers were very critical of the United States after 9/11. For every two news stories, opinion articles or photographs that supported the United States, there were three that opposed it (33 to 21). Moreover, the caricatures or cartoons (40 total) overwhelmingly are critical of the United States.

The political environment can have an important influence on the negativity of the images of the United States in the Palestinian media. When President Clinton was in Gaza in 1998, the American flag and the Palestinian flag flew together in the streets and were displayed in the newspapers. However, when the United States invokes its veto power in the Security Council in favor of Israel, the American and Israeli flags are burned in the streets of Gaza and inflammatory articles against the United States work their way onto the front pages of the newspapers.

REFERENCES

al-Quds Newspaper, Sept., Oct., Nov., Dec., 2001.
al-Hayat al-Jadidah Newspaper, Sept., Oct., Nov., Dec., 2001.
A.J. Greimas. *Sémantique Structurale*, Paris, Larousse, 1966.

Honorable Lady, we are sorry for what had happened. However, it is time now for your government to review its policies towards our problems. Hayat, 14

Down with the international terrorism. Hayat, 16

We stand by the United States in fighting Terrorism. Hayat, 18

Who is not with us is against us. Hayat, 19

Western and Zionist media. Hayat, 25

I brought you the map of the focus of terrorism. You must only attack. Hayat, 29

Justice without borders. Quds, 15

Quds, 12

Coalition against terrorism. *Quds, 20*

American Hamburger... *Quds, 19*

Quds, 20

Quds, 18

Quds, 19

My Lord I cannot disobey you because I know you can chain my hands *Quds, 21*

October 2001

No for the freedom of press (al-Jazeera) in the third world. We are all with the CNN. *Hayat, 16*

Ben Laden picture: Wanted Dead or Alive Sharon Picture: Loved Dead or Alive *Hayat, 3*

This is not enough.... You must fight terrorism 100%. Hayat, 12

State Terrorism: Palestinians must eliminate terrorism 100%.. Hayat, 27

Our war is against terrorism and those who are not with us are against us. Hayat, 5

Occupation is the climax of terrorism. Fighting terrorism. Hayat, 13

O, This is not Taliban. This is our ally Sharon fighting terrorism .Hayat, 7

Thank your God because you are an Israeli. Lists of terrorism . Hayat, 22

Listen I do not allow you to curse me. You support Sharon the butcher, hero of massacres, the enemy of peace, terrorist and killer and you say that you fight terrorism. Hayat, 9

The Only Peace. Quds, 5

Chapter 17

SEPTEMBER 11 AND TURKISH MEDIA

Orhan Gökçe and Birol Akgün

$\mathbf{R}$ight after the twin towers of the World Trade Center were hit by the two hijacked airplanes, Turkish media outlets began covering the terrorist incidents. Turkish TV stations include four state-owned TRT channels and more than a dozen of privately owned stations, and a couple of 24-hour news networks, including CNNTURK and NTV. The total daily circulation of newspapers in Turkey is three million, and the newspapers represent varying interests and ideological cleavages in the society ranging from mainstream big newspapers to the radical left and conservative Islamists.

Because of technical difficulties and unavailability of records of the TV networks in Turkey, we had to rely mainly on the printed press for our analysis. Thus, four daily newspapers — *Milliyet, Zaman, Radikal* and *Yeni Safak* — were selected to represent the varied Turkish press. Although these newspapers openly declare that they are politically independent, *Milliyet* was selected because it represents the mainstream media in the country; *Zaman* is generally considered to be center-right; *Radikal* is center-left and *Yeni Safak* is moderate Islamist. In terms of daily circulation, Milliyet and Zaman sell 400,000 copies per day, Yeni Safak 150,000 and Radikal 50,000. Despite some limitations, we believe that the analysis of the four newspapers will provide a fairly balanced view of how 9/11 was framed by the Turkish press.

The time period of our study is from Sept. 12 to Oct. 12, the third day of the war in Afghanistan. Staff reports, columnists' writings, commentaries and interviews constituted the main research materials for this analysis.

METHODOLOGY

Quantitative and qualitative content analyses have been extensively used in social sciences, especially in communication studies (Berelson, 1952). The essence of the content analysis is classification and categorization. As Berelson (1952: 147) states, "content analysis stands or falls by its categories."

In our analysis, we classified by case and by topic. By case we mean the number of 9/11 related news items, and by topic we mean selecting and emphasizing certain aspects of the events, since journalists many times do not present the reality as it is but rather tend to make some aspects of the events more salient by using subjective frameworks in defining, interpreting and evaluating the topic under consideration (Entman, 1993). In the case of Turkish media, 9/11 was often framed as a "clash between the West and Islam," or as "America's Middle East Policy," "Turkish-American Relations" and the "New World Order."

Two coding forms were developed. The first includes general topics, political actors, their identities, how they are related and how they are treated in the texts of the news. The second coding form aims to determine how an event (a statement, a speech or a reaction) is referenced. Basically, the news in the papers can be divided in three sub-categories:

- News related to background and development of the terrorist attacks and suspected perpetrators
- News related to statements and reactions by political figures
- Views and interpretations

RESULTS

During the time period of the study, a total of 1,889 items appeared in the four newspapers regarding September 11. In terms of coverage of the news, *Radikal* seemed to show more interest (30.6%) followed by *Zaman* (26.7%), *Yeni Safak* (21.8%) and *Milliyet* (21.0%).

When we compared the number of news and commentaries, again a clear distinction can be observed among the newspapers. In terms of the number of commentaries *Yeni Safak* and *Radikal* outnumber the other two dailies. The fact that newspapers carried 9/11 to their commentary pages can be seen as the evidence that Turkish media paid great attention to the terrorist attacks in the US.

The frequency of 9/11-related news and commentaries was very high in the early days but declined almost by two-thirds after two weeks. The stories focused mostly on describing the attacks and the possible perpetrators. More specifically, here are the topics and number of stories for each.

The planning, execution and long-term implications of the terrorist attacks were the most frequently emphasized topics in the Turkish press, especially in the early days. Like other media around the world, the Turkish press was primarily interested in answering the "who, how, why and which" questions. News related to planning and execution stages of the terrorist attacks appeared in 645 times.

The "surprise" element of the terrorist attacks against the United States also was emphasized in the Turkish press. This is illustrated in the headlines, such as "America in a shock" and "America is shaken to the roots." One of the most repeated names among the possible suspects was Osama bin Laden. Although some other groups or organizations, including the CIA, were mentioned as possible perpetrators, the press focuses most on bin Laden. The focus on bin Laden stems partly because his name was mentioned by U.S. President George W. Bush in his September 15 address to the nation.

The Turkish press relied heavily upon American sources, such as CNN international, for information about bin Laden. *Milliyet* described him as "extraordinarily genius" and as a "terrifyingly fanatic" person who had been trained by the CIA during the Afghan war against Soviets in the 1980s (*Milliyet*, Sept. 14, 2001). Bin Laden was presented as a bloody fanatic terrorist leader with a large terrorist network that was allegedly responsible for 3,000 deaths in 34 different countries.

However, there were considerable variations among the newspapers in terms of the way bin Laden was presented. While *Milliyet* heavily focused on bin Ladin early on, publishing his picture on the front page, *Radikal* and *Zaman* used very cautious language without further comment.

Yeni Safak, on the other hand, avoided naming a perpetrator until the suspects were captured or when the United States presented strong and convincing evidence. *Yeni Safak* argued that a man living in remote Afghan mountains could not execute such a high-tech terrorist attack, and the paper cautiously stayed away from openly using the name of bin Laden. The newspaper saw the identification of bin Laden as American propaganda. Recalling the Kennedy assassination, the paper implied that the real suspects can be perhaps found within ranks of the U.S. government.

Although the U.S. government's policy of officially charging bin Ladin for the attacks has been interpreted by some as a clever strategy of personification of the enemy in order to mobilize international support in its fight against the international terrorist networks (Kuntze, 2003: 251), the Turkish press did not seem to be entirely convinced. In the days that followed, the Turkish press and political elites increasingly displayed skepticism regarding America's plan for deposing the Taliban regime in Afghanistan. Indeed, opinion makers in Turkey more and more came to believe that America had a secret agenda and Turkey should not participate in America's war, especially in the case of Iraq, Turkey's neighbor. Later, in the wake of adverse public opinion, the Turkish parliament failed to approve the government's bill for granting American troops the right of passage just before Iraq war. There is no doubt that the press played a critical role in rejecting this bill.

President Bush's explanations for and comments about 9/11 played an influential role in setting the agenda of the Turkish press. The press often made reference to the antagonisms between "Western civilizations and Islamic world." The press also reported on the president's use of the word "crusade" and his official apology to Muslims for this mistake. Bush's comments praising Islam as a peaceful religion were reported extensively in the news and commentary sections of the Turkish newspapers.

American leaders' repeated declarations that perpetrators will be punished according to the "war power act" were reported 140 times in the press during the time of the study. But the Turkish press was not in total agreement with the American official policy. Many stories and commentaries were critical of the American policy of war against Afghanistan, which left an impression that American government officially equated Islam with violence and terror. The Turkish press also questioned the motives of the United States (fighting terrorism or domination of the Middle East) and blamed the United States for ignoring the long-standing Palestinian issue. In addition, the press questioned the legality and legitimacy of a U.S. invasion that wasn't backed up with a clear mandate from the United Nations.

The decision of the Bush government to go to a war in Afghanistan was justified and explained by the Turkish press mostly in line with the arguments used by Bush's address to the nation on September 15. They included the following: (1) the Taliban is a radical, fanatic and brutal fundamentalist group of people that constitute a real threat to the world, (2) the United States needs to restore law and order and the establish democracy in Afghanistan; (3) Modern civilization is under attack by Taleban; (4) Terrorism must be eradicated; (5) The United States has a right to use its military power against its enemies; and (6) The supporters and sponsors of the terrorism must be fought and punished like terrorist themselves.

While those writers who supported American intervention mostly used the arguments underlined by Bush and his cabinet members, there were another group of columnists who were not persuaded by these arguments. On the contrary, they persistently opposed the war in Afghanistan and developed their own explanations for America's intention of the war. For many of them, the Afghanistan operation was designed to control Afghanistan, a strategically located Islamic country, not to fight terrorism. They also believed that America had a hidden political agenda, which is to dominate the Islamic lands and control its oil reserves. Moreover, they also argued that Afghanistan was just a beginning and that the United States will likely expand its list of enemy regimes to include Iraq, Syria and Iran. These writers frequently portrayed Bush as having a "cowboy mentality" bent on revenge.

REFERENCES

Berelson, Bernard (1952): Content Analysis in Communication Research, New York.

Entman, Robert M.(1993), "Framing: Toward Clarification of a Fractured Paradigm," *Journal of Communication,* vol.43. Nu., pp. 51-55.

Kuntze, Maren (2003): "Vision und Endkampf Zwizchen Gut und Böse," Freund- und Feindbilder waehrend der Krise am Bispiel von FAZ und NZZ," In Beuther, M./J. Butter/ S. Fröhlich/ I. Neverla/ S. A. Weichert (Hrsg.): Bilder des Terrors Terror der Bilder? Köln, pp. 238-268.

Part IV

AUSTRALIAN &
AFRICAN MEDIA

Chapter 18

MUSLIMS AND ARABS IN AUSTRALIAN MEDIA SINCE 9/11

SCOTT POYNTING & GREG NOBLE

Ethnocentrism and orientalism have been part of the landscape of the Australian press since its inception, so in some ways anti-Arab and anti-Muslim racism has always gone with the territory. Since the early days of the White Australia Policy in 1908, the masthead of the Sydney magazine *Bulletin* bore the motto: "Australia for the White Man" until it was removed in 1961. Arabs were not white, though some struggled strategically to accumulate the measures of this whiteness (Monsour, 2002; Hage, 1998).

Media vilification of non-Christian "heathens" has just as long a history in Australia. Afghan cameleers, for example, who came to Australia with their animals in the nineteenth century and enabled transport through the desert, were subjected to press racism across the country. The editor of the *Coolgardie Miner*, F. C .B. Vosper, fomented anti-Afghan racism in his newspaper on the Western Australian goldfields, and in 1894 he set up the Anti-Afghan League. In 1903, the Broken Hill *Barrier Truth* in western New South Wales, editorialized against the "Afghan menace," asserting that the Afghans threatened the morals of the community (Cleland, nd).

Of course, such taken-for-granted xenophobia can turn into the active assemblage of an enemy image in time of war. In 1885, the colony of New South Wales sent a contingent in support of the British Empire's campaign in the Sudan. The *Sydney Morning Herald* earlier that year published a letter from Sir Edward Strickland, KCB, urging the Australian colonies to raise such a contingent, to fight in the Sudan against "England's and all Christendom's old enemies, the Saracens" (Hutchinson and Myers, 1985).

We argue in this chapter that the upsurge of anti-Arab racism and "Islamophobia" in Australia after 9/11 arose, as did similar episodes during the 1991 Gulf War, from the exacerbation of existing tendencies, which have been manifest in everyday racism, both before 1991 and in the intervening period. We also argue that there are causal connections, however complex, multi-causal and indirect, between populist politics exploiting xenophobia in symbiosis with manipulated and generally tamed media, and repressive arms of the state, responding to and dependent upon both of these. Thus, we shall see how security services' raids at dawn are conducted in the company of tabloid journalists, who lend legitimacy as well as publicity, to the story that here something is being done about terrorism. At the same time, politically opportunist and sensationalist paper-selling "attacks" in headlines lead to and give ideological license to racist attacks in shops, streets and workplaces.

GULF WAR ONE

During the Gulf War, the tabloid press and high-profile opinion-making presenters on commercial television and talkback radio demanded that Iraqi Australians and virtually all Arab-background immigrant community leaders declare their allegiance to Australia, and that they both repudiate and apologize for the evils of Saddam Hussein's regime, which a number of the Iraqi Australians had themselves fled (Human Rights and Equal Opportunity Commission, 1991). There was a clear assumption that anyone identifying or identifiable as Arab or Muslim was disloyal and even dangerous until proven otherwise: an "enemy within." In practice, no amount of protestation of commitment to Australia and its values would suffice to allay this suspicion. Those ethnic and religious leaders from the targeted communities, who, desperate for respectability and some peace for their constituents, played the game of declaring their fealty before the cameras and microphones, unwillingly acceded to the ongoing logic of this being continually demanded and never enough.

Concomitantly, there was an outbreak of racist hate crime in Australia against Arabs, Muslims, or those who appeared so to the attackers. The Hawke Labor Government urged "tolerance" toward these minorities under the longstanding Australian policy of multiculturalism, although it did little to act effectively against racial vilification or attacks and neither did state governments (Human Rights and Equal Opportunity Commission, hereafter HREOC, 1991; Newell, 1990; Hage, 1991).

Women were especially targeted as victims. Many Muslim women wearing their *hijab*, or traditional headscarf, in public places, were assaulted, abused and had strangers of both genders, but usually men, grabbing at their scarves to tear them away. Most of the victims were not Iraqi; some were not even Arab but, rather, were South-East Asian. But such confusions of the object of racial hatred are not unusual in the history of Australian racism. There was an outbreak of incidents of people in traditional Muslim clothing or of "Middle Eastern appearance" being spat upon or more violently assaulted in the street, of incidents of arson, vandalism, threats, harassment and other racist attacks directed by "white-thinking" people against this newly identified fifth column which was seen to be subverting the nation from within. It was as if there were now manifold "borders" internal to the nation rather than around its perimeters, to be patrolled against the non-Christian, non-Western, "third-world-looking" outsiders who might endanger the good life from among our midst (Hage, 1998; 31/1/02).

The Prime Minister's appeal during the Gulf War for "us" to be "tolerant" only served to underscore who was in a position to tolerate and who was to be magnanimously tolerated (or not) (Hage, 1991). This "tolerance" message, basically one of forebearance and forgiveness of the deviance of cultural difference, was carried by the editorials and opinion sections of the more liberal newspapers; those marketing more nationalist and xenophobic fare called for defense of "our way of life," enforcement of assimilation and eternal vigilance against these internal outsiders.

THE RESISTIBLE RISE OF XENOPHOBIA AND DEMISE OF MULTICULTURALISM

The decade between the Gulf War and the so-called "War on Terror" saw the demise of political bipartisanship over multiculturalism in Australia and a concerted attack on cultural diversity and the rights of minorities. "Political correctness" — allegedly propagated by cosmopolitan, urban, intellectual "elites" ignoring the will and the suffering of ordinary "mainstream" people — was under assault. This rightwing ideology, successfully imported from the United States, appealed especially to those social groups alienated and marginalized by the effects of globalization and to those experiencing dislocation and disempowerment.

In 1996, the assimilationist, anti multiculturalist ex-Liberal Party candidate Pauline Hanson was elected to federal parliament for the seat of Oxley on the urban fringe of the Queensland capital, Brisbane. She stood as an independent, following her expulsion from the Liberals after unguarded comments about "handouts to Aborigines" and other racist remarks. The One Nation party that she subsequently founded attracted huge media attention and garnered up to 10 percent of the vote in several state elections, in addition to the federal one, by opposing immigration and rearticulating the racism of the old "white Australia policy." Their supporters object, as did the *Bulletin* a hundred years ago, to immigration, especially from "non-Christian countries," and accuse immigrants of bringing unemployment, crime, corruption, communal strife, disease, among a list of social ills. At the 1998 election in which John Howard's Coalition government was elected, neither they nor the Labor Party voiced significant opposition to the mounting xenophobia and racism. By 2001, One Nation was almost defunct, having been rendered redundant by the governing Liberal-National Coalition's adoption of much of its ideology and many of its policies, such as those against asylum seekers and against Aboriginal self-determination.

DOG-WHISTLING

The 2001 federal election campaign was marked by "dog whistle politics," a concept and practice imported, like the attack on "political correctness," from the United States. (As we write, it has now been exported to the United Kingdom in their national election campaign of 2005, with the same Australian "spin doctors" who advised John Howard coaching British Conservative leader Michael Howard in the strategy. If it gains less purchase on that ground, it will largely be because the latter Howard does not have the benefit of incumbency.) The notion of "dog-whistling" involves sending a particularly sharp message that calls clearly to those intended and goes unheard by the rest of the population, like a high-pitched dog whistle audible to the canine but not the human ear.

Prime Minister Howard's key election slogan of 2001, amid a manufactured crisis about asylum-seeking "boat people" creating popular hysteria around August of that year, was, "We will decide who comes to this country and the circumstances in which they come." This skillfully conveyed, to a particular "we," a message that deliberately went beyond the words. Ostensibly it was a reasonable statement about national sovereignty that almost goes without saying in a contemporary nation state. At the inaudible level, it spoke to those disaffected, disoriented and displaced by local effects of globalized economic restructuring — those whose insecurity and ignorance leaves them susceptible to populist claims that their relaxed and comfortable past had been stolen away by cosmopolitan "politically correct" elites and the "multicultural industry," by favoring Asian and Middle-Eastern immigrants, refugees, and by privileging Aborigines. Thus, it silently but successfully promised barriers against the unassimilable, the irrevocably different races or cultures — non-Christian, non-white, non-Western — against whom the previous supporters of One Nation had raised their voices.

Such "dog-whistle politics" was abetted by "dog-whistle journalism" (Poynting and Noble, 2003). Throughout 2000 and up to August 2001, the media presented a seemingly endless and unstoppable flow of refugees and asylum seekers invariably described as "Middle-Eastern" arriving on Australian territory off the coast of Western Australia. In fact, the numbers were well within Australia's planned immigration provision for refugee intake of 12,000 per annum. The moral outrage was supposedly directed at their purported "queue jumping" and at the predatory industry of "people smuggling" (Poynting, 2002). In this reporting on the "boat people," the media were depending upon and accepting information supplied by government ministers and officials (Stani, 27/1/00). This dependence was increasingly cultivated and exploited by government media managers.

Critical journalist Nadya Stani demonstrates how the media fixed on the means in which the asylum seekers came to Australian territory instead of reporting what they were fleeing from. Stories invariably originated from press releases and briefings by the Department of Immigration and Multicultural Affairs, and its Minister, Philip Ruddock. The reports focused on the illegal and predatory nature of "people smuggling," the supposed leapfrogging of presumed orderly queues of applicants for asylum, the allegedly privileged background of those able to pay the people smugglers for their unlawful conveyance. They overwhelmingly used the language of fear and eschewed the standpoint of the asylum seekers (Stani, 27/1/00).

THE "TAMPA CRISIS"

This pattern of representation was amplified into a moral panic, reaching a crescendo with the "Tampa Crisis" from August 2001. Oppositional voices were effectively silenced or drowned out as politically correct liberal whining. Christine Jackman in Sydney's Murdoch tabloid *Daily Telegraph* pronounced: "The so-called humanitarians screeching 'racist' at anyone who questioned the right of the 438 on the Tampa to automatic entry should explain what is so humanitarian about indulging people-smuggling." She went on to use the term "people-smuggler" twice more in the piece, as well as "human cargo." (Jackman, 14/9/01: 17). Similarly, rightwing *Telegraph* columnist Piers Akerman managed to fit "people smuggler" and "queue jumper" into one sentence, and many more such into the rest of one opinion piece: "Plucked from a people smuggler's leaky ferry, the principally Iraqi and Pakistani queue jumpers have shown little civility towards representatives of the country where they hope to settle" (Akerman, 4/10/01: 22).

On Aug. 26, 2001, a leaky ferry, the *KM Palapa*, carrying more than 430 asylum seekers, mainly from Afghanistan, began to sink in the Indian Ocean. Those on board were rescued by the *MV Tampa*, a Norwegian freighter, about 75 nautical miles from Australia's Christmas Island and almost four times that far from the Indonesian port of Merak (Marr and Wilkinson, 2004;

Senate Select Committee on a Certain Maritime Incident, 2002). The Captain, Arne Rinnan, decided to head for Christmas Island, as many of the asylum seekers were ill and in poor condition. He radioed Australia for medical assistance, but none was provided. Having entered Australian territorial waters, Captain Rinnan was abruptly threatened by an officer of the Department of Immigration and Multicultural Affairs with the punishment meted out to people smugglers under the Migration Act — including the possibility of huge fines and confiscation of the vessel — if he did not turn around and head toward Indonesia (Marr and Wilkinson, 2004; Burnside, 23/1/02). With an election fast approaching, the government had apparently resolved to stop these asylum seekers from reaching Australian land. As Julian Burnside puts it, "This odd decision has never been explained, except with the rhetoric of 'sending a clear message to people smugglers and queue jumpers that Australia is not a soft touch.'" Burnside infers that the Prime Minister was calculating that "a show of toughness against helpless refugees would be electorally popular amongst the large number of Australians who had responded positively to aspects of Pauline Hanson's unattractive platform" (Burnside, 23/1/02).

The *Tampa* was interdicted four miles from Christmas Island, boarded and taken over by Australian SAS forces, in what Rinnan and others later characterised as an act of piracy. From this point, in a deliberate and significant strategy, communications were strictly limited by the Australian military. Eventually after more than a week of stand-off, the asylum seekers were transferred to an Australian naval vessel, for subsequent transportation to the impoverished Pacific island of Nauru, which struck a multi-million dollar deal to incarcerate and assess the asylum seekers there, allowing the Prime Minister to keep his promise that the asylum seekers aboard the Tampa would not set foot on Australian soil.

This populist venture immediately registered in the opinion polls, and election campaign headlines began to reflect messages like "Howard's Tampa-led recovery" and "Tough time for Labor as nation rallies to PM." News reports and images of the asylum seekers were tightly controlled via the Australian military. Lawyer Julian Burnside, who argued the case for the asylum seekers' challenge in the Federal Court to the government's actions, later wrote:

> The press were (sic) not allowed anywhere near the ship. Despite repeated requests from lawyers and others, no Australian was allowed to speak to any of the refugees. The physical circumstances meant that no images of individual refugees were available. At best, film footage showed distant images of tiny figures under an awning on the deck of the ship. By the same technique, the stories of the refugees were

suppressed. ... Although the misery of the refugees' situation was obvious enough none of them could be seen as human beings (Burnside, 23/1/02).

The deliberateness of this strategy may be assessed in the light of the revelation on April 17, 2002, at the Senate Select Committee on a Certain Maritime Incident, by Brian Humphreys, director general of communications strategies in the Government's Public Affairs and Corporate Communication: "Immigration had concerns about identifying potential asylum seekers, and so we got some guidance on ensuring there were no personalizing or humanizing images." The refugees were not to be allowed to be seen in the Australian media as human beings, as individuals with life stories.

Other crucial images were doctored and misrepresented during the election campaign, in the now infamous "children overboard affair." On Oct. 6, another unseaworthy vessel, a fishing trawler laden with 223 Middle Eastern asylum seekers, was intercepted by the Australian naval frigate, *HMAS Adelaide*, in Australian waters off the west coast. Shots were fired across its bows and it was boarded. Over the following day, Navy personnel tried in vain to prevent the vessel from sinking, so that it could be towed out of Australian waters. As the boat finally did sink, asylum seekers, including children, had to be rescued from the water. A video was taken by navy personnel. That very day, a Canberra bureaucrat told the People Smuggling Task Force that asylum seekers had thrown their children overboard in an attempt to prevent the Adelaide turning their vessel back (Marr and Wilkinson, 2004). The assertion was repeated publicly many times by the Defence Minister, the Prime Minister, and those campaigning for them, and it was echoed in tabloids and talkback across the continent. It has now been shown to be falsification (Senate Select Committee on a Certain Maritime Incident, 2002). It has been demonstrated that images from the video depicting children in the water, shown on national television by the Defence Minister during the election campaign, were cut down so as to excise the view of the boat sinking in the background and were misrepresented as being of the previous day when the incident of throwing the children into the sea was claimed to have occurred. It also has been proved that the Prime Minister's office and that of the Defence Minister were warned soon afterwards by Navy personnel conveying firsthand knowledge of the falsehood of the story they were presenting, which they nevertheless continued to defend as true until well after the election (Senate Select Committee on a Certain Maritime Incident, 2002).

Prime Minister Howard repeated, "I don't want, in Australia, people who would throw their own children into the sea. I don't" (*Four Corners*, 15/4/02). He told Alan Jones's commercial radio audience on Sydney's highest-rating talkback program on Oct. 8, "I don't want in this country people who are prepared, if those reports are true, to throw their own children overboard" (Wilkinson, 16/2/02: p. 28).

As commentator Hugh Mackay put it, "the 'children overboard' incident ... show[s] us just how vulnerable Australians have become to political spin." He argues that "we wanted to believe the kids had been thrown overboard, because we had already been worked over by a slick propaganda machine that had created a 'refugee crisis' out of a couple of hundred people rescued by the Tampa" (Mackay, 16-17/2/02: 31). "We" were helped in that belief by those tabloid column-writers such as Piers Akerman who, in rival columnist and radio talkback host Mike Carlton's less than charitable words, "swallow and regurgitate the Government's deceit, all the while denouncing the gullible bleeding hearts of the chardonnay-swilling liberal media elite" (Carlton, 16-17/2/02: 24). Carlton was (in vain) anticipating contrition from Akerman after the "children overboard" misrepresentation was revealed, since at the time Akerman had written, "As for those who threw their children into the sea on Sunday and the malcontents who trashed the Manoora — it must be made absolutely clear that not only is such behavior totally unacceptable but will in fact mitigate (sic) against any future consideration for admission into Australia" (Akerman, 9/10/01: 16).

Such was the timing and execution of the media manipulation, that newspaper headlines first became able to denounce this decisive "children overboard" fabrication on the very morning of the election. By then, the "War on Terror" dominated the news, and the media would instead be exercised to connect ideologically the U.S. foreign policy objectives of "regime change" in Afghanistan and then Iraq.

AL-QAEDA DOWNUNDER

We have argued elsewhere (Noble and Poynting, 2003; Poynting et al, 2004) that years of representing the Arab/Muslim Other as backward, uncivilized, barbaric, violent, terroristic, mysogynistic and other demonic qualities received their "ideological payout" with the attacks of 9/11 and the ensuing "War on Terror." The media-fed criminalization of Arab-Australian youth since the 1990s (Collins, Noble, Poynting and Tabar, 2000) could be ideologically validated in hindsight, with its purveyors adopting a "told-you-so" tone, and the themes could now be called upon to enhance the credibility of the wider discourse of Arab and Muslim deviance which rapidly subsumed it. "Act of War" was the *Daily Telegraph* headline after shots blamed on Lebanese youth gangs were fired at a western Sydney police station in 1998, and exactly those words headed the *Telegraph*'s front page on Sept. 12, 2001 (Noble and Poynting, 2003). Similarly, the huge media story about "ethnic gang rape" in Sydney by immigrant youth of Lebanese or Muslim background, echoing similarly constructed stories in France (Poynting et al, 2004), could now lend credence to the rationalization that the recently noticed oppression of women by the Taliban justified their vengeful overthrow. Just as the same inherent criminality of Arabs and Muslims in Australia could now be seen at work more globally, so the global terror would now be seen at work in Australian suburbs.

For days after 9/11, articles in the *Telegraph* on the events in the United States and their consequences were captioned "Act of War," even before "war on terror" was declared. Thereafter, the banner "War on Terror" has continually reappeared in the tabloid. Three days after the airliner attacks in New York, Washington and Pennsylvania, *Telegraph* columnist (and now editor) David Penberthy wrote an opinion piece that is worth quoting at some length for the exemplary way it presents itself as rational and tolerant, and for the sentiments which nevertheless show through. It is also conveys quite accurately the mood of intolerance and irrationality that had descended on Australia, and the linking of ideological elements which accompanied it.

> Whatever tiny shred of goodwill that still existed in this country towards Muslim Australians probably disappeared at the same time the first hijacked passenger jet smashed into the World Trade Center.
>
> Those who seek to portray John Howard as a bigot for his stand on the Tampa now find themselves in something smaller than a minority; equally those who accuse Premier Bob Carr of flirting with race politics through his stand on crime are free to meet in a telephone booth and talk among themselves.
>
> This galvanising of public opinion is not rational. ...
>
> In the minds of most Australians, all of these issues have merged into one.
>
> A series of events has overlapped, the result of which is blanket, unprecedented hostility to anyone who would seek to defend Islam and its adherence.
>
> It explains why, as the Lebanese gang rape scandal started to unfold, there was such acrimony directed towards [Mufti of Australia] Sheik Hilaly, over his call for a seat in State Parliament to be found for a Muslim, not to mention his absurd suggestion that because the gang rapists were Australian born, their criminal actions reflected more on their new homeland than on their ancestry. ...
>
> It explains why, when the Tampa arrived in Australian waters,

carrying 434 people from Muslim Afghanistan. most Australians did not want to hear any stories from those on board. They just wanted them to go away. (Penberthy, 14/9/01: 27)

Here we have an ideological chain of equivalence, recognized as irrational and yet endorsed as understandable: terrorism, ethnic crime gangs, Islam, misogynist violent crime, Muslim ethnic-religious leader, Middle-Eastern asylum seekers.

In October 2001, as the United States mounted war in Afghanistan, stalwart opinion columnist Piers Akerman lauded the Australian military "preparing to go to sea in the service of their country." The enemy in each case was equated:

Some are going to the Middle East, to provide back-up to the civilised world's war against terrorism; others are going to the edges of our territorial waters to dissuade people-smugglers from bringing their cargoes of illegal immigrants to our shores. (14/10/01: 95)

The *Daily Telegraph,* on the previous day, had printed in its editorial column stories, since discredited, about rescued asylum-seekers in custody aboard an Australian Navy ship threatening to harm their children. Sententiously, it proclaimed, "Criticism that Australia lacks compassion since the introduction of the Border Protection Act should not foster guilt over our revulsion at those who care so little for their own children." It continued, "While on board, SAS members were able to place under surveillance a suspected agent of the Osama bin Laden terrorist network" (*Daily Telegraph*, 13/10/02: 24). The letters to the editor reflected similar concerns. The same letter-writer from Currumbin Waters who had fretted from 1,000 km away about Sydney's "ethnic gangs" in August now asked, "What uncivilised barbarism is this? ... placing children's lives at risk." The *Telegraph* pointedly headed this letter section "Terrorism on the seas" (*Daily Telegraph*, 11/10/02: 27). As there was never a subsequent report about the suspected Al Qaeda terrorist being arrested or tried, we can only assume that the suspicions or the report were as unfounded as the inventions about parents harming their children. We nevertheless see through this process how, as with the moral panic about ethnic crime, the demonization of the asylum seeker achieves its "ideological payout" with the terror attacks of 9/11.

On Oct. 12, 2001, the *Telegraph* frontpage headline screamed, "TERROR AUSTRALIS: Bin Laden groups in our suburbs," and the article detailed raids on homes of Arab and Muslim immigrants in Western Sydney by the Australian Federal Police and the Australian Security Intelligence Organisation. It reported that "more than a dozen men from Egypt, Jordan and Tunisia currently applying for refugee status, have been identified as having connections or membership with radical Al-gama Islamiya, Al-Maqdesi, Al-Dawa and Al-Nahda groups" (Miranda, 12/10/01:1,4). The editorial of that day headlined, "Entry is a privilege not a right," and warned of "up to a hundred operatives in Sydney" suspected of raising funds for "bogus charities that have been found to have links to terrorist networks." It urged "firm and immediate action" and cautioned that "the existence of these groups should sound a warning over the standards required to gain entry to Australia (*Daily Telegraph* 12/10/01: 20).

Since then, there has still not been a report of any charges, let alone a trial, for any terrorism-related offence in connection with the highly publicized raids. Of course, inadequate law always can be blamed as the reason: a cartoon in the *Telegraph* depicted a judge in his wig sitting on the sofa between four bearded, turban-wearing Taliban-like figures, drinking cups of tea with five such visitors while saying to his wife, bearing the tea tray, "I'm sorry dear — I told them it was okay to stay" (Brown, 12/9/01: 33).

If the turban or the veil become the symbol for the "uncivilized barbarism" imagined by writers of letters to the editor and opinion leaders in the tabloid press, it is reasonable to conjecture a causal connection with the fact that these become targets for the acts of racial hatred outlined earlier in this article. Piers Akerman's column, titled "Opening our doors to a wave of hatred," was accompanied by Löbbecke drawing of a women in a chador with a brick wall instead of human eyes showing through the gap. Akerman began by marshalling the September 11 events for an attack on Australian multiculturalism: "The terrorist attack on the U.S. should provide a wake-up call to Australia to re-examine its policy of multiculturalism."

He concluded:

> When we look within Australia we find a separatist clique unsure whether it follows religious or cultural practices.
>
> A beard, a scarf, a headdress or the length of a sleeve or dress are all important to some of these people and the supporters of multiculturalism tell other Australians that they are the ones who must exhibit tolerance when they are spat upon or cursed for wearing ordinary clothing in keeping with the dominant culture.
>
> It is the Muslims who must show tolerance to others here and in other Western nations otherwise they will always be separate (Akerman, 18/9/01).

In an ideological inversion, the "ordinary" people of the dominant culture in Australia appear as being spat upon by the Muslims, and the latter are presented as evincing intolerance. Yet the same newspaper recognized, in two small column inches ambiguously headed "Muslim backlash," that it was Muslims being "abused, threatened and attacked, with one mosque alerting police to a firebomb threat. Many reports have come from women, targeted because of their head scarves" (*Sunday Telegraph* 16/9/01: 9). The *Sun-Herald* recognized that it was indeed "women with veils" being spat upon (Devine, 11/11/02).

After the Bali bombings in October 2002, ASIO and Australian federal police operatives again mounted raids on suburban homes of Muslim citizens — this time mainly Australians of Indonesian origin in Sydney, Perth and Melbourne (Poynting et al, 2004). Below identification sketches of suspects in the Kuta attacks, the *Australian* published the frontpage headline, "Hunt for faces of terror," followed by "ASIO raids target JI sleeper cell" (Powell and Chulov, 31/10/02: 1). As with the 2001 raids, there have been no charges laid and no arrests made on terrorism-related matters, although there was an arrest over a visa infringement. Neighbors of one home raided at dawn in a Perth working-class suburb reported the timber door being splintered with sledge hammers and windows being smashed by a gun-bearing squad wearing black helmets, balaclavas, goggles and flak jackets, issuing from two four-wheel drive vehicles (*Daily Telegraph*, 31/10/02: 7). A 17-year-old, whose home in Perth was invaded, told of the trauma she experienced along with her three brothers and sisters, one only four years old, who "saw balaclava-clad officers thrust their machine guns in [their] faces" (Dunn, 31/10/02).

In a simultaneous operation in Sydney, some 15 operatives confiscated mobile phones, computers, disks, passports, bank statements, and personal documents such as marriage and birth certificates, just as in the raids the previous year, along with — bizarrely — a copy of the *Daily Telegraph* reporting the Bali attack (Morris and Rowlands, 31/10/02: 7). One Sydney family was "effectively held prisoner for five hours" (ABC News Online, 31/10/02), according to those held captive. In bursting into the home of a businessman in Greenacre in south-west Sydney, one of the agents said to him, "You are one of JI." The man said that he had not heard of Jemaah Islamiah, the group being blamed for the Bali terrorist attacks, until the Kuta nightclub bombings occurred. ASIO seized computers, documents and business records (Morris, Cameron and Cornford, 1/11/02: 7).

A man whose home in Sydney's south-west was also raided by 15 officers with guns and a sledgehammer said that he had no connections whatever with Jemaah Islamiah, although he had attended two or three speeches made by alleged JI leader in Sydney (Karvelas, 31/10/02: 7; Morris and Rowlands, 31/10/02: 7). ABC Radio's *AM* program (31/10/02) reported that "What appears to have been a key to the raids ... is that men in the target families had been to lectures given by Abu Bakar Ba'asyir, the alleged spiritual leader of Jemaah Islamiah, suspected in the Bali bombing."

The front page of the *Sydney Morning Herald* on Nov. 5 had an article telling how the previous week's security service and federal police raids were justified by the seizure of the Muslim equivalent of a parish newsletter denouncing Hollywood and promiscuity, laden with double meanings and expressing sympathy toward Osama bin Laden (Morris and Thompson, 5/11/02: 1). The newsletter was called *Al Haq*, which "translates as Truth." So, incidentally, did *Pravda*. Just as many labelled as "communists" and "fellow travelers" during the Cold War had not the slightest connection with the Communist Party nor with Stalinism, so not everyone branded a Muslim terrorist (or terrorist supporter or sympathiser) will prove to be one. Most will not, as in these armed ASIO raids where citizens had their doors broken down and guns pointed at their heads — a perfectly proportionate precaution, some will say, in the "war on terror"; a small price (for others) to pay for the defence of freedom, civilization and democracy.

Nevertheless, the suppression of "terrorists" serves an important function in the maintenance of the prevailing hegemony. The effect goes well beyond those raided. The swoops were clearly intended to send an intimidatory message to whole communities to which those raided belong. For that very reason, the media were taken in tow in both the 2001 and 2002 raids. On several occasions the media identified the families concerned, and they were consequently subjected to vigilante-style harassment. The raids were useless for intelligence-gathering purposes, and no-one raided was charged for terrorist offenses. This can hardly have been their underlying purpose unless they were extremely bungled. Their purpose was obviously to reassure the white, Christian "mainstream" that something was being done about these terrorists or terrorist sympathizers in our midst, and to frighten the targeted communities into keeping a low profile. The mainstream media literally went along with this.

This, too, is a form of terror, as is the gentler form of persuasion in the shape of fear of the ubiquitous enemy, propagated by the repressive arm of the State and purveyed by its ideological apparatuses, above all the mogul-dominated media and those who mirror them.

This chapter has traced a "signification spiral" — or rather a series of them — amplified and disseminated via the Australian media since 9/11, whereby a new "other" is constructed as the folk demon of our time. In the ideological slippages of the racist imagination, Middle Eastern has become conflated with Arab, Arab with Muslim, Muslim with misogynist, misogynist with rapist, rapist with gang, gang with terrorist, terrorist with "boat people," "boat people" with barbaric, and so on in endless chains of equivalence connoting criminality, irrational violence, and evil. We have learned in the same media of the effects of such chaining. These very media will just as important in the taking apart of these chains.

REFERENCES

ABC News Online (31/10/02) ABC News Online (31/10/02) "ASIO raids slammed as 'publicity stunt,'" ABC News Online, 31 October, 8: 42am AEDT.

Akerman, P. (18/9/01) "Opening our doors to a wave of hatred," *Daily Telegraph*, 18 September, p. 22.

Akerman, P. (4/10/01) "Cargo bound by definition," *Daily Telegraph* 4 October, p. 22.

Akerman, P. (9/10/01) "Publicity stunts self-defeating," *Daily Telegraph* 9 October, p. 16.

Akerman, P. (14/10/01) "Pay no mind to paranoid hippies," *Sunday Telegraph* 14 October, p. 95.

Brown, W. (12/9/01) "I'm sorry dear - I told them it was okay to stay" [cartoon], *Daily Telegraph*, 12 September, p. 33.

Burnside, J. (23/1/02) "Refugees: The Tampa Case," *Web Diary* 23 January. http://old.smh.com.au/news/webdiary/2002/01/23/FFXNANTZRWC.html

Carlton, M. (16-17/2/02) "About face: toadies' backflips promise best laughs in years," *Sydney Morning Herald* 16-17 February, p. 24.

Cleland, B. (nd) "Racism and the Muslim Community in Australia," http://members.tripod.com~Bregava/australia01

Collins, J., Noble, G., Poynting, S. and Tabar, P. (2000) *Kebabs, Kids, Cops and Crime: Youth, Ethnicity and Crime*. Sydney: Pluto Press.

Daily Telegraph (11/10/02) "Terrorism on the seas" [letters], 11 October, p. 27.

Daily Telegraph (12/10/01) "Entry is a privilege not a right" [editorial], *Daily Telegraph* 12 October, p. 20.

Daily Telegraph (13/10/02) "Vindication of our line in the sand" [editorial], *Daily Telegraph* 13 October, p. 24.

Daily Telegraph (31/10/02) "Like scenes from a movie," *Daily Telegraph*, 31 October, p. 7.

Devine, M. (11/11/02) "Where security counts, tolerance goes two ways," *Sun Herald*, 11 November, p. 27.

Four Corners (15/4/02) "To Deter or Deny" [Debbie Whitmont, reporter], 15 April. http://www.abc.net.au/4corners/archives/2002a_Monday15April2002.htm

Hage, G. (1991) "Racism, Multiculturalism and the Gulf War," *Arena*, 96, pp. 8-13.

Hage, G. (1998) *White Nation: Fantasies of white supremacy in a multicultural society*, Sydney: Pluto Press.

Hage, G. (31/1/02) "A contagious mix of fear and paranoia," *Canberra Times*, 31 January, p. 11.

Human Rights and Equal Opportunity Commission (HREOC) (1991) *Racist Violence: Report of the National Inquiry into Racist Violence in Australia*, Australian Government Publishing Service, Canberra.

Hutchinson, F. and Myers, F. (1885) *The Australian Contingent: A History of the Patriotic Movement in New South Wales and an Account of the Despatch of Troops to the Assistance of the Imperial Forces in the Soudan.* Sydney: Thomas Richards, Government Printer.

Jackman, (4/9/01) "Don't sigh too soon Australia, it's not over yet," *Daily Telegraph* 4 September, p. 17.

Karvelas, P. (31/10/02) "Raid man denies link to Bashir's network," *Australian* 31 October, p. 7.

Mackay, H. (16-17/2/02) "Numbed voters take spin doctors' orders," *Sydney Morning Herald* 16-17 February, p. 31.

Marr, D. and Wilkinson, M. (2004) *Dark Victory.* Sydney: Allen and Unwin.

Miranda, C. (12/10/01) "TERROR AUSTRALIS: Bin Laden groups in our suburbs," *Daily Telegraph*, 12 October, pp. 1,4.

Monsour, A. (2002) "Whitewashed: the Lebanese in Queensland, 1880-1947." Pp. 16-36 in G. Hage (ed), *Arab Australians Today.* Melbourne: Melbourne University Press.

Morris, L., Cameron, D. and Cornford, P. (1/11/02) "Police told man: you are one of JI," *Sydney Morning Herald*, 1 November, p. 7.

Morris, L. and Thompson, M, (5/11/02) "Belmore newsflash: Bin Laden, icon of the holy struggle," *Sydney Morning Herald*, 5 November, pp. 1,7.

Morris, R. and Rowlands, L. (31/10/02) "Father denies link to feared group," *Daily Telegraph*, 31 October, p. 7.

Newell, P. (1990) *Migrant Experience of Racist Violence: A Study of Households in Campbelltown and Marrickville.* Sydney: Human Rights and Equal Opportunities Commission.

Noble, G. and Poynting, S. (2003) "Acts of War: military metaphors in the representation of Lebanese youth gangs," *Media International Australia: Culture and Politics, 106*, February, pp. 110-123.

Penberthy, D. (14/9/01) "Making sense of the irreconcilable," *Daily Telegraph* 14 September, p. 27.

Powell, S. and Chulov, M. (31/10/02) "ASIO raids target JI sleeper cell," *The Australian* 31 October, p. 1.

Poynting, S. (2002) "Bin Laden in the Suburbs: Attacks on Arab and Muslim Australians before and after 11 September." *Current Issues in Criminal Justice, 14*,1, July, pp. 43-64.

Poynting, S. and Noble, G. (2003) "Dog-whistle Journalism and Muslim Australians since 2001" *Media International Australia: Culture and Politics, 109*, November, special issue, "The new 'others': western media and society post-9/11," eds L. Green and L. Jacka, pp. 41-49.

Poynting, S, Noble, G., Tabar, P. and Collins, J. (2004) *Bin Laden in the Suburbs: Criminalising the Arab Other.* Sydney: Institute of Criminology.

Senate Select Committee on a Certain Maritime Incident (2002) Hansard 25-26 March, 4-5, 11-12,16,17,18 April, 1, 2 May, http://www.aph.gov/au/senate/committee/ s-maritInc.htm

Stani, N. (27/1/00) "How the Media Treats Ethnic Diversity," *Media Report*, Radio National, Australian Broadcasting Corporation, 27 January. http://www.abc.net.au/rn/talks/8.30/mediarpt/stories/s97348.htm

Sunday Telegraph (16/9/01) "Muslim backlash" *Sunday Telegraph*, 16 September, p. 9.

Wilkinson, M. (16/2/02) "Tampering with the evidence" *Sydney Morning Herald* 16 February, pp. 23, 28.

Chapter 19

BETWEEN SCYLLA AND CHARYBDIS: 9/11 IN SOUTH AFRICAN MEDIA

Nicolene Botha & Arnold S. De Beer

Like elsewhere in the world, 9/11 stung South Africa. The shared sense of shock and outrage that unified media and people alike, especially in the West, was high on the national news agenda. For weeks reports, punditry, and predictions dominated the media: Who did it? Why? How would the United States react? How would the Islamic world react? What were the implications for the world, for Africa, and for South Africa?

The views of world leaders were sought, and, rather surprisingly, politicians in many countries who shared a patchy past with the United States — including Syria, Libya, Iran, Iraq, Cuba, "and even the Taliban rulers of Afghanistan" (*Dispatch Online*, 2001 September 13) — expressed their sympathies with the American people. Libyan leader, Moammar Gadhafi, proclaimed:

> "[I]rrespective of the (read: the Arab world's) conflict with America, it is our human duty to show sympathy with the American people, and be with them at these horrifying and awesome events which are bound to awaken human conscience" (*Beeld*, 2001 September 12, p. 9).

North Korea, which is listed by the United States as a "sponsor of terrorism," called the attacks "very regretful and tragic," and added that the country "is opposed to all forms of terrorism" (*Die Burger*, 2001 September 14, p. 2). Palestinian leader Yasser Arafat not only condemned the attacks, but donated blood to help the victims of 9/11 (*Beeld*, 2001 September 13, p. 10). It was noted that many of these countries' reactions "were tempered with cautions about U.S. foreign policy — and, no doubt, the awareness of their own vulnerability" (*Dispatch Online*, 2001 September 13).

African leaders likewise communicated their solidarity with the United States. The Organization of African Unity called it "horrific terrorist attacks that have caused enormous loss of human life and destruction" and expressed "the full solidarity and the deepest condolences of the OAU and the entire people of Africa over this tragedy which affected not only the people of the USA, but humanity as a whole [Translated]" (*Beeld*, 2001 September 22, p. 2). Nigerian President Olusegun Obasanjo said "[w]e must all resolve that there will be no hiding place for terrorists. If this can happen to the most powerful nation of the world, those of us who are less powerful must make sure that we are always at alert"(IOL, 2001 September 13).

The *Daily Nation* of Kenya called the attacks "abhorrently savage" and maintained that such actions only served to further alienate "the forces dedicated to reasonable ways of ensuring justice in the world." Many other African leaders, such as Presidents Abdelaziz Bouteflika of Algeria, Blaise Compaore of Burkina Faso, Alpha Oumar Konare of Mali, and John Kufuor of Ghana, all sent messages expressing their sympathy and dismay about what had happened (IOL, 2001 September 13).

Many of the African countries that criticized the attackers "have large Muslim populations and share a sense of Third World solidarity with the Arab world." While denouncing the attacks, they implored the United States and President George W. Bush to show restraint in their quest for revenge. In this context the Kenyan weekly *East African* noted that "thanks to partisan American and Western press coverage, the popular image of a terrorist as a Muslim, preferably of Arab origin, with fundamentalist persuasion, is being firmly entrenched in the world mind." Nigeria's *This Day* added: "We don't want to look back twenty years from now at a world devastated by racial and religious conflict and wonder if it could have been avoided." And an editorial column in South Africa's *Sunday Independent* urged the rest of the world to "save United States from itself" (IOL, 2001 September 17).

SOUTH AFRICA'S REACTION

The South African media reported extensively on the reaction of the government, which mirrored the shock and anger expressed by the greater part of the global community and pledged its support in their fight against terrorism.

President Thabo Mbeki unequivocally denounced the attack (*Rapport*, 2001 September 16, p. 1). "No sane person anywhere in the world has any doubt but that this catastrophe should not be repeated anywhere else in the world, and that all humanity should act together to achieve this result" (Mbeki, 2001 September 28).

Mbeki's sentiments were shared by the ruling African National Congress (ANC), whose spokesman, Smuts Ngonyama, said that his organization was appalled by the attacks. "We regret the loss of innocent lives in these senseless attacks ... such attacks can only create instability worldwide." He also offered his party's support to the United States "in their efforts to deal with the crisis" (Dispatch Online, 2001 September 12).

Various opposition parties and other community groups also denounced the attack in the media, generally agreeing that a clear and decisive message should be sent that the world would not tolerate a reign of terror. Douglas Gibson, chief whip of South Africa's opposition party, the Democratic Alliance (DA), expressed his indignation at the fact that the "almost unbelievable events" in the United States took place less than one week after the joint decision at the World Conference Against Racism in Durban to fight intolerance (*Dispatch Online*, 2001 September 12). "We have what amounts to a declaration of war on the United States ... The attack on the leader of the free world is an attack on all democracies around the world."

Expressing his dismay at the tragic events, United Democratic Movement (UDM) leader Bantu Holomisa cautioned that "[t]he possible links to the situation in the Middle East have yet to be confirmed, but if it proves accurate, it should emphasize once and for all that the situation requires a global and united effort by the whole international community" (IOL, 2001 September 13).

On the other hand, some South African observers cautioned that Bush's plans to launch a military campaign against essentially anonymous and amorphous groups of people with a variety of ideological convictions in order to bring an end to global terrorism would be fruitless (Van der Westhuizen, 2001, September 28, p. 15), and to attack Afghanistan, a small desolated tract of land, would be to "look for fleas on a dog." Referring to the "disastrous humanitarian tragedy unfolding in Afghanistan," South African Deputy Foreign Minister Aziz Pahad called on the United States to show care and restraint in its use of military force against civilians and the social and economic infrastructure of the country (*Mail & Guardian*, 2001 October 31).

TO SUPPORT OR NOT

As the world started thinking about the implications of being either for or against America, the distinction between sympathy and unconditional support became increasingly clear (*Die Burger*, 2001 September 21, p. 13). Not everybody was prepared to give the United States a blank cheque without knowing what would be expected of them or how long they would be expected to participate in whatever America would plan to do. Former President Nelson Mandela denounced the attack, but warned Bush to think carefully if he planned retribution against the attackers, saying that America should avoid any actions that would be just as unpopular as those of the attackers (*Rapport*, 2001, September 16, p. 1).

These remarks were indicative of a growing sense of apprehension in South Africa, which was further acerbated by Bush's rather Messianic proclamation that "[e]ither you are with us, or you are with the terrorists" (Bush, 2001 September 20). To South Africa, at least according to media reports and editorials, this was a Hobson's choice.

SOUTH AFRICA'S PRECARIOUS POSITION

Superficially, there was all the reason in the world to unconditionally support the United States in its endeavors, but the situation in South Africa was, and still is, far more complex.

Economically, the United States is the largest investor in South Africa, with bilateral trade and investment relationships that were rapidly growing (Mills, 2003). South Africa especially depends on North America and Europe for more than 60 percent of its gross national product. "In other words, in terms of its foreign policies, the Republic [of South Africa] cannot move too far away from the direction that the broad West takes [Translated]" (*Die Burger*, 2001 September 14, p. 2).

Strategically, South Africa's geographical position could not be underestimated, especially in times of crisis (*Die Burger*, 2001 September 14, p. 2). "With the Islamic fundamentalists widely gaining ground in Egypt, with its Suez Canal, amongst others, geopolitical scenario's become possible which may greatly increase the importance of the Cape sea-route [Translated]." This warning from the Afrikaans Cape Town daily sounded not unlike those made in apartheid years about the need to "safeguard the West" from Communism.

Politically, Mbeki needed U.S. support for his New Partnership for Africa's Development (Nepad) initiative, which aims to solicit trade concessions, aid, and international investment as a reward for a commitment to good governance and democratization (Mills, 2003). Without extensive involvement of the United States, these goals would be unattainable.

Militarily, the power and prowess of the South African National Defense Force had strongly plummeted since the ANC government came to power in 1994, and its knowledge and experience of terrorism had vastly diminished (*Die Burger*, 2001 September 14, p. 2). Moreover, the defense force was neither equipped nor logistically capable for active involvement in a war in Afghanistan.

Ideologically, a crucial consideration was the country's mostly moderate Muslim community, which, however, included organizations that could be considered to contain "dangerous fundamentalists" — for example, Quibble and Pagad (*Die Burger*, 2001 September 14, p. 2). A too strong showing of support for the United States could, according to *Die* Burger, cause an upsurge of terrorist activity in South Africa rather than solving the problem.

THE MUSLIM COMMUNITY

South Africa, often referred to as the "Rainbow Nation," is a multi-ethnic country where a conflux of African, Western, and Eastern cultures co-exist — and sometimes collide. While only about 1 million of the country's 44 million citizens are Muslim (Steyn, 2001 October 16, p. 3), which is about 2.2 % of the total population, the large Islamic community living in the Western Cape region represents 33 percent of the total population (Botha, 2001 July). This figure is growing, as Islamic proselytizing efforts are extending beyond the Asian population towards the coloured and black communities (Morrison, 2001 November 15). Not surprisingly, the reaction of the Islamic community became a popular topic for many South African news reports after 9/11, for even though this community is relatively small, its members are socially active, politically vocal, and generally very influential (Mills, 2003). More importantly, a few of its members were known to be associated with various extremist groups across the globe.

From the onset, the South African Muslim community condemned the attack on the United States, but they were also very concerned. "Because of what America is doing in the aftermath of the attack, people are getting the impression that every Muslim and Arab throughout the world is a terrorist," Sheikh Achmat Sedick, secretary-general of the Muslim Judicial Council, said (*Sunday Times*, 2001 September 12). His fears were not unfounded, for within a few hours after the attack in America one of the oldest mosques in Cape Town received a bomb threat. He himself was personally threatened, and he received offensive telephone calls and hate mail.

Many ordinary Muslims felt the attack should serve as a wake-up call for the United States — that the country should consider why anybody would go to such extremes (*Sunday Times*, 2001 September 12). A journalist for a Muslim community radio station said: "Bush should be thinking: 'Why would someone do this, and what forces someone to go to such extremes?' He should look at the cause and not the symptom. Tuesday's attack was a symptom of a disease." A social science teacher maintained that "America had had a hand in some of the greatest human rights violations in the world — and had many enemies ... This should be an indication to America that they are doing something wrong. And that these people did not do what they did without a reason" (*Sunday Times*, 2001 September 12).

THE MILITANT FACTIONS

In the global context, these attitudes were nothing out of the ordinary. What was a cause of concern for South Africans, however, was America's interest in at least two specific Islamic organizations, namely Qibla and Pagad (People Against Gangsterism and Drugs), both of which had been classified by the CIA as terrorist organizations (Botha, 2005 p. 9).

Qibla, a small radical group with strong anti-American sentiments, was inspired by Iran's Ayatollah Khomeini and sought to establish an Islamic state in South Africa (Cordesman & Burke, 2001). Qibla supported the black consciousness movement during the anti-apartheid struggle, had a special relationship with the Pan African Congress (PAC), and still has strong bonds with Iranian intelligence services (Botha, 2005 p. 9).

Pagad was founded in 1995 to fight crime and especially drug trafficking in the Western Province (Botha, 2005 p. 10). Supporting the idea of a violent jihad in order to establish an Islamic state, Pagad launched a volley of terror attacks between 1996 and 2000, resulting in 472 instances of shooting and bombing, and the deaths of 24 people, many of them innocent bystanders (Gottschalk, 2005 February). Although their activities have been severely curtailed by law enforcement since 2001, American security agencies still suspect Pagad and its front organizations — e.g., Muslims Against Global Oppression (Mago) and Muslims Against Illegitimate Leaders (Mail) — of having ties with radical Islamic elements in the Middle East (Sullivan, 2001 p. 25).

THE SOUTH AFRICAN CONNECTION

Within days after 9/11, reports started to appear in the media about South Africa's alleged involvement in the attack. Interestingly, the first report about such a "connection" was about a hoax e-mail, which contained a false CNN article claiming that South Africans were responsible for the attack (IOL,

2001, September 13). According to this e-mail, U.S. Secretary of State Colin Powell had indicated that the South African government itself could be involved in the attack and that "some of the masterminds might be in hideaway in South Africa," as he cited strong ties between South Africa and Libya. The South African government rapidly responded and called it "simply and utterly a hoax."

The gravity of these accusations — although only a hoax — became apparent in reports that were published on the same day stating that the United States suspected the existence of al-Qaeda cells in South Africa (Steyn, Van Wyk & Khumalo, 2001, September 23, p. 1). The United States called for co-operation by South African intelligence services in the collection of information about terror organizations: "Pagad and its armed G-Force, as well as the obscure terror group Qibla are on America's list of organizations with possible ties to Muslim extremists in the Middle-East [Translated]." The United States requested the closure of South Africa's borders to terrorists who would try to enter the country to hide there, as was the case in 1998 when Khalfan Khamis Mohamed, a confidant of Osama bin Laden, sought refuge in Cape Town after his involvement with the bombing of the American embassy in Tanzania. He was arrested and extradited to the United States, where he was convicted and sentenced to life in prison (Steyn, 2001, September 22, p. 2).

YOUSUF DEEDAT

Subsequent reports claiming that the South African intelligence agencies were investigating organizations such as the Islamic Propagation Centre International (IPCI) in Durban, which is closely associated with the family of Osama bin Laden, drew the connection with al-Qaeda even closer (Munusamy, 2001 September 23, p. 1). Yousuf Deedat, who caused an uproar at the World Conference Against Racism in Durban a few days before 9/11 when he distributed anti-Semitic leaflets featuring an image of Adolf Hitler, was quoted as saying that he and his late father, Muslim scholar Ahmed Deedat, had often met bin Laden since 1986, and found him to be "quiet-spoken, respectful and humble" (Naidu, 2001 September 16, p. 3). The bin Laden family donated more than $3 million over eight years for the acquisition of a building for the IPCI, the printing of the Koran in English and Zulu, as well as the printing and distribution of other Islamic literature, and allegedly paid the 45-year-old Yousuf Deedat a monthly salary of $100,000 while he was secretary general of the IPCI. In appreciation of their generosity, the Deedats named their building in Durban after the bin Laden family.

Although there was no indication that either Yousuf Deedat or any of the other Muslim organizations was in any way associated with 9/11, they became links between South Africa and global terrorism (Gibson, 2001 September 20, p. 2). In fact, Deedat had discouraged his fellow-Muslims from volunteering to enter the war in Afghanistan, for which he was severely criticized by members of the Muslim community, who claimed he was "just afraid of his assets being frozen by the U.S." (Tabane, 2001 October 8). Nevertheless, the media expressed the concern that such links could cause internal tension, as it might force South Africans to look differently at their Muslim compatriots (Gibson, 2001 September 20, p. 2). Also, if the South African government should have decided to support the retributive attacks on Afghanistan in which innocent Muslims were killed, this tension could have reached boiling-point.

FRIENDSHIP WITH "ROGUE NATIONS"

Reports also expressed concern that South Africa's friendship with countries such as Libya and Cuba, both of which are regarded by America as supporters of terrorism, could come in the way of the cordial relationship between South Africa and the United States (Steyn, 2001 September 22, p. 2).

The friendships between South Africa and the "rogue countries" are long-standing, dating from the apartheid era, when they each supported the liberation struggle, while countries like the United States supported the apartheid government and classified the now ruling ANC as a terrorist organization. When former American President Bill Clinton had visited South Africa during Nelson Mandela's term in office, Mandela told him that he had invited the leaders of Cuba, Libya and Iran to visit the country. In a joint news conference, Mandela told critics of his friendship with these countries that they could "jump in a pool," and added that "[w]e should not abandon those who helped us in the darkest hour in the history of this country. Not only did they support us with rhetoric, they gave us the resources for us to conduct the struggle and to win" (*The Examiner*, 1998 March 28).

ANTI-AMERICAN SENTIMENTS

Because of America's historical association with the apartheid government as well as its stance towards the ANC, there still exists a strong anti-American and anti-Western sentiment amongst many black South Africans

(Mills, 2003). This animosity was visible in some of the ANC members' reaction to 9/11. Eastern Cape Premier Makhenkesi Stofile said he felt that the hijackers who flew the airplanes the World Trade Center and the Pentagon "were perhaps guerrillas and not cowardly terrorists" and that the United States should "look into itself" for the cause of the attacks (Dispatch Online, 2001 September 15). Stofile was quickly brought into line with the official ANC view and retracted his comments.

Ebrahim Ismail Ebrahim, ANC chair of Parliament's Foreign Affairs committee, expressed the opinion that indiscriminate attacks by the United States would create a "generation of terrorists" and said that the committee did not think that "an attack on the people of Afghanistan, because of the actions of some of the leadership of the Taliban movement, can be justified" (Michaels, Mkhwanazi, Ebersohn & Fabricius, 2001 September 17). He said that the attacks could not be justified "by any stretch of the imagination," but accused America of being arrogant when they dealt with less influential nations. They had also "done nothing" to solve the problems in the Middle East, but instead, by siding with Israel, "even to the extent of vetoing simple UN resolutions such as a request by the Palestinians for international observers in the conflict zone — the U.S. has sent a message to Palestinians that their cause was a hopeless one."

These remarks reaffirmed Mbeki's unenviable position: While showing support for the United States, he also had to pacify his support base both locally and in the rest of Africa. Consequently, many of the ANC's statements in connection with the 9/11 attack were designed to appease the South African electorate, as well as to counter African perceptions that South Africa "operates economically and politically as little more than an embassy for Western views on the continent" (Mills, 2003). According to Greg Mills, who is National Director of the South African Institute of International Affairs, "Pretoria's response is thus a difficult balancing act, one between keeping close enough to the United States to have a voice, but shrill enough to keep its credentials in Africa and among the South."

Official Position

Early on the South African media speculated about what South Africa's policy and role should be in the unfolding drama, stating that although it would be best if the country could officially remain neutral, it could not regard itself as an island unaffected by events in the rest of the world (*Die Burger*, 2001 September 15, p. 26). Moreover, such neutrality should at least show goodwill towards the United States. "Depending on how the conflict played out, this might be an unattainable luxury. And under such circumstances the government should very soberly and very calculatedly consider the country's objective interests [Translated]."

A week after 9/11, Mbeki officially made the government's position known. He announced that South Africa would cooperate in any international venture to prosecute those responsible for the terror attacks, but that the country would not militarily support retributive attacks on Afghanistan (Lackay, 2001 September 20, p. 2). He also agreed to the resolution of the United Nation's Security Council which compelled member countries to prosecute terrorists within their counties' borders (*Rapport*, 2001 September 13, p. 2). According to the resolution, countries that did not comply could expect military action against them.

The main area of involvement was South Africa's assistance to the United States in the search for and investigation of possible suspects (Munusamy, 2001 September 23, p. 1). Intelligence and security agencies immediately processed the names, identikits and passport numbers of more than 200 people — most of them from Arab descent — which they had received from American investigators. The state intelligence agencies conducted searches through Home Affairs and airline records to trace whether the suspected terrorists were in the country or had any association with South Africa (Munusamy, 2001 September 23, p. 1). The government also pledged to tighten airport security and border control, to exchange information and monitor suspected terrorist organizations and their movements, including the IPCI, and to extradite suspects. Furthermore, the Reserve Bank instructed South African banks to track and report on transactions with terror organizations (*Rapport*, 2001 September 13, p. 2)

The government decided against offering the U.S. military assistance, because although they recognized America's right to prosecute the terrorists (Lackay, 2001 September 20, p. 2), they were concerned that United States might unfairly target Islamic countries — many of which had longstanding friendships with the South African government — in their response to the terror attacks (Munusamy, 2001 September 23, p. 1). Such a step might also have created domestic tension in certain community sectors, which is also the reason why the government refrained from widely publicizing the scope of its cooperation with the United States (*Rapport*, 2001 September 13, p. 2). Furthermore, the government felt that military action was not the way to address global terrorism and that the United States instead should search for an understanding of the motivation for the attacks as well as make a concerted effort to resolve conflicts worldwide (Lackay, 2001 September 20, p. 2). The results of an instant opinion poll by the internet news service News24 indicated that South Africans agreed with the government's view about military aid, as 72 percent of the respondents indicated that they were against South Africa becoming militarily involved in any planned counterstrikes by the United States (*Beeld*. 2001 September 21, p. 4).

In an open letter to Mbeki, Tony Leon, as leader of the official opposition, lambasted the government for its policy stance, saying that the country should rid itself of "immoral and degrading friendships with despots and oppressors" and rather focus on building friendly relationships with democracies "sharing our values" (Leon, 2001 September 21, p. 13). He continued that although there was reason to criticize the foreign policies of the United States and the West and that the government was correct in placing the interests of its people first, it remains crucial for the sake of the country's long-term interests to "stand up for human rights and democracy ... If we are prepared to use our influence over Mugabe, it will carry more weight when we ask the USA to use its influence over Israel. If we condemn Palestinian terror, our condemnation of Israeli military excesses will carry more weight." Leon stressed that South African foreign policy should be cleansed of "moral duplicity and hypocrisy" and that the attacks on the United States had provided just such an opportunity.

THE WAR ON TERROR

The pending American attacks on Afghanistan drew loud cries of disapproval form especially the Muslim community. About two weeks before the attacks, the organization Muslims Against Illegitimate Leaders (Mail) claimed that it expected up to 5,000 people would volunteer to fight against the United States, despite South Africa's promise to prevent any "mercenaries" from departing its soil (Bester, 2001 September 28, p. 10). Bester quoted Bush's ultimatum and warned that "South Africa must prevent that any support, of any nature, is offered to Afghanistan, as the question: 'friend or enemy?' might just occur to the USA."

Such sentiments did not deter Muslims who saw the attacks by the United States as a war on Islam. *The Star* interviewed a seafood merchant and his two sons who said they saw themselves as "members of the al-Qaeda movement and are ready to defend their religion Islam, which they say is under attack from Americans" (Tabane, 2001 October 8). "If the call comes tomorrow, every single Muslim will go and defend the religion. You have not seen anything like it. It will be so horrific that the world cannot stop it. I must be prepared to go and kill, otherwise I have to leave the fold of Islam. Every Muslim has al-Qaeda in their hearts. We love al-Qaeda because we know what they do. Everyone of us is a time bomb." When reminded that the South African government prohibited the recruitment of people to fight overseas, the brothers warned that "South Africans risk a civil war — if they do that."

Shortly after the first strikes against Afghanistan, U.S. Secretary of State General Colin Powell contacted Mbeki, who, as the chairman of the Non-Aligned Movement, was considered as an important player in the Afghanistan crisis, to inform him of the events (Seale, 2001 October 9, p. 3). *The Sunday Independent* reported that government officials "appeared relieved ... that when President George W. Bush called President Thabo Mbeki to thank him for his unequivocal condemnation of the terror attacks on the U.S., he did not ask for military assistance" (Fabricius, 2001 October 22).

Predictably, the South African community had mixed reactions to the eventual strikes by the United States (Van der Westhuizen, 2001 October 9, p. 3). The government itself refrained from commenting, except to say that its was keeping an eye on the situation, but the South African Communist Party (SACP) and the Congress of South African Trade Unions (Cosatu) denounced the offensive, saying that it would contribute to a vicious circle of violence, as it will lead to retaliatory attacks, which will undermine global peace and stability.

"It is disconcerting that the USA attacked Afghanistan without convincing the world that bin Laden was responsible for the attacks on the USA. The United Nations as an independent body should have taken the lead in resolving the impasse between Afghanistan and the USA," Zwelinzima Vavi, General Secretary of Cosatu said (Van der Westhuizen, 2001 October 9, p. 3). The SACP felt the suspects should have been prosecuted based on proof and according to international law. The PAC responded that terrorism must be fought under the supervision of the UN, and that no country or coalition should be allowed to act unilaterally to punish terrorism. The Palestinian Solidarity Committee condemned the attacks "because as in all wars, it will bring misery to the most oppressed and poorest of people ... It is criminal to spend huge amounts of money on wars when you consider the global starvation, poverty and need for medicines against Aids."

Conversely, the DA fully supported the attacks, praising Bush for his "commendable conduct" (Van der Westhuizen, 2001 October 9, p. 3). "From any perspective he has lead the USA wisely, and while his does this, he deserves the support of all decent people." Cassie Aucamp of the AEB ("Afrikaner Unity Movement") also supported the strikes, "because they were executed with precision, which will limit the loss of life, and because the video-recording of bin Laden clearly showed that more attacks were planned." He called on the government to express its support for the United States as "aloof neutrality" could be detrimental to the country.

Two days after the strikes against Afghanistan, *Die Burger* reported that the government was considering the possibility of banning the Muslim organizations Qibla and Pagad (Seale, 2001 October 10, p. 2). Aziz Pahad, Deputy Minister of Foreign Affairs, stressed that such action would not be an attack on Islam, as the two organizations only represented a small extremist minority.

Members of the Muslim community subsequently marched on the American consulate in Cape Town, accusing the government of supporting a war against Islam and waving posters with slogans such as "Mbeki sack your blairy bushy terror-able bosses," "Root out terrorism and not innocent Afghans," and "Bush: wanted dead or alive" (Cruywagen, 2001 October 12, p. 2). A member of the public expressed the opinion that the strong police presence at the protest was proof that "the government obeyed American instructions." In its statement, Pagad accused the United States and Great Britain of being judge, jury and executioner, while world leaders idly looked on. The Workers Organization for Socialist Action (Wosa) said America was attacked because of all the "crimes against humanity" they committed and that they were unleashing powers they would not be able to control.

The United States shortly afterward indicated that it might require military assistance from South Africa and "would expect such assistance forthcoming" (Fabricius, 2001 October 22). This showed that the American government was either ignorant of or indifferent to Mbeki's plight. Merely allowing American warships to use South African harbors could have been interpreted as "an act of hostility against Islam and would probably stir up Muslim extremists such as Pagad in South Africa," according to Jakkie Cilliers, the head of the Institute for Security Studies in Pretoria (Fabricius, 2001 October 22).

NELSON MANDELA

The intensity of the emotions around these issues was illustrated by the scathing attacks on Nelson Mandela for expressing his support for the strikes against Afghanistan after talks with Bush in Washington (SABC News, 2002 January 2). He repeated this view in December when he visited Durban's Grey Street mosque, saying that Osama bin Laden should be captured and tried, and that the al-Qaeda network as well as other terrorist strongholds should be destroyed.

Angry Muslims responded by saying he "had no right to label bin Laden a terrorist when he had not been convicted in a court of law" (SABC News, 2002 January 2). The Muslim Youth Movement accused him of not being committed to the rule of law, which demands a trial before conviction (Khan, 2002 January 5). He was criticized for "not displaying the statesmanship and even-handedness that characterizes his politics."

The PAC, a long-time ally of the Qibla movement, also lashed out at the former president (Mamaila, 2001 November 14). "Does Mandela condone the death of children, women and the elderly in Afghanistan while patron of the Nelson Mandela Children's Fund in South Africa? Or does he want to tell us to believe that the life of children in Afghanistan is cheaper than that of children in South Africa?" The PAC said that Mandela's call for the "flushing out of terrorists" showed just how determined he was to please Bush.

In early January 2002, Mandela issued an apology for his previous "vociferous and unqualified support to the U.S.-led coalition's war on terrorism in Afghanistan," saying that his initial statements had been "one-sided and overstated" and that he regretted giving the impression that he was "insensitive and uncaring about the suffering inflicted upon the Afghan people and country" (Khan, 2002 January 5). This was considered by some to be a move to "appease a constituency that has always been important to the ruling African National Congress (ANC)."

Muslims welcomed his apology and the leading newspaper *Business Day* praised him, saying that "[b]y humbling himself and revisiting his position on the bombing campaign, Madiba (Mandela) has once again demonstrated his greatness in a world where politicians' egos often get in the way of reason and good judgment" (Khan, 2002 January 5). John Stremlau, a professor of International Relations at the University of the Witwatersrand in Johannesburg, also described it as "a very sensible approach" and said that "[t]he war on terrorism should not divide South Africans among themselves."

Shortly after Mandela's apology, (former) Vice President Jacob Zuma told a meeting of Muslims at a mosque in Durban that the word "terrorism" was interpreted differently by different sectors of the community (Joubert, 2002 January 5, p. 2). "He found it unacceptable that the West regarded the attack on America as terrorism, but had no problem with the Allied attacks on Afghanistan, in which innocent people are dying." The DA warned that Zuma was playing a very dangerous game (IOL, 2002 January 4). DA chairman Joe Seremane said these comments looked as if the government was trying to distance itself from Mbeki's initial exemplary statements that South Africa has a role to play in the fight against terrorism. "Quibbling over definitions creates the impression that he (Zuma) might be supporting Osama bin Laden — surely this is not the case?" According to Ross Herbert, Africa Research Fellow at the South African Institute of International Affairs, it appeared as if Zuma was also trying to placate Muslim voters (Essop, 2002 January 8, p. 2).

Probably the most controversial remark from a South African pertaining to the war on Iraq came from Nelson Mandela: "If (Iraqi President) Saddam Hussein was not carrying out the UN instructions and resolutions ... I will support them (the UN) without resignation, but what I condemn is one power with a president who can't think properly and wants to plant the world into holocaust" (Bell, 2003 January 30). He asserted that Bush wanted Iraq's oil and that British Prime Minister Tony Blair's support had made him the U.S. "foreign minister." He also insinuated that the United States ignored the United Nations because its secretary-general, Kofi Annan, was black. "They never did that when secretary-generals were white."

The reaction of South African political leaders to this diatribe again stressed the political divide in the South African community. While the PAC and the UDM applauded Mandela's stance, other leaders thought it inappropriate (Bell, 2003 January 30). PAC Deputy President Motseko Pheko said his party had repeatedly condemned the American war plans. "We believe the U.S. is making itself a bully in the world and that they are the cause of this war ... why should it demand other countries disarm when it does not?" Bantu Holomisa said he wished that Mandela "was still president of this country," and added that Mandela had "questioned the rationale behind Bush's desire to attack Iraq, when Mbeki's government was 'pussyfooting' around the issue."

Tony Leon, leader of the DA, said he "respectfully disagrees with the way Former President Mandela has characterized the issue," while the New National Party (NNP) said it understood Mandela's concerns, but that he had damaged a good argument by "playing the race card" (Bell, 2003 January 30). The Inkatha Freedom Party was "amazed" about the "viciousness" of Mandela's attack, saying the "the issue is not as simple as Mr. Mandela is trying to make it."

President Thabo Mbeki (2003 January 26) stated his views on the proposed attack on Iraq in an article that was published in the *Sunday Times*. While opposed to the use of weapons of mass destruction, and thoroughly in favor of the destruction of any such munitions that Iraq might have, he was "not aware of any information that would suggest that Iraq has been in serious breach of UN resolutions. Nothing credible has been said that any such breach has occurred to justify war." He also stressed that "[t]he very countries that are threatening Iraq over weapons of mass destruction themselves own large quantities of these weapons. They say nothing whatsoever against Israel's weapons of mass destruction. Of course, from their point of view, the matter has nothing to do with principle. It turns solely on the question of power. We disagree."

The editorial column in the same newspaper stated that while there was not enough evidence of a breach of United Nations disarmament instructions to justify an invasion by the United States and its allies, they still planned to continue doing so (*Sunday Times*, 2003 January 26). "What is most perplexing is not that the U.S. and Britain are planning to invade Iraq, but that they are prepared to do so without the sanction of the UN. Not only is the belligerence of Washington and London in danger of physically destabilizing the Middle East, but it is destroying the very notion that world matters belong in the court of world bodies."

The Afrikaans Sunday newspaper *Rapport* (2003 February 9, p. 22) noted that even before the war in Iraq had started, South Africans were deeply divided about the issue. "What is upsetting in the case of the Iraq/America conflict is the possibility that a war that actually has nothing to do with South Africa will confuse and confound our people to such an extent that we soon will be unable to agree on the solutions to our own problems. Or that the war will become the a new source for mistrust and alienation [Translated]." The newspaper criticized people like ANC spokesman Smuts Ngonyama who said Colin Powell's arguments to the UN were "irrelevant" and "fabrications," and called on the government to "stop trying to play mediator in Iraq." "Regardless of how badly a war can harm South Africa and Africa, our country simply is not in the league of countries capable of stopping a war. The uncertain times ahead will demand greater political leadership than that exhibited by both South Africa's government and the opposition leaders."

At least three political parties — the DA, NNP and Freedom Front — warned that South Africans will regret anti-American statements that could be understood as pro-Iraqi (Du Toit, 2003: February 23, p. 15). Professor Willie Breytenbach at the University of Stellenbosch commented that even if one should agree with Mandela's view of Bush, it is for the sake of Nepad probably not a good position to take. "If you want large sums of money from someone, it might be better not to step on his toes."

About South Africa's attempt to stop the war in Iraq by sending a group of experts in biological and chemical weapons to the country, Dr. Wouter Basson, project leader of the previous government's chemical and biological warfare program, said it was a "senseless" exercise, as well as "utterly arrogant" (Jansen, 2003 February 23, p. 15). He said it was nonsense that Iraq had the ability to threaten America with weapons of mass destruction. "What is a weapon of mass destruction? It means that you bedevil everything with hundreds of thousands of casualties. Apart from a nuclear bomb, such a thing does not exist. Moreover, America has the weapon that comes closest to a nuclear bomb. It is the Daisycutter bomb that they used in Afghanistan [Translated]." He continued that Bush should not say that it was a global issue. "He must not say it is for our safety. Iraq can do absolutely nothing to South Africa."

Iraq Attacked

When the United States attacked Iraq, Mbeki expressed his regret, with presidential spokesman Bheki Khumalo calling it a "blow to multilateralism" (IOL, 2003 March 20). NNP Foreign Affairs spokesperson Boy Geldenhuys stressed the importance of South Africa's neutrality. "Humanitarian aid must be encouraged but South Africa should at all cost not be seen to support Saddam Hussein," he said. "We hope the targets will be the military targets and not civilians." Still, after the attacks on Iraq, the editorial column of *Rapport* (2003 March 30, p. 14) said South Africans should be proud of the way the government had taken a stand and had tried to contribute to a solution for the sake of world peace. "Indeed, South Africa played a leading role and it must have improved our stature worldwide."

Conclusion

Like the rest of the world, the South African politicians, media and public were stunned by the scope and magnitude, as well as the audacity, of the 9/11 attack on America. If it was simply a case of being either with the United States or with the terrorists, of simply choosing to be on the side of the cowboy with the white hat, then South Africa's 9/11 tale might have been simple, maybe even boring. However, because of the spectrum of cultural, political, racial, and religious divides in the country, South African President Thabo Mbeki had no other choice than not to choose at all, and do it in such a way as not to offend anybody.

Perhaps *Die Burger* said it best: "It is a fact that the government had to practically squeeze the country through the narrow straight between Scylla en Charybdis. Yet it seems as if the chosen direction was mostly the correct one" (*Die Burger*, 2001 October 5, p. 8).

References

Beeld. (2001, September 12). Terroriste aanval op VSA Ghaddafi veroordeel aanvalle, bied hulp aan, p. 9.
Beeld. (2001, September 13). Kalm bly, p. 10.

Beeld. (2001, September 22). OAE vra wêreld om teen terreur te veg, p. 2.

Beeld. (2001d, September 21). "SA se wapens moet hier swyg," p. 2.

Bell, G. (2003, January 30). *Madiba's attack on Bush surprises opposition.* Retrieved November 6, 2005, from Independent Online: www.iol.co.za/index.php? click_id=6&art_id=qw1043940421806B261&set_id=1.

Bester, C. (2001, September 28). SA moet dié huursoldate keer. *Die Burger*, p. 10.

Botha, A. (2001, July). The Prime Suspects? The Metamorphosis of Pagad. *Monograph* 62. Retrieved October 24, 2005, from Institute for Security Studies: www.iss.co.za/Pubs/Monographs/No63/Chap2.html#Anchor-Historical-55000.

Botha, A. (2005). Pagad: A Case Study of Radical Islam in South Africa. *Terrorism Monitor* 3(17):9-11. Retrieved 2005-09-29 from The Jamestown Foundation: http://jamestown.org/ terrorism/news/uploads/ter_003_017.pdf.

Bush, G.W. (2001, September 20). *Address to a Joint Session of Congress and the American People.* Retrieved October 11, 2005, from The White House: www.whitehouse. gov/news/releases/2001/09/20010920-8.html.

Cordesman, A.H. & Burke, A.A. (2001). *A New Strategy for Dealing with Terrorism in the Middle East—Working Draft.* Retrieved October 16, 2005, from Centre for Strategic and International Studies: http://www.csis.org/burke/saudi21/ MEterror.pdf.

Cruywagen, V. (2001, October 12). SA regering steun oorlog teen Islam, sê betogers. *Die Burger*, p. 2.

Die Burger. (2001, September 14). Koalisie teen terreur groei, p. 2.

Die Burger. (2001, September 21). Wie help Amerika in stryd teen terreur? Wêreld geskok, simpatiek, maar steun nie noodwendig militêre optrede. p. 13.

Die Burger. (2001, October 5). Hoe SA hom in huidige krisis moet posisioneer, p. 8.

Die Burger. (2001, September 15) Nou is dit tyd vir koel koppe, p. 26.

Dispatch Online. (2001, September 13). *Editorial Opinion: Hope of rescue.* Retrieved October 11, 2005 from Dispatch Online: http://www.dispatch.co.za/2001/ 09/13/editoria/ ALEADER.HTM.

Dispatch Online. (2001, September 12). *Mbeki: unite against terrorism.* Retrieved October 18, 2005 from Dispatch Online: http://www.dispatch.co.za/2001/ 09/12/southafrica/embeki.htm.

Dispatch Online. (2001c, September 15). *Premier withdraws US terror comments.* Retrieved October 27 from Dispatch Online: http://www.dispatch.co.za/2001/09/ 15/easterncape/ ACOMMENT.HTM.

Du Toit, Z.B. (2003, February 23). Onsekerheid oor Nepad word ál groter. *Rapport*, p. 5.

Essop, P. (2002, January 8). Zuma se stelling oor terreur "nie teenstrydig," p. 2.

Fabricius, P. (2001, October 22). US expects military aid from SA on demand. Retrieved November 2, 2005, from Sunday Independent: http://www.iol.co.za/ index.php?set_id=1&click_id=13&art_id= ct20010922192508207S12361.

Gibson, E. (2001, September 20). Aanvalle in VSA "gaan Afrika bloedneus op geldsakkie slaan" *Beeld*, p. 2.

Gottschalk, K. (2005, February). Vigilantism v. the State: A case study of the rise and fall of Pagad, 1996–2000. *ISS Paper 99*. Retrieved October 10, 2005 from Institute for Security Studies: http://www.iss.co.za/pubs/papers/99/paper99.pdf.

IOL. (2001, September 13). *Africa's leaders united in outrage at terror*. Retrieved October 22, 2005, from Independent Online: http://www.iol.co.za/index.php?set_id=1&click_id= 68&art_id=ct20010913105513115A162659.

IOL. (2001, September 17). *African voices caution US against rash reply*. Retrieved October 22, 2005, from Independent Online: http://www.iol.co.za/index.php?set_id= 1&click_id=68&art_id=qw1000732264572B232.

IOL. (2001, September 13). *Government dismisses "newsflash" blaming SA*. Retrieved October 24, 2005 from Independent Online: http://www.int.iol.co.za/index.php?set_id= 1&click_id=13&art_id=qw1000389302881B225.

IOL. (2002, January 4). *DA slams Zuma's "dangerous game."* Retrieved November 5, 2005 from Independent Online: http://www.iol.co.za/general/newsview.php?art_id=qw1010152440408 B254&click_id=13&set_id=1.

IOL. (2003, March 20). *Mbeki regrets the start of war in Iraq*. Retrieved November 6, 2005 from Independent Online: www.int.iol.co.za/index.php?sf=2813&set_id= &sf=2813&clickid =3&art_id=qw1048135501125B262&set_id=1.

Jansen, H. (2003, February 23). "Missie is verwaand, sinloos" – Basson. *Rapport*, p. 15.

Joubert, J.J. (2002, January 5). SA moet weer besin oor terreur Zuma Word glo verskillend verstaan. *Die Burger*, p. 2.

Khan, F. (2002, January 5). *Mandela to apologize for supporting U.S. on terror war*. Retrieved November 5, 2005 from Common Dreams News Center: http://www.commondreams.org / headlines02/0105-01.htm.

Lackay, A. (2001, September 20). SA steun stryd teen terrorisme, maar nie met militêre hulp. *Beeld*, p. 2.

Leon, T. (2001, September 21). "Los die onderdrukkers." *Beeld*, p. 13.

Mail & Guardian. (2001, October 31). SA govt "concerned" by Afghan deaths. Retrieved October 23, 2005 from *Mail & Guardian:* http://www.mg.co.za/articledirect.aspx?articleid=226881&area=%2farchives_online_edition%2f.

Mamaila, K. (2001, November 14). PAC raps Mandela for his support for US. Retrieved November 5, 2005 from *The Star*: http://www.iol.co.za/general/newsview.php?art_id=ct20011114203145234P253654&click_id=13&set_id=1.

Mbeki, T. (2001, September 28). Ordinary US citizens offer a lesson to South Africa. Retrieved October 18, 2005 from *ANC Today* 1(36): http://www.anc.org.za/ancdocs/anctoday/ 2001/at36.htm.

Mbeki, T. (2003, January 26). War in Iraq is a question of power, not principle. Retrieved November 6, 2005 from *Sunday Times*: http://www.suntimes.co.za/articles/article-specialreport.aspx?ID=ST6A115361.

Michaels, J., Mkhwanazi, S., Ebersohn, F. & Fabricius, P. (2001, September 17). SA divided over reprisal attacks. Retrieved November 2, 2005 from *The Star*: Independent Online: http://www.iol.co.za/index.php?set_id=1&click_id= 13&art_id=ct20010917212506961U260697.

Mills, G. (2003). The view from South Africa. *In the National Interest* 12(10). Retrieved October 26, 2005 from *In the National Interest*: www.inthenationalinterest.com/ Articles/vol2 issue10/vol2issue10millspfv.html.

Morrison, J.S. (2001, November 15). *Africa and the war on global terrorism*. Testimony before the U.S. House of Representatives, International Relations Committee - Subcommittee on Africa. Retrieved October 1, 2005-10-01 from House of Representatives: www.house.gov/ international_relations/107/76191.pdf.

Munusamy, R. (2001, September 23). SA joins hunt for terror suspects - Intelligence agencies comb records for 200 people on US "wanted" list. *Sunday Times*, p. 1.

Naidu, B. (2001, September 16). SA activist's bin Laden ties. *Sunday Times*, p. 3.

Rapport. (2001, September 16). SA hulp aan VSA tasbare intelligensie-steun soos na Nairobi-bom, sê Netshitenzhe, p. 1.

Rapport. (2001, September 13). SA werk volstoom saam teen terreur, Steun Amerika se pogings; sal sterk boodskap in VN oordra, p. 2.

Rapport. (2003, February 9). Irak verdeel SA, p. 22.

Rapport. (2003, March 30). Waar gaan die wêreld heen? p. 14.

SABC News. (2002, January 2). *Mandela withdraws support for USA war in Afghanistan*. Retrieved November 5, 2005 from SABC News: http://www.sabcnews.co.za/ south_africa/ general/0,2172,25967,00.html.

Seale, T. (2001, October 9). Powell laat weet Mbeki kort ná aanval. *Die Burger*, p. 3.

Seale, T. (2001, October 10). Regering kan Pagad en Qibla in SA verbied. *Die Burger*, p. 2.

Steyn, P. (2001a, October 16). SA Moslems wat wil gaan veg "wys hoe VSA misgetas het." *Beeld*, p. 3.

Steyn, P. (2001, September 22). VSA het SA se inligting nodig oor terro-geld. *Beeld*, p. 2.

Steyn, P., Van Wyk, J.J. & Khumalo, F. (2001, September 23). bin Laden-sel in SA gesoek. *Rapport*, p. 1.

Sullivan, J.P. (2001). Gangs, hooligans, and anarchists—the vanguard of Netwar in the streets. In: Arquilla, J. & Ronfeldt, D. (Eds.), 2001. *Networks and Netwars: The future of terror, crime and militancy*. Santa Monica: RAND. Retrieved October 3, 2005 from RAND Organisation: http://www.rand.org/publications/MR/ MR1382/MR1382.ch4.pdf.

Sunday Times. (2001, September 12). SA Muslims condemn attack - and urge US to consider causes. Retrieved October 20, 2005 from *Sunday Times*: http://www.sundaytimes.co.za/ 2001/ 09/12/voicemuslims.asp.

Sunday Times. (2003, January 26). The new world disorder. Retrieved November 6, 2005, from *Sunday Times*: http://www.suntimes.co.za/articles/article-specialreport.aspx?ID= ST6A115360.

Tabane, R. (2001, October 8). Johannesburg family ready to join jihad. Retrieved November 2, 2005 from *The Star*. http://www.int.iol.co.za/index.php?set_id= 1&click_id=13&art_id= ct20011008215417460R320119.

The Examiner. (1998, March 28). Mandela tells critics "go jump in a pool." Retrieved October 30, 2005 from *The Examiner*. http://archives.tcm.ie/irishexaminer/ 1998/03/28/fhead.htm.

Van der Westhuizen, C. (2001, September 28). "Terug na Koue Oorlog": Bush se beleid kan dié era laat herleef, sê kritici. *Beeld*, p. 15.

Van der Westhuizen, C. (2001, October 9). Bush kry lof en kritiek uit SA. *Die Burger*, p. 3.

Part V

NORTH & SOUTH
AMERICAN MEDIA

Chapter 20

HOW U.S. TV JOURNALISTS TALK ABOUT OBJECTIVITY IN 9/11 COVERAGE

Kirsten Mogensen

Watching CNN on September 11, 2001, in the United States I noticed that all the American sources involved in the discussions during the first 24 hours were people expressing mainstream American views. The sources were witnesses, intellectuals, experts, and present or former government officials from the Democratic Party as well as the Republican Party, but there were no sources expressing views considered politically incorrect. We know from other media that there were extremist views among Americans, but the supporters of such views were not allowed to express themselves on CNN or on the major networks.

The extremist views can be divided into two major groups. The first consisted of views that Muslims in general were a threat to the social fabric of American society. These people expressed anger against American Muslims in local radio talk or call-in programs and in interpersonal conversations. In Louisiana, where I lived at the time, an owner of a local sandwich bar was harassed as a result of such a radio show. Fortunately, in this case a group of responsible people concerned about the possible backlash against Muslims helped stop the harassment.

The other group of extremist views came from Americans who, to some degree, expressed sympathy for the terrorists. Easterbrook (2001) mentions as examples a talk show host who said the September terrorists were brave; a professor who called the United States a terrorist nation; another professor who, on September 11, told his university class that anyone who would blow up the Pentagon would have his vote; a composer who called the World Trade Center destruction "the greatest work of art ever"; and a novelist who said that George W. Bush and Osama bin Laden were interchangeable. According to the law, people are allowed to express such views if they are willing to risk being unpopular, and in a crises situation the public may react aggressively. However, while citizens have a right to speak, the media have no obligation to present extremist views, and on 9/11 major American news networks allowed only people outside the United States, such as Palestinians, to express support for the terrorists.

But why were extremist views excluded from CNN and other major networks? After all, the influential journalists at these news networks subscribe to ethical standards such as those expressed by the Society of Professional Journalists (Day 2002: 445-446). They included statements like: "Journalists should ... tell the story of the diversity and magnitude of the human experience boldly, even when it is unpopular to do so ... examine their own cultural values and avoid imposing those values on others ... support the open exchange of views, even views they find repugnant ... give voice to the voiceless; official and unofficial sources of information can be equally valid" in the name of public enlightenment, justice and democracy.

American journalists often talk about "objectivity" as an ideal, meaning that they "strive to keep their personal preferences and opinions out of the news stories, to achieve balance in coverage, and to relay on credible and responsible news sources. According to this traditional view, the ethics of news writing is concerned with facts and impartiality in the presentation of those facts" (Day 2002: 36).

In contrast, Merrill, who is an advocate of existential journalism, argues that "all reporters must be selective, and this selectivity involves being subjective — selecting and using information that fits their existing ideas as to what constitute news" (Merrill 1997: 121). He adds: "All productive thinking, observing and communicating are driven by the observer's interest and respect for the essence of what is being observed and reported." As an ideal, "good and ethical reports are truthful, unbiased, full and fair" (Merrill 1997: 174). Some people assume that the reason CNN and American network journalists chose not to be objective in their coverage of 9/11 was that their viewers were in a state of shock and crisis (Greenberg 2002), where the combination of sadness and anger easily could result in violence or other forms of unacceptable behavior (Schramm 1965; Minkdak & Hursh 1965; Neal 1998). But this study asks the journalists who covered these events how they interpreted the journalism norm of objectivity during the first hours when their nation was the victim of a seemingly ongoing terror attack.

METHOD

This article is part of an ongoing project for the Reilly Center for Media & Public Affairs at The Manship School of Mass Communication, Louisiana

State University, about how CNN and the networks covered the September 11 crisis. A content analysis of the first eight hours was published in Greenberg's *Communication and Terrorism: Public and Media Responses to 9/11* (Mogensen, Lindsay, Li, Perkins and Beardsley 2002). The project also includes a narrative analysis of the first 24 hours on CNN (Mogensen 2003). Even though there were differences in the coverage at the various TV networks and CNN, the overall narrative was pretty much the same given the nature of the events. An overview of CNN's coverage is provided below.

This article is based on personal interviews with 37 journalists who covered the events on 9/11 for ABC, NBC, CBS, CNN, MSNBC and FOX News. The interviews were conducted in the interviewee's own newsroom between January and March 2002 using a flexible, semi-structured questionnaire containing eight open-ended questions. Seven members of the LSU faculty did the interviews working alone or in groups. Five of them had a background in practical journalism, so they were familiar with journalistic norms.[1]

Interviewees — including reporters, producers, editors, anchors, and vice presidents of news operations — were asked to describe how they reacted initially and how they worked through the 24 hours that followed. The interviewees were allowed to talk freely about anything that they found important with respect to coverage during the first couple of days. When they described situations of special interest to us, the interviewers would ask them to elaborate more on the topic, and a few times a discussion developed between an interviewer and an interviewee. The interviews lasted between 20 and 80 minutes. All interviews were recorded, transcribed by secretaries, and analyzed for themes and issues using the computer program Atlas.ti.

Based on analysis of the interviews, the following presentation will focus on five aspects of objective and balanced reporting:

1. Balanced sourcing
2. Legitimate views
3. Patriotism
4. Conformity to reality
5. Concern about viewers' reactions

FIVE STAGES

The media coverage can be divided into five distinct stages. There were, of course, overlapping themes and sources as well as a replay of footage from one stage to the next, but the stages differed within two important ways: major events and types of sources interviewed or giving public statements.

The stages were:

1. *The catastrophe*. Chaos and horror. 8:49 a.m. to approx. 6:40 p.m.
2. *Control and national unity*. Approx. 6:40 p.m. to 9:10 p.m.
3. *Rescue work*. Approx. 9:10 p.m. to 12:30 a.m.
4. *International*. Approx. 12:30 a.m. to 6 a.m.
5. *Mourning begins*. Approx. 6 a.m. to 8:49 a.m.

The terrorist attacks were staged events that monopolized the agenda on 9/11, but the influence on the coverage of that agenda changed through the five stages.

During the first stage, news was constantly breaking, and government officials left their offices in fear. Journalists saw it as their primary task to inform the American public and the rest of the world about what happened and to find sources that could provide interpretations.

The second stage had important symbolic massages in which political communicators reassured the public that the social system had not collapsed, that the legal government was in control, and that people could count on their neighbors because Americans behaved in a civilized manner and helped one another during a difficult time. They also told the public that the United States was the best place in the world with its freedom and justice and that nobody would succeed in destroying the American way of life because the United States is a strong military nation.

In the third stage, CNN to a large degree served as a channel for information from the rescue officials to the public — especially to the relatives of victims but also to other citizens who wanted to help.

In the fourth stage, most of the national political communicators left the spotlight, and CNN presented news from around the globe. Some journalists used these nightly hours to experiment with longer and more narrative formats than those from breaking news stories.

The fifth stage marked a new day, and when the format suggested that the situation was under control and government officials were able to tell the public what to expect next.

Tables 20.1 shows that who was interviewed or who gave statements to reporters or anchors on CNN. Within each stage, the unit of analysis is one clock-hour, meaning that one interviewee may be counted more than one time in a stage, but only once within a clock-hour. The table does not include replays, and it does not include eyewitnesses or relatives of victims (Mogensen 2003).

Overall, the results show that U.S. government and political officials are quoted much more often than ordinary people, whose role is usually limited

Table 20.1
Title of Persons Interviewed on CNN
(Number of Persons)

Title	Stage 1	Stage 2	Stage 3	Stage 4	Stage 5	Total 24 Hours
Former government officials, including former NATO commander	20	8	5	1	3	37
Rescue officials and NYC mayor and NY governor (including spokespeople for hospitals, firefighters, police officers, volunteer organizations and Pentagon, when the focus of the interview or statement is the rescue effort)	11	3	8	4	11	37
U.S. political leadership: Congress and President Bush and his spokespersons	11	9	5	1	0	26
International leaders	4	0	0	9	2	15
U.S. Administration: Current government officials (except the President, the NY top leadership, rescue officials and members of Congress)	0	5	0	2	1	8
Terrorism expert	3	0	1	4	0	7
Airline officials and aviation safety experts	2	0	1	1	0	4
Other official	3	1	2	3	0	8
Eyewitnesses and relatives of victims*	22	0	14	13	6	55
TOTAL**	76	26	36	38	23	199

*The estimates for eyewitnesses and relative are from the Vanderbilt archives.
**Table excludes replays.

to talking about how the tragedy affected them or their families. Sources that might offer views or opinions that conflict with U.S. official sources were rarely interviewed.

The table also shows that eyewitnesses played an important role in the first stage, when viewers were eager to hear what had happened. In the second period the national leaders staged a massive demonstration of their leadership, control and unity, and they received full attention from CNN.

When the rescue work came into focus, officials responsible for this work naturally were interviewed together with eyewitnesses and relatives of victims. International leaders were more prominently covered during the evening hours and expressed their support for the United States. Many international leaders expressed support for the United States. In fact, according to CNN's Tom Fenton, vice president and deputy managing editor of International Newsgathering, some of them contacted CNN and asked to have statements broadcast because they wanted to distance their countries from terrorism.

The next morning, officials connected to the rescue operation were more frequently interviewed. As expected, the use of interviewees and public statements generally mirrored the focus of attention. However, somewhat surprising is the finding that former government officials played a major role during the first stage. One might have expected eyewitnesses and current leaders to dominate. One possible explanation for this finding is that current leaders were too busy assessing the situation to participate in interviews, so the media turned to former government officials, at least initially. Not surprisingly, the research shows that most of the officials are also established, consensus-seeking politicians, diplomats and former governments officials.

FINDINGS OF THE INTERVIEWS

Balanced Sourcing

Since the days of Daniel Defoe and James Franklin, liberal journalists have fought for their right to present provoking information and opinions to the public. With the development of professionalism and social responsibility in the 20th century, it became a norm for many journalists to balance such opinions. As Hamilton and Krimsky put it (1996: 13):

> One of the fundamental journalistic rituals is "balance." Journalists do not report what one person purports to be the truth, however compelling that truth may seem. They gather varying opinions. So when it comes to reporting their mother's love, journalists quote the views of others who agree or disagree. In this way they earn the status of impartial observer.
>
> The concept of balance nicely fit the adversarial nature of the American democratic system.

The tendency in many news stories is to find "'duelling experts' who have staked out views at distant poles" (Hamilton and Krimsky 1966: 14). However, as every child has learned on the playground, the seesaw can be brought into balance not only by placing equally heavy weight on each end, but also by placing all the weight in the center. Balanced news reports presenting distinct opinions staked at distant poles are fundamentally different from balanced news reports relying on only mainstream opinions. Usually, the first type of balanced news reporting is common in liberal democracies, while the latter have similarities with the one-sided news reporting in more authoritarian systems.

Interviewed on their 9/11 coverage, our informants generally insisted on being fair and balanced, and, when asked to elaborate, they explained how instead of creating balance between opposing views they chose to interview well-informed sources with balanced views. Five journalists working in CNN's booking department in Atlanta provided us with an insight into the procedures for selection of sources to be interviewed on the air. The booking department has a database that at the time contained information about about 50,000 potential interviewees. Right after the first attack on the World Trade Center, the group started brainstorming about relevant information and analyses needed. The first requirement to the sources was that they had the knowledge needed and that they would not speculate.

> We don't want to put somebody on the air that says something that's premature or that somebody that doesn't have all the facts ... In breaking news like that, the inclination is to speculate. And we like to stay as far away from speculating ... I heard that over and over again in the first few days.

As a rule, one of the journalists in the booking department will do a pre-interview with guests before they go on air. During this pre-interview, each source is asked questions that the journalist expects the anchor to ask, and the interviewee's reactions are typed into the computer. When news is breaking, its sometimes difficult to pre-interview, but if sources are on air for the first time, CNN will pre-interview. The staff also searches in the databases to see if the credibility of the sources has ever been challenged.

> I might think, I've booked this great guest and then Gail does the pre-interview and does a dead body search and finds out that the guest isn't legitimate ... Or in talking to him, he or she comes up with a comment out of left field we weren't expecting. We thought they were objective analysts which turns out they're not so that we do need to bring somebody else.

In its ordinary news coverage, the booking department seeks to balance views and is especially careful about balance between major political groups.

[We are] carefully looking at who we're booking and what their background is and where they fall on issues, and even if someone is Democrat, you know they may fall one way on an issue that most Democrats don't fall. We're aware of all of that and we listen, and if somebody says one thing and it's cleared up, you can put the other side on, you know ... We won't just sort of let a one-sided opinion stand ... We sort of check and balance ourselves [but in] breaking news it's just getting, finding, you know, the right people and just the daily day-to-day.

This balance check on ordinary news coverage is carried out in connection with each show, and the fact that there is no time for such balance checks during breaking news may be a reason for concentrating on "balanced sources." One of the extreme viewpoints that were seemingly not allowed to be aired on the major TV networks on 9/11 was blaming Islam for the terrorism, which would easily lead to anger and backlash against the American Muslims. Here's another comment from a CNN booking department spokesperson:

You were asking, if we would book somebody who's angry at Muslims? Well that's not balanced, that's not what we do

Major TV networks had a similar policy. NBC's host on the "Today Show," Matt Lauer, said:

I mean you have to be balanced. ... I'll give you an example of being not balanced. It would be easy on that day to say ... look what they have done to us! Now we are going to go get the bastards. You know, that we are going to go find them, and we are going to get them. ... That's what you can say on talk radio and you can say that on ... some cable news networks, but we can't say that. Fair and balanced, you know.

A few Americans who could not get on the air in a regular way tried to cheat. According to Executive Producer and Director Al Ortiz of CBS Special Events:

There was a call from one fellow who ... was giving a description of what he was supposedly seeing and then started a rant about how the CIA had done this and ... Assad had done this, and he thought, he was on the air, but he was being pre-interviewed by one of my producers.

However, it was only American sources that had to be balanced. When it came to foreign sources, CNN was back to balancing between opponents such as the fighting groups within Afghanistan. According to Tom Fenton:

> We were in the northern alliance territory. We were also in the Taliban
> territory. You know we were balanced.

When it came to showing international reactions to the events, American television covered a more open exchange of views — even views they found repugnant, such as pictures of celebrating Palestinians. Some viewers felt that the news networks should not have shown those pictures, because they provoked anger against the Palestinians. But the journalists argued that it was necessary to provide the viewers with a trustworthy account of the international reactions. One of them was Bill Shine, network executive producer of FOX News:

> That tape, I think ... gave Americans another aspect that, you know,
> there are people out there that don't like us ... There are people out
> there who think today is a great day.

In short, the American TV journalists definition of "balance" on 9/11 excludes controversial opinions or extreme views from Americans, but that practice does not apply to non-Americans. This practice of distinguishing between national and foreign sources has interesting consequences. TV coverage managed to place the most disturbing viewpoints outside the United States, where they were not threatening to national cohesion but created an image of "we" versus "them."

Legitimate Views

The findings for how TV journalists define "balanced" led us to look closer at what they considered were appropriate ways for Americans to respond to the terror. The anchors at the main TV networks wanted to tell the viewers what happened in a calm way. Around them in the studios and control rooms, camera people and producers broke down in tears when the second plane hit World Trade Center; others were screaming when the Pentagon was hit, and most were stunned when the towers fall apart. As Matt Lauer put it:

> When we ... started to see the pictures of people running as the building
> was collapsing behind them, it was very easy to realize that this was a
> feeling of panic that was going to sweep the nation. It was also
> personally the hardest moment for me.

Several journalists spontaneously referred to the old fairy tale about

Chicken Little as a symbol of the role they didn't want to play. FOX News Anchor Jon Scott said he just wanted to crawl under the desk, but

> At some point ... it occurred to me that if everybody did play Chicken Little, then the terrorist won and that was exactly what they were trying to do. Hence the name. They want to instill terror in people.

As indicated, the anchors did not see themselves as detached journalists reporting the facts neutrally. They interpreted the events as a fight between the terrorists and the United States, and in that fight they felt loyal to the nation. They would not let the terrorists win, and they felt no obligation to talk to American supporters of terrorism. Many of them were personally touched by the events. MSNBC Anchor Lester Holt experienced for the first time in his more than 20 years as a journalist that half of his brain was not focused on the coverage because he was concerned about the safety of his children, who went to school near World Trade Center:

> This was a story that didn't have two sides to it. You didn't have to worry about being impartial.

Anchor Shepard Smith of FOX News also did not find the viewpoints of the terrorists legitimate:

> Every story you cover has two sides; this one didn't ... There is nothing I could think of that we, as a people or ours as a government, could have done to make anyone be able to shape the argument that it would have been OK to retaliate in such a manner. Therefore, this conflict in my mind didn't have two sides.

Matt Lauer agreed:

> There was nothing partisan about this story. ... This was black and white ... This was evil.

What those comments indicate and what was supported by the content analyses was that viewpoints supporting terrorist were considered unfair and evil with no legitimate right to be voiced in the broadcasts during the first day and night. However, one may argue that the terrorists got their message across (Deppa 2001). They set the media agenda in form of attacks, according to. Senior Executive Producer Steve Friedman of CBS.

> I believe they attacked at a time when they knew all three network

morning shows   were going to be on live. So they knew they would get live coverage right away... They wanted the pictures of those towers on fire.

Question: Do you think that they (the terrorists) are good communicators in their own way?

Yeah, I think they are masters of impact ... I think you are going to see more and more spectacular attacks ... if they make it. For I do believe that our job is to kill them before they kill us ... Our job is to ask questions; our job is to tell people what is going on. But we don't have to be down the middle on everything. That's ridiculous.

Patriotism

The coverage of 9/11 has been widely criticized for being too patriotic. This patriotism revealed itself through the naming of programs (e.g., *America Attacked, Attack on America* and *America Under Attack*) and graphic images (e.g., wrapping the programs in white, blue and red colors, using flags as decorations and so on). Do journalists think they can be objective and patriotic at the same time? Robert Dembo, director of National News, Assignment Desk, at NBC thinks they can.

I did not drape my desk with American flags even though it is on camera. I did not do those things; it is not appropriate. Even though the United States may be attacked, it is our role to remain as objective as we possibly can, and I think we did ... If you slap a flag on your vest, it is making it very difficult to certainly appear to be objective, let alone to be objective.

However, Dembo found that journalists as a whole are patriotic and sees it as a fundamental part of being a journalist.

The journalist's job is a critical part of the democratic process, so I think it would be right for us to bristle at the suggestion that one should be surprised that a journalist is a patriot.

Similar views were expressed by our informants on the other major TV networks. Paul Friedman, executive vice president at ABC, said patriotism became part of the story because Americans instantly started waving the flag and singing "God Bless America." ABC made it a policy for its staff not to wear pins or buttons with flags on air because the network did not want the individual members of the staff to be seen as more or less patriotic depending on whether they were wearing a flag. Friedman said:

> [The coverage was] certainly more patriotic than usual. I don't know if
> it was less objective ... I don't think we at least were guilty of any being
> non-objective because of any patriotic issues. I think it was more ... in
> the case of not going hard on the   story.

Bill Felling, national editor at CBS, commented on the naming of
coverage:

> The facts are the facts. We are under attack. This is a country; we are
> citizens of this country. There is a *we*. I mean we are part of the *we* ... It's
> patriotic ... but is also accurate. If it were patriotic and inaccurate, that
> would be jingoistic, but it's not. It was accurate and ancillary patriotic in
> the same sense. Although I ... don't think we should be wearing flag [on
> our] lapels and all of that. I mean I don't want to be in a position where
> I somehow don't feel as though I should be questioning the
> government. I am here to be an adversary.

In general, the journalists saw themselves as part of a society that had
been attacked. They felt that they provided a public service to that society,
that seeking and reporting the truth were a critical part of the democracy, and
that their role as watchdogs in relation to the government was a sign of this
loyalty to the nation and its people. Objectivity to these journalists did not
imply detachment from the nation.

Conform to Reality

According to Merrill, "Journalistic objectivity connotes a relationship
between symbol and reality with virtual correspondence of meaning, or
harmonizing, being the result." Merrill also says that journalists should want
their stories to "be as thorough and accurate as possible, to conform
maximally to reality" (Merrill 1997: 117). All reporters must be selective in
their choice of facts for their stories, but the "reporter's attitude basically
determines objectivity" (Merrill 1997: 119).

Does the reporter diligently attempt to covey reality in words or
pictures? Does he demand of himself to be as thorough, accurate,
disinterested, fair and balanced as humanly possible? On 9/11 the reporters
at Ground Zero were faced with grim realities. What was their attitude to
presenting the full story?

ABC Correspondent Don Dahler told us about two cases where he
deliberately chose not to tell the public newsworthy facts because he was

concerned about the consequences. When interviewed six months after 9/11, he was satisfied with his choice in one of the cases, while he was still bothered by the other.

Dahler lived near the World Trade Center. He was watching "Good Morning America," when he heard the loud noise of an airplane and shortly after the huge explosion from American Airlines Flight 11 crashing into the North Tower. He called ABC, was put on the air almost immediately and reported from his fire escape via the telephone most of that morning. He described what he saw:

> In reporting, objectivity is more ... a function of not putting forth a personal agenda ... Objectivity was not an issue because all I was doing was reporting what I was seeing ... I would try to just give it as succinct and clear a description as possible.

However, he decided not to include in his description the fact that people jumped from the World Trade Center.

> I knew that there were viewers who had loved ones in those buildings so ... I made the decision to not report that. And the way I justified that to myself was [that] I couldn't confirm ... that these were people jumping ... It was only my eyes telling me this. So I opted not to mention it ... It was a decision I made at the time for my own personal standards.

Six months later and after having received positive responses from his bosses and the viewers, Dahler was satisfied with this decision. The viewers were told by others about the people jumping, but ABC chose not to show pictures of people leaping to death from the burning towers. Dahler felt more uncertain about not having reported another event that happened later that day when he was at Ground Zero.

In the company of a federal agent, he took refuge in a technology store that had been heavily damaged by dust and water. While he was there, he saw firefighters reaching through the bars taking cameras off the shelves. Dahler found that distasteful. When he asked a fireman for his opinion on the looting, the source said that the cameras would be thrown away anyway and the insurance would pay for it, so the firefighters might as well use them to document their own experience.

Dahler did not think the public would like to hear that the firefighters, who were seen as heroes, looted the shops. He knew it was not a story the first day when everybody was choked up because of the enormity of what happened, but a few days later he discussed the story with his producer, who said that there were too many larger stories to do and that with thousands of firefighters those looting were just a few bad apples. In fact, some firefighters were later sentenced for looting. Dahler did not report the story, but six months later he talked about self-censorship.

> It bothered me personally; just my sense of integrity was kind of offended by it … So that was a moment of censorship, and it was a real struggle for me … To this day … there's a part of me that says, 'I'm a little bothered by glossing over that.' And even my justification now, I'm not sure what I would have done with it … I've heard from the producers that I've talked to, that there was a real sense of what the public needed to hear, and a part of that was reassurance.

Reporters from all the major TV networks and CNN made similar decisions regarding the appropriateness of certain information while covering the events on Ground Zero. Gary Tuchman of CNN did not talk about body parts like a foot or a hand from a victim but preferred to talk about "remains." Molly Falconer of FOX News would not show people screaming at the hospital but focused on the treatment and help they received. Photographers chose not to film suffering people burning to death, and, even if they did, the major networks would not show those pictures. Journalists at all the major news networks were concerned about "tone" and "taste" and about the feelings of the viewers when they explained why they did not report the full story.

Concern About Viewers' Reactions

Our informants generally supported the norm of objectivity. As Executive Producer Paul Slavin of ABC World News Tonight put it:

> You can never be totally objective. All you can do is recognize what your biases are and where and try and minimize them as best you can.

However, as this article has pointed out, there were in fact points at which journalists consciously choose not be objective, neutral, or impartial, and they often explained their actions by referring to the feelings of the viewers. Jim Murphy, executive producer on CBS Evening News, said:

> People are so strongly moved by what happened that you know there is a lot of irrational reaction to what we do. And you have to think about that.

Question: Well, what do you think about that? Do you think about it, or do you try to say, "I have to be objective?"

Well, I am pretty much past thinking about it now. In the beginning you have to think about it because part of your job is to serve your audience. You are trying to just beat objective journalism ... but we are not robots. You have to be concerned about how the whole country is reacting and what they are dealing with. I mean it was a huge trauma. So you couldn't just [say] on the first day: Good evening, this was probably your fault! The history of Western civilization has lead to a complete dismissal of the Islamic world and its culture, and it decided to strike back. ... It wouldn't be right. It also wouldn't be objective either ... We didn't consciously sit here and say, "Damn it! I love my country, and this is what the news is going to look like." I think that that was just a purely visceral natural reaction of a group of people who felt like everyone else here that they were attacked. We also live here ... It is difficult under those circumstances to just say I am going to be completely deliberate.

CONCLUSION

American journalists in their everyday reporting seek to be objective in their reporting. They want to tell the full story and they strive to be impartial, fair and balanced. However, they also value democracy, and when these two values collide, the journalists would often forego neutrality in reporting. By condemning the terror on civilians, they reminded their viewers of the norms shared by the United States and most of the international community.

The loyalty of the American journalists toward their nation and its people lead them to make editorial decisions that helped create a "we" different from the criminals and their supporters. In order to create such a "we," they chose to focus on mainstream American opinions and neglected to a large extent extremist views as well as unacceptable behavior among Americans. Such unacceptable opinions and behavior became part of "them."

These findings support many theories of mass media, particularly social system theories, which see the mass media as producing content that helps support and maintain a social system (Demers 1996; Donohue, Tichenor and Olien 1973). A interesting question for future research is whether such findings can be applied during the first 24 hours of other crises, when viewers are in a state of shock and fear.

CHAPTER ENDNOTE

[1] I am grateful to the participating journalists at ABC, NBC, CBS, NBC, MSNBC and FOX News for sharing their insights. I also want to thank the following LSU staff and faculty for their contributions to this article: Ronald L. Snipes, Linda Rewerts, Anne Cunningham, Ralph Izard, Susan Brown, Laura Lindsay, Mike Beardsley, Jay Perkins.

REFERENCES

Booking Department, CNN. Group interview conducted by Jay Perkins and Kirsten Mogensen. Atlanta, January 24, 2002.

Dahler, Don. Personal interview conducted by Anne Cunningham. New York, March 7, 2002.

Day, Louis Alvin (2002). *Ethics in Media Communications – Cases & Controversies*. California: Thomson/Wadsworth.

Dembo, Robert. Personal interview conducted by Susan Brown and Kirsten Mogensen. New York, March 8, 2002.

Demers, David (1996). *The Menace of the Corporate Newspaper: Fact or Fiction?* (Ames: Iowa State University Press, 1996).

Deppa, Joan (2001). *Broadcasting & Cable* (9-17-2001). USA: 4.

Deppa, Joan (1994). *The Media and Disasters. Pan Am 103*. New York: New York University Press.

Donohue, George A., Tichenor, Phillip J., & Olien, Clarice N. (1973). "Mass Media Functions, Knowledge and Social Control," *Journalism Quarterly, 50*: 652-659.

Easterbrook, Gregg (2001). "Free Speech Doesn't Come Without Cost," *The Wall Street Journal*, 5. November 2001.

Falconer, Molly. Personal interview conducted by Laura Lindsay and Mike Beardsley. New York, February 12, 2002.

Felling, William (called Bill). Personal interview conducted by Susan Brown. New York March 7, 2002.

Fenton, Tom. Personal interview conducted by Jay Perkins and Kirsten Mogensen. Atlanta, January 24, 2002.

Friedman, Paul E. Personal interview conducted by Anne Cunningham and Ralph Izard. New York, March 7, 2002.

Friedman, Steve. Personal interview conducted by Susan Brown and Kirsten Mogensen. New York, March 7, 2002.

Gasser, Hans-Peter (2002) "Acts of terror, 'terrorism' and International humanitarian law," IRRC, September 2002, vol. 84:547-570.

Greenberg, Bradley S., Linda Hofschire and Ken Lachlan (2002): "Diffusion, Media Use and Interpersonal Communication Behaviors" in Bradley S. Greenberg (ed.) *Communication and Terrorism. Public and Media Responses to 9/11*. New Jersey: Hampton Press: 3-16.

Hamilton, John Maxwell, and George A. Krimsky (1996) *Hold the Press: The Inside Story on Newspapers*, Baton Rouge: Louisiana State University Press.

Holt, Lester. Personal interview conducted by Kirsten Mogensen. New Jersey March 7, 2002.

ICRC (31-10-2002). "What does humanitarian law say about terrorism?" (http://www.icrc.org/) 10/7/2004.

Lauer, Matt. Personal interview conducted by Kirsten Mogensen, Susan Brown, Ralph Izard and Anne Cunningham. New York March 8, 2002.

Merrill, John C. (1997). *Journalism Ethics: Philosophical Foundations for News Media*, New York: St. Martin's Press.

Mindak, W. H. & Hursh, G. D. (1965). "Television's Functions on the Assassination Weekend" in B. S. Greenberg & E. B. Parker (Eds.): *The Kennedy Assassination and the American Public: Social Communication in crises*, Stanford, CA: Stanford University Press: 130 -141.

Mogensen, Kirsten, Laura Lindsay, Xigen Li, Jay Perkins and Mike Beardsley (2002). "How TV News Covered the Crisis: The Content of CNN, CBS, ABC, NBC and Fox" in Bradley S. Greenberg (ed.): *Communication and Terrorism - Public and Media Responses to 9/11*. New Jersey: Hampton Press: 101-120.

Mogensen, Kirsten (2003). "From Chaos to Mourning: Five Stages in the Coverage on CNN on September 11, 2001," paper presented at the Danish Organization for Communication and Media Research, SMID, Æro, October 27-28, 2003.

Murphy, Jim. Personal interview conducted by Susan Brown. New York, March 7, 2002.

Neal, Arthur G. (1998): *National Trauma & Collective Memory — Major Events in the American Century*. New York: M.E. Sharpe.

Ortiz, Al. Personal interview conducted by Susan Brown and Kirsten Mogensen. New York, March 7, 2002.

Schramm, Wilbur (1965): "Communication in Crisis." In B. S. Greenberg & E. B. Parker (Eds.): *The Kennedy Assassination and the Public: Social Communication in Crises*, Stanford, CA: Stanford University Press: 1-25.

Scott, Jon. Personal interview conducted by Laura Lindsay and Mike Beardsley. New York, February 12, 2002.

Shine, Bill. Personal interview conducted by Laura Lindsay and Mike Beardsley. New York, February 12, 2002.

Siebert, Fred (1956) "The Libertarian Theory" in Fred Siebert, Theodore Peterson and Wilbur Schramm *Four Theories of the Press*, Urbana: The University of Illinois Press: 39 - 72.

Slavin, Paul. Personal interview conducted by Anne Cunningham. New York, March 7, 2002.

Smith, Shepard. Personal interview conducted by Laura Lindsay and Mike Beardsley. New York, February 12, 2002.

The Commission on Freedom of the Press (1946) *A Free and Responsible Press: A General Report on Mass Communication: Newspapers, Radio, Motion Pictures, Magazines, and Books*, Chicago: The University of Chicago Press.

Tuchman, Gary. Personal interview conducted by Jay Perkins and Kirsten Mogensen. Atlanta, January 24, 2002.

Vanderbilt University News Archive. Vanderbilt University, http://tvnews.vanderbilt.edu/ April 3, 2002.

Chapter 21

September 11 in Canada: Representation of Muslims in The Gazette

Ross Perigoe

The attacks of 9/11 shocked Canadians as much as they did citizens of other Western nations. Within minutes of the collapse of the twin towers, the office of Canada Prime Minister Jean Chrétien issued a press release describing himself as "stricken" by the news. In the 101-word statement, he developed an astonishing eight Orientalist themes and frameworks that would be repeated by world leaders over the subsequent days and months.

This analysis looks at the representation of Muslims over a 20-day period in Montreal's English language newspaper *The Gazette* immediately following the attacks of 9/11. *The Gazette* published a special edition within 4 hours of the attacks, describing the events with the banner headline, *War on America*. The research demonstrates how, in the moment of crisis, leaders and others characterized the events and so naturalized general fear and suspicion of Muslims that an attack on Afghanistan became a part of the discourse without there being an interrogation as to whether violence on Afghans would be a productive first step in George Bush's "War on Terror."

It begins with a review of the methods to be used in this analysis. That is followed by a description of *The Gazette* newspaper, its cultural battle for readers, and a brief contextualization of coverage of events in Afghanistan over the preceding six months. The texts are then examined using Critical Discourse Analysis to interpret the attacks by each of the four distinct constituencies who spoke. The chapter concludes with an analysis of the long-term legal and societal implications. What we see in this analysis is a remarkably complex but, nevertheless, coherent and unified series of textual productions that led toward the production of the Muslim as a weak, disorganized victim in the West and as treacherous misogynists in the East.

FRAMEWORK FOR THE ANALYSIS

This analysis explores how previously established ideology is applied to new events; how it catalyzes and seals the boundaries of the nation, defining those who belong and those who don't. The work is grounded in an epistemological framework that adopts an Althusserian (1971) understanding of ideology as a false consciousness propagated by the ruling elites (Lewis, 2002); and Hall's et al. (1977, p. 333) interpretation of Gramsci's (1971) description of hegemony as a form of consensual, rather than coercive, reduction of power by the elites on the masses. The study is predicated on the belief that mass media play a large role in reproducing ideology, belief systems and values in a social order. The media's power in the ideological framing of events is centralized (Foucault, 1980). Thus, racism presumes the normalization and the perpetuation of elite White domination — through textual production — by rhetorical and discursive means.

Bulhan (1985 p. 13) defines racism as

> the generalization, institutionalization, and assignment of values to real and imaginary differences between people in order to justify a state of privilege, aggression and/or violence. Involving more than the cognitive or affective content of prejudice, racism is expressed behaviourally, institutionally, and culturally. The ideas or actions of a person, the goals or practices of an institution and the symbols, myths or structure of a society are racist if (a) imaginary or real differences of race are accentuated; (b) these differences are assumed absolute and considered in terms of superior, inferior; and (c) these are used to justify inequity, exclusion or domination.

Thus, racism presumes the normalization and the perpetuation of elite White domination — through textual production — by rhetorical and discursive means. Both Content Analysis and Critical Discourse Analysis were used in analyzing 362 racially implicated articles in *The Gazette* newspaper over a 20-day period, from Sept. 11-30, 2001. Content Analysis served as a method for early identification of the types of rhetoric and discourses, their number and frequency. It was followed by the application of Critical Discourse Analysis to evaluate the specific language of the various "voices" which appeared as quotes within the text. The work of van Dijk (1991, 1993, 1998a, 1998b) Foucault (1980), Hall (1982), and Karim (2003) are important methodological guides. They note that who gets to speak, about what and when are of critical importance in the study of the representation of minority groups.

In this study, four groups were organized by their power constituencies or "voices." These were Leaders, whose discourses focused largely on elite White dominance; (White) Victims whose quotes reflected a form of post traumatic stress disorder; Muslims whose victimization was distinguished by gender and geography; and finally Journalists, who, in the absence of anyone else to quote, gave their own opinions. In terms of racist production, the most problematic of the four groups was the Journalists, who produced what I have come to describe as "deliberative" racism. This will be expanded upon in a subsequent section on racist production and the Journalists themselves.

THE GAZETTE NEWSPAPER

Like most of Canada's newspapers, *The Gazette* is a morning publication. It is a folio-style newspaper, printing 136,000 copies per weekday and 173,000 on Saturdays, making it the eighth largest newspaper in Canada in terms of circulation. It is also Canada's oldest continuously operating daily newspaper, having been started in 1778.

Gazette marketing brochures boast that over a seven-day period, 632,000 people read the paper at least once.[1] Considering that there are only 757,000 English speakers in the province,[2] it is fair to say that a large proportion of the population reads *The Gazette* at least once a week, although a significant number of *The Gazette's* readers are Allophones whose mother tongue is neither English nor French. More than 80 percent of *Gazette* readers read only the one newspaper; thus, they rely on *The Gazette* exclusively for their daily consumption of textual information.[3] Perhaps most important in terms of this study, though, is *The Gazette's* claim that it reaches a majority of English language decision makers — i.e., managers, owners, professionals and executives in the Montreal area.[4] *The Gazette* belongs to a number of news services, including Canadian Press/Presse Canadienne; Associated Press; Reuters; Agence France Presse; The New York Times; and Bloomberg News.

Over the past two decades, *The Gazette* has presented a series of conflicted ideological positions because of changes in ownership. The relatively laissez-faire ownership of the Fisher and Balfour families under the Southam Publications corporate banner, where editorial opinion was left to the discretion of the individual paper's publisher in each location, was replaced by oversight by a passionately Conservative owner in Conrad Black's Hollinger Corporation when it was purchased a decade ago. The paper reverted to a position of unqualified support of the Liberal Party of Canada when the Southam chain was re-sold in 2000 to the Asper family, who own CanWest Global Communications Corporation. In 2001, CanWest

Global owned 37 daily newspapers, including *The Gazette*, most of them under the Southam Publishing banner, as well as an English-language TV network in Canada and holdings abroad.

Under the Aspers, most particularly CEO Israel Asper, the newspaper became a vociferous supporter of Israel in the Middle East on the editorial pages of *The Gazette*. Just over a week after the 9/11 attacks, David Asper, son of the owner and a director of CanWest Global, attacked Muslim leadership in the Middle East for "demonizing" the West, "brainwashing their children" and allowing for "brutal dictatorships who are driven by fanatical Islamic objectives." *The Gazette* article continued, quoting Asper:

> "They train their populations from the earliest ages to hate us for what we stand for and to be willing to heave themselves in deathly attacks upon us," he said. ... "They cry poor, appeal to our humanitarian instincts, take our well-meaning aid and then arm themselves so as to do us harm. And they openly celebrate when they achieve that end, whether it be one death or thousands." ... Asper lashed out at the West's fanatical enemies in the Middle East who "believe that our business world is a godless, worthless and vile place."[5]

Less than a year later, in October of 2002, Israel Asper attacked his own newspaper chain as well as other Canadian media when he said in a speech in Montreal, "much of the world media, in covering the Arab-Israeli conflict, have abandoned the fundamental precepts of honest reporting. They have adopted Palestinian propaganda as the context for their stories."[6] This pro-Israel position did not diminish even after Israel Asper died in October of 2003.

Less than a year later, in September of 2004, the Canadian Broadcasting Corporation (CBC) Television news reported that Asper's Southam News Service was violating a contractual agreement with Reuters News Service by adding the word "terrorist" in news copy, to describe Palestinian attacks on Israelis.[7] Additionally, the Canadian Islamic Congress has evaluated articles published for the past six years. *The National Post*, CanWest's flagship national newspaper, was ranked every year of its existence as containing the highest amount of anti-Muslim rhetoric. *The Gazette* ranked as the second or third worst in Canada for five of the past six years. For the last year reported, in 2003, *The Gazette* was ranked as the fifth worst (or, to put it inversely, the second best) of the six newspapers studied.[8]

Statistics Canada (2004) reports that by 2001, "Canada had 4 million visible minorities. ... accounting for 13.4 percent of the total population. Projections show that by 2016, visible minorities will account for one-fifth of Canada's population."[9] Muslims in the Montreal region now number over one hundred thousand, and Islam is Canada's second largest religion, having surpassed Judaism.[10]

The Gazette management is not unaware of the need to reach readers whose mother tongue is neither English nor French. The newspaper's current advertising campaign slogan — *The Gazette* IS Montreal — is supported by photographs of visible minorities reading the paper. Actions at *The Gazette*, however, speak volumes. A month before 9/11, *The Gazette* terminated its board of editorial contributors, among them Salam Elmenyawi, chairman of the Muslim Council of Montreal. Three months after 9/11, Elmenyawi told *The Globe and Mail* newspaper that "I suspect the Muslim approach and point of view is no longer welcome" at *The Gazette*.[11] It was not until 2002 that *The Gazette* hired its first ever Arabic-speaking journalist. She was dismissed a year later as a part of budget cutbacks.

PRE-9/11 COVERAGE

The fact that Montrealers and, indeed, Canadians more broadly were caught completely by surprise by the 9/11 attacks is understandable. An examination of *The Gazette* for the 11 days in September leading up to the attacks revealed no mention of either Osama bin Laden or al-Qaeda. Indeed, the only mentions of Afghanistan appeared three times in coverage during the preceding six months.

In March 2001, Bamiyan Province of Afghanistan was the site where the Taliban blew up two statues of the Buddha, dating from the 7th century or earlier. The larger statue, at 53 metres, was the tallest Buddha known. Afghan leader Mullah Mohammed Omar justified these actions by declaring that the statues were "an offense to Islam."[12] In August 2001, 24 Christian missionaries were jailed for proselytising the Christian faith in Afghanistan.[13] On September 8, Northern forces leader Ahmed Shad Masood was assassinated by al-Qaeda operatives, thus eliminating the Taliban's most powerful opponent in Afghanistan. In retrospect, it is believed this cemented the relationship between the Taliban and al-Qaeda,[14] although the name al-Qaeda did not appear in the coverage of the assassination at the time.

These were the only major news stories readers of *The Gazette* received in the six months leading up to the 9/11 attacks. As a group, they produced a textual reading of a rigid, doctrinaire, religious Afghan leadership, intolerant of other religions and engaged in civil war. While they were a narrow reading of life in Afghanistan, they were hardly a motivation for war. Within a month of the attacks, however, American, British, Australian and Canadian troops had been mobilized and the bombing had begun.

Tuchman (1978) notes that, when reporters are confronted with the extra-ordinary, they tend to adopt routine behavior — attending press conferences and interviewing authority figures. When details are sketchy and the magnitude of the threat unknown, the press searches for leadership, reassurance of normalcy and for context. Thus, in the first hours after the attacks, the Canadian press looked for guidance from its political leadership. Indeed, one of the most interesting elements in examining the representation of Muslims throughout this period appeared on the day of the attacks.

The Gazette realized the magnitude of this event, and not wanting to be a full day behind the electronic media (since the attacks took place at 9 a.m. and the next regularly scheduled paper would not be in the hands of consumers until 6 a.m. the following day) worked feverishly to put out a special edition.[15] On Sept. 11, barely four hours after the World Trade Centers had collapsed, *The Gazette* published a special 16-page edition. Within those 16 pages, largely consisting of photographs and no advertisements, the Prime Minister's statement to the press was printed, in whole or in part, three times: once as part of the main story[16]; another as part of a national reaction to the events[17]; and, finally, as part of an international round-up of leaders' comments.[18] This repetition clearly showed that *The Gazette* was searching for an interpretation of the attacks and for confirmation that the government was in control of the situation. Most of the Prime Minister's statement was published again, a fourth time, the following day, in the normal Sept. 12 edition of the newspaper.

Whether intentional or not, the text of the Prime Minister's statement had a large say in the press release which was distributed. We can surmise that the Prime Minister wrote the statement himself, by the misuse of the word "stricken" in the first sentence. The past tense of "to strike" in the passive voice is "I was struck," not "I was stricken." In his brief (101-word) press release to the media, Chrétien outlined an extraordinary number of discourses — eight in all — that would inform the future textual reading of the attacks. Here is the statement by Jean Chrétien on Sept. 11, 2001.

> I was stricken by news and television pictures coming from the United States this morning.[19]
>
> It is impossible to fully comprehend the evil that would have conjured up such a cowardly and depraved assault upon thousands of innocent people. There can be no cause or grievance that could ever justify such unspeakable violence. Indeed, such an attack is an assault not only on the targets but an offence against the freedom and rights of all civilized nations. We stand ready to provide any assistance that our

American friends may need at this very, very difficult hour and in the subsequent investigation.[20]

After spending his first sentence explaining what his topic would be, Chrétien's second sentence evoked five separate textual codings. The Prime Minister began his statement using the Discourse of Orientalism, the theme most frequently resorted to throughout the period of study. "It is impossible to fully comprehend" (Orientalism's mystery, treachery, exoticism, and inexplicability) "the evil" (a religious judgment) "that would have conjured up" (an allusion to magic) "such a cowardly and depraved assault ..." (minimization) "upon thousands of innocent people" (the discourse of innocence).

The remainder of the text contains one discursive thought per sentence. First he minimizes the motivation of the hijackers. "There can be no cause or grievance could ever justify such unspeakable violence." He then turns to the themes of an attack on civilization. "Indeed, such an attack is an assault not only on the targets but an offence against the freedom and rights of all civilized nations." And he concludes with a hegemonic declaration of solidarity. "We stand ready to provide any assistance that our American friends may need at this very, very difficult hour and in the subsequent investigation."

With these 101 words, then, repeated over a two-day period (*The Gazette* reprinted the Prime Minister's statement in their Sept. 12 edition), the ideological framing of eight discourses had been set. These powerful thematic frameworks would be the major reference points around which Canadians would construct our understanding of the attacks and by which we would frame our response to them. Later, in a speech to Canada's House of Commons, Chrétien would reiterate several of these themes, expressing hegemonic solidarity with Canada's allies, while reminding Canadians of who "we" are.

> We will stand with our allies, we will do what we must to defeat terrorism. However, let our actions be guided by a spirit of wisdom and perseverance, by our values and our way of life. As we press the struggle, let us never, ever, forget who we are and what we stand for.[21]

Thus, from the very earliest of days, the discourses developed by Chrétien would serve as the framework for Leaders to interpret the attacks. The most prominent of these discourses were an Attack on Civilization; Solidarity and Status Quo; Incredulity; and the Discourse of War. Other themes were developed by George Bush. They included the Discourses of Christianity (versus Islam by way of references to the Crusades); and with

Western Justice (Osama bin Laden was "wanted dead or alive"[22]). The parallel between 9/11 and Pearl Harbor was particularly important for the Americans, interpreted as it was an attack by the East on innocent civilian and military targets, by air, without provocation, and leading to war.

These metaphors, while they all appeared in the pages of *The Gazette*, were not used to justify the war in Afghanistan in which Canada would ultimately participate. Nevertheless Bush's rhetorical approaches certainly touched the American people, giving him an approval rating of 90 percent, highest in the 50 years of polling.[23]

WHITE VICTIMS

The second group to be given a voice became increasingly forceful in the days immediately after 9/11. Those who witnessed the attacks, either in person or on television, were so traumatized by the events and the frequency of their repetition, that their quotes occupied an important part of newspaper coverage for several days. The need to express publicly their sense of victimization was something that newspapers like *The Gazette* afforded their readers, and it offered them a cathartic experience. Interviewees responded with passion and eloquence.

Clearly, when a newspaper publishes examples of how others are feeling, readers tend to feel better about their own mental condition. On the other hand, the grieving process naturalizes behaviors and itself can lead to racist behavior. One person, a waitress in a restaurant near the Canadian-American border, found that picking on someone else was a feeble attempt at trying to feel better about oneself. "People are feeling their own mortality. They are looking for someone to point the finger at, trying to make themselves feel better because it's someone else's fault."[24] Other people used words like "vulnerability,"[25] "insecurity"[26] and "mourning their own mortality"[27] to explain the depth of their emotional abyss. A freelance art director from Lachine told *The Gazette* reporter Donna Nebenzahl that he dreamed he was driving on the highway following a plane in flames. "It's the possibility of war, the not knowing what's coming next that is freaking me out. In a way, it's even scarier now."[28]

The deconstruction of victim-oriented stories in which they largely did the talking, closely approximated the categories of five stages of grieving which Elizabeth Kubler-Ross (1969) identified in her book *On Death and Dying*. These are shock and disbelief; denial; anger, resentment; depression; and acceptance. Interestingly, Kubler-Ross's final stage, acceptance, simply does not appear in the 20-day period of study. Coming to terms with this trauma took much longer than the short period of examination. Thus, the discourses that White Victims adopted included the discourses of Denial and Surreality (interpreting the attacks as a surreal movie); the Discourse of Denial and Blamelessness (as victims emphasized innocence); The Discourse of Anger and of Personal Safety (a fear which was palpable and routinized); The Discourse of Revenge (such as the sign directed at Muslims in the New York City window, "We're coming Motherf----ers"[29]); The Discourse of Racial Profiling (the quote, "If ... he's got ... a fan belt around that diaper on his head, that guy needs to be pulled over and checked,"[30] was never repudiated by *The Gazette*); of Sadness and Depression; and the Discourse of Fear and Moral Panic — all of these were printed in the pages of *The Gazette* and were employed to construct an emotional response to the attacks. Most importantly, they produced, reproduced and naturalized the notion of revenge.

THE VOICES OF MUSLIMS – 'GOOD' AND 'BAD'

In analyzing the Voice of Muslims, it becomes apparent that not one but two distinct voices were generated by the press, or what Karim (2003) describes as the depiction of "Good" Muslims and "Bad" Muslims. This creation of a bi-polarity permeates the entire discourse on Islam, and, indeed, the framework of George Bush's "War on Terror"; the bi-polarity of the conflict between Good and Evil; East and West; fear and freedom; right and wrong; justice and tyranny.

The textual interpretation of Muslims varied, depending upon location and gender. Here, "Good" Muslims were all Western Muslims and Eastern women. They were described as sharing common beliefs — fearful of reprisals, peaceful but disorganized, weak and victimized. "Bad" Muslims (Eastern males) were unrepentant of the 9/11 attacks, unfathomable zealots, and misogynists. Good Muslims in this context disavowed the tactics of al-Qaeda, describing the hijackers as "demonically possessed."[31] Bad Muslims supported Osama bin Laden and justified the attacks. What is produced, then, is a textured and nuanced ideological reading that stereotypes "Bad" (Eastern male) Muslims as treacherous and crazed; while applying reductionist generalizations to "Good" Muslims, who, while they were treated sympathetically, are nevertheless portrayed as victimized and submissive. Jiwani (2004) also found this to be true. She noted that Journalists applied Orientalism (Said 1979, 1997) when she searched for the use of the term "hijab" in several Canadian newspapers immediately following the 9/11 attacks.

The Gazette carried many examples for both the "Good" and "Bad" Muslim groups. In the article *Where equality is "obscene": Conservative Pakistani clerics vow to crush women's rights* ,[32] Gannon quotes a Muslim woman in Pakistan describing the abused women who come to her shelter. "Their self-esteem is not there. They think of themselves something akin to the animals."[33] Meanwhile, there is an undercurrent of resistance. Referring to the Taliban leadership, the woman says, "'They know that if their (Afghani) women know their rights, they won't be able to control them,' she says, smiling beneath the shawl."[34] The notion of rescue of women is raised in the text here and, combined with a number of quotes from Eastern Muslim women that expressed fear of the impending attacks from the West, the attitudinal distance between them and their Muslim male counterparts is striking.

Misogyny is developed in the same article by Gannon when she quotes a Pakistani cleric Maulana Sakhi Badshah: "'Women should stay in the home,' he shouts. 'These people say that men and women are equal. Of course, they are not. Women cannot be as smart as a man.'"[35] Gannon then quotes another cleric who refers to feminist organizations that enter Afghani villages. "'Don't allow these sinful women to enter our villages,' roars Maulana Zia-ul Haq, a cleric in Banda, a village in the Dir district (of Pakistan). 'If you see any one of them, just take her home and forcibly marry her. If she is a foreigner, kill her.'"[36] Cooke (2002, p. 468) describes the technique of quoting clerics to produce "(I)n the Islamic context, the negative stereotyping of the religion as inherently misogynist (that) provides ammunition for the attack on the uncivilized brown men."

Only once during this period does *The Gazette* note contributions of the East, in a feature article that takes a swing at Islam in its title, *Twisting the faith: Islam is a serene religion, but can be warped into a form of totalitarianism,* Gazette staffer Paul Waters writes,

> And Muslims are indeed members of an old and proud civilization. They led the world in science, medicine, mathematics, astronomy and navigation from the 7th century until the Renaissance. Their scribes preserved and commented on the classical works of the Greeks, and their cities had paved roads, working sewage systems and public street lighting at a time when Europe's illiterate petty princelings lived in comfortless stone and wooden forts. It must be galling for the inheritors of that legacy to be condescended to by a people whose most visible cultural accomplishments include such ornaments as Porky's, punk rock and Survivor.[37]

In contrast with the strident portrayal of Eastern Muslim males, Naber (2000) writes that North American Muslims were virtually "invisible." She maintains that Muslims have attempted to blend in to society and did not organize themselves on the basis of religion. Nevertheless, because *The Gazette* published a total of 108 statements by Eastern Muslims and 109 from Western Muslims during this period, some conclusions can be drawn.

The first is that women were almost invisible both East and West. Only 7 of the 56 (or 12.5%) of all Western Muslims interviewed were women — not much better than the 5 of 101 (or 5 %) in the East. Second, Western Muslims who were interviewed were almost exclusively employed and authority figures in their community. In this sense, the Muslims interviewed were displaying the Western Protestant ethic of personal industry, which allows them to be embraced by a society dominated by the ideology of hard work.

Third, there was not only a sense of impending victimization but of inevitability of attack. On the first full day of reporting, Sept. 12, *The Gazette* ran the following headline: *Arabs brace for a backlash: Members of Middle Eastern communities prepare for the outrage of the intolerant.*[38] Muslims appeared resigned to attacks and beatings. This resignation is summarized in the quote by airport worker Michael Rezkala (note that his occupation forms an essential part of his personal description): "(He) says he's become inured to the bigotry. 'For sure it's going to happen, we are going to get blamed for this. Every time there's a plane crash, Arabs are the ones who are suspected.'"[39] This headline and others, such as *Montreal's Pakistani Muslims feel the heat: "We are here; we are not the terrorists,"*[40] embodied a plea for reason and peaceful coexistence; and at the same time, signaled that Muslims expected trouble.

This framing created the expectation that the attacks were not only inevitable, they were also justified — since even the Muslims themselves expected them. The predicted attacks did occur. Bahdi (2003) reports that the Montreal police department recorded 40 instances of racist attacks on Muslims in the 30 day period after 9/11. The number of reported attacks on Muslims throughout Canada in the year after the 9/11 attacks compared with the previous year increased 17-fold, from 28 to 481.[41]

VOICE OF THE JOURNALIST

The final grouping, the Voice of the Journalist, appeared only after the previous three Voices had been thoroughly examined. Even after the representation of Muslims had been thoroughly examined in terms of the quotes from Leaders, (White) Victims and Muslims, there remained a great deal of representation of Muslims still unaccounted for. It was then that it became clear that, in the absence of other voices to quote, the Journalists used their own ideas to fasten on several frameworks to cast Muslims in a negative light.

The primary discourses for Journalists were the immigration system and public safety and security. Columnist Elizabeth Bromstein described her feelings of seeing a man in a turban — more likely a Sikh than a Muslim. "I am in the Place des Arts metro station. I see three men, one of them wearing a turban. I start to shake. I want to get out of the station but force myself to get on the train."[42] Bromstein's intention may have been to give voice to racist thoughts so as to discount them. But the impact of her words can also be used to naturalize racism itself.

On other occasions, Journalists attempted to set the agenda for their readers. A *Gazette* editorial of Sept. 14 reads, "Fortunately, the anti-Muslim backlash has been less than first feared ... Such tolerance is encouraging."[43] In addition to predicting and accepting the inevitability of violence against Muslims, *The Gazette*, because it had not recognized that any violence against Muslims was unacceptable, decided there was no story. In the final 11 days of the study, *The Gazette* never reported on violence perpetrated against Muslims in Montreal, despite the evidence that beatings were continuing. An attack on a Sikh gas station attendant was reported on twice (Sept. 18 and 29),[44] even though the attack had happened on Sept. 15. But there was no news concerning Montreal Muslims and attacks after Sept. 18, 2001, until the end of the study period 11 days later.

Early in the coverage, an erroneous front page report linking the hijackers with illegal entry into the United States from Canada was never retracted. On Sept. 13, *Gazette* reporters wrote that five of the hijackers had entered the United States through Canada.[45] Within a matter of days, it became clear that all the hijackers had entered the United States legally from a variety of points of origination, none of them Canada. But no retraction appeared. Instead, *Gazette* Columnists explained the hijackings on a combination of inept airline security; "sloppy"[46] immigration policies; porous borders; and an immigration and refugee screening system that is "a joke."[47] *Gazette* Columnist Brian Kappler wrote,

> Perhaps it will turn out that this week's terrorists didn't make use of Canada's refugee process at all. The report about Canada (being the entry point for 5 hijackers) may be wrong. The hijackers may have been in Canada illegally. They may have been sixth-generation Canadian citizens. But the idea that this week's hijackers may have been refugee claimants sprang at once to the minds of many Canadians familiar with

the current system; that fact alone suggests that we already admit to ourselves just how sloppy the existing system is. There's already abundant evidence that every escaped killer, Triad gang-lord, terror mastermind, fugitive con-man, and "snakehead" people-smuggler around the globe knows full well what a soft touch Canada is.[48]

In this way, immigration and terror were linked in Canada.

Racist topics raised by Journalists also included the question of the ultimate fate of Osama bin Laden. Journalists in *The Gazette* who had written about the sanctity of human life as they mourned the loss in the 9/11 attacks had no difficulty discussing the killing Osama bin Laden, using a variety of verbs and euphemisms to describe his demise. While there were no references to bringing Osama bin Laden to trial, there were descriptions of how, once he was caught he would be "exterminated"[49] as one dispatches vermin. After his capture, Journalists described bin Laden's fate as being "eliminate(d),"[50] "taken out"[51] or "kill(ed)."[52] Meanwhile, bin Laden had escaped, they reported, "on a donkey, 'whose droppings led anywhere from Lebanon to Yemen to the Sudan.'"[53]

The type of text that Journalists largely employed in producing and reproducing the discourse of White elite domination were Columns. This study indicates that researchers identified 5.8 examples of racist discourse per 1,000 words in Columns, while News textual production of racist themes generated 3.2 examples per 1,000 words. This was particularly surprising since News reporters were obliged to report the words of Leaders, who adopted metaphors such as the Crusades and Pearl Harbor. Columnists work under less deadline pressure, producing texts every second day or even more infrequently. This additional time allows columnists writers to craft their arguments, to develop balance and to challenge conventional thought. And yet the production of racist discourses was at its highest in those areas where it could have been the lowest, or at least contained balance by adding anti-racist sentiments. These judgments, which produced such high amounts of racism, are what I have termed "deliberative racism" — suggesting a conscious will on the part of the writer to judge others and find them inferior.

Other reporters, based in the Far East, participated in the creation of Muslim men as ignorant and messianic. The Taliban were described as "ignorant psychotics,"[54] living in "rat's nest of international thugs,"[55] willing to use nuclear warheads if they had them[56]; the madrassah or school, was a "Jihad Factory ... (producing) ... the perfect Jihad machines."[57] On Sept. 22, Ansary wrote, "When you think Taliban, think Nazis. When you think bin Laden, think Hitler."[58] Karim (2003) notes this characterization of Islam as producing fundamentalist terrorists is no more valid than a characterization of all Christians as fundamentalist terrorists after the blowing up of the Alfred P. Murrah federal building in Oklahoma City. He points out that the Christian fundamentalists were characterized as being well beyond the mainstream of Christian fundamentalism, while Islamic fundamentalists were grouped with both terrorism and with mainstream Islamic interpretation.

IMPACT OF THE COVERAGE

In Canada, coverage of the attacks produced, for White Canadians, feelings of insecurity, vulnerability and suspicion of the Muslim community. In a poll undertaken by the Canadian Broadcasting Corporation three weeks after the attacks, over a third of Canadians polled (37%) reported they had more negative feelings toward "Arabs" than previously; and 50 percent said they agreed with the statement, "Given current circumstances, I think that it is acceptable that airline, police, and customs officials give special attention to individuals of Arabic (sic) origin."

Nearly a year later, in August 2002, the Canadian Broadcasting Corporation commissioned a similar survey and discovered that the percentage agreeing with the above statement had declined by only 2 percent, to 48 percent.[59] Ismael and Measor (2003) examined a variety of magazines and newspapers in Canada and found that virtually all media had accepted the ideology of the status quo — accepting the Leaders' interpretation of the 9/11 attacks as a civilizational conflict and ignored questions such as the legal legitimacy of an attack on Afghanistan.

On Dec. 18, 2001, the Canadian Government passed Law C 36, the Anti-Terrorism Act[60] for implementation between that date and Jan. 6, 2003. Scholars have described it as "hastily drafted"[61] and have decried the provisions, which allow the Canadian government to hold suspected terrorists for an indefinite period without notifying the suspect of the charges and evidence.[62] This led to the detention of Adil Charkaoui, a Moroccan-born permanent resident in Canada, in a Montreal jail for 20 months before his release; and of the torture of Canadian citizen Maher Arar in a Syrian jail on suspicion of his involvement with terrorist operations — a charge later shown to be unfounded.

Canadians have since measured their actions somewhat more carefully. Instead of plunging headlong into the Iraq War, as they had in Afghanistan, the Canadian government offered additional troops to the coalition in Afghanistan and, thus, allowed the forces of other countries to be deployed in the Iraq campaign without committing troops directly itself.

SUMMARY

This chapter set out to discover how Muslims were represented in the crisis period immediately after the 9/11 attacks. It showed not only that all types of Voices (Leaders, White Victims, Muslims and Journalists) participated in the representation, but that Orientalist interpretations of Muslims were naturalized so as to perpetuate elite White domination. Largest among these groups were Journalists, specifically, columnists. They produced more racist rhetoric and discourses than any other textual producer, what has been termed "deliberative racism."

That being the case, the impact of *The Gazette's* position should not be overstated. On Sept. 29, 2001, Gazette columnist Brian Kappler wrote, "A poll published in La Presse yesterday showed 33 per cent of Canadians — including 40 per cent of Quebecers — believe the main cause of the September 11 horror was 'American policy in the Mideast.' How can so many people believe that? How can anyone believe it?"[63] This opinion may be attributable to the tone with which French language media were taking, or it may be that *The Gazette*, in supporting the America position in the impending war, was ignoring a sentiment among Quebecers that there was more to the attacks than was being reported. No one should suggest that the alarming increase in attacks on Muslims in Canada was solely attributable to coverage by *The Gazette* newspaper, any more than the suggestion that *The Gazette* was uniquely responsible for sending Canadian troops off to war in Afghanistan.

But what is clear is that *The Gazette* participated in the construction of a reading of the 9/11 attacks as worthy of retribution, violence and deaths of others who were as innocent as those who died in the World Trade Center, the Pentagon, and a field in Stoney Creek Township in Pennsylvania.

CHAPTER ENDNOTES

[1] *The Gazette is* Montreal, sales brochure, September 2002.

[2] Government of Canada. *2001 Census: Community profiles, population statistics,* available at. www12.statcan.ca/english/profil01/Details/details1pop1.cfm?SEARCH=BEGINS&PSGC =24&SGC=24462&A=&LANG=E&Province=24&PlaceName=Montreal&CSDNAME= Montr%E9al&CMA=&SEARCH=BEGINS&DataType=1&TypeNameE=Census%20Metr opolitan%20Area&ID=639

[3] *The Gazette is* Montreal, sales brochure, September 2002.

[4] Ibid.

[5] Carol Howes, Feds must revamp policy to boost security: Asper, *The Gazette*, (Montreal), September 19, 2001, Final Edition, p. A8.

[6] Israel H. Asper, Media have abandoned honesty on the Middle East: Many journalists have simply adopted Palestinian propaganda as their context, *The Gazette* (Montreal), October 31, 2002.

[7] Newspapers accused of misusing word 'terrorist', Sept. 17, 2004, CBC News. http://www.cbc.ca/story/canada/national/2004/09/17/canwesterrorist040917.html

[8] Canadian Islamic Congress, (2005) Anti Islam in the Media. www.canadianislamiccongress.com/rr/rr_2003.php#comparison

[9] Canada, Canada's ethnocultural portrait. The changing mosaic: Visible minority population. Three-fold increase since 1981. http://www12.statcan.ca/english/census01/products/analytic/companion/etoimm/canada.cfm#threefold_increase

[10] Ibid.

[11] CanWest Global: Courage and Consequences: The Casualties. http://www.yourmedia.ca/modules/canwest/courage/courage.shtml

[12] Photos document destruction of Afghan Buddhas. http://edition.cnn.com/2001/WORLD/asiapcf/central/03/12/afghan.buddha.02/

[13] Christian Aid Workers Arrested in Afghanistan. August 17, 2001 http://www.cswusa.com/Reports%20Pages/Reports–Afghanistan.htm#Christian%20Aid%20Workers%20Arrested%20in%20Afghanistan

[14] Carol Giacomo, "U.S. says bin Laden likely culprit in Masood death," Middle *Eastern Times 38*, (Reuters, 2001). http://www.metimes.com/2K1/issue2001-38/reg/us_says_bin.htm

[15] Interview with Jack Romanelli, Managing Editor, *The Gazette* (Montreal), January 31, 2004.

[16] Michael Shenker, 'Christ, this is awful': Terrorist attack brings down New York Trade Centre, *The Gazette* (Montreal), September 11, 2001, Final Edition, p. 3.

[17] Elizabeth Thompson, Canada's capital on alert: U.S. embassy evacuated, RCMP seal off Parliament, *The Gazette* (Montreal), September 11, 2001, Final Edition, p. 14.

[18] 'The new evil in our world': World leaders unite to express revulsion and horror at terror attacks on U.S. *The Gazette* (Montreal), September 11, 2001, Final Edition, p. 15.

[19] Elizabeth Thompson, Canada's capital on alert.

[20] Michael Shenker, 'Christ, this is awful': (Note that this version edited out the first sentence, which situated the context of the press release.)

[21] Elizabeth Thompson, Canada stands with U.S.: But Chrétien says country's actions will be tempered by Canadian values, *The Gazette* (Montreal), September 18, 2001, Final Edition, p. A7.

[22] James Bone, An inspiration for extremists *The Gazette* (Montreal), September 20, 2001, Final Edition, p. B3.

[23] Mike Blanchfield, Terrorists' assets frozen: Bush orders seizure of funds of 27 individuals and groups, *The Gazette* (Montreal), September 25, 2001, Final Edition, p. A1 / FRONT."

[24] Catherine Solyom, The Maine connection: Did Terrorists slip through this town on way to attack U.S. targets? *The Gazette* (Montreal), September 16, 2001, Final Edition, p. A8.

[25]Donna Nebenzahl, People seeking shelter in prayer: Horror of attacks ignites a crisis of heart and spirit, September 20, 2001, Final Edition, p. A4..

[26]Susan Semenak, Coping in fallout of terror, *The Gazette* (Montreal),September 27, 2001,Final Ed., p. A1.

[27]Donna Nebenzahl, People seeking shelter in prayer.

[28]Ibid.

[29]Mark Lepage, 'They don't know what to say', *The Gazette* (Montreal), September 29, 2001, Final Edition, p. B4

[30]Sorry for remark, *The Gazette* (Montreal), September 21, 2001, Final Edition, p. A15.

[31]Lisa Fitterman Montreal's Pakistani Muslims feel the heat: 'We are here; we are not the Terrorists' *The Gazette* (Montreal), September 21, 2001, Final Edition, p. A13.

[32]Kathy Gannon, Where equality is 'obscene': Conservative Pakistani clerics vow to crush women's rights, *The Gazette* (Montreal), September 13, 2001, Final Edition, p. C7.

[33]Ibid.

[34]Ibid.

[35]Ibid.

[36]Ibid

[37]Paul Waters, Twisting the faith: Islam is a serene religion, but can be warped into a form of totalitarianism, *The Gazette* (Montreal), September 15, 2001, Final Edition, p. B1 / BREAK.

[38]Susan Semenak, Michelle Lalonde and Irwin Block, Arabs brace for a backlash: Members of Middle Eastern communities prepare for the outrage of the intolerant, *The Gazette* (Montreal), September 12, 2001, Final Edition, p. A13.

[39] Ibid.

[40]Lisa Fitterman, Montreal's Pakistani Muslims feel the heat: 'We are here; we are not the Terrorists' *The Gazette* (Montreal), September 21, 2001, Final Edition, p. A13.

[41]More tolerant than we realize, *National Post*, Thursday October 30, 2003. From 2000 to 2002, the number of reported anti-Muslim incidents has gone from 28 to 481 to 155. So, yes, there was a spike in 2001.

[42] Elizabeth Bromstein, Feeling racism's imperceptible grip, *The Gazette* (Montreal), September 19, 2001, Final Edition, p. A4.

[43]Tolerance and Extremism. *The Gazette* (Montreal), September 14, 2001, Final Edition, p. B2.

[44]Bush calls for restraint as fears of backlash rise, *The Gazette* (Montreal), September 18, 2001, Final Edition, p. B6.and, Scott Thomsen, 'I'm an American!' says man accused of killing Sikh, *The Gazette* (Montreal), September 29, 2001, Final Edition, p. A18.

[45]Paul Cherry And William Marsden, Cross-border terror: Five hijackers entered U.S. through Canada; Early evidence points FBI to New England and Florida *The Gazette* (Montreal), September 13, 2001, Final Edition, p. A1 / FRONT.

[46]Brian Kappler, Lax refugee policy now under critical spotlight, *The Gazette* (Montreal), September 13, 2001, Final Edition, p. A17

[47]Brian Kappler, No time for empty rhetoric by leaders, *The Gazette* (Montreal), September 20, 2001, Final Edition, p. A7.

[48]Brian Kappler, Lax refugee policy now under critical spotlight.

[49]Arthur Kaptainis, Donne had it right: Focus on the human toll, and remember we are all responsible for our actions, *The Gazette* (Montreal), September 12, 2001, Final Edition, p. B3.

[50]Chris Cooper, Steve Levine, Daniel Pearl, Hugh Pope, Carla Anne Robbins and Neil King Jr., 'Kill me, my ideas go on forever: Any strike against Osama bin Laden will be tricky. To succeed, it will have to eliminate not just him, but the core leaders of his network, which extends to about 40 countries around the world, *The Gazette* (Montreal), September 15, 2001, Final Edition, p. B4.

[51]Ibid.

[52]Lenny Savino and Nancy San Martin, Two hijackers known to FBI, *The Gazette* (Montreal), September 17, 2001, Final Edition, p. A3. "CBS News reported last night that President Bill Clinton in 1998 secretly signed an order allowing the Central Intelligence Agency to kill bin Laden."

[53]Hilary Mackenzie, "Taliban to bin Laden: get out: Afghanistan's hard-line regime is forcibly blocking its own people from leaving the country, even as its leader, Mullah Mohammed Omar, asks its most notorious guest to move on.", *The Gazette* (Montreal), September 28, 2001, Final Edition, p. A1 / FRONT

[54]Tamim Ansary, "Bomb Afghanistan back to Stone Age? It's been done," *The Gazette* (Montreal), September 22, 2001, Final Edition, p. B7.

[55]Tamim Ansary, Bomb Afghanistan back to Stone Age?

[56]Sarah Lubman and Andrew Duffy, "Pakistan seen as loose, nuclear-armed cannon," *The Gazette* (Montreal), (September 19, 2001), Final Edition, p. B1 / BREAK.

[57]Jeffrey Goldberg, "Taking courses at jihad school: All-Islamic classes," *The Gazette* (Montreal), (September 15, 2001), Final Edition, p. B1 / BREAK.

[58]Tamim Ansary, Bomb Afghanistan back to Stone Age?

[59]September 11th: One year later. September 11th in Hindsight: Recovery and Resolve http://www.cbc.ca/september11/content_files/text/poll_nw.html

[60]Government of Canada: Updates to Justice Laws Web Site http://laws.justice.gc.ca/en/A-11.7/2187.html accessed October 28, 2005.

[61]Jeff Sallot, Civil liberties at risk, ex-CSIS head says, *National Post*, November 27, 2003, p. A8.

[62]Michelle Macafee, Arab and Muslim Canadians endure year of collective blame after attacks, *Canadian Press*, Monday, September 02, 2002.

[63]Brian Kappler: U.S. did not deserve attacks: Blaming the victim is morally unjust, *The Gazette* (Montreal), September 29, 2001, Final Edition, p. A8.

REFERENCES

Althusser, L. (1971). *Lenin and Philosophy and other essays.* London: New Left Books.

Ansary, T. "Bomb Afghanistan back to Stone Age? It's been done," *The Gazette* (Montreal), (September 22, 2001), Final Edition, p. B7.

Bahdi, R. (2003). See no exit: Racial profiling and Canada's war on terrorism. *Osgoode Law Journal, 41*(2&3), 293-317.

Blanchfield, M. Terrorists' assets frozen: Bush orders seizure of funds of 27 individuals and groups, *The Gazette* (Montreal), September 25, 2001, Final Edition, p. A1 / FRONT.

Bone, J. An inspiration for extremists *The Gazette* (Montreal), September 20, 2001, Final Edition, p. B3.

Bromstein, E. Feeling racism's imperceptible grip, *The Gazette* (Montreal), September 19, 2001, Final Edition, p. A4.

Bulhan, H. A. (1985). *Frantz Fanon and the psychology of oppression.* New York and London: Plenum Press.

Bush calls for restraint as fears of backlash rise, *The Gazette* (Montreal), September 18, 2001, Final Edition, p. B6.and, Scott Thomsen, 'I'm an American!' says man accused of killing Sikh, *The Gazette* (Montreal), September 29, 2001, Final Edition, p. A18.

Canadian Islamic Congress, (2005) Anti Islam in the Media. http:// www.canadianislamiccongress.com/rr/rr_2003.php#comparison

CanWest Global: Courage and Consequences: The Casualties. http:// www.yourmedia.ca/modules/canwest/courage/courage.shtml

Cherry, P. & Marsden, W. Cross-border terror: Five hijackers entered U.S. through Canada; Early evidence points FBI to New England and Florida *The Gazette* (Montreal), September 13, 2001, Final Edition, p. A1 / FRONT.

Christian Aid Workers Arrested in Afghanistan. August 17, 2001. http:// www.cswusa.com/Reports%20Pages/Reports- Afghanistan.htm#Christian%20Aid%20Workers%20Arrested%20in%20Af ghanistan.

Cooke, M. (2002). Saving brown women. *Signs, 28*(1), 468-470.

Cooper, C. Levine, S. Pearl, D. Pope, H. Robbins C.A. & King N. Jr., 'Kill me, my ideas go on forever': Any strike against Osama bin Laden will be tricky. To succeed, it will have to eliminate not just him, but the core leaders of his network, which extends to about 40 countries around the world, *The Gazette* (Montreal), September 15, 2001, Final Edition, p. B4.

Fitterman, L. Montreal's Pakistani Muslims feel the heat: 'We are here; we are not the Terrorists' *The Gazette* (Montreal), September 21, 2001, Final Edition, p. A13.

Foucault, M. (1980). *Power/Knowledge: Selected interviews and other writings 1972-1977.* New York: Pantheon Books.

Gannon, K. Where equality is 'obscene': Conservative Pakistani clerics vow to crush women's rights, *The Gazette* (Montreal), September 13, 2001, Final Edition, p. C7.

Giacomo, C. "U.S. says bin Laden likely culprit in Masood death," Middle *Eastern Times 38*, (Reuters, 2001). http://www.metimes.com/2K1/issue2001-38/reg/us_says_bin.htm

Goldberg, J. "Taking courses at jihad school: All-Islamic classes," *The Gazette* (Montreal), (September 15, 2001), Final Edition, p. B1 / BREAK.

Government of Canada. *2001 Census: Community profiles, population statistics.* http://www12.statcan.ca/english/profil01/Details/details1pop1.cfm?SEARCH=BEGINS&PSGC=24&SGC=24462&A=&LANG=E&Province=24&PlaceName=Montreal&CSDNAME=Montr%E9al&CMA=&SEARCH=BEGINS&DataType=1&TypeNameE=Census%20Metropolitan%20Area&ID=639

Government of Canada. Canada's ethnocultural portrait. The changing mosaic: Visible minority population. Three-fold increase since 1981. http://www12.statcan.ca/english/census01/products/analytic/companion/etoimm/canada.cfm#threefold_increase

Government of Canada: Updates to Justice Laws Web Site http://laws.justice.gc.ca/en/A-11.7/2187.html

Gramsci, A. (1971). *Selections from the prison notebooks* (Q. Hoare & G. Nowell-Smith, Trans.). London: Lawrence and Wishart.

Hall, S. (1982). The rediscovery of 'ideology': return of the repressed in media studies. In M. Gurevitch, T. Bennett, J. Curran & J. Woollacott (Eds.), *Culture society and the media* (pp. 55-90). London: Methuen.

Howes, C. Feds must revamp policy to boost security: Asper, *The Gazette*, (Montreal), September 19, 2001, Final Edition, p. A8.

Ismael, T. Y., & Measor, J. (2003). Racism and the North American media following 11 September: The Canadian setting. *Arab Studies Quarterly, 25*(1 & 2 Winter/Spring), 101-136.

Jiwani, Y. (2004). Gendering terror: Representations of the Orientalized body in Quebec's post September 11 English-language press. *Critique: Critical Middle Eastern Studies, 13*(3), 265-292.

Kappler, B. Lax refugee policy now under critical spotlight, *The Gazette* (Montreal), September 13, 2001, Final Edition, p. A17

Kappler, B. No time for empty rhetoric by leaders, *The Gazette* (Montreal), September 20, 2001, Final Edition, p. A7.

Kappler, B. U.S. did not deserve attacks: Blaming the victim is morally unjust, *The Gazette* (Montreal), September 29, 2001, Final Edition, p. A8.

Kaptainis, A. Donne had it right: Focus on the human toll, and remember we are all responsible for our actions, *The Gazette* (Montreal), September 12, 2001, Final Edition, p. B3.

Karim, K. H. (2002). Making sense of the "Islamic Peril": Journalism as cultural practice. In B. Zelizer & S. Allan (Eds.), *Journalism after September 11th* 101-116. London and New York: Routledge.

Karim, K. H. (2003). *Islamic peril: Media and global violence.* Montreal: Black Rose Books.

Kubler Ross, E. (1969). *On death and dying.* New York: Macmillan.

Lepage, M. 'They don't know what to say', *The Gazette* (Montreal), September 29, 2001, Final Edition, p. B4.

Lewis, J. (2002). *Cultural studies: The basics.* London, Thousand Oaks, CA and New Delhi: Sage.

Lubman S, & Duffy, A. "Pakistan seen as loose, nuclear-armed cannon," *The Gazette* (Montreal), September 19, 2001, Final Edition, p. B1 / BREAK.

Macafee, M. Arab and Muslim Canadians endure year of collective blame after attacks, *Canadian Press*, Monday, September 02, 2002.

Mackenzie, H. "Taliban to bin Laden: get out: Afghanistan's hard-line regime is forcibly blocking its own people from leaving the country, even as its leader, Mullah Mohammed Omar, asks its most notorious guest to move on," *The Gazette* (Montreal), September 28, 2001, Final Edition, p. A1 / FRONT

More tolerant than we realize, *National Post,* Thursday October 30, 2003.

Naber, N. (2000). Ambiguous insiders: An investigation of Arab American invisibility. *Ethnic and Racial Studies, 23*(1), 37-61.

Nebenzahl, D. People seeking shelter in prayer: Horror of attacks ignites a crisis of heart and spirit, *The Gazette* (Montreal), September 20, 2001, Final Edition, p. A4

Newspapers accused of misusing word 'terrorist', Sept. 17, 2004, CBC News. www.cbc.ca/story/ canada/national/2004/09/17/canwesterrorist040917.html www.canadianislamiccongress.com/rr/rr_2003.php#comparison

Photos document destruction of Afghan Buddhas. http://edition.cnn.com/2001/ WORLD/asiapcf/central/03/12/afghan.buddha.02/

Romanelli, J. Personal Communication with Managing Editor, *The Gazette* (Montreal), January 31, 2004.

Said, E. (1979). *Orientalism.* New York: Vintage Books.

Said, E. (1997). *Covering Islam: How the media and the experts determine how we see the rest of the world.* New York: Vintage Books.

Sallot, J. Civil liberties at risk, ex-CSIS head says, *National Post,* November 27, 2003, p. A8.

Savino, L. & San Martin, N. Two hijackers known to FBI, *The Gazette* (Montreal), September 17, 2001, Final Edition, p. A3.

Semenak, S. Coping in fallout of terror, *The Gazette* (Montreal), September 27, 2001, Final Ed., p. A1.

Semenak, S. Lalonde, M. & Block, I. Arabs brace for a backlash: Members of Middle Eastern communities prepare for the outrage of the intolerant, *The Gazette* (Montreal), September 12, 2001, Final Edition, p. A13.

September 11th: One year later. September 11th in Hindsight: Recovery and Resolve http://www.cbc.ca/september11/content_files/text/poll_nw.html

Shenker, M. 'Christ, this is awful': Terrorist attack brings down New York Trade Centre, *The Gazette* (Montreal), September 11, 2001, Final Edition, p. 3.

Solyom, C. The Maine connection: Did Terrorists slip through this town on way to attack U.S. targets? *The Gazette* (Montreal), September 16, 2001, Final Edition, p. A8.

Sorry for remark, *The Gazette* (Montreal), September 21, 2001, Final Edition, p. A15.

The Gazette is Montreal, sales brochure, September 2002.

'The new evil in our world': World leaders unite to express revulsion and horror at terror attacks on U.S.*The Gazette* (Montreal), September 11, 2001, Final Edition, p. 15.

Tolerance and Extremism. *The Gazette* (Montreal), September 14, 2001, Final Edition, p. B2.

Thompson, E. Canada's capital on alert: U.S. embassy evacuated, RCMP seal off Parliament, *The Gazette* (Montreal), September 11, 2001, Final Edition, p. 14.

Thompson, E. Canada stands with U.S.: But Chrétien says country's actions will be tempered by Canadian values, *The Gazette* (Montreal), September 18, 2001, Final Edition, p. A7.

van Dijk, T. A. (1991). *Racism and the Press*. London and New York: Routledge.

van Dijk, T. A. (1993). *Elite discourse and racism*. Newbury Park, CA: Sage.

van Dijk, T. A. (1998a). Context models in discourse processing. In H. van-Oostendorp & S. Goldman (Eds.), *The construction of mental models during reading*. 123-148. Hillsdale, NJ: Erlbaum.

van Dijk, T. A. (1998b). *Ideology: A multidisciplinary approach*. London: Sage.

Waters, P. Twisting the faith: Islam is a serene religion, but can be warped into a form of totalitarianism, *The Gazette* (Montreal), September 15, 2001, Final Edition, p. B1

Chapter 22

SEPTEMBER 11 AND THE U.S. IMAGE IN LATIN AMERICAN MEDIA

Sallie Hughes & Jesus Arroyave[1]

In this essay, we explore the impact of 9/11 and the subsequent wars in Afghanistan and Iraq on Latin Americans' opinions of the United States. We do this through the use of country-level survey data and a content analysis of newspaper coverage in a sample of countries where the U.S. image is more or less positive than the regional average.

The survey results show that, when the 18-country region is taken as a whole, opinions of the United States dropped significantly after 9/11 and the wars. Opinions improved only in one country: Panama.

Additional analysis shows that Latin Americans who held a more positive image of the United States after the terrorist attacks and the wars generally were more likely to live in countries that (1) had a better experience with neoliberal economic reforms promoted by Washington; (2) have leaders who profess a belief in the free trade model of the 1990s; (3) depend more on remittances sent home by immigrants in the United States; and (4) experienced lower levels of deportation of their citizens from the United States after 2000. An analysis of newspaper coverage of the United States reinforced these findings: Images of the United States are more positive when discussing domestic politics, culture, education, science and technology, but equally negative when covering immigration, economic integration or the U.S. war on terrorism.

However, we found some anomalies. Mexico is the most notable example. Despite high levels of immigration, visitation, economic integration, a free-trade agreement and a shared 2000-mile border, Mexicans' image of the United States is among the lowest in the region. A review of newspaper articles suggests this is partly because Mexicans quickly rejected President George Bush's pre-emptive strike doctrine, which conflicts with Mexico's long-standing support of non-interventionism in foreign affairs. The low numbers also may stem from the fact that greater economic integration has not brought prosperity for the majority of Mexicans and from concern over mistreatment of Mexican immigrants in the United States.

This essay explores the causes of Latin Americans' opinion of the United States by analyzing data in four general categories: (1) economic liberalization, (2) personal interaction across borders, (3) attitudes about the Iraq War and U.S. handling of international conflicts, and (4) Latin American media images of the United States. First, we present country-level data on the U.S. image across time in 18 Latin American countries where the Latinobarómeter survey has been conducted since 1995. Next, we test the influence of factors associated with economic integration, personal contacts, and perceptions of the War on Terrorism on general country-level perceptions of the United States in a series of multiple regressions. Finally, we discuss how elite media representations of the United States reinforce our argument that 9/11 aggravated an already troubled relationship.

THE U.S. IMAGE IN LATIN AMERICA

Public opinion toward the United States in Latin America has shifted over time, depending upon world conditions, policies and priorities of the incumbent U.S. presidential administration, and the internal conditions of the region or a particular country.[2] Some authors argue that the region is undergoing a wave of anti-Americanism unseen since the invasions and revolutions of the 1950s and 1960s (Ballve 2005, McPherson 2003). Yet, while the image of the United States has declined markedly since 2000, there is a great deal of variation in country-level appreciation of the United States before and after 9/11. Our compilation of country-level data from the annual Latinobarometro surveys in 18 Latin American countries between 1995 and 2005 is shown in Table 21.1.[3]

When the region is taken as a whole, the percentage of respondents who expressed a "good" or "very good" opinion of the United States peaked in 2000, before the attacks of Sept. 11, and then declined 12 percentage points between 2000 and 2005, from an average of 73 percent of residents per country expressing a "good" or "very good" opinion of the United States in 2000 to 61 percent in 2005. Opinions showed significant declines in 11 countries. Five showed little or no change. And opinions improved in only one country: Panama, which showed a 8 percentage point increase. (The Dominican Republic is excluded from this analysis because it wasn't surveyed until 2004.)

Although the overall trend showed a decline, there were considerable

Table 21.1
OPINION OF THE UNITED STATES
BY COUNTRY AND YEAR
(Percent of "Good" and "Very Good" Responses)

Country	1995 or First Year*	2000	2001	2003	2004	2005	First Year /2005 Difference
Argentina	31	53	38	30	31	32	1
Bolivia	48[a]	69	55	45	41	50	2
Brazil	66	68	54	50	50	53	-13
Chile	75	73	70	58	61	57	-18
Colombia	36[a]	71	76	68	73	70	34
Costa Rica	59[a]	81	84	75	80	75	16
Dominican R	85[b]	NA	NA	NA	85	74	-11
Ecuador	69[a]	77	85	68	77	66	-3
El Salvador	53[a]	82	84	80	84	81	28
Guatemala	34[a]	78	80	67	77	77	43
Honduras	55[a]	87	89	80	81	87	32
Mexico	67	72	63	41	41	53	-14
Nicaragua	62[a]	89	84	69	69	68	6
Panama	70[a]	75	89	80	82	83	13
Paraguay	76	79	70	50	62	48	-28
Peru	79	72	75	69	72	71	-8
Uruguay	50	58	51	46	44	38	-12
Venezuela	59	65	68	59	55	41	-18
TOTAL	63	73	71	61	64	61	-2

Survey Question: I would like to know your opinion about the United States. Do you have a very good, good, bad or very bad opinion of the United States?

*First year data were collected: [a]1996, [b]2004.

variations across countries. Residents of Central American countries and the Dominican Republic held the most positive opinions of the United States in 2005. The Andean countries were in a middle range, with Bolivians and Venezuelans more critical of the United States than residents of Peru, Colombia, Ecuador and Chile. Residents of South American countries expressed the lowest assessments of the United States, with Argentines being most negative. Mexico, belying its geographic proximity to the United States and Central America, was in a lower-middle position in 2005, although the U.S. image in Mexico had improved substantially over 2004. Colombians held more positive views of the United States than other South Americans.

What accounts for these differences? Several authors who have addressed negative perceptions of the United States distinguish between "external" causes linked to U.S. foreign policy decisions, military action or economic domination, and "internal" causes linked to political, economic or cultural conditions within a particular country (Shlapentokh and Woods, 2004; Shlapentokh, Shiraev and Woods, 2005; Tai, Peterson and Gurr, 1973). While these categories are useful, the transnational linkages between Latin America and the United States encouraged us to re-conceptualize the possible explanations. We will assess the strength of explanations stemming from market-based economic reform in the region since the "Washington consensus" promoted economic liberalism throughout the region in the 1980s and 1990s, changing levels of direct human contact through immigration and visitation of the United States, and more focused feelings about the U.S. role in Iraq and international conflicts.

ECONOMIC LIBERALIZATION

As Latin American economies reeled in the 1980s, an agreement emerged in U.S. policy circles about the economic measures that could best respond to the inflation, deficits, debt, and lagging productivity that plagued many Latin American countries. The "Washington Consensus," as the economic package became known, responded mostly to the preferences of the U.S. Treasury Department and international financial organizations, such as the International Monetary Fund, in the context of debt reduction negotiations with developing countries (Santiso, 2004: 831). The policy recommendations, sometimes imposed as part of loan agreements, but often supported by domestic finance ministers trained in the United States, included deep spending cuts, trade opening, privatization of state-owned enterprises, de-regulation, and liberalization of exchange rates, capital markets and prices.

Several Latin American presidents decided the best way to proceed was through "shock treatment," suddenly ending currency and price supports while selling off state companies such as telephone companies and banks. At the same time, they cut import tariffs and quotas, and ended subsidized exchange rates for industry. Economic liberalization and open-trade curbed inflation and budget deficits in several countries, but by 2000 it became apparent that balanced budgets and freer trade were not enough to spur economic development. Unemployment, poverty and wealth gaps remained stubborn or increased. In the 2000s, the Washington Consensus and many of the domestic politicians who supported them were out of favor in Latin America. Specifically, newly elected governments in Argentina, Venezuela, Brazil, Uruguay, Bolivia and Ecuador cut ranks and criticized the neoliberal model. Santiso writes (2004: 828-829) that "the reform impetus inspired by the Washington Consensus has stalled and given way to widespread doubts about future developmental strategies. Two decades of market-oriented reforms in Latin America ended equivocally, marked with a general sense of unease and frustration. Once-promising emerging market economies have been rocked by a series of shocks" (Santiso, 2003).

According to the Economic Commission for Latin American and the Caribbean (ECLAC), the average annual GDP growth rate for the region was 3.8 percent between 1995 and 2005, lower than the region's pre-crisis performance of 5.5 percent between 1950 and 1980. GDP growth was also far below what was necessary to address persistent inequality, rising poverty and increasing unemployment. There was variation in growth levels by country, however. Averaging over the decade, the best annual GDP performances occurred in the Dominican Republic (5.3%), Chile (4.6%), Costa Rica (4.3%), Panama (4.2%) and Nicaragua (4.1%). The worst performers were Venezuela (1.1%), Paraguay (1.5%), Argentina (1.9%), Brazil (2.4%) and Colombia (2.4%). Posting a middle range of average annual GDP growth were Ecuador (2.6%), Mexico (2.7%), El Salvador (2.9%), Uruguay (3.1%), Bolivia (3.3%), Guatemala (3.4%) and Honduras (3.4%).

GDP per capita grew even more modestly than overall GDP, suggesting that inequality increased over the decade, according to ECLAC data created on the basis of official country-level figures (constant 1995 prices). GDP per capita grew an average of just 1 percent annually between 1995 and 2005. Real wages essentially stagnated at the regional level between 1995 and 2005, although government wage data reported to the Economic Commission on Latin America in many cases does not capture rural wages or wages of the underemployed. Real wages reported here then are mostly for the most-secure, urban portion of the Latin American population. They grew by only 0.2 percent annually between 1995 and 2004. Again, the regional figure masks substantial differences in wage performance at the country level. Wages declined most annually in Venezuela (-3.0%), Uruguay (-3.4%), Brazil (-1.2%), Paraguay (-0.5%), Peru (-0.5%) and Argentina (-0.3), while they grew most annually in Bolivia (3.4%), Nicaragua (2.7%), Chile (2.4%) Colombia (2.2%), Costa Rica (1.5) and Mexico (1.1%). Wage data were not reported for six countries.

Performance on urban unemployment was also troubling. Again, using

ECLAC data from official country sources. The average annual rate from 1995 to 2004 was 9.6 percent across 18 countries, but the trend was toward growing unemployment in the second half of the decade under study. This measure also masks underemployment because millions of Latin Americans' work fewer than 40 hours or in unregulated and untaxed jobs such as street sales or unlicensed assembly jobs. Unemployment varied by country. Mexico reported the lowest average annual level of urban unemployment (3.6%), followed by Guatemala (4.1.%), Costa Rica (6.1%), Honduras (6.2%), Bolivia (6.6%) and El Salvador (6.9%). The highest levels of urban unemployment were reported in Argentina (16%), Panama (15.9%), Dominican Republic (15.5%), Colombia (15.2%), Venezuela (123.6%) and Nicaragua (12.6%). Brazil (8.0%) Chile (8.1%), Peru (8.9%), Paraguay (9.3%) and Ecuador (10.7%) reported middle levels.

The percentage of people living under the poverty line decreased only slightly across the region (ECLAC, 2004; 62, 63). From the early 1990s to the early 2000s, the best dates available, poverty declined a total of 3.6 percent across the 18-country sample. Change in the number of people living under the poverty line showed a great amount of variation by country, however, 40.3 percentage points. Countries where poverty increased the most between 1989-90 and 2001-2002 were in South America: Argentina (+20.5%), Paraguay (+17.8%) Bolivia (+9.8%) and Venezuela (+8.8%). Poverty decreased the most in Chile (-19.8%), Panama (-14.6%), Brazil (-10.5%), Guatemala (-8.9%) and Mexico (-8.3%). The least amount of change in poverty occurred in Ecuador (1.4%), Colombia (-1.9%), Uruguay (-2.5%), Honduras (-3.5%), Nicaragua (-4.2), El Salvador (-5.3%), Costa Rica (-6.0%) . The population under the poverty line in Peru increased 7.2 percent between 2001 and 1998, the only comparative dates available. There were no comparative figures for the Dominican Republic.

In absolute terms, countries with the highest percentage of people living under the poverty line in 2001-2002 were Honduras (77.3%), Nicaragua (69.4%), Ecuador (63.5%), Bolivia (62.4%), Paraguay (61%), Guatemala (60.2%), Peru (54.8%) and Colombia (50.6%). Countries with the lowest percentage of people living under the poverty line that year were Uruguay (15.4%), Chile (18.8%), Costa Rica (20.3%) and Panama (25.3%). Middle range poverty levels were reported in Brazil (35.8%), Mexico (39.4%), Argentina (41.6%), the Dominican Republic (44.9%), Venezuela (48.6%) and El Salvador (48.9%).

Considering GDP, GDP per capita, real wages, urban unemployment and the population living under the poverty line, Latin America's economic progress after the Washington Consensus consolidated around market-based economic reform and opening to free trade was halting at best. From the mid-1990s to the mid-2000s, GDP posted an average annual increase of 3.8 percent, but that did not translate smoothly into gains for the wider population because of high levels of wealth concentration and sporadic economic shocks in larger economies. The average annual growth rate in GDP per capita was 1.0 percent and the average annual change in real wages was 0.2 percent, considering mostly urban and formal sector employees. The average annual rate of mostly urban unemployment across the period was 10.2 percent. Poverty decreased by 3.6% across the region between 1989-1990 and 2001-2, the latest period for which data are available. The trend line on poverty was unclear.

A composite of the five economic measures are presented in Table 21.2. The composite is an additive scale and the components are not standardized. A higher score indicates better economic performance, and the range across countries is 56.5 points with Argentina posting the worst performance and Chile posting the best. The composite was created as follows: average GDP growth rate + average GDP per capita growth rate + average real wage growth rate − average urban unemployment − change in population under the poverty line across the decade. The best performers, in order, were Chile, Mexico, Guatemala, Costa Rica, Panama and Brazil. The countries that performed worst, in order, were Venezuela, Argentina, Paraguay, Uruguay, and Peru. In a middle range were Brazil, Ecuador, the Dominican Republic, Nicaragua, Honduras, and El Salvador.

By the early 2000s, national politicians began to react to the lackluster record of market-based reforms led by the United States. Presidents expressed doubts or openly split with Washington on market reforms and free trade in Argentina, Bolivia, Brazil, Ecuador and Venezuela. Another measure of adherence to the model of the Washington Consensus would be to look at which countries had entered free trade agreements with the United States by 2005. Eight of the 18 countries in our sample had entered a trade agreement with the United States in the 1990s or 2000s, signaling their political elites' faith in the free trade model. They were Mexico in 1994, Chile in 2003, and Costa Rica, the Dominican Republic, Guatemala, Honduras, Nicaragua and El Salvador in 2006.[4] Negotiations for a wider U.S.-led regional agreement that would include South America, the Free Trade Agreement of the Americas, had stalled and seemed dead in early 2006.

PERSONAL CONTACTS

While studies of tourism and cultural exchange are somewhat speculative and often ambivalent when discussing effects, U.S. policy since the Cold War has certainly assumed that the greater the contact between societies and cultures,

Table 21.2
ECONOMIC PERFORMANCE
BY COUNTRY OVER A DECADE
(from 1995 to 2004/2005)

Country	Avg Annual GDP Growth Rate	Avg Annual GDP Growth Rate Per Capita	Avg. Annual Real Wage Change*	Avg. Annual Urban Unemploy ment Rate	Change in Population under Poverty Line	Index of Economic Performance†
Argentina	1.9	0	-.0.3	16	20.5	-34.9
Bolivia	3.3	0.8	3.4	6.6	9.8	-8.9
Brazil	2.4	1	-1.2	8	-10.5	4.7
Chile	4.6	3.1	2.4	8.1	-19.8	21.8
Colombia	2.4	0.2	2.2	15.2	-1.9	-8.5
Costa Rica	4.3	2	1.5	6.1	-6	7.7
Dominican R	5.3	3.4		15.5		-6.8
Ecuador	2.6	0.7		10.7	1.4	-8.8
El Salvador	2.9	0.9		6.9	-5.3	2.2
Guatemala	3.4	0.8		4.1	-8.9	9
Honduras	3.4	0.6		6.2	-3.5	1.3
Mexico	2.7	1.1	1.1	3.6	-8.3	9.7
Nicaragua	4.1	1.4	2.7	12.6	-4.2	-0.2
Panama	4.2	2		15.8	-14.6	5
Paraguay	1.5	-1.2	-0.5	9.3	17.8	-27.3
Peru	3.7	1.8	-0.5	8.9		-3.9
Uruguay	3.1	-0.1	-2.2	13.1	-2.5	-9.8
Venezuela	1.1	-0.6	-3	13.6	8.8	-24.9
TOTAL	3.8	1	0.2	9.6	-3.6	-4

* Estimated
† Higher is better performance. Categories are not standardized. Index=Avg DGP Growth Rate + Avg GDP Per Capital Growth Rate + Avg Real Wages - Avg Urban Unemployment - Change in Population under the Poverty Line.

the greater empathy between the participants (Frey 2005; Archer, Cooper and Ruhanen 2005: 55, 56; Kraft 2000: 350-353; Kim and Prideaux 2003). Throughout the Cold War, U.S. policy was to invite "multipliers" of public opinion to the United States for educational exchange and tourism in the hope of positively influencing their opinion of the country. Once in the United States, however, the experience might or might not be a positive one. While Camp reports the influential and apparently positive role of education abroad in forming Mexico's economic and political elite, Frey notes that visits by Asian elites in the 1950s sometimes produced negative feelings (Frey 2005; Camp 2002; see also Coombs 1964). We postulated that personal contact through immigration, visitation for tourism or educational endeavors, or money sent by friends or relatives in the United States (in and of itself and as a proxy for having U.S. connections) are other ways Latin Americans could form opinions of the United States.

While there have been several waves of Latin American immigration to the United States historically, the country has experienced a sustained increase in immigration from Latin America beginning in the 1980s. This is due to conditions in the expelling countries, including poor economic conditions and various forms of civil unrest in several countries, as well as demand for labor in the United States and the maturation of immigration networks initiated in earlier immigration streams (Suarez Orozco and Paez 2002). According to a Pew Hispanic Center study of government immigration data, however, the increases peaked in 1999 (Passel and Suro 2005).

Does the level of person-to-person contact with U.S. citizens and society influence Latin Americans' image of the United States? In what way? We collected data on the country-of-origin of Hispanics in the United States, remittances sent by immigrants in the United States to their home countries, visas issued for admittance into the United States, and deportations (e.g., removals) by country of origin over a 10-year period.

While, of course, not all people of Latin American origin in the United States have relatives abroad, the ranking of Hispanics by country-of-origin and comparison to the overall population in that country offer indicators of the strength of Latin Americans' personal connection to the United States. The data come from the 2000 U.S. Census, which has not been updated at the country level since that time, and the Population Conference Bureau (2005). Mexicans have the strongest personal connections to the United States, followed by people of Caribbean countries and then Central Americans, who are trailed distantly by South Americans. Hispanics of Mexican origin are most numerous in the United States (58.2%), followed by U.S. Hispanics with origins in Puerto Rico (9.6%), Cuba (2.5%), the Dominican Republic (2.2), El Salvador (1.9%), Colombia (1.3) and Guatemala (1.1%). Hispanics with ties to the remainder of the countries of Latin America make up less than 1 percent of total Hispanics in the United States.

Although the geographic pattern remains, the strength of ties shifts somewhat when comparing numbers of Latin American origin peoples in the United States to the population in their country-of-origin. Mexicans and Mexican Americans in the United States equal 19.3 percent of the population of Mexico. Puerto Ricans in the United States, because of facilitated travel and legal migration status, are the equivalent of 87.3 percent of the population of Puerto Ricans living on the island. Cubans and Cuban Americans in the United States equal 11 percent of the island's population, while Salvadorans in the United States are the equivalent of 9.5 percent of the population of El Salvador and Dominicans in the United States equal 8.6 percent of their home country's population. Hispanic populations with ties to the remainder of the Central American countries are equivalent to 2 to 3 percent of their home country's populations, while South Americans in the United States are equal to between 0.1 to 1 percent of their home countries' populations.[5]

Remittances sent by U.S. immigrants to their relatives at home are another way personal ties could influence Latin Americans' image of the United States. The countries with the highest levels of remittances sent home from the United States in 2004 were Mexico ($16.6 billion), Colombia ($3.17 billion), El Salvador ($2.5 billion), Brazil ($2.5 billion) and the Dominican Republic ($2.3 billion), according to the World Bank's World Development Indicators. Countries that received the least were Uruguay ($34.7 million), Bolivia ($65.6 million), Paraguay ($138.2 million) and Argentina ($265.7 million). While remittances only reach a portion of each country's population, dividing the total remittances by a receptor country's total population is a better indicator of the importance of money sent by relatives in the United States. When viewed through this lens, the relative weight of remittances by country becomes more clear. Particularly, the importance of remittances in the Central American countries and the Dominican Republic emerges.

Remittances sent by Latin Americans living abroad have been growing steadily for most of the countries in the region, an average annual growth rate of 38 percent between 1999 and 2004. Remittance growth did not stop after 9/11; there was only a dip. In many countries, growth in the early 2000s stems from the use of immigration to the United States as a survival strategy during economic crises and stagnation. The increase in remittances sent home by Argentines was startling, as professionals and blue collar workers went abroad once their businesses were lost in the 2001-2003 crash. The growth of remittances sent to Central America is the result of migration responses to civil wars in the 1980s that became institutionalized, and natural disasters in the 1990s and 2000s that spawned new immigration streams, most recently after Hurricanes Stan and Wilma in 2005. Analysts believe immigration responses to crises become permanent, at least in the medium term (Suro 2003). The growth in Mexican remittances is the result of long-term structural changes that increased immigration, including the uprooting of migrants in southern Mexico, the aging U.S. workforce, consolidated networks linking sender and receiver communities, and chronic underemployment in Mexico.

Visitation, as opposed to more permanent immigration, is another way Latin Americans can experience personal contact with U.S. citizens or society. The decline in visas issued to all kinds of visitors from Latin America to the United States after 9/11 was well-publicized, but less known is that the decline leveled off in 2003 above where it had been six years earlier. Visas for Latin Americans were growing at the rate of about 250,000 per year before 9/11, according to U.S. government data. They then dropped steeply in 2002 and 2003. However, the number of visas granted to Latin American visitors increased in 2004 and never returned to pre-1997 levels even adjusting for the full change in government record-keeping that might have inflated post 1997 Mexican visas. The decline in visas granted affects particularly Argentina, Brazil and Venezuela, not the region as a whole.

Visas declined between 1995 and 2004 at an annual rate of 4.3 percent for Argentina, 3.9 percent for Brazil, 2.8 percent for Venezuela, 1.4 percent for Uruguay and 1.1 percent for Chile. They grew most in Mexico, but a change in record-keeping accounts for much of the 26.5 percent growth, followed by El Salvador (13.5%), Honduras (8.3%), Ecuador (5.1%), Panama (4.9%), Guatemala (4.6%), Colombia (4.6%), Nicaragua (4.1%), Costa Rica (3.7%), Peru (3.5%), (Bolivia (2.7%) and the Dominican Republic (0.9%). Argentina's case is notable and not related to 9/11. Prior to its deep economic crisis in 2001-2003, Argentines held preferred status and could enter the United States without a visa. The U.S. State Department and Department of Justice ended the Argentina visa waiver program on Feb. 21, 2002, "due to the current economic crisis in Argentina and the increase in the number of Argentine nationals attempting to use the program to live and work illegally in the United States" (U.S. Department of Justice, 2002). The number of Argentines visiting the United States legally almost halved between 2001 and 2002, accounting for 30 percent of the total decline in visas granted that year. The decline in visas awarded to Argentines, Brazilians, and Venezuelans accounted for 61 percent of the total drop.

There is also a perception that the number of deportations of Latin Americans with no visa or who had overstayed a tourist visa in order to work increased after 9/11, but a closer examination of the data from the U.S. Department of Homeland Security calls into question that generalization for the region as a whole. While "removals of aliens" were at a historic high in 2004 for the 18-country Latin American sample, the average annual level of deportations from 2001 to 2004 was actually 2 percent lower than the average annual level of deportations from 1998 to 2001. This is largely because deportations into Mexico went down 8 percent over the two periods.[6] However, there also was a large variation in change by country. The percentage increases in average annual deportation levels pre- and post 9/11 were highest for South American countries and Costa Rica, followed by Guatemala and Honduras.

In summary, the citizens of many Latin American countries maintain strong personal ties to the United States through immigration, money received from family members in the United States, or visitation for tourism or educational exchange. Data on Hispanics in the United States, the amount of money they send home and its relative impact by country, and change over time in deportations and visitation levels suggests that there was some disruption of these ties for Mexico and Central America after 9/11, but that this disruption did not affect all forms of ties nor was it permanent. There was greater disruption for South Americans, who had been entering the United States in larger numbers prior to 9/11 because of economic or political crises in their countries of origin, but certainly in the case of Argentina and probably in the cases of Brazil, Bolivia and Uruguay, we know that the reason for greater barriers to visitation and immigration was economic rather than heightened national security.

IRAQ AND INTERNATIONAL CONFLICTS

Thus far we have focused on material explanations, both economic and personal. What about opinions specifically about U.S. actions in the War on Terrorism?

This variable is almost assuredly a component of the general attitude towards the United States in the region, but it is worth exploring as an independent variable and then determining its relative weight in relation to other hypothesized explanations via a series of regression models. Table 21.3 presents the results of two questions from the 2004 Latinobarómeter survey gauging respondents' sentiments about U.S. actions in Iraq and the U.S. government's handling of international conflicts generally. Because opinions are variable, we averaged both measures as an index. The table reports the percentage in each country that held a positive opinion.[7]

The responses reveal an overwhelming rejection of U.S. actions in the war on terror, ranging from 4.5 percent support for U.S. actions among Argentines to 35.5 percent support in Panama. The 18-country total level of

Table 21.3
INDEX OF POSITIVE OPINIONS ON
U.S. HANDLING OF IRAQ AND WORLD CONFLICT
(in percent)

Country	Iraq	International Conflict	Index
Argentina	3	6	4.5
Bolivia	8	14	11
Brazil	10	13	11.5
Chile	9	16	12.5
Colombia	15	33	24
Costa Rica	25	37	31
Dominican R	21	36	28.5
Ecuador	22	26	24
El Salvador	20	28	24
Guatemala	16	24	20
Honduras	26	41	33.5
Mexico	4	9	6.5
Nicaragua	14	23	18.5
Panama	29	42	35.5
Paraguay	11	18	14.5
Peru	15	26	20.5
Uruguay	5	7	6
Venezuela	23	31	27
TOTAL	15	23	19

*The index averages country-level responses to the following questions: Do you strongly agree, agree, disagree or strongly disagree with the following: (1) The actions of the United States in Iraq and (2) How the government of the United States is managing conflict in the world.

Source: Latinobarometer 2004, reported in Lagos (2004)

approval of 19 percent is 45 percentage points lower than for Latin Americans' overall assessment of the United States. At the country level, the geographical spread noted in the general opinion of the United States and presented in Table 21.1 is basically replicated, with the exception of Venezuela, probably because opponents of President Hugo Chavez, who support the United States, are numerous enough to effect the country-level ranking on this measure. It is interesting that the countries with the most-recent historical experiences of U.S. intervention, including Guatemala, El Salvador, the Dominican Republic and especially Panama, which the U.S. invaded in December 1989, show higher than average levels of support for U.S. actions. U.S. legacies of military interventionism or support for military dictatorships in the region might be related to the low level of support for U.S. invasions in the Middle East, but it does not appear to explain the variation across countries.

STATISTICAL ANALYSIS

Which of the possible explanations for Latin Americans' opinions of the United States are most powerful?

To answer this question, we created an index of country-level opinion of the United States from 2003, 2004 and 2005 by averaging the scores to stabilize random fluctuations and then regressed the index on indicators of economic performance, trade ties, personal ties and attitudes about U.S. actions in the War on Terrorism. Table 21.4 presents Pearson correlations and Table 21.5 presents a series of regression models to estimate the predictors with and without the presence of the war opinion component.

There are three points we would like to make about the Pearson correlations before turning to the regression models. First, the economic performance index is highly correlated with the presence of a trade agreement with the United States, a relationship we believe will lower the power and level of significance of the economic performance index in the regression models. Second, the number of U.S. Hispanics as a percentage of the population in the country of origin is positively but not significantly correlated to the U.S. image, but it is highly and significantly correlated to other indicators of personal ties (remittances as a percentage of the population in the country of origin, post-9/11 versus pre-9/11 removals as a percentage of the level of removals in 2004, and change in annual visas across the decade). We believe the high correlations suggest interactive effects that increase the power and change the direction of the Hispanics variable in the regressions.[8] Last, the correlations offer us little guidance in determining whether remittances belong in the realm of person-to-person ties along with other indicators of immigration and settlement, or belong to the realm of economic performance and trade since they are the result of survival strategies compelled by recently poor economic performance which in turn is highly correlated to the presence of a trade agreement with the United States.

Turning to the multiple regressions, all of the explanatory models are

Table 21.4
Pearson Correlations

	1	2	3	4	5	6	7
1. Good U.S. Image (2003-2005)	1	.47**	.59**	0.11	.56**	-.57**	0.25
2. Economic Performance Index	.47**	1	.69**	0.33	0.37	-0.36	.45*
3. U.S. Trade Agreement	.59**	.69**	1	.54**	.62**	-0.39	.50**
4. U.S. Hispanics as Percent of Home Country	0.11	0.33	.54**	1	.64**	-.60**	.87**
5. Remittances per Population in Home Country	.56**	0.37	.62**	.64**	1	-.57**	.54**
6. Post 9/11 Removals - Pre 9/11 Removals, as a % of 2004	-.57**	-0.36	-39	-.60**	-.57**	1	-.71**
7. Change in annual visas	0.25	.45*	.50**	.87**	.54**	-.71**	1
8. View of U.S. Performance on Iraq and World Conflict	.87**	0.19	0.4	0	0.36	-.50**	0.15

n=18; *p<.05; **p<.01

significant and powerful.[9] The full model (model three) explains 94.8 percent of the variation in country-level attitudes toward the United States. Removing trade agreements as a predictor (model four), the explanatory power increases slightly to 95.4 percent. The standardized multiple regression coefficients (β) in models three and four tell us that Latin Americans' opinions of U.S. actions in the War on Terrorism — holding all else constant — is what most explains the overall image of the country in the region. However, remittances, personal ties through immigration, removals of Latin American citizens from the United States, and economic performance during a decade of market-based economic reform and integration are also important predictors.

The first two regression models explore the importance of Latin Americans' opinion of the War on Terrorism further by removing it from the explanatory model. They provide support for the assertion that economic and personal ties are powerful even without considering opinions of 9/11. Alone, they explain 85.6 percent of the variation of Latin American opinion of the United States. We believe that the structural explanations of U.S.-promoted economic reform and personal ties to the United States are more

Table 21.5
IMAGE OF U.S. REGRESSED
ON INDEPENDENT VARIABLES
(Standardized Regression Coefficients)

Independent Variable	Model 1	Model 2	Model 3	Model 4
View of U.S. handling of Iraq and World Conflict Index	- -	- -	.54**	.64**
Economic Performance Index	.40**	0.13	0.15	.19*
U.S. Trade Agreement	- -	.52**	0.16	- -
U.S. Hispanics as a Percent of Home Country's Population	-.66**	-.81**	-0.28	-.26*
Remittances per Home Country Population	.61**	.41**	.42**	.35**
Average Annual Change in Visas	-0.22	-0.17	-0.08	-0.07
Removals from U.S. Pre- v. Post 9/11 as a Percent of 2004	-.60**	-.67**	-.27*	-.19*
Adjusted R-Square	.72**	.86**	.95**	.95**

*$p<.05$; **$p<.01$ (one-tailed tests)

powerful for explaining the U.S. image in the region than the full regression models suggest and must be taken into account by anyone seeking to explain why Latin Americans' views of the United States are more negative today than in the late 1990s.

For additional evidence to support this interpretation of the data, we turned to how elite Latin American newspapers in three countries — two with comparatively negative opinions of the United States and one with a comparatively positive view — present information about the United States.

CONTENT ANALYSIS

Newspapers are thought to both reflect and influence elite opinion. Reporting routines in Latin America appear to be closely indexed to the actions and opinions of governing elites (Waisbord, 2000; see also Hughes, 2006). Although empirical study of newspaper effects is less common for print media than for television, Lawson argued that changing frames in Mexican newspapers helped legitimize the work of nongovernmental organizations and participation outside of the single-party Mexican state during that country's political transition (Lawson, 2002). A similar argument could be made for the Brazilian press in the late 1980s (Straubhaar, Olsen and Nunes, 1993). In both countries, television was highly biased in favor of the political status quo. Today in Latin America, partisan bias and sensationalism commingle in the television news of many countries (Boas, 2005, Hughes and Lawson, 2004; Hughes, 2006; Arriaga, 2002; Torrico, 2002). In Mexico, after the end of the PRI regime in 2000 and the market-driven transformation of television news since the late 1990s, elites still trust information from newspapers more than television. The 2003 Latinobarometer poll in Mexico, which asked an unusually large battery of questions on media use, found that people with higher levels of education trusted newspapers more as a source of political information than any other medium, including television.[10]

For these reasons, and because there is no archive of Latin American media content similar to Lexis-Nexis, we chose to analyze representations of the United States in three elite newspapers located in countries that vary by country-level opinion of the United States. In Mexico and Argentina, where country-level opinion was comparatively negative, we analyzed articles in *El Universal* and *La Nación*. *El Universal* is Mexico's leading circulation daily, excluding sports tabloids. Ideologically, the newspaper sits between the left-leaning *La Jornada* and the more conservative *Reforma*. In Argentina, *La Nación* is the second-highest circulation newspaper in the country following *Clarín*, which has a broader market appeal, and the sports tabloid *Crónica*. *La Nación*, which is center-right ideologically, is considered a newspaper read by political elites. It contrasts with the smaller circulation, left-oriented newspaper *Página/ 12*. In recent years it has been at odds with the President Nestor Kirschner, a loud critic of U.S. economic policy in the region. *La Prensa Libre* in Guatemala is the circulation leader in the country after the crime tabloid *Nuestro Diario*, which it also owns, and is also center-right ideologically (WAN, 2005: 143, 326, 459; Hughes, 2006, Chapters 6 and 10).

To select the articles, we created a sample of 12 days, one per month, in the constructed week format for each year from 2000 to 2005. We chose one of the days in 2001 to coincide with the aftermath of Sept. 11; it was Sept. 15. In Mexico we coded all articles mentioning the United States that were listed on the newspaper Web site as being on the front page for the print edition on the date in the sample (www.eluniversal.com.mx/ edicion_impresa.html). For Guatemala (www.prensalibre.com.gt) and Argentina (www.lanacion.com.ar), we used the Web sites' archive functions to locate the sample dates and then coded every article that mentioned the United States that appeared in the date's index. This produced the following sample of coded articles: Mexico: n=88; Guatemala: n=43; and Argentina:

n=97. The total sample size was 228.

To operationalize the variables found to influence Latin Americans' opinions of the United States, we first created a variable measuring the primary topic of the news article using an emergent method of data analysis to identify the topics and then recoded the list of topics into five domains of coverage, including issues related to economic integration (international trade, organizations and banks; the exchange rate; and the Argentine economic crisis), immigration (immigration or U.S. Hispanics), the War on Terrorism (U.S. foreign policy in the Middle East, the wars in Afghanistan and Iraq, and the War on Terrorism generally), a societal-cultural domain (religion, science and technology, education, tourism, sports, entertainment, arts or crafts), and a political domain that excluded issues related to the War on Terrorism (elections, other politics, political violence, governing, and foreign policy in Latin America excluding Cuba or Venezuela). The first author coded the entire Guatemala and Argentina sample a second time for this variable using summaries of the articles written by the second author and performed reliability checks. Cohen's Kappa for this variable was .875.

To measure how the articles portrayed the United States, we created five dummy variables coded for presence or absence of the following characteristics: United States presented as an aggressor, United States presented as a victim, United States presented as a friend to the home country, and criticism of the United States within the article. We also coded whether overall U.S. image was negative. The first author double-coded 11 percent of the sample for these variables and reliability checks were performed. Cohen's Kappa for the dummy variables ranged from .913 to 1.0. We then created a six-point Likert Scale (0-5) using each of the five dummy variables and excluded two — the United States as friend and as victim — after correlations on the sum of the items indicated the two variables were measuring a different dimension of media representations than the other three. From the remaining three variables we constructed a four-point Likert Scale (0-3) which was then used to create "good, very good" and "poor, very poor" categories of U.S. image presented in the Latin American newspaper articles.

The analysis consisted of the simple cross-tabulations, which are presented in Table 21.6. The United States was presented best in articles about societal and cultural issues (93% of articles) and then in articles about domestic politics (78.6% of articles). We found that the U.S. image was poorest in articles about the War on Terrorism, immigration, and economic integration. The percentage of articles reflecting a poor image of the United States across the coverage areas was 44.1 percent for articles related to the War on Terrorism, 44.2 percent for articles on issues related to economic

Table 21.6
Percent of Stories in a Domain That Present a Poor Image of the United States

Coverage Area	Poor/Very Poor Image
Immigration	45.7
Economic Integration	44.2
War on Terrorism	44.1
Domestic U.S. Politics	21.4
Societal-Cultural	7
Other	33.3
AVERAGE	35

n=228 (newspapers in Mexico, Guatemala, Argentina)
Note: Results are weighted by publication sample size. Weighted n=411.

integration and 45.7 percent on articles related to immigration.

Breaking down the results by newspaper, the Mexican newspaper presented the United States poorly in 81.8 percent of articles on issues related to economic integration, 73.3 percent of articles related to the War on Terrorism and 60 percent of articles about immigration. The Argentine newspaper presented the United States poorly in 37.5 percent of articles on issues related to economic integration and 42.4 percent of articles on the War on Terrorism. Only three articles on immigration were in the Argentina sample and they all presented a good image of the United States. Finally, the Guatemalan newspaper presented a poor image of the United States in 50 percent of immigration articles, 41.7 percent of articles related to economic integration, and 28.6 percent of articles related to the War on Terrorism.

CONCLUSION

This study of Latin Americans' views of the United States has found that blaming 9/11 for negative opinions of the United States in the region is too simplistic. Analysis of country-level data finds that attitudes toward the United States are the result of experiences with U.S.-led economic reform in the 1990s and increasing personal ties forged mostly through immigration. Analysis of elite newspaper coverage of the United States in a smaller sample of countries finds support for this interpretation. Coverage of the United States in the war on terrorism, economic integration, and immigration were equally negative.

Latin American reactions to 9/11 and the War on Terrorism are conjunctural, though perhaps not ephemeral. They reinforce longer-term dynamics rather than represent a rupture in the U.S.-Latin American relationship. In the living memory of many Latin Americans is distrust growing from U.S. support for military dictatorships or direct intervention across the region, but also the goodwill forged by economic aide under John F. Kennedy's Alliance for Progress. Should the current U.S. administration decide that Latin America is again worth paying attention to, it might remember each of these historical experiences as it decides how to improve the U.S. image in the region both among the people and within their media.

CHAPTER ENDNOTES

[1]The authors would like to thank our colleague Gonzalo Soruco for valuable comments during the course of writing this chapter. We would also like to gratefully acknowledge Daniel Lund, CEO of MUND Américas, for the use of the Mexican national data from the 2003 Latinobarometer survey.

[2]There is a not a large empirical literature on mass opinion of the U.S. image in Latin America, but McPherson (2003), Dugas (2005), and Shlapentokh and Woods (2004) provide some insights. There is a rich literature on the criticism of intellectuals in the region and elite opinions. See work by Eduardo Galeano, for example (1973; 2001).

[3]Methodologies for the country surveys is found in Corporación Latinobarómetro (2005: 81). Sixteen polls cover 100 percent of the adult populations of their countries. Chile's survey covers 80 percent and Paraguay's survey covers 97.4 percent. Confidence is 95% and sampling error runs from +/ 2.4% to +/- 3.1% depending on the country. Controls for construct equivalence across national and cultural groupings were not discussed.

[4]The target date for implementation of the Central American free Trade Agreement (CAFTA) was 2006. All countries had ratified CAFTA except Costa Rica by July 2005. Office of the United States Trade Representative. (2005, Dec. 30). "Statement of USTR Spokesman Stephen Norton Regarding CAFTA-DR Implementation." Accessed Feb. 2, 2006 at http://www.ustr.gov/Document_Library/Press_Releases/2005/December/Statement_of_USTR_Spokesman_Stephen_Norton_Regarding_CAFTA-DR_Implementation.html

[5]Puerto Ricans and Cubans have not been included in other analyses because their home countries are not part of the Latinobarometer survey data, which operationalizes our dependent variable. However, their weight in the U.S. Hispanic population necessitated their inclusion in this discussion.

[6]Mexico is the United States' neighbor and largest source of immigrants by far, so it is not surprising that the largest number of its citizens were deported. However, some of those deported to Mexico may actual have been Central Americans hoping to stay close to the U.S. border to make another try into the United States, but the number is impossible to determine.

⁷No other questions related to U.S. actions regarding terrorism were available. Both measures were strongly and evenly correlated to the index. Iraq: .983 (p = .000). Conflict: .951 (p = .000).

⁸The Mexican exception – high immigration and low opinion of the United States – may also influence the direction of the standardized regression coefficient.

⁹The high levels of explained variance should be interpreted cautiously, because the number of independent variables to the number of cases is high, which inflates R-square and other regression values.

¹⁰MUND Americas, Latinobarometer national survey for 2003. Data provided by MUND CEO Daniel Lund. The full Latinobarometer sample is not available publicly. Question: What is the source of information that you most trust to inform you about politics? Responses for people with some university education to post-graduate education: Daily newspaper, 28.5%; radio, 27.2%; television, 18.1%; no one, 16.3%; friends and family, 9.0%; other 21.4%; don't know, 44.4%. n=1200.

REFERENCES

Archer, B., C. Cooper, et al. (2005). The positive and negative impacts of tourism. *Global tourism*. W. F. Theobald.

Arriaga, J. (2002). "La nota roja: Colombianización o Mexicanización periodística." *Sala de Prensa* 6(2).

Ballvé, M. (2005). "A New Wave of Anti-Americanism." *NACLA Report on the Americas* 38(6): 37-42.

Boas, T. (2005). Television and neopopulism. Media effects in Brazil and Peru. *Latin American Research Review* 40(2): 27-49.

Camp, R. A. (2002). *Mexico's mandarins: Crafting a power elite for the twenty-first century.* Berkeley, University of California Press.

Coombs, P. H. (1964). *The fourth dimension of foreign policy; educational and cultural affairs.* New York, Published for the Council on Foreign Relations by Harper & Row.

Dugas, J. C. (2005). Case: Colombia: Colombian attitudes towards the United States after 9/11. America. Sovereign defender or cowboy nation. V. Shlapentokh, E. Shiraev and J. Woods. Aldershot, Hampshire, United Kingdom, Ashgate Publishing Limited: 71-90.

Economic Commission for Latin America and the Caribbean (2005 November). *Panorama Social de Amierica Latina,* 2004. Accessed Feb. 4, 2006, at www.eclac.cl

Frey, M. (2003). "Tools of Empire: Persuasion and the United States's Modernizing Mission in Southeast Asia." *Diplomatic History* 27(4): 543-568.

Galeano, E. (1973). *Open veins of Latin America. Five centuries of pillage of a continent.* New York, Monthly Review Press.

Galeano, E. (2001). *Upside-down: A primer for the looking-glass world.* New York, Picador USA.

Hughes, S. (2006) *Newsrooms in conflict. Journalism and the democratization of Mexico.* University of Pittsburgh Press.

Hughes, S. and C. Lawson. (2004). "Propaganda and crony capitalism. Partisan Bias in Mexican Television news." *Latin American Research Review* 39(3): 81-105.

Kim, S. and B. Prideaux (2003). "Tourism, Peace, Politics and Ideology: Impacts of the Mt. Gumgang Tour Project in the Korean Peninsula." *Tourism Management* 24(6): 675-685.

Kraft, H. J. S. (2000). "The Autonomy Dilemma of Track Two Diplomacy in Southeast Asia." *Security Dialogue* 31(3): 343-356.

Lagos, M. (2004). The image of the United States in Latin America. The Miami Herald's Americas Conference. Miami, Florida, Corporación Latinobarómetro.

Latinobarómetro, C. (2005). *Informe Latinobarómetro 2005*. Santiago, Chile.

Lawson, C. (2002.) *Building the fourth estate. Democratization and the rise of a free press in Mexico*. Berkeley: University of California Press.

McPherson, A. (2003). *Yankee No! Anti-Americanism in U.S.-Latin American Relations*. Cambridge, Massachusetts.

Passel, J. S. and R. Suro (2005). *Rise, Peak and Decline: Trends in U.S. Immigration 1992-2004*. Washington, D.C., The Pew Hispanic Center.

Population Reference Bureau (2005). *World population data sheet of the Population Reference Bureau*. Accessed Feb. 12, 2006, at www.pbr.org

Santiso, C. (2004). "The contentious Washington Consensus: reforming the reforms in emerging markets." *Review of International Political Economy* 11(4): 828-844.

Santiso, J. (2003). *The political economy of emerging markets: actors, institutions, and financial crises in Latin America*. New York, Palgrave.

Shlapentokh, V. and J. Woods (2004). "The threat of international terrorism and the U.S. image abroad." *Brown Journal of World Affairs* x(2): 167-179.

Shlapentokh, V., J. Woods, et al. (2005). *America: Sovereign defender or cowboy nation?* Burlington, VT, Ashgate Publishing Company.

Straubhaar, J., O. Olsen and M.C. Nunes. (1993) "The Brazilian Case: Influencing the Voter." In T.E. Skidmore (ed.), *Television, Politics and the Transition to Democracy in Latin America*. Baltimore: Johns Hopkins University Press: 118-136.

Suárez-Orozco, M. M. and M. M. Páez (2002). *Latinos: remaking America*. Berkeley, University of California Press.

Suro, R. (2003). Remittance senders and receivers: tracking the transnational channels. Washington, D.C., Inter-Am. Dev. Bank and Pew Hispanic Center: 17.

Tai, C. S., E. J. Peterson, et al.. (1973). "Internal versus External Sources of Anti-Americanism: Two Comparative Studies." *Journal of Conflict Resolution* 17(3): 455-488.

Torrico, E. (2002). "El sensacionalismo: Algunos elementos para su comprension y analisis." *Sala de Prensa* 6(2).

Waibord, S. (2000). *Watchdog journalism in South America. News, Accountability and Democracy*. Columbia University Press.

AFTERWORD

Cees J. Hamelink

W riting the afterword for the preceding pages is like playing the "encore" after the concert audience has left. Such a wealth of information and analysis has been offered that readers need no more.

Nevertheless, I would like to conclude here with a brief reflection on the troublesome encounter of journalism with complex realities. There can be little doubt that 9/11 was both a manifestation of the complexity of contemporary history and an event that had to be mediated to worldwide audiences through the instrument of journalism. This does raise the question of how reliable such mediation can be. Several factors seem to erect impediments to reliable mediation of complex realities.

Journalism is above all else observation. As we know from perception psychology, the human observation of reality is biased and inadequate. Humans are inclined towards a "rapid closure of perception." They look at events and people in prejudicial — often stereotypical ways — and tend to rapidly confirm their initial impressions. As a result, all human perception including journalistic observation is inherently unreliable despite professional training and experience.

The time, attention and expertise that the mediation of complex reality requires is often not available. There are the well-known pressures of time (always in short supply), competition (growing with the expanding commercialization of news media), lack of resources (among others to invest in investigative journalism), and insufficient levels of specialized topical expertise (most dramatic is often the absence of historical knowledge) among journalists.

The narrative structure of the news also is an interesting obstacle. To promote a degree of objectivity in reporting, trainee-journalists around the world are taught the 5Ws formula of What, Where, When, Who and Why. In actual practice, this formula often obstructs reliable mediation. This is particularly the case since answering the Who and Why questions tends to lead to speculation. More often than not there are no readily available answers to "who did it?" and "what were the motives?" There are, however, stories offered to journalists that would seem to provide such answers.

The sources of these stories are often the so called "spindoctors." They are the experts who know how to fabricate reality in an attractive news format. They are the prime sources of much unreliable mediation. The crucial question is why journalism is so often their easy victim. How can "mediacomplicity" with the spinners be explained?

Some factors can be singled out. There is the convenience of just relaying materials that are very skillfully produced. There is the often unequal battle between the professional "perception managers" and the smaller number of journalists. Often the reality as fabricated by the spindoctors matches with the political preference or patriotic sentiments of the mediators.

Next to journalistic inadequacies there is reality itself as a prime factor. If one expects reliable mediation by journalists, the assumption is likely to be that there is a single reality out there that only needs to be reliably covered. But reality out there is chaotic, multi-layered and lacks transparency. Reality — whether natural of social — is like a tropical rain forest. Nothing is what is seems to be; all elements are interdependent; there are no linear cause-effect connections; minute changes can have enormous effects; and little if anything can be predicted with a measure of certainty. In news reporting, this implies that for most events — and among them is 9/11 — there are different stories to be told, with sometimes conflicting interpretations. There is hardly ever one single frame that tells it all and many different frames can all be true at the same time!

Journalists will try to avoid this complexity and legitimize this by referring to the unwillingness of their audiences to live with different truths within one story. This is indeed a serious consideration: Do audiences want a multi-layered version of reality?

As T. S. Eliott once wrote "mankind cannot bear too much reality." What to do if the news audience prefers the clarity of single realities over chaos? The famous dictum by U.S. Sen. Hiram Johnson that in war truth is the first victim is closely followed by the observation (phrased by philosopher Ronald Dworkin) that the second victim is the desire to be told the truth. Certainly, citizens need reliable mediators, but the mediators also need "good citizens." The quality of journalism is closely tied to the quality of its audiences.

Can the encounter between journalism and complex reality ever grow into reliable mediation? This will require that both journalists and their audiences learn to live with complexity and uncertainty. On the road toward reliable mediation of reality, both parties will have to accept that reality "out there" will continue to escape human understanding.

NAME INDEX

A

Adam, Konrad, 96
Akerman, Piers, 265, 268, 270
Al-Zawari, Ayman, 44
Angang, Hu, 191
Angell, David, 44
Arafat, Yasser, 63, 277
Asper, Israel, 322
Atta, Mohammed, 129, 235

B

Badshah, Maulana Sakhi, 328
Bertz, Bill, 213
Beuve-Méry, Hubert, 84, 92
bin Laden, Osama, 29, 42, 43, 46, 65, 68,
    100, 101, 111, 123, 131, 140, 147,
    148, 151, 152, 154, 157, 161, 164,
    178, 206, 208, 213, 215, 219, 223,
    224, 228, 234, 244, 256, 270, 273,
    283, 289, 290, 301, 323, 326, 327,
    331, 337
Blair, Tony, 62, 149, 187
Bone, James, 44, 326
Bouteflika, Abdelaziz, 278
Breytenbach, Willie, 292
Bromstein, Elizabeth, 330
Brown, Derek, 45
Brzezinski, Zbigniew, 141
Bumei, Ren, 196, 202
Burnside, Julian, 266
Bush, George W., 31, 85, 87, 90, 101, 104,
    238, 250, 256, 278, 288, 301

C

Castro, Fidel, 188

Charkaoui, Adil, 332
Chavez, Hugo, 353
Cheney, Dick, 213
Chomsky, Noam, 33, 60
Chrétien, Jean, 319, 324
Churchill, Winston, 44
Cilliers, Jakkie, 289
Clinton, Bill, 90, 211, 284, 331
Compaore, Blaise, 278
Cviic, Steven, 70

D

d'Ormesson, Jean, 87
Dagong, Zhao, 196, 202
Dahler, Don, 312
Dan, Cheng, 198-200
Dederichs, Mario R., 99
Deedat, Yousuf, 283, 284
Defore, Daniel, 306
Dembo, Robert, 311
Deqiang, Han, 198, 201
Diekmann, Kai, 95
Duan, Feng, 192, 204
Dyke, Greg, 39

E

Ebrahim, Ismail Ebrahim, 285
Eisenhower, Dwight, 44
Endo, Yoshio, 215
Eyal, Jonathan, 46

F

Falconer, Molly, 314
Fan, He, 192, 204
Farouk, King, 232

SUBJECT INDEX

Canada, 8, 14, 16, 23, 140, 220, 319, 321, 322, 325, 326, 329-333, 337-340

Canadian Broadcasting Corporation (CBC), 14, 18, 218, 322, 332, 339

Canadian Islamic Congress, 322, 337

Canadian Press, 321, 324, 332, 339

Canberra Times, 275

CanWest Global Communications Corporation, 321

Cape Town, 280, 281, 283, 289

capitalism, 18, 31, 47, 89, 156, 157, 189, 361

capitalist-like economy, 172

caricature, 241, 249, 250

catastrophe, 6, 38, 42, 44, 46, 47, 86, 96, 106, 127, 133, 247, 249, 278, 304

Catholics, 222

CBS (Columbia Broadcasting System), 303, 308, 310, 312, 314, 317, 331

CBS Evening News, 314

CCP, 186, 189, 197, 199

censor, 224

censorship, 18, 123, 159, 216, 314

Central Intelligence Agency (CIA), 140, 245, 256, 282, 308, 331

Channel 4, 39

Chechen, 113, 165

Chechnya, 141, 165, 195

Chicago, 120, 136, 138, 214, 317

Chile, 342, 343, 345-347, 351, 353, 362

China, 7, 10, 12, 23, 90, 169, 171-176, 181, 182, 184-187, 189, 191-202, 206, 207, 209, 212-215

China Daily (Zhongguo Ribao), 173, 174, 181, 182, 184, 185

China International Broadcasting Station, 191

Chinese Youth, 189

Christian, 154, 161, 162, 177, 221, 236, 261, 263, 264, 273, 323, 332, 337

Christian fundamentalism, 332

Christianity, 154, 155, 159, 325

Christmas Island, 265, 266

church, 137, 154, 155, 236

civil liberties, 110, 124, 332, 339

Civil War, 109, 215, 287, 323

civilization, 32, 87, 114, 149, 150, 154, 192, 196, 199, 204, 216, 221, 257, 273, 315, 325, 328

civilized, 35, 95, 148-150, 158, 160, 177, 192, 216, 304, 324, 325

Clarín, 357

clash of civilizations, 96, 155, 158, 159, 161, 181, 183-185, 249

class, 44, 102, 190, 234, 239, 242, 244, 248, 249, 272, 301

CNN.com, 229, 323, 339

CNNTURK, 254

Cold War, 89, 93, 94, 124, 139, 178, 185, 189, 194, 195, 215, 273, 347, 348

collateral damage, 108, 126, 142

Colombia, 9, 342, 343, 345-347, 349-351, 353, 361

columnists, 244, 258, 330, 331, 333

communication, 2, 9-15, 17, 19-24, 49, 93, 109, 120, 134, 136, 141, 160, 170, 171, 184, 185, 191, 229, 234, 239, 240, 254, 258, 267, 302, 303, 316, 317, 339

communism, 89, 94, 142, 143, 194, 197, 280

communist, 85, 89, 139, 140, 142, 172, 181, 186, 273, 288

comparative, 9, 11, 22, 23, 124, 146, 149, 150, 160, 185, 346, 362

conflict, 9-11, 16, 31, 59, 68, 107-112, 116, 117, 120, 121, 123, 126, 134, 141, 144, 159, 161, 179, 201, 207, 213, 221, 231, 244, 247-249, 277, 278, 285, 292, 305, 310, 322, 327, 332, 352, 353, 355, 356, 361, 362

Confucianism, 181

Congress, 4, 104, 244, 279, 282, 288, 290, 294, 304, 322, 337

construction of reality, 18, 106, 136, 158

content analysis, 22, 169, 173, 174, 185, 186, 255, 258, 303, 320, 341, 356

Coptic, 236

Costa Rica, 342, 345-347, 351-353

counterterrorism, 210, 212, 213, 240

credibility, 99, 231, 239, 268, 307

crisis, 13, 39, 49, 99, 112, 120, 124, 131, 134, 136, 152, 185, 191, 202, 203, 206, 210, 264, 265, 279, 280, 288, 302, 303, 317, 319, 326, 333, 339, 345, 351, 358

critical discourse analysis, 319, 320

Crónica, 357

crusade, 87, 154, 155, 159, 161, 246, 257

Cuba, 158, 187, 188, 277, 284, 349, 358

cultural studies, 13, 16, 19, 145, 339

current affairs, 23, 33

cyberspace, 11, 20, 197, 199

D

Dagbladet, 10, 124
dailies, 39, 96, 97, 150, 173, 255
Daily Express, 33
Daily Mail, 33
Daily Mirror, 33, 39
Daily Nation, 278
Daily Telegraph, 33, 39, 40, 265, 269-272, 274, 275
Dallas Morning News, 105
Danes, 86
deliberative racism, 331, 333
Delo, 12, 146, 150-156, 159-162
democracy, 13, 14, 18, 31, 83, 89, 109, 110, 113, 120, 136, 140, 148, 151, 152, 162, 178, 181, 196, 197, 199, 202, 223, 239, 249, 257, 273, 287, 302, 312, 315, 362
democratic process, 90, 311
Democratic Party, 212, 301
Democrats, 100, 308
demonize, 215
denial, 233, 234, 326, 327
Denmark, 13, 239
Department of Homeland Security, 351
depression, 192, 326, 327
Der Spiegel, 101, 102
Der Standard, 154, 155
destruction, 39, 79, 87, 194, 197, 207, 214, 215, 221, 244, 245, 278, 291, 292, 301, 323, 339
destructive, 19, 224
Detroit Free Press, 221
Die Burger, 277, 280, 281, 285, 288, 293-297
Die Welt, 95, 96
diplomatic relations, 171, 172, 184
disbelief, 30, 95, 104, 148, 157, 233, 234, 326
discourse analysis, 22, 319, 320
discourse of anger, 327
discourse of denial and blamelessness, 327
discourse of fear and moral panic, 327
discourse of war, 325
discrimination, 244-246
disenchantment, 236
dislike, 233, 238
Disney, 19
Dispatch Online, 277, 279, 285, 294
dissent, 32, 34, 35, 233
dissociation, 233, 236
diversity, 169, 263, 276, 302

DNA, 218
Dnevnik, 150
dollar, 86, 207, 208, 214, 266
Dominican Republic, 342, 343, 345-347, 349-351, 354
Dresdner Bank, 96
Dubai, 218
Durban, 279, 283, 290

E

e-mail, 282, 283
East African, 278
East and West, 327, 329
East Jerusalem, 242
East Timor, 172
Eastern Muslims, 328, 329
economic liberalization, 342, 344
economic structure, 169
economy, 17, 22, 46, 91, 110, 111, 117, 131, 133, 134, 163, 172, 177, 178, 181, 182, 186, 190, 192, 204, 206, 362
Ecuador, 342, 343, 345-347, 351, 353
editorial, 9, 10, 43, 64, 84, 99, 100, 110, 112-114, 116, 117, 120, 121, 130, 135, 151, 153, 156, 157, 160, 161, 173, 176, 177, 209, 210, 238, 270, 271, 278, 292-294, 315, 321-323, 330
editorial board, 9, 10
Egypt, 9, 23, 227, 228, 233, 236, 237, 239, 240, 244, 270, 280
El Mundo, 110, 111, 116-118
El País, 110-112, 114-118, 120
El Salvador, 342, 345-347, 349-351, 353, 354
El Universal, 357
election(s), 14, 45, 90, 95, 142, 144, 233, 238, 239, 263, 264, 266-268, 358
elite, 6, 38, 40, 49, 98, 120, 144, 185, 191, 231, 249, 268, 320, 321, 331, 333, 340, 342, 349, 356, 357, 359, 361
embassy(ies), 46, 70, 74, 95, 116, 129, 142, 79, 192, 207, 211, 212, 221, 227, 230, 237, 283, 285, 324, 340
embassy bombings, 70
English language, 86, 319, 321
Enron, 192
environment, 19, 34, 54, 70, 71, 90, 170, 250
ETA, 29, 109, 110, 113, 116
ethics, 2, 11, 13, 59, 249, 302, 316, 317
ethnocentrism, 261

Gwadar, 213

H

Hamas, 228, 235
Hamburger Morgenpost, 95
hating America, 240
headline, 40, 95, 97, 99, 101, 110, 116, 139-
141, 160, 162, 187, 189, 190, 269, 270,
272, 319, 329
heathens, 261
hegemony, 11, 21, 154, 155, 192, 216, 273,
320
Herzegovina, 155
highjackers, 221
hijab, 228, 262, 327
Hindus, 178
Hindustan Times, 218
Hispanics, 349, 352, 354-356, 358
history, 10, 14, 16, 23, 39, 44, 49, 52, 56, 63,
73, 81-83, 85, 95, 99, 147-149, 157,
159, 161, 165, 172, 177, 180, 221, 230,
231, 248, 261, 263, 275, 284, 315, 361,
363
Holland, 204, 239
Hollywood, 45, 86, 157, 273
Honduras, 342, 345-347, 351-353
Hong Kong, 16, 197, 207
horror, 35, 47, 49, 84, 113, 147, 148, 158, 177,
190, 304, 324, 326, 333, 339, 340
human drama, 139, 164
human rights, 9, 11, 94, 110, 123, 151, 152,
159, 172, 197, 199, 215, 247-249, 262,
275, 282, 287
Hutton Inquiry, 39
hyperpuissance, 86, 87, 90

I

ideology, 6, 38, 48, 109, 141, 156, 158, 173,
184, 263, 264, 320, 329, 332, 340, 362
immigration, 100, 162, 263, 265-267, 330,
331, 341, 344, 349-352, 354, 355, 358-
360, 362
impact, 7, 30, 34, 36, 41, 46, 53, 55, 57, 58,
61, 62, 67, 75, 76, 78, 80, 98, 107, 141,
142, 163, 170, 177, 182, 227, 311, 330,
332, 333, 341, 352
income, 188

incredulity, 325
India, 23, 169, 171-176, 178-181, 183, 217,
218, 220-223, 239
Indian TV news, 218
Indonesia, 23, 87, 153, 169, 171-176, 179,
180, 183, 237, 239, 266
Information Age, 18
informed commentary, 22
injustice, 32, 115, 149, 244, 248
institutions, 45, 109, 134, 140, 157, 179, 190,
192, 207, 209, 214, 227, 362
integrity, 200, 314
intellectuals, 13, 87, 183, 189, 197, 202, 223,
232, 243, 249, 301, 342
international affairs, 12, 19, 90, 194, 285, 290
international communication, 11-15, 19, 23,
24, 93, 136
international conflict(s), 14, 342, 344, 352,
353
international law, 45, 100, 179, 187, 247, 288
international relations, 12, 17, 22, 23, 153,
191, 192, 199, 290, 296
international terrorism, 105, 131, 144, 188,
192, 248, 362
International Association for Mass
Communication Research (IAMCR),
23, 239
International Criminal Court, 93
International Herald Tribune, 93, 102, 103,
218
International Monetary Fund, 344
Internet, 18, 30, 54, 83, 86, 164, 173, 192,
198, 200, 202, 204, 209, 219, 228-230,
234, 235, 286
Interviews with journalists, 22
Intifada, 34, 112, 120, 237, 246
invasion, 9, 18, 34, 35, 48, 111, 124, 197, 198,
212, 213, 257, 292
investigative journalism, 13, 156, 363
invisibility, 339
IPAC, 235
Iran, 17, 87, 99, 157, 177, 185, 206, 208, 213,
258, 277, 284
Iran hostage crisis, 99
Iraq, 2, 9, 11, 17, 18, 20, 24, 29, 34, 35, 39, 47,
48, 87, 88, 91, 100, 109, 126, 139, 143,
144, 158, 172, 188, 189, 193, 194, 198,
199, 201, 206, 211, 218, 223, 224, 238-
240, 247, 257, 258, 268, 277, 291-293,
295, 332, 341, 342, 344, 352, 353, 355,
356, 358

Iraq War (of 2003), 2, 11, 18, 20, 24, 88, 144, 218, 223, 238, 240, 257, 332, 342
Ireland, 12, 13, 22, 29, 38, 39, 43, 46, 49, 221
Irish Independent, 39
Irish Republican Army (IRA), 31, 69
Irish Times, 38-40, 42, 46-50
Islam, 141, 154, 155, 159, 160, 164, 172, 179-181, 191, 230, 243, 246, 249, 255, 257, 269, 270, 287, 289, 294, 308, 322, 323, 325, 327, 328, 331, 337, 339, 340
Islamabad, 208, 213, 216
Islamic Propagation Center International (IPCI), 283, 286
Islamophobia, 261
Israel, 12, 54, 90, 125, 153, 163, 188, 195, 228, 231, 233, 235, 237, 238, 243-245, 247-250, 285, 287, 322
Israeli conspiracy, 180
Italy, 55, 83, 93, 153
ITV, 39

J

Jakarta Post, 173, 180, 185
Jammu, 180, 181
Japan, 7, 16, 23, 71, 169, 171-176, 182, 183, 199, 201, 206, 207, 209-212, 215, 216
Japan Echo, 209
Japan Times, 16, 209, 210
Jemaah Islamiah, 272, 273
Jewish, 235, 237
Jiang Zemin, 182, 187, 203
Jiao Guobiao, 198, 201
Jiefangjun bao, 189
jihad, 17, 29, 43, 47, 180, 234, 239, 282, 297, 331, 338
Jinmao Tower, 182
Jordan, 227, 228, 239, 270
Journal of Conflict Resolution, 362
journalism, 9-16, 19, 21-23, 25, 30, 31, 34, 36, 37, 39, 49, 51, 52, 83, 135, 136, 156, 171, 184, 185, 213, 220, 232, 240, 264, 275, 302, 303, 315-317, 338, 361-364
journalist(s), 8, 10-16, 22, 31-33, 35, 36, 41, 45, 51, 60, 81, 104, 106, 110-112, 123, 124, 126-128, 132-134, 148, 157, 165, 170, 193, 204, 207, 208, 213, 216, 217, 219-224, 231, 236, 243, 255, 262, 265, 281, 301-304, 306, 307, 309-312, 314, 315, 321-323, 327, 329, 331, 363, 364

journalistic practice, 22
justification, 34, 114, 116, 140, 142, 223, 231, 314

K

Kabul, 165, 208, 215, 216
Karachi, 173, 207
Kashmir, 16, 172, 180, 181, 207, 222
Kenya, 9, 278
KM Palapa, 265
Kobe, 209
Kosovo, 89, 90, 134, 207, 208, 237
Kuala Lumpur, 173
Kuwait, 34
Kyodo News, 214
Kyoto, 90, 93, 211

L

La Jornada, 357
La Nación, 357
La Prensa Libre, 357
labor, 262, 264, 266, 349
Labor Party, 264
land mines, 94
Laotian, 212
Latin America, 22, 99, 342, 344, 345, 349, 351, 356-358, 360-362
Latinos, 362
law, 13, 45, 90, 100, 121, 125, 140, 147, 151, 153, 179, 187, 212, 227, 247, 257, 271, 282, 288, 289, 301, 316, 317, 332, 337
Le Figaro, 87, 92
Le Monde, 85, 87, 88, 90, 92, 153
Lebanon, 99, 147, 230, 235, 239, 331
Legislative Council, 242, 243
Lexis-Nexis, 357
Liberal Party, 263, 321
Libééération, 86, 91, 92
Libya, 190, 228, 277, 283, 284
live broadcast, 75
London, 10, 12, 25, 30, 33, 35-39, 44, 46, 82, 83, 136, 141, 163, 184, 185, 222-224, 239, 240, 292, 337-340
London bombings, 35
London Review of Books, 33
loyal, 124, 142, 310

M

Madrid, 15, 106, 116, 121, 194

magazine(s), 10-12, 32, 83, 96, 141, 146, 156-158, 185, 207, 209, 211, 212, 215, 216, 218, 261, 317, 332

Mainichi Daily News, 173

Mainichi Shimbun, 182, 210

mainstream media, 54, 124, 142, 162, 177, 254, 273

Malaysia, 23, 169, 171-176, 179, 183, 201

Mali, 278

Manhattan, 30, 43, 46, 62, 63, 66, 79, 104, 113, 137, 140, 147, 165, 209, 249

Manila, 173

Marcos regime, 172

marginalization, 222

mass communication, 2, 9, 11-13, 15, 20, 21, 23, 24, 49, 141, 170, 234, 239, 302, 317

mass media, 4, 11, 12, 16, 18, 19, 22, 49, 104, 122, 134, 147, 148, 158, 169, 184, 185, 216, 231, 240, 315, 316, 320

media content, 15, 357

media coverage, 6, 7, 9, 18, 19, 21, 22, 29, 34, 35, 38, 96, 121, 123, 124, 134, 169-172, 186, 199, 218, 222, 223, 241, 303

media discourse, 106, 144, 156

media event(s), 6, 18, 51-53, 55, 56, 58, 60-62, 64, 67, 70, 74, 75, 80-83, 122, 132

media ownership, 163

media production, 41, 158

media professionals, 20, 41

mediation, 56, 107, 159, 363-365

Melbourne, 14, 24, 272, 275

Merak, 265

Messiah, 24

Messianic, 158, 280, 331

Mexico, 11, 153, 341, 342, 344-347, 350-353, 357, 359, 361, 362

Middle East, 7, 31, 34, 68, 69, 74, 87, 91, 116, 135, 177, 179, 180, 219, 222, 227, 228, 230-233, 235, 237, 239, 240, 242, 244, 246-248, 255, 257, 270, 279, 282, 285, 292, 322, 354, 358

Migration Act, 266

militant(s), 34, 152, 157, 165, 180, 206, 236, 282

military, 29, 34, 56, 59, 71, 73, 79, 86, 88, 90, 97, 100, 101, 105, 109, 110, 114, 115, 124, 126, 143, 151, 157, 161, 165, 171, 178, 180, 183, 188, 190-193, 206-216, 235, 246, 257, 266, 270, 275, 279, 286-289, 293, 294, 304, 326, 344, 354, 360

Milliyet, 254-256

minorities, 262, 263, 322, 323

minority, 53, 61, 177, 178, 269, 289, 320, 322, 338

misinformation, 108

missile defense, 44, 46, 93, 212

missionaries, 323

Mladina, 12, 146, 148, 156, 158-161

modernity, 83, 163

modernization, 12

Mogamma, 233

monopoly, 125, 145, 163

Montreal, 14, 321-333, 337-340

moral panic, 265, 270, 327

Morocco, 87, 231

Mossad, 88, 245

mourning, 44, 49, 95-97, 113, 140, 224, 243, 304, 317, 326

MSNBC/MSNBC.com, 193, 229, 303, 310

multiculturalism, 16, 161, 262, 263, 271, 274

Mumbai, 217, 218

music, 83, 94

Muslim insurgency, 172, 177

Muslim Judicial Council, 281

Muslim leadership, 322

Muslim population, 171-173, 221

Muslim(s), 8, 14, 34, 35, 86, 88, 95, 97, 100, 102, 123, 154, 155, 162, 171-173, 177-181, 183, 192, 201, 219, 221, 222, 234, 236, 237, 239, 243, 244-246, 249, 257, 261-263, 268-276, 278, 281-284, 287, 289, 290, 296, 301, 308, 319, 321-324, 327-333, 337, 339

N

Nablus, 243, 245

narrative, 32, 42, 43, 48, 52, 56, 62, 74, 76, 135, 146, 147, 149-153, 159, 161, 232, 303, 304, 363

narrative flow, 52, 62, 76

national identity, 120, 170, 239

national interest, 296

National Missile Defense, 44, 212

NATO, 12, 96, 99, 113, 116, 118, 124-126, 129, 130, 140, 142, 149, 151, 161, 162, 165, 212, 304

R

Rabaat, 233
race, 83, 141, 197, 269, 291, 320
racial profiling, 327, 337
racism, 158, 159, 261-264, 274, 279, 283, 320,
    321, 330, 331, 333, 338, 340
Radikal, 254-256
radio, 11, 14, 30, 55, 95, 138, 140, 150, 158,
    164, 229, 231, 240, 241, 262, 268, 276,
    281, 301, 308, 317, 357
radio stations, 95, 140
Rainbow Nation, 281
Ramadan, 244
Ramallah, 243
Rapport, 278, 280, 286, 292-296
rationalize, 242, 247
rbc.ru, 164
readership, 39
reality effects, 52, 56, 75, 76, 80, 81
Red Cross, 246
Reforma, 357
refugees, 157, 208, 264, 266, 267, 274
Reilly Center for Media & Public Affairs, 302
religion, 21, 141, 154, 169, 172, 184, 195, 221,
    230, 232, 257, 287, 323, 328, 329, 340,
    358
Religion Newswriters' Association, 21
representation of Muslims, 8, 319, 324, 329,
    330
Republican Party, 301
Republicans, 31
rescue of women, 328
resistance, 157, 228, 249, 328
resources, 31, 164, 186, 187, 206, 241, 246,
    284, 363
Reuters, 108, 120, 321-323, 338
revenge, 88, 98, 99, 152, 190, 191, 217, 258,
    278, 327
risk, 69-72, 74, 79, 105, 116, 118, 211, 270,
    287, 302, 332, 339
rogue states, 47, 87, 188, 192
role of media, 105
Roman Catholic, 154, 155, 172, 177
Russia, 15, 90, 140, 153, 165, 187, 188, 191,
    195, 213, 239
Rwanda, 185, 210
Rwandans, 86
Ryder Cup, 44

S

SAJA, 219, 220
Saladin, 245
salience, 40, 41, 49, 126
Samoobrona, 142
Samtiden, 132, 136
San Jose Mercury News, 105
Satan, 46, 227
satellite, 19, 34, 39, 122, 218, 230-232, 240
Saudi Arabia, 91, 125, 239, 244
scientists, 231
Scotland, 13, 30
Scripps Howard News Service, 38
security, 36, 42, 45, 47, 69, 91, 93, 94, 96, 98,
    99, 104, 105, 109, 115, 123-125, 129-
    131, 148, 151, 181-185, 187, 191, 206,
    210-213, 217, 218, 228, 237, 238, 245,
    247, 248, 250, 262, 270, 273, 274, 282,
    286, 289, 294, 295, 322, 330, 338, 351,
    352, 362
Seiron, 216
self-censorship, 123, 216, 314
Self-Defense Force, 183
semantic(s), 154, 155, 242
semiotic(s), 8, 22, 241, 242
sentiments, 123, 179, 269, 279, 282, 284, 287,
    331, 352, 364
Serbs, 237
Shanghai, 182
Shiite, 208
Siemens, 96
Sikhs, 178
Sinai Peninsula, 228
Six Day War, 228
Sky News, 39
Slovenia, 12, 16, 146, 149, 150, 154, 155, 160-
    163
social science, 24, 282
social system theories, 315
Social Democrats, 100
socialization, 118
Society of Professional Journalists, 302
sociologist, 102, 141, 155
solidarity, 31, 34, 35, 46, 54, 59, 85, 95, 97,
    99, 101, 102, 116, 125, 140, 141, 148,
    154, 161, 179, 242, 243, 278, 288, 325
Somalia, 100, 231, 237
sorrow, 219, 223, 243

T

The Gazette, 8, 319-331, 333, 337-340
The Great Satan, 227
The Guangming Daily, 189
The Nation, 45, 61, 201, 207, 256, 257, 263, 309, 310, 312, 320
The National Post, 322
The New Straits Times, 173, 179, 184
The People's Liberation Army paper, 189
The Southern Weekend, 186
The Sun, 39, 272
The Times, 38-40, 42-44, 47, 48, 112, 179
thematic analysis, 146, 147
Third World, 113, 278
This Day, 95, 278, 314
threat, 7, 47, 69, 70, 72-74, 89, 99, 105, 106, 109, 113, 122, 129, 130, 142, 149, 153, 179, 194, 214, 235, 257, 272, 281, 301, 324, 362
Tianamen, 181
Today Show, 308
Tokyo, 16, 24, 173, 206-209, 211, 212, 214, 216
tone, 42, 46, 47, 59, 64, 113, 140, 173-175, 178, 179, 181, 182, 197, 268, 314, 333
tone of coverage, 173-175
topic, 41, 173, 213, 255, 281, 303, 325, 358
torture, 332
totalitarian, 158
Toyota, 19
trade volume, 172, 179
tradition, 84, 91, 110, 232
transnational, 9, 19, 29, 30, 37, 93, 121, 134, 135, 231, 240, 344, 362
trauma, 52, 82, 122, 147, 210, 272, 315, 317, 326
TRT, 254
Trybuna, 142
Tunisia, 271
Turkey, 9, 10, 23, 153, 201, 237, 254, 256, 257
Turkish media, 8, 254, 255
TVS, 137, 146-151, 160, 161
Twin Towers, 30, 35, 79, 85, 88, 101, 102, 104, 149, 151, 157, 160, 214, 218, 230, 235, 236, 254, 319

U

U.S. Department of State, 196
U.S. Embassy, 142, 179, 230, 237, 324, 340
Ulemas Council, 180

UN resolutions, 285, 291
unilaterism, 144
union, 15, 87, 93, 94, 100, 115, 116, 118, 138, 171, 178, 195
United Democratic Movement, 279
United Kingdom, 14, 29, 31, 65, 124, 138, 186, 199, 264, 361
United Nations, 35, 88, 94, 105, 110, 126, 181, 188, 210, 212, 230, 240, 257, 288, 291, 292
United Nations Security Council, 105
United States, 4, 9, 12-14, 17, 18, 29-31, 33-35, 43-47, 54, 56, 65, 70, 71, 73, 79, 84-102, 110, 111, 114-119, 122-126, 128, 129, 131, 133, 138, 141-145, 147-149, 151-155, 157, 161, 162, 164, 165, 169, 171-184, 186-199, 201, 209, 212, 213, 215, 217, 218, 220, 227, 228, 231, 232, 235, 237-239, 242-250, 256-258, 263, 264, 269, 270, 277-281, 283-289, 291-293, 301, 302, 304, 306, 309-311, 315, 324, 330, 341-344, 347-362
urban, 10, 44, 72, 171, 263, 345-347
Uruguay, 342, 345-347, 350-353
USA Today, 105, 234, 240
Uzbekistan, 153, 213
values, 2, 23, 29, 32, 44, 47, 54, 56, 58, 86, 94, 96, 99, 101, 122, 139, 144, 154, 161, 162, 185, 188, 194, 197, 217, 240, 262, 287, 302, 315, 320, 325, 340, 355

V

Večer, 12, 150
Venezuela, 342, 345-347, 351, 353, 358
Verdens Gang, 125
VG, 125, 127-132
Viacom, 19
Vietnam War, 198, 212
viewers, 32, 34, 55, 57, 62, 65, 66, 70, 76, 95, 147, 209, 218, 231, 236, 302, 305, 309, 313-315
violence, 19, 31, 33, 44, 89, 97, 100, 105, 107-109, 112, 113, 115, 121, 157, 158, 180, 190, 191, 193, 221, 239, 243, 246, 257, 274, 275, 288, 302, 319, 320, 324, 325, 330, 333, 338, 358
Voice magazine, 211, 212
VRT, 9, 55, 59

W

wage(s), 47, 180, 345-347
Wall Street, 65, 117, 214, 316
Wall Street Journal, 316
war, 2, 6, 9, 11, 16-20, 24, 25, 29, 31-37, 43-45, 49, 68, 87-91, 93-97, 99-102, 104, 105, 107-109, 111-115, 117, 118, 120-126, 134, 136, 139, 141, 142, 144, 148-154, 156-161, 164, 169, 170, 172, 177, 178, 180, 183, 185, 187-189, 191-195, 197-199, 201, 203, 206, 210, 212, 213, 215, 216, 218, 219, 222-224, 227, 228, 238-240, 243, 246, 247, 250, 254, 256-258, 261-263, 268-270, 273-275, 279, 281, 284, 287, 289-292, 295, 296, 319, 323, 325-327, 332, 333, 337, 341, 342, 347, 348, 352, 354, 355, 358-360, 364
War on America, 33, 164, 319
War on Terror, 29, 102, 123, 136, 141, 142, 169, 172, 192, 222, 263, 268, 269, 273, 287, 319, 327, 352
warning, 69-72, 74, 96, 98, 153, 228, 271, 280
Washington, 3, 4, 15, 25, 30, 33, 36, 44, 46, 62, 76-79, 89, 98, 101, 124, 128, 139, 140, 165, 177, 178, 184, 190, 192, 196, 211, 213, 216, 227, 229, 230, 234, 239, 243, 246, 247, 269, 289, 292, 341, 344-347, 362
Washington Consensus, 344-347, 362
Washington, D.C., 25, 139, 177, 184, 362
Washington Times, 213
watchdog, 2, 362
weapons of mass destruction (WMD), 34, 39, 194, 291, 292
Western media, 10, 31, 142, 190, 207, 215, 216, 219, 222, 231, 233, 275
Western Muslims, 327, 329
Western nations, 47, 271, 319

Western powers, 42
Westernization, 146
White Australia Policy, 261, 263
White Victims, 326, 327, 333
wire services, 139, 164
women, 10, 99, 202-204, 262, 269, 271, 272, 290, 327-329, 337
workers, 44, 56, 63, 65, 164, 177, 289, 323, 337, 350
world opinion, 234
World Trade Center (WTC), 30, 33, 34, 42-44, 46, 47, 51, 54, 56, 57, 59, 62, 63, 65-68, 70, 71, 73, 76, 78, 79, 88, 102, 113, 122, 124, 129, 131, 137, 139, 140, 142, 177, 180, 182, 183, 205-207, 209, 211, 212, 214, 220, 229, 248, 254, 269, 285, 301, 307, 309, 310, 313, 333
World Trade Organization (WTO), 190
World War II, 44, 108, 122, 142, 172, 227
World War III, 95
Wprost, 139

X

xenophobia, 261-264
Xinjiang, 213

Y

Yemen, 231, 331
Yokosuka, 211

Z

Zaman, 254-256
Zionism, 44
Zionist, 245